Keetie Roelen, Richard Morgan and Yisak Tafere (Eds.)

Putting Children First
New Frontiers in the Fight Against Child Poverty in Africa

About CROP

CROP, the Comparative Research Programme on Poverty, is a response from the academic community to the problems of poverty. The programme was initiated by the International Social Science Council (ISSC) in 1992, and the CROP Secretariat hosted by the University of Bergen (UiB) was officially opened in June 1993 by the Director General of UNESCO, Dr Frederico Mayor. In 2018, the ISSC merged with the International Council for Science (ICSU) to become the International Science Council (ISC).

In recent years, poverty-related issues have moved up on the international agenda, with poverty eradication now defined as the greatest global challenge facing the world today. In co-operation with the ISC and the UiB, CROP works with knowledge networks, institutions and scholars to establish independent and critical poverty research in order to help shape policies for long-term poverty prevention and eradication.

The CROP network comprises scholars engaged in poverty-related research across a variety of academic disciplines. Researchers from more than a hundred different countries are represented in the network, which is coordinated by the CROP Secretariat at the University of Bergen, Norway.

The CROP series on *International Studies in Poverty Research* presents expert research and essential analyses of different aspects of poverty worldwide. By promoting a fuller understanding of the nature, extent, depth, distribution, trends, causes and effects of poverty and poverty-related issues, this series will contribute to knowledge concerning the prevention and eradication of poverty at global, regional, national and local levels.

CROP Secretariat, University of Bergen

P.O Box 7800, 5020 Bergen, NORWAY

Email: crop@uib.no

Website: www.crop.org

Keetie Roelen, Richard Morgan
and Yisak Tafere (Eds.)

PUTTING CHILDREN FIRST

New Frontiers in the Fight Against Child Poverty in Africa

Bibliografische Information der Deutschen Nationalbibliothek
Die Deutsche Nationalbibliothek verzeichnet diese Publikation in der Deutschen Nationalbibliografie; detaillierte bibliografische Daten sind im Internet über http://dnb.d-nb.de abrufbar.

Bibliographic information published by the Deutsche Nationalbibliothek
Die Deutsche Nationalbibliothek lists this publication in the Deutsche Nationalbibliografie; detailed bibliographic data are available in the Internet at http://dnb.d-nb.de.

ISBN-13: 978-3-8382-1317-0

ibidem-Verlag, Stuttgart 2019

copyright © CROP, 2019

Alle Rechte vorbehalten

Printed in the EU

Contents

List of Figures

List of Tables

List of Tables

INTRODUCTION

Keetie Roelen, Richard Morgan and Yisak Tafere

1. Introduction

Child poverty is devastating in its effects and presents one of the most urgent challenges for any society. Poverty in all its dimensions is detrimental for early childhood development (Walker et al. 2007) and leads to often irreversible damage for the lives of girls and boys, locking children and families into intergenerational poverty. Confronting child poverty is an ethical and practical necessity; fulfilling the rights of children, including adolescents, by lifting intersecting deprivations and through expanding opportunities can unlock vast economic and social dividends.

Despite important strides in the fight against poverty in the past two decades, child poverty remains widespread and persistent. Worldwide and throughout Africa, children are much more likely to be poor than adults are. Poverty rates are highest among children in sub-Saharan Africa; one in five children grow up in extreme monetary poverty (UNICEF and World Bank, 2016), and two-thirds of children in the region experience multidimensional poverty (OPHI, 2017), including high rates of mortality and malnutrition; poor living conditions and educational outcomes; and often high risks of exposure to different forms of violence. One in four children in the Arab States—which include Northern Africa—experience multidimensional poverty. Estimates suggest that by 2030, nine out of ten children suffering from extreme monetary poverty will be living in sub-Saharan Africa (UNICEF, 2016).

A fast-changing world means that the face of child poverty and its drivers are ever-evolving. While the majority of poor children can still be found in rural areas, the world is growing increasingly urban (UN, 2014), posing new challenges to children and their families in terms of navigating their lives and livelihoods. Undernutrition remains a global challenge, with 174 million children estimated to be malnourished in 2010 (Black et al., 2017). High unemployment and scant provision of good-quality basic services challenges families' abilities to provide an enabling environment for their children, and for adolescents to move safely from childhood into adulthood. The onset of climate change, environmental shocks and ongoing conflict have led to an age of displacement across the region (see UNICEF, 2015), presenting a huge challenge to fighting poverty for those most vulnerable.

In 2015, the world explicitly committed itself to the eradication of child poverty. Target 1.2 in Sustainable Development Goal (SDG 1) calls for the eradication of poverty in all its forms for individuals of all ages, making the elimination of child poverty "a universal commitment as well as an urgent global priority" (Harland, 2016: 8). Combatting child poverty in Africa calls for nuanced understandings of the complex realities that children face, and effective and innovative policy responses for boys and girls across their life courses. This edited volume brings together applied research from across the continent, aiming to contribute to academic understandings and to appropriate and effective policy initiatives. It is based on the framing of and contributions to the international conference *Putting Children First: Identifying Solutions and Taking Action to Tackle Poverty and Inequality in Africa* that was held from 23–25 October 2017 in Addis Ababa. The conference included 150 researchers, practitioners, policy makers and civil society activists involved in the fight against child poverty. This edited volume reflects a bridging of debates on how to address child poverty in Africa from across academic and policy spaces, and aims to push the frontiers by challenging existing narratives, exploring alternative understandings of the complexities and dynamics underpinning child poverty and—crucially—examining policy options that work to reduce it.

This volume presents new and applied research from across the continent in three themes, namely (i) manifestations of child poverty, (ii) child-sensitive social protection, and (iii) transitions from childhood into adulthood. Policy makers, practitioners and researchers joined by the Global Coalition to End Child Poverty identified these as key themes within which more evidence was needed, particularly for bringing research into the policy sphere.

2.   Key themes in the fight against child poverty

2.1. Manifestations of child poverty

An important first step towards achieving SDG 1 and the eradication of child poverty involves the identification of children who are living in poverty and understanding their needs and vulnerabilities. The availability of data and efforts to measure and map child poverty has led to a rapid expansion in the evidence base on children's living conditions as well as causes and trajectories out of poverty. It is now widely accepted that different measures lead to differential estimates of poverty and identify different groups of children as being poor (Roelen, 2017). This is exemplified by the recent estimates published by the World Bank and UNICEF, and by Oxford Poverty & Human Development Initiative (OPHI). It is therefore crucial that different measures are used in complementary ways and that advances are made to further improve them. Important strides forward include UNICEF's Multiple Overlapping Deprivation Analysis (MODA) (Plavgo and Milliano, 2014), the extension of OPHI's Multidimensional Poverty Index (MPI) to children (OPHI, 2017) and recent global estimates of monetary child poverty by the World Bank and UNICEF (Newhouse et al. 2016). All of these provide crucial impetus to policy efforts towards reduction of child poverty (UNICEF and the Global Coalition to End Child Poverty, 2017).

Notwithstanding the important strides in child poverty measurement, current quantitative understandings overlook important psychosocial and relational issues that are core components of children's experiences of living in poverty. It has long been asserted, for example, that shame lies at the 'irreducible, absolutist core' of poverty (Sen, 1983: 159) and has been shown to be a cross-cultural experience (Walker et al., 2013) also affecting children (Dornan and Oganda-Portela, 2016).

Knowledge gaps also persist with respect to malnutrition and hunger, arguably among the most pressing issues facing children and undermining their rights and opportunities. Malnutrition, especially in the first two years of life, poses a serious threat to children's physical and cognitive development with potentially irreversible and cumulative damaging effects that persist during their life-cycle (Smith and Haddad, 2015). A greater understanding of its interactions with other dimensions of child poverty and deprivation is required.

Any assessment of poverty, including child poverty, also needs to acknowledge its dynamic nature. A recognition of the non-static nature of poverty has long been a key argument for adopting more longitudinal approaches to its study (Baulch and Hoddinott, 2000). The need for understanding movements in and out of poverty is compounded by African children increasingly facing multiple shocks in an age of climate change (UNICEF, 2014a), urbanisation (Ruthstein et al., 2016), and conflict. These new realities change the experiences of poverty and the nature of children's vulnerabilities. Most crucially, they change the necessary responses to prevent falls into poverty, and to promote moves out of it.

Furthermore, while the acknowledgement that measurement of child poverty needs to be based on complementary and dynamic approaches reflects the recognition that child poverty is complex and multi-faceted, the focus on rigid and quantified categorisations of poverty can be considered to undermine nuanced understandings of children's lives. Taking account of complex realities for children in research and child poverty assessments may require a more open-minded approach.

Contributions in this volume in relation to this theme reflect on the advances made in terms of complementary measurement. The early chapters challenge existing narratives underpinning poverty measurement. They illuminate poverty's complexities—particularly in relation to measuring child nutrition—and explore alternative understandings using new conceptual and analytical entry points.

Firstly, **Elizabeth Ngutuku** challenges conventional approaches to understanding child poverty and vulnerability, arguing for and applying a "rhizomatic" approach that aims to defy categorisation and give explicit voice to children in articulating their experiences. Drawing on in-depth case study research, she offers compelling insight into children's lived experiences in Kenya and highlights that the nature of childhood poverty is complex, fluid and highly inter-relational. The contribution by **Grace Bantebya-Kyomuhendo, Elaine Chase and Florence Muhanguzi** also highlights the need for moving beyond standard measures and understandings of child poverty by offering a fine-grained analysis of the pervasiveness of poverty-induced shame and children's strategies for managing such shame. Spatial analysis in Uganda and the United Kingdom suggests that shame is omnipresent in children's lives and that children adopt complex strategies for managing this.

Winnie Sambu and Katherine Hall provide detailed longitudinal analysis of an area of child deprivation that remains a challenge across the African continent, namely hunger and malnutrition. They undertake descriptive and regression analysis across three household survey data sets in South Africa, finding a strong interaction between poverty, hunger and lack of dietary diversity. Their research also highlights the complexities and stringent data requirements for investigating issues of hunger and malnutrition. The chapter by **Oluwaseyi Dolapo Somefun, Joshua Odunayo Akinyemi and Clifford Odimegwu** extends the analysis of malnutrition by examining the relationship between child stunting, family structure and community characteristics across countries in sub-Saharan Africa. Parental presence appears to be a strong factor in child nutrition, although it can only mildly offset the effects of widespread poverty at community level.

Tassew Woldehanna and Yisak Tafere provide testimony to the importance of undertaking longitudinal and mixed methods analysis of child poverty. Their dynamic analysis of children's multiple overlapping deprivations in Ethiopia confirm the devastating impact of household shocks such as death of livestock and loss of unemployment. They find education of caregivers to be crucial for mitigating such shocks. The qualitative analysis shows that quantitative measures of deprivation are in line with children's perspectives of poverty and offers valuable additional insights into the psychosocial side of poverty and exclusion.

2.2. Child-sensitive social protection

In the last decade, social protection has become a central part of global and national development agendas and is now widely recognised as one of the foremost interventions within the policy package for fighting child poverty (UNICEF and Global Coalition to End Child Poverty, 2017). Child-sensitive social protection (CSSP) encompasses programmes that aim to maximise positive impacts on children and to minimise potential unintended side effects (DFID et al., 2009). This includes both direct interventions (i.e. child-focused or targeted) and indirect interventions such as social pensions, public works (Roelen and Karki Chettri, 2016). Its role in advancing child wellbeing and rights in Africa is widely recognised, such as during the sixth International Policy Conference on the African Child held in Addis Ababa in 2014 (ACPF, 2014).

An expanding evidence base provides testimony that social protection—and cash transfers in particular—can improve food security and dietary diversity, increase school enrolment, reduce child labour and improve access to health services (Bastagli et al., 2016). However, less poverty does not necessarily go hand-in-hand with lower rates of malnutrition. Despite significant improvements in food security in South Africa in conjunction with stark reductions in child poverty (Delany et al., 2016) and rapid expansion of cash grants for children, malnutrition remains widespread (Devereux and Waidler, 2017). This disjuncture between poverty reduction and improvements in child nutrition has strong ramifications for policies aiming to reduce malnutrition, not least for social protection.

Evidence increasingly suggests that the provision of cash alone is not a 'magic bullet.' More nuanced understandings of the impact of social protection on children have led to debates on the most effective and appropriate social protection instruments for improving child outcomes, including in the area of nutrition (De Groot et al., 2017). The need for more integrated approaches that combine cash with other types of services is widely recognised and increasingly tested, sometimes referred to as "cash plus" programmes (Roelen et al., 2017). Such interventions often incorporate communication and information to empower parents and caregivers and promote care, feeding and hygiene practices that are likely to be positive for children. Exactly how different modalities can be brought together into more comprehensive packages of support in a cost-effective way requires more learning and debate.

Contributions in this volume consider the role of social protection in addressing malnutrition, explore the role of "cash plus" programming, and highlight the need for multisectoral and holistic responses. The research that is presented also emphasises the importance of design and implementation of interventions in effecting change for children (see also Bastagli et al., 2016), including the frequency and size of transfers, as well as understanding and addressing the crucial role of contextual and structural barriers.

The contribution by **Stephen Devereux, Coretta Jonah and Julian May** reflects on options for making policies more child- and nutrition-sensitive, including social protection, in light of the 'food security paradox' in South Africa. In line with findings by Sambu and Hall, they find strong associations between poverty and malnutrition, but also explore other factors including maternal care and healthy environments to explain largely stagnant malnutrition rates against falling poverty rates. Programmes that take a holistic approach and includes material and non-material support are considered key for addressing the nutrition challenge in South Africa.

Nicola Hypher, Luke Harman, Kerina Zvobgo and Oluwatosin Akomolafe explore the potential of "cash plus" approaches for improving nutrition and provide a comprehensive review of impacts of various programmes from across the continent. "Cash plus" interventions are found to improve care knowledge and practices across the board, and reduce stunting and wasting in a few cases. This chapter also elaborates on policy implications, highlighting the importance of appropriate design and effective implementation and taking into account context and structural barriers. The importance of design and implementation for social protection to affect children is also evident from the contribution by **Billow Hassan, Stephen Mutiso and Munshi Sulaiman**. Their research investigated how different frequencies and amounts of cash transfers as well as labelling of transfers has a differential effect on children's outcomes in Somalia. They find that lump-sum transfers that are labelled as business grants do increase business income, assets and food security more than small cash transfers do, but that they have limited impacts on children. This in turn may reinforce the need for consideration of complementary interventions alongside economic support to households that are poor.

2.3. Transitions from childhood into adulthood

Young people are the fastest-growing demographic group in Africa, accounting for 547 million people in 2015 and estimated to increase to almost one billion by mid-century (UNICEF, 2014b). This demographic shift gives rise to questions about which actions are needed to convert the "youth bulge" into a "demographic dividend." Many countries have witnessed a generational shift with young people now having gained more years of schooling than their parents at the same age. New technologies are rapidly changing young people's experiences and aspirations.

Adolescence is a critical turning point at which pre-existing inequalities can translate into lower life chances that persist into adulthood. It is also a further critical window of opportunity during which policies aiming to support young people's development may help equalise opportunities and generate high economic and social returns for both these individuals and their societies (Sheehan et al., 2017). Interventions for this rising demographic of young people are central to Africa's ambitions for inclusive and sustainable growth.

Fostering employment features heavily in debates about youth and transitions into adulthood. Youth unemployment presents a major challenge in countries across the region. This challenge raises questions about job creation and about the role of entrepreneurship and self-employment as well as young people's own aspirations (Ayele et al., 2017). Access to information and markets is crucial, with the use of rising technology such as cell phones facilitating mobility through the expansion of social networks (Porter et al., 2012). Programmes to promote employment, individual capabilities and skills training have been crucial in increasing young people's access to labour markets and maintaining positive outcomes in the long run (Dekker and Hollander, 2017). At the same time, youth employment programmes are criticised for being too heavily grounded in individualistic notions of the problem and overly reliant on interventions addressing the supply of labour while ignoring the structural lack of demand (Flynn et al., 2017).

Adolescence represents a time of life-changing decisions, growing responsibilities and increasingly pronounced social roles. During this stage in life, gender norms often become more important and accentuated. These norms can affect access to schooling, learning outcomes and aspirations, and roles and responsibilities with respect to paid work and unpaid care. They may also relate to experiences of bullying and other forms of violence (Winter, 2016). The SDGs direct attention towards one particular form of violence against adolescents, namely child, early and forced marriage. In addition to increasing the likelihood of gender-based violence, child marriage is also associated with poorer early childhood development among those born to mothers aged less than 18 years of age (Efevbera et al., 2017).

Contributions in this volume in relation to the theme of transitions from childhood into adulthood investigate young people's experiences of finding work, negotiating widespread forms of physical and psychological violence and the role of social connectedness in support of safe transitions. The contributions highlight how the life phase of adolescence is one that requires many strategies to negotiate highly intricate sets of interactions between family members, peers, community members and authority figures. It becomes evident that policy interventions only have a chance of success when accounting for the context and wider systems within which young people seek to shape a life of their own.

Firstly, the contribution by **Nikhit D'Sa, Sarah Press, Anna Du Vent, Ahmed Farahat, and Sita Conklin** offers a critical reflection on the role of youth livelihood development interventions and argues for a greater role for peers, family and communities in strengthening their impact. Based on an assessment of youth education and livelihood projects in Burkina Faso, Egypt, Ethiopia, Malawi and Uganda, they find that family and community members act as gatekeepers for young people to enhance their skills and find work, and that youth have to negotiate strong negative stereotypes within families and communities regarding their level of motivation and dedication. Further consideration of the issue of youth employment is offered by **Gina Porter, Kate Hampshire, Alister Munthali and Elsbeth Robson** as they explore the role of physical and virtual mobility in young people's lives in Malawi. They find that limited physical mobility as a result of poor infrastructure and weak access to transport greatly shape the locations and types of work that are available to young people. Mobile phones may offer opportunities for some to establish and strengthen connections in support of finding work, but contextual factors limit such opportunities. Overall they find that rurality, gender and disadvantageous economic conditions undermine the possibilities that physical and virtual mobility that may afford youth in finding employment.

The contribution by **Nicola Jones, Marie Francoise Umutoni, Bekele Tefera, Ernestina Coast, Workneh Yadete, Roberte Isimbi, Guday Emirie and Kassahun Tilahun** moves on to provide detailed insights into experiences of violence among adolescents in Ethiopia and Rwanda. Their work provides evidence for the pervasiveness of violence at home, in school and within communities. Both boys and girls experience beatings, bullying and punishments, particularly in school. Certain forms of violence are particularly gender-specific, including child marriage in Ethiopia and labia elongation in Rwanda. The research is a powerful reminder of the complex lives of children and adolescents, and the need for multisectoral responses in ensuring safe and secure transitions to adulthood.

Finally, **Marlene Ogawa, Shirley Pendlebury and Carmel Marock** investigate the role of social connections, relationships and social capital in the transition to healthy adulthood in South Africa. Through a careful examination of a programme that aimed to help young people to achieve their aspirations by strengthening their social connectedness, they show that greater connectedness can be beneficial for many and present a turning point for some in terms of moving out of poverty. Nonetheless, their contribution is also a potent reminder of the structural conditions of poverty and that addressing these is a complex task which needs multi-sectoral and multi-stakeholder collaboration.

References

ACPF (2014). Outcome Document. Advancing Child Wellbeing in Africa through Social Protection: A Call for Action. Addis Ababa: ACPF.

Ayele, S., Khan, S. and J. Sumberg (2017). "Africa's Youth Employment Challenge: New Perspectives." *IDS Bulletin* 48(3): 1–12.

Bastagli, F., Hagen-Zanker, J., Harman, L., Barca, V., Sturge, G., Schmidt, T., and L. Pellerano (2016). *Cash transfers: what does the evidence say?* London: ODI.

Baulch, B. and J. Hoddinott (2000). "Economic Mobility and Poverty Dynamics in Developing Countries." *The Journal of Development Studies.* 36(6): 1–24.

Black, M. M., Walker, S. P., Fernald, L. C. H., Andersen, C. T., DiGirolamo, A. M., Lu, Cet al. (2017). "Early Childhood Development Coming of Age: Science through the life course." *The Lancet, 389* (10064): 77–90.

De Groot, R., Palermo, T., Handa, S., Ragno, L. P., and A. Peterman (2017). "Cash Transfers and Child Nutrition: Pathways and Impacts." *Development Policy Review* 35(5): 621–643.

Dekker, M. and S. Hollander (2017). *Boosting Youth Employment in Africa: What works and why?* Synthesis report for the INCLUDE/MFA conference 30 May 2017. The Hague: INCLUDE Secretariat.

Delany A., Jehoma S. and L. Lake (eds) (2016).) *South African Child Gauge 2016.* Cape Town: Children's Institute, University of Cape Town.

Devereux, S. and J. Waidler (2017). *Why does Malnutrition Persist in South Africa Despite Social Grants?* Food Security SA Working Paper Series No. 001. South Africa: DST-NRF Centre of Excellence in Food Security.

DFID, HelpAge International, Hope & Homes for Children, Institute of Development Studies, International Labour Organization, Overseas Development Institute, Save the Children UK, UNDP, UNICEF and the World Bank (2009). *Advancing Child-Sensitive Social Protection.* New York: UNICEF.

Dornan, P., and M. J. Oganda Portela (2016*). Do Feelings of Shame Undermine Children's Development?* Oxford: University of Oxford.

Efevbera, Y., et al. (2017). "Girl Child Marriage as a Risk Factor for Early Childhood Development and Stunting." *Social Science & Medicine.* 187(2017): 91–101.

Flynn, J., Mader, P., Oosterom, M. and S. Ripoll (2017)." Failing Young People? Addressing the Supply-side Bias and Individualisation in Youth Employment Programming." IDS Evidence Report 216. Brighton: IDS.

Harland, C. (2016). *Child Poverty: What Drives It and What It Means to Children Across the World.* London: Save the Children.

Newhouse, D., Suarez-Becerra, P., Evans, M. and Data for Goals Group (2016). *New Estimates of Extreme Poverty for Children.* Policy Research Working Paper 7845. Washington DC: World Bank.

OPHI (2017). *Children's Multidimensional Poverty: Disaggregating the Global MPI.* Oxford: Oxford Poverty and Human Development Initiative (OPHI).

Plavgo, I. and M. Milliano (2014). *Multidimensional Child Deprivation and Monetary Poverty in Sub-Saharan Africa.* Innocenti Working Paper No. 2014-19. Florence: UNICEF Office of Research.

Porter, G., et al. (2012). "Youth, Mobility and Mobile Phones in Africa: Findings from a Three-Country Study." *Information Technology for Development.* 18(2): 145–162.

Roelen, K. (2017). "Monetary and Multidimensional Child Poverty: A Contradiction in Terms?" *Development and Change.* 48(3): 502–533.

Roelen, K., Devereux, S., Abdulai, A-G., Martorano, B., Palermo, T. and P. L. Ragno (2017*). How to Make 'Cash Plus' Work: Linking Cash Transfers to Services and Sectors.* Innocenti Working Paper WP-2017-10. Florence: UNICEF Office of Research.

Roelen, K and H. Karki Chettri (2016). *Improving Social Protection's Response to Child Poverty and Vulnerability in Nepal.* Brighton/Kathmandu: IDS/Save the Children Nepal.

Rutstein, S., Staveteig, S., Winter, R. and J. Yourkavitch (2016). *Urban Child Poverty, Health, and Survival in Low- and Middle-Income Countries.* DHS Comparative Reports No. 40. Rockville, Maryland: ICF International.

Save the Children (2018*). The War on Children: Time to End Grave Violations Against Children in Conflict.* London: Save the Children International.

Sen, A. (1983). *Poor, Relatively Speaking.* Oxford Economic Papers. 35(2): 150.

Sheehan, P., et al. (2017). "Building the Foundations for Sustainable Development: A Case for Global Investment in the Capabilities of Adolescents." *The Lancet* 390(10104): 1792–1806.

Smith, L.C. and L. Haddad (2015). "Reducing Child Undernutrition: Past Drivers and Priorities for the Post-MDG Era." *World Development,* 68: 180–204.

UNICEF and Global Coalition to End Child Poverty (2017). *A World Free from Child Poverty*. New York: UNICEF and Global Coalition to End Child Poverty.

UNICEF (2016). *The State of the World's Children 2016: A fair chance for every child*. New York: UNICEF.

UNICEF and World Bank (2016). *Ending Extreme Poverty: a focus on Children*. New York: UNICEF and World Bank.

UNICEF (2015). *Unless We Act Now: The impact of climate change on children*. New York: United Nations.

UNICEF (2014a). *The Challenges of Climate Change: Children on the Front Line*. Innocenti Insight. Florence: UNICEF Innocenti Office of Research.

UNICEF (2014b). *Generation 2030: Africa*. New York: UNICEF.

United Nations (2014). *World Urbanization Prospects: The 2014 Revision*. United Nations Department of Economic and Social Affairs. New York: United Nations.

Walker, S. P., Wachs, T. D., Meeks Gardner, J., Lozoff, B., Wasserman, G. A., Pollitt, E., and J.A Carter, (2007). "Child development: risk factors for adverse outcomes in developing countries." *The Lancet, 369*(9556): 145–157.

Walker, R., Kyomuhendo, G. B., Chase, E., Choudhry, S., Gubrium, E. K., Nicola, J. Y., Lodemel, I., Leemamol, M., Mwiine, A., Pellissery, S. and Y. A. N. Ming (2013). "Poverty in Global Perspective: Is Shame a Common Denominator?" *Journal of Social Policy*, 42(2): 215–233.

Winter, F. (2016). *Shaping Aspirations and Outcomes: Gender and Adolescence in Young Lives*. Young Lives Policy Paper 9. Oxford: Young Lives.

PART ONE
Manifestations of Child Poverty

CHAPTER 1
Beyond Categories: Rhizomatic Experiences of Child Poverty and Vulnerability in Kenya

Elizabeth Ngutuku

1. Going beyond categories in understanding child poverty experience

By the year 2014, it was estimated that there were 21,064,614 children below the age of 18 in Kenya, 49 percent of the total population in the country (KNBS and UNICEF 2017: 102). Child poverty and deprivation is an important lens through which children and childhood in Kenya is understood and an average child in Kenya is seen as a poor child (UNICEF and Government of Kenya 2014: 8). In the combined Third, Fourth and Fifth State Party Report to the United Nations Committee on the Convention on the Rights of the Child (UNCRC), the Kenyan government noted that in Kenya, children "are not only vulnerable to poverty [but] poverty tends to affect children more than any other age group" (GoK, 2012b: 31).

Child poverty and vulnerability in Kenya has been understood and measured through various lenses including categorical approaches, monetary and multi-dimensional measures. For example, the category "Orphaned and Vulnerable Child" (OVC) is used in understanding the experience of children with poverty and vulnerability. According to the Social Protection Sector Review, in 2012, 3.6 million children were orphaned or classified as vulnerable in Kenya (GoK 2012); of these, one million children were orphaned, having lost one or both parents. HIV/AIDS has also shaped the context in which child poverty and vulnerability is experienced. According to UNICEF's 2015 State of the World's Children Report (2014: 56), in 2013 there were roughly 190,000 children living with HIV/AIDS in Kenya; 1.1 million children were orphaned by AIDS and 2.5 million other children were orphaned by other causes. There is therefore sometimes a conflation between being orphaned and living in poverty, based on the assumption that households with OVCs tend to be poor, and households that are child-headed are more vulnerable due to lack of endowments.

It is widely acknowledged that child poverty goes beyond income deprivation, and that it is multi-dimensional and affects children differently from adults (Abdu and Delamonica 2018; Delamonica 2014; Roelen 2017). More recently, methods that combine monetary and multi-dimensional perspectives have been utilised in estimating child poverty in Kenya (KNBS and UNICEF 2017: 83). These measures are based on children's rights, which are universal and indivisible, and are embedded in the United Nation Convention on the Rights of Children (UNCRC) (UN 1989). These rights-based approaches utilise specific rights, commonly known as constitutive rights, to child poverty, and these rights are given equal weight. They include health, nutrition, education, information, water sanitation and housing (Delamonica 2014). Deprivation of rights in these areas are considered manifestations of poverty.

In 2014, the Government of Kenya (GOK) and UNICEF used the Bristol Index, a rights-based approach that measures child deprivation in relation to access to clean water, health, food, medical care, education, and information (GoK and UNICEF 2014: xvi). Accordingly, as noted in *Situation Analysis of Children and Adolescents in Kenya: Our Children, Our Future* (2014), they found that 7.8 million children were deprived of access to safe drinking water. 15.8 million children were deprived of access to improved sanitation, and 13.1 million had inadequate shelter. At the same time, 5.3 million children aged 6–17 years old were deprived of adequate education. In addition, 20 to 30 percent of children were still not completing primary education, including 400,000 who never enrolled even after the re-institution of the policy of free primary policy in education (ibid.). In health, 1.1 million children who were younger than 2 years old had not received all recommended vaccinations, and 2.1 million children were stunted (ibid.: xvi).

More recently, another right-based approach has been used, namely the Multiple Overlapping Deprivation Analysis (MODA), which "identifies children as poor if they are deprived in basic goods and services that are crucial for them to survive, develop, and thrive" (UNICEF and KNBS 2017: 8). MODA focusses on the child and not the household, by measuring whether and how many needs of a child are met and how the child may experience multiple deprivations simultaneously (Plavgo and Milliano 2018). Poverty is seen as affecting children differently from adults and this measure is also based on life-stage specific needs. The approach has been lauded for paying attention to the processes of accessing services instead of solely relying on statistics. It also utilizes qualitative data to understand the experiences of children (Chzhen et al. 2016; KNBS and UNICEF 2017). In a first ever MODA study in Kenya in 2017, 45 percent of all children in Kenya—9.5 million children—were seen as "severely deprived in at least 3 or more basic needs for their wellbeing" and therefore multi-dimensionally poor (ibid.: 25).

2. Understanding child poverty and vulnerability differently

Even though rights-based approaches acknowledge the multi-dimensional nature of child poverty, I argue that in themselves they do not capture the complex experience of child poverty. There is a need to do research that opens possibilities for complex experiences of poverty and produces new understandings. Additionally, there is a need for an approach that focusses on finer textures of children's experiences beyond deprivation and the dominant categories of poor and vulnerable children (e.g. OVC). For instance, among rights-based approaches, only specific indicators of material deprivation are utilised, as this is deemed important to ensure that the measure can be grasped by policy makers (Abdu and Delamonica 2018). In addition, only deprivations that are underpinned by constitutive rights are incorporated, leaving out other rights-based deprivations such as child labour. Other indicators, regardless of their importance to children's lives and their rights, are seen as spuriously correlated and potentially undermining the measure's validity (Abdu and Delamonica 2018: 887). Similar issues also apply to categorical approaches that use entirely qualitative indicators of poverty and vulnerability. In the policy sphere, categories are used to define groups who are assumed to share particular qualities; this makes it reasonable to subject them to the same outcomes of policy (Bakewell, 2008: 436).

While important for policy and programme thinking, I contend that categories may eschew diversity and gloss over experiences that deviate from well-known categories (Reynolds 2014: 138). While Urban (2016) concurs that research should be useful for policy, she notes that a focus on ends(in this case policy considerations) rather than the means, points to the power of discourse for framing what is seen as useful science in policy discussions. She notes that policy makers would want perspectives that articulate global impacts of a phenomenon, and that providing solutions and justifications through good science are seen as secondary (2016: 110). As a result, complex experiences may be overlooked. Even within more qualitative approaches to research, one of the difficulties in capturing the lived experiences of child poverty and vulnerability has been the lack of voice of children. Caregivers tend to speak on children's behalf. For example, Boyden et al. (2003) noted the absence of children's voices in programmes on child poverty arguing that, "there is [far] too little understanding of how children experience poverty, what impoverishment means to them" (21). Tafere (2012) made a similar observation that little attention had been given to children's perspectives of poverty.

I concur with the authors above that children's voices would enable a better understanding of lived experiences of child poverty and vulnerability. I however also draw from James (2007), who noted that we should be careful about methodological pitfalls when invoking children's voice. This is because children's voices may be edited or smoothed over by adult voices, may be influenced by power relations, may be contradictory, and children's silence may indicate voice (Mazzei 2007; Spyrou 2016). All of this requires methods attuned to properly capturing such voice.

Drawing from my one-year research on child poverty and vulnerability in Siaya, Kenya in 2016–2017, I enter into the debate of children's lived experiences of child poverty and vulnerability in two ways. First, I offer a perspective on the methodology I utilised to investigate the complex lived experiences of child poverty and vulnerability in Kenya, and how I moved beyond studying the dominant categories of children who are living in poverty and vulnerability. I elaborate on how I used rhizomatic mapping for capturing complexity and connectivity in children's experiences, instead of relying on linear perspectives of measurement and categorization. Secondly, I provide four illustrations of the experiences of child poverty and vulnerability that point to a need for going beyond current thinking and practice in categorization.

3.   Researching like a Rhizome: Theoretical and methodological considerations

I explored the experiences of child poverty and vulnerability in three interrelated spaces in children's lives, namely the household, the school and programmes of support to vulnerable and poor children. Deleuze and Guattari's (1987) philosophy of rhizome guided my understanding of children's experience as well as well as the methodology for the research.

Deleuze and Guattari used the image of a rhizome to reflect a reality that is not linear or hierarchical, but heterogeneous and complex. A rhizome is a non-arboreal plant that grows laterally and unpredictably and whose different nodes proliferate in the ground. Examples of rhizomes include ginger, grass, among others (Deleuze and Guattari 1987). They contrast a rhizome with a tree which is hierarchical, with a root and trunk system of growth. According to Deleuze and Guattari (1987), a rhizome is governed by several principles that can be used in analysing diverse realities in society. Here I explore three principles that guided my research and the arguments in this chapter. These are the principles of connectivity, multiplicity and cartography.

Connectivity refers to a rhizome only being composed of lines that are connected with each other in complex ways. Seeing things rhizomatically therefore means focusing on the connections between and within what might otherwise be seen as discrete entities. Guided by this principle, I explored the interconnected nature of the experiences of children.

The principle of multiplicity means that a rhizome does not grow in a unilinear way, but that it is non-hierarchical, and its multiple nodes can be connected to other nodes forming an "assemblage" (Deleuze and Guattari 1987: 7). Such a principle enabled me to capture the interaction of complex factors in the experience of children, instead of a linear approach of causes and effects of poverty. I explored how this multiplicity of experience is formed around diverse processes and factors including material lack, gaps in policies, social relations and norms.

The principle of mapping or a cartography guides the overall narrative in the chapter. Deleuze and Guattari noted that a "the rhizome pertains to a map that must be produced, constructed, a map that is always detachable, connectable, reversible, modifiable, and has multiple entryways and exits" (1987: 21). Thus, I see the experience of children as a map, and emphasize connections rather than separations, unlike the common categorical practices of research. Like a map, the experiences of children that I explore here can have multiple entry points as well as exits and can be read differently. Such a perspective enables an understanding of the dynamism of the experience of child poverty and vulnerability, and how it shifts along diverse axes and contexts (Carducci et al., 2011).

Rhizomatic thinking determined the way I encountered and selected children during the research. I chose to research in Siaya, a county characterized as one of the poorest in Kenya. I carried out the research with children and young people aged 0–22 years old, who were supported by different poverty programmes, and other children who were described as poor in the community. I worked intensively with about 90 children through households, and with more than 100 others through various interactions, mainly in schools.

In researching the experiences of children like a rhizome, I utilised methods that were emerging (I'Anson, 2013), and that enabled a perspective into connections in the experiences of children. Researching like a rhizome meant that perspectives from one encounter guided successive encounters. I utilised several child-centred ethnographic methods "to meet children in their experience" (Smith and Greene 2015: 205). These included go-along and in situ interviews, semi-autobiographical essays, participant diaries, creative writing, photo narratives and observations.

These multiple methods enabled me to go beyond spoken voice and to capture the multiplicity of perspectives in children's voice (Jackson and Mazzei 2009) and experience as it unfolded during the research process. This is what I have called "listening softly" to children's voice. This also meant that the methods were not just aimed at triangulating the perspectives by children, but at capturing emerging perspectives. Data synthesis was dynamic and continuous, where reading data from diverse methods enabled me to follow emerging leads. Martin and Kamberelis (2013) argue that "mapping affords opportunities to read data as complex, connected networks rather than as sets of discrete relations between and among variables" (676).

In listening with care (George 2010), I obtained consent from teachers and caregivers to engage with children, but also obtained permission from children. Researching voice differently was also an ethical approach. For example, while I recognized that silence could mean power issues between children and myself, I also used other methods to understand the silence (Syprou 2016).

4.   Stepping out and stepping into the categorical practices in research

In the initial research stages, I was operating with a categorical perspective. In selecting children, I started with children who were already considered to be poor because they were either orphaned, were fostered by relatives or were staying with grandmothers, or had been recruited into programmes on the basis of the fact that they were described as poor. But during my research, it emerged that the status of children changed throughout, therefore disrupting my earlier categorical thinking.

There was no local name for a poor and vulnerable child in the Luo community in Siaya. Several informants noted that these were "children whom we know how they live" and this meant children living in difficulties. Such a description also draws from local repertoires of living well as having all needs met. In some cases, these children were described as *Nyithindo machandore,* children who are suffering, or children who were receiving *kony* (assistance) from programmes of support. But these children were distinguished from those that were receiving assistance by being fostered by relatives for example. In many cases, children themselves did not describe themselves as poor but noted various challenges they faced like lack of food or school supplies. In some cases, older children also used metaphors to describe their experience. One of the metaphors they used was "we are just like this," a phrase that shows a person without material resources. I argue that it is not so much the notion of deprivation that was emphasized in these local repertoires of a poor and vulnerable child but rather the experience of being a suffering child.

As the process of data collection unfolded, my methods enabled me to encounter other experiences and children that I had not factored in my research. Categories did not therefore entirely frame the research. For example, new children were referenced during the discussions or encounters with teachers, household members or other children, and some emerged during my daily reflection on emerging perspectives or through my reflection on data.

In stepping in and out of categorical thinking, I use four examples to illustrate the experiences of children in the research site. Despite assigning identifiers or categories, my intention is not to present core characteristics of children in a particular group. I however note that some categories may conform to the known categories of poor children in research, policy and practice. Referencing categories while disavowing them might look like I am caught in my own argument. Analytically, the aim of taking a particular description as a starting point is to illustrate how that experience connects diverse processes, factors and categories. Showing the interconnections and entanglements within and across groups shows the complexity within these categories or what McCall (2005: 1773) had earlier called intra-categorical complexities. However, in this chapter, my aim is to show how complex experiences may be downplayed by focusing on specific dominant categorization of poor and vulnerable children.

5.   Children "staying on their own", child-headed households and on status transit

I tell the story of these children through the lens of two families. These children were cared for by their siblings and were "staying on their own", or conventionally termed as child-headed households. I however delve further into this dominant category to reveal that it is a fluid, complex and a dynamic category.

In the first family, three children in my research were living with an elder brother Oluoch[1] who was 24 years old. They had started staying on their own when Oluoch was 17 years old, following the death of their mother. In his version of the story, Oluoch did not start narrating his experiences starting with the death of his mother but from his mother's accident and sickness that wiped out family resources. After staying in their grandmother's house, his uncle who relocated to the village from the city forced them out of the grandmother's house. While Foster et al. (1997) noted that these households are transient based on the ability of

---

1   All the names used are pseudonyms to protect the identity of children and caregivers.

the extended family to organize themselves to take care of the children, in this case, several factors come into play to determine whether children are taken in or not.

Due to challenges with school fees, community members encouraged Oluoch to join a low quality vocational school, commonly known as polytechnics. However, he declined and insisted that he deserved high school education like his peers. The fluidities and ruptures in his experience were further evident when a well-wisher who was supporting him with school fees became widowed and Oluoch dropped out of school again. Another node was added to his status and experience when he was employed as a domestic worker and moved in with the family together with his three siblings.

Oluoch narrated that he eventually received support with school fees from a non-governmental organization (NGO) and he combined schooling with working as a domestic worker. However, this support, while positive, brought with it a new set of vulnerabilities and dynamics. Without paying attention to his caregiving roles, the NGO recruited him as a volunteer and so he lost his job as a domestic worker and consequently his accommodation. They were then forced to rent a small house in the centre.

Within the context of struggling to survive and sometimes stigma in the community, Oluoch had instructed his siblings not to disclose their orphan status. He stated, "We are very strong, and nobody knows my brothers are orphans." Oluoch's position challenges the stereotype of children cashing in on the status of orphanhood for material support (e.g. see Fassin, 2013; Ansell, 2016 and Cheney, 2017). While the refusal of label as an orphan may liberate oneself from stigma, it also comes with loss of privileges that may accompany this label. For example, some children who were known to the teachers as orphans would be excused from paying school fees.

Oketch's narrative, a 20 year-old male in high school, is a story that was often told interspersed with loud silences. Yet, similar to Oluoch, it is also dynamic. He described himself as "living on his own" from an early age after his four maternal aunts, his father, mother and grandmother died in that order, and when having left school to work for several years. Death and "being alone" were the vernaculars of his narrative as revealed through his semi-autobiographical essays, interviews in situ and observations. A close reading of his narrative however revealed a need to nuance the sensibility of being alone because the head teacher in his school and the cook were acting as his surrogate parents by supporting with food and school fees, applying for fee bursaries and approaching support organizations on his behalf. This mirrors the experiences of several other children in the research site, with school staff acting as caregivers.

Though narrating himself as alone, Oketch was also a de facto caregiver to his step-sister, Stella, whose mother had died. Stella had earlier been placed in a children's home but was later withdrawn by Oketch's cousin. Four months later the cousin died, leaving Stella with their cousin's wife, who was 21 years and already a mother of two. The whole family including Stella then moved to stay with the mother of their cousin's wife. The 42 year-old woman was overly burdened because she was also taking care of her other daughter and her child. On a later encounter with Oketch, Stella had moved to stay with him because their cousin's wife had left to look for a job, and she had told Oketch that they were no longer related. Indeed, the cousin's wife had earlier on asked me when I asked her about Stella; "who will pay her [Stella's] school fees? The one who was supporting her died."

Further encounters revealed that Oketch had approached the children's home to take Stella back, but Stella refused. Eventually in 2017, Stella started living with their grandmother's sister in another community. Given the fact that the woman is elderly, a possible death could introduce new vulnerabilities or signal another practical, material or status-transit and mobility. This mobility was evident in his brother Oketch: two years after my research when I visited in 2018, he was no longer staying on his own but had moved in with a well-wisher in the community. While he was silent when I asked him why he moved, a staff member in his school told me that Oketch was frequently falling sick and teachers thought there was a bad omen in their home. This fear of witchcraft was obviously a new line in understanding his experience of mobility.

I argue that one can never put a full stop to the experience of being simultaneously an orphaned child, a child caregiver, a circulated or fostered child and a poor child in status transit; all of these loosely appended to the status of being orphaned or a lone/and/or a member of a child headed household.

6. Ambiguities in fostered child category: "This is a child that God brought to us"

I encountered several children who had been placed with different caregivers for support. For some, this was due to death of their parents, while for others it was because their mothers had re-married elsewhere or were perceived as needy. Fostering does not necessarily presuppose that the foster parents are well off; the choices were sometimes guided by the notions of kin relations or what emerged during my research as notions of "my blood" where relatives felt compelled to support needy children within their kinship network (see also Cheney, 2016).

These caregivers therefore experienced the burden that accompanies caring under resource-constrained circumstances especially in providing food and educational support to children. Children who are fostered may slip through the net of support from organisations or even state support because of assumptions regarding the economic capacity of adoptive parents. My research revealed a need for going beyond observable household assets in determining children's needs, as children who are fostered may not benefit from these assets. For example, while Chzhen et al. (2016) noted that some types of children's needs may differ from adults' needs, they noted that lack of housing for children can be proxied by lack of housing for adults because housing is a shared asset. However, my research revealed this was not always the case.

Otieno is a 11 year old boy fostered by his grandmother. After an analysis of an essay he wrote, and my household observations, I discovered that he was not sleeping in the good house that I had seen when visiting their home. Instead, he slept in a separate old house which served as a kitchen that he described as "surrounded by a bush which has a snake and the roof is leaking." He was not willing to disclose the reason for his stay in the kitchen, but my research assistant attributed this to a practice in the Luo culture that prescribed that pre-pubescent or pubescent boys and girls could not sleep in the same house with their sexually active caregivers. While this practice was originally attributed to limited sleeping space and poverty, over the years, it had been appropriated as a sexual taboo, thereby affecting the well-being of children. Several children in this community were therefore either sharing sleeping space with chicken or other cattle in the kitchen, or their essays and diaries showed that they had to go each evening to sleep with their friends who had a separate house. Girls bore the brunt of this because boys in some cases had separate houses.

While this deprivation was occasioned by the need to comply with cultural norms, it also shows the complexities of giving voice to children and caregivers in poverty research. This is because when I asked Otieno's caregiver whether she lived in the same house with the fostered children, she did not mention that the children slept in a separate house. Similarly, Otieno did not reveal this either in interviews and discussions. Chaizhen (2016: 341) says that parents may underreport the extent of deprivation to comply with societal norms and that estimating the full extent of this bias in reporting is difficult. However, guided by my rhizomatic methodology where I read the focus group and individual interview against Otieno's essay and my own observations and further discussions with key informants, I was able to capture these perspectives which were otherwise hidden.

Children sometimes move from one relative to another on a continuous basis, based on the perceived ability of the relative to help, suffering in the foster family or as a result of missing their biological families. However, children appeared ambivalent about this experience. Donald, a 20 year-old and a de facto caregiver to four siblings, noted: "My sister has stayed with two sets of relatives and she suffered. If a relative said, [let me go with this girl], my parents would oblige. .... one enjoys an opportunity to take tea in the morning." Earlier interactions with his sister had revealed that she was over-worked and sexually assaulted in one of the families where she was fostered, and she eventually gave birth and dropped out of school.

The fact that children have to make choices between staying in potentially harmful situations and an opportunity to have tea or eat breakfast points to the precariousness of their situation. The danger for Donald's sister also emerged through connecting experiences rhizomatically to diverse biographic factors, ranging from having uneducated parents without a sustainable livelihood strategy, and his father having been fostered and having been evicted together with his family after the caregiver died. Adding to this biography was the breakdown of the social contract between these children and the state, which had not provided adequate support to these children (Okwany and Ngutuku, 2018).

Fostering children is often done for purposes of reciprocity, with the expectation that children will provide support to caregivers. For elderly caregivers, a key motivation is their need for company. Two caregivers who were hosting a fostered child noted: "this is the child that God brought to us." The child reciprocated support with his high school fees by watching over their home and supporting the elderly grandparents. A narrative by another caregiver fostering a 12 year-old girl shows that this need for reciprocity is however tangled with need for child protection. As she noted: "The mother to Linah, (12 years old) was needy and was working for me. When the mother was leaving, I asked her if I could stay with Linah, so she could help me at night". In going beyond categories however, one can take a different line in reading Linah's narrative to explore her entangled experience. Linah straddles another identity label that I explore later; an "outsider" child, because she was not the biological child of the husband to her mother. Earlier it was reported that due to this, the stepfather had physically assaulted her, and she had been staying with relatives before she accompanied the mother to work for the current caregiver.

The research also revealed that children who do not reciprocate to their caregivers may be vilified and were often returned to their original home. Abebe (2010: 466) has argued that the nature of the relationship between the foster parent and the deceased relative determines how well children will be treated. For example, a caregiver who had taken in four children after her neighbour died noted that her neighbour was a good friend and so when the neighbour died, she took in her children. Another caregiver who had fostered her brother's son noted: "my brother was good to my mother and when he died, I took good care of his children." This voice was contradictory, however, since this same caregiver explained that she had previously returned a sister of this fostered child back to her extended family because of indiscipline.

The narratives discussed in this section therefore indicate that the experiences of children may vary. It also reveals that we should focus on the dynamics of the process of fostering and seek to understand how this practice has metamorphosed within specific contexts of generalized economic insecurity and poverty as well as agency by children in such care arrangements. Following Carsten (2004), these everyday practices of people in fostering are also important.

7.   Fluidities of being labelled an "outsider" child

The status of a child labelled "outsider" is one of the defining experiences of children that I interacted with. In the Luo community, children are labelled "outsiders" when fathered by another man other than the husband to the mother. The notions of being an outsider in this context were fluid since children could be seen as an 'insider' while in their natural father's household but an outsider if the mother remarried and took them along. Children born to unwed mothers were also seen as outsiders when the mother married into new households.[2] When such children are left in their maternal relatives' home, they may also be exposed to further stigma. This same label was ambivalent since one could be an orphaned, an outsider child as well as a fostered or circulated child simultaneously. Each of these statuses obtain different salience in terms of vulnerability depending on the context.

For example, Linda, a 15 year-old girl, was seen as "outsider" while in her stepfather's household. After the death of her father, her mother remarried and left the children under the care of paternal relatives because the new husband did not want the burden of care. The paternal relatives neglected the children and so the mother took them to her new matrimonial home, where they faced further neglect. Linda and her siblings were placed with other relatives who could not provide proper care for them. Eventually Linda was fostered by non-kin, to get education support, in exchange for her services as a child minder. An important node in the experience of these children is the local notions of inheritance and culture. Such children are imagined in the local repertoires as "taking away the luck" of the legitimate children, meaning benefitting from resources that belong to the bona fide heirs. Their experience should also be connected to the state laws and legal provisions since the Kenya constitution (2010) provides that a father should assume parental responsibility whether married to the mother or not. The husband should also take responsibility whether he is biological father or not.

While the older children may be aware of this label of being an "outsider", the younger children were informed that they were staying

---

2   Even though I use the word outsider as a comprehensive word, discussions with my informants reveal that there are different labels given to these children in the local language, determined by if they were born to unwed mothers, married with the mother into a new home, etc.

with maternal grandparents to provide them company or to benefit from better schools, and they appropriated the same view and voice in our discussions. However, reading through their diaries, essays and drawings, it was revealed that even the young children see this practice as unjust. Otieno, an 11 year-old boy in class four, said during an interview session that he was providing company to his grandmother; however, later he described in his essay, that he as a child was struggling on his own. He noted that, "this boy, his mother does not care about him and has left him to struggle on his own." Otieno and his brother felt like they are struggling on their own, even though they are described as fostered, living with a grandmother who was not only widowed but also suffered from a stroke and HIV/AIDS; the household also had an uncle's wife who sometimes refused to cook for them. My analysis reveals a need for a non-simplistic reading of this situation of apparent neglect. Some grandmother carers to these fostered children noted that while their daughters or daughters in law, even though married elsewhere, would have wanted to look after their biological children, they were also struggling economically and dependent on their maternal households or husbands for support.

8.   Children on itinerary with projects and scouting for Good Samaritans

In this section, I provide a perspective on children who were "following after projects" or "scouting for good Samaritans" as one of the emergent characteristics of children that may not be captured using conventional methods. Within the Kenyan landscape of child care where there is limited support by the state, several NGOs are working in support of children in poverty. These programmes have made children to develop new behaviours of continually being on the lookout for projects as they seek support. This finding concurs with Mcdonald (2009: 40) who argues that specific institutional arrangements like programmes of support in this case, may influence the experience of children.

Alidi who was seven years by the time we met had lost both parents and with his two sisters, were left under the custody of their 20-year-old brother, then 18 years old. They did not have a house of their own, since culture stipulates that the house is abandoned after the death of parents, and they lived in a rented make-shift house next to the lake. The brother, like the rest in this community, lived precariously and relied on small scale fishing where he rented both the fishing gear, boat and also rented the fishing route from other fishermen. Alidi had been moving from one relative to another; for example, after his mother's death, he stayed with his aunt in Nairobi and later went back to the village to stay with his brother. In 2016, when we met, he was once again staying with his brother and his sister, since one of their younger sisters had become sick and died a year earlier. Alidi, who also had HIV/AIDS, another node in the experience of poverty, was occasionally going to the hospital alone to collect medication that were provided by the state for free. After some time, he went again to live with another aunt after his brother was arrested by the police.

Despite the precarious situation that Alidi experienced at his brother's home, he was yet again forced to go back to stay with the brother because he was enrolled in a programme which supports poor children. To comply with the criteria of being resident in the community, the community worker prevailed upon Alidi's aunt to allow him to go back to live with his brother. By the time we met, though recruited to the project, he was not receiving any support. Fitting into the organization's set criteria for support by being in the community is one of the registers governing poor children and their caregivers (Foucault 1980). It interacted with Alidi's material condition to influence childcare options available. This situation was the same for several other children supported by programmes who indicated that they were not allowed to stay with well-off relatives in other communities, even though the programmes were not meeting their needs adequately.

Mobilities by children and fostering within the context of projects have also acquired new meanings and connotations. For example, in one of the research sites, there was one organization that was supporting girls' education, and three girls engaged in these programmes. To meet the targets, communities in this project site were encouraged to bring girls who were not going to school, even those living in different parts of the country. Donor reporting called for the staff to mobilise beyond the project catchment area to get the required numbers. While seemingly problematic, such mobilities emerged as positive for some children who were negotiating their citizenship rights to education at these two levels of the non-state actors and kin-based support.

However, within the context of what I call "adoption for projects," foster care giving practices may be reconfigured and children might encounter specific vulnerabilities within these arrangements, since some foster carers do not assume full rights of care. For the case of Purple, who was 16 years and in high school, the foster caregiver (her aunt) provided food and maintained contacts with Purple's mother, asking her to provide partial fees and other supplies. However, the foster caregiver revealed tensions in such fostering when she noted, "I brought my niece who has been out of school and approached the project to support. But her family thinks that I took in their child to support, feeding her is my contribution." Her niece was also expected to reciprocate by providing support in the household. Discussions with Purple indicated that these partial rights and expectations were stressful because her guardian family often constructed her as lazy and as cashing in on the guardian's wealth, threatening to take her back to her mother.

Children who were not receiving support have also developed sensibilities of survival by hanging around the projects or "looking for good Samaritans," as they called it. For example, Aisha, a 15 year-old orphaned girl who had been out of school for a year due to lack of school fees, was hanging out near a girls' education project, hoping to get education support. She had moved from her aunt's home back to the community when her friends were recruited. She noted that her grandmother, in yet another form of symbolic "hanging around," had been nagging her to scout for donors, and her younger brother was also said to be moving around looking for *wazungu* (white people) to support his education. Later in 2017, I was informed that Aisha had moved from the brother's place, perhaps looking for another project. One can therefore conclude that while the other enduring characteristics like orphanhood and economic hardship may look like the underlying reasons of movement for these children, failure to account for this experience may deflect attention from the entangled practices within programmes and how they influence the experience of child poverty and vulnerability this way.

9. Discussion: Understanding children's experience without packaging it

The narratives presented in this chapter indicate that the experiences of child poverty and vulnerability are complex and fluid. This supports a need to explore experiences in situ and as a cartography, as I did in this research. In favouring an approach that enables an exploration of the quotidian experiences of children beyond numbers and multi-dimensionality, I have responded to the calls by several authors to understand children's experience differently.

The application of rhizomatic methods in this research constitutes a social critique that contributes towards disrupting our common sense knowledge on child poverty and vulnerability experience (Honan 2004). These methods engage the application of linear methods of investigation, which may lead to a situation where categories are seen as discrete, and yet it is our research methodologies that create the discrete reality.

In demonstrating the difficulties in tidying up the experience of children, the illustrations show rhizomatic entanglements and engage with important questions of who these children are and how they are known. It also shows how children sometimes act beyond the way they are constructed and categorized. I have also offered glimpses of how children may occupy fluid categories at the same time. A child can simultaneously occupy interacting categories of children orphaned, children fostered or circulated, "outsider children", child caregivers, children on status transit, and itinerant children. This supports Minha-ha's assertion that even though we may always want to "separate, contain and mend, categories always leak" (1989: 94).

Some authors have noted that the emphasis on fluidity runs the risk of overlooking the structural power at work. For example, Gigengack (2014: 8) when arguing against the construction of street children as a fluid category, noted that it was only at the level of the theory that the category looked porous but not in the actual day to day lives of children. However, arguing for a need to go beyond categories in this research was not just a theoretical manoeuvre; it was enabled by my continued engagement in the community where I witnessed specific experiences change, transmute and others emerge for specific children. The discussions support the argument by McDonald (2009) that social theory and social policy should work hand in hand with understanding child poverty and vulnerability. It also supports Tafere's (2012: 23) argument that children's contributions should respond to ontological, epistemological and methodological challenges childhood studies are facing.

The contingent and fluid experience of child poverty does not mean that we cannot know poor and vulnerable children, but rather that we can know them in complex ways. I also hold the view that theorising and doing child poverty research differently should not be seen to be at odds with policy or what Abdu and Delamonica (2018) term as a "theoretical curiosum" (882). In going beyond "science as usual" (Harding 1991: 1) in understanding children's reality, I see this level of engagement that draws from my data as alive and reflexive (Reynolds 2014). Energised by other researchers who have used rhizomatic methodologies to understand diverse reality in children including play, identity and education among others (e.g Honan, 2007, Gabi, 2013, St Pierre, 2004), I am optimistic about the potential of the rhizomatic approach leading to a better understanding of child poverty experience.

10. Signposts for policy

While rhizomatic methodologies do not provide a road map for policy and practice because of their emphasis on multiple entry points, I provide potential signposts for policy and practice. A key question I pose is: how can we still theorise or understand the fluidity of experience of children, without rendering child poverty and vulnerability experience meaningless to policy and programmes of support?

10.1.   Context-based research and interventions

I point to a need for attention to contextual differences and idiosyncrasies of children's experiences. Such an approach however goes beyond simple contextual differences, which may be quite obvious, to an approach that reveals the entanglement of fluid and contingent differences within each specific setting. Such an idiosyncratic approach may look elusive, fragmented and disorderly, challenging established criteria for categorizing, which is important for policy. However, research that is attentive to context and specificity of experience, and one that attends to children's voice can yield important insights for our understanding of what it means to live as a poor child in specific contexts. It is an approach that behoves us to map reality as we encounter it, but not to rely on predetermined maps.

Goethals et al. (2015) suggest we approach the context with an attitude of "I completely do not know," thereby creating spaces for complex and ambiguous experience. Such an approach can make visible some experiences like children seen as "outsiders," who may be living out of the focus of the "sharp lights of policy" (Bakewell, 2008: 450). Taking a middle ground from Goethals et al. (2015) and finding out how specific contexts may make some experiences more plausible than others, would be a stepping-stone to better knowing children.

In addition, walking the route of addressing child poverty cannot be indifferent to the processes in diverse contexts that influence it. Such an approach should reveal not only how children may be multiply disadvantaged but also the processes and non-linear relationships between the different experiences of child poverty and vulnerability in these contexts.

10.2.   Anti-essentialist categorisation

While categories may be important for specific policy makers and programme implementers, I recommend that these categories should not be seen as fixed, but these generalizations could be seen as temporary ways or a beginning of a journey; they help with community entry and then mapping the experience of the children on the ground. Min-ha (1989), points to a need to decentre categories, to question them, work within them and even go beyond them.

Useful questions that could guide programming and policy would be: how do we factor in possible changes in the experience of children, or what needs to be changed in the way programmes work, to better capture fluid and emerging experience of children? What other categories or experiences might exist within a particular context? What other experiences are being eschewed by the fixed category? What else is silenced in this context and how can experience that deviates from the normal be captured? This means that predetermined categories do not drive the agenda, but project implementers are open to what is available on the ground.

References

Abdu, Maryam, and Enrique Delamonica, 2018. "Multidimensional Child Poverty: From Complex Weighting to Simple Representation." *Social Indicators Research: An International and Interdisciplinary Journal for Quality-of-Life Measurement.* Vol 136(3): 881–905.

Abebe, Tatek 2010. "Beyond the 'Orphan Burden': Understanding *Care for* and *by* AIDS-Affected Children in Africa." *Geography Campus* Vol 4, No 5.

Ansell, Nicola 2016. "Once upon a Time …: Orphanhood, Childhood Studies and the Depoliticisation of Childhood Poverty in Southern Africa." *Childhood* Vol. 23, No 2.

Bakewell, Oliver 2008. "Research Beyond the Categories: The Importance of Policy Irrelevant Research into Forced Migration." *Journal of Refugee Studies,* Vol. 21, No. 4.

Boyden, Jo, Eyber, Carola, Feeny, Thomas and Caitlin Scott 2003. "Children and Poverty: Experiences and Perceptions from Belarus, Bolivia, India, Kenya and Sierra Leone." Christian Children Fund Poverty Series.

Carducci, Rozanna, Kuntz, Aaron, Gildersleeve, Ryan and Penny Pasque 2011. "Disruptive Dialogue Project: Crafting Critical Space in Higher Education." *UCLA Journal of Educational and Information Studies.* Vol 7 No 2.

Chzhen, Yekaterina, de Neubourg Chris, Plavgo, Ilze and Marlous de Milliano 2016. "Child Poverty in the European Union: The Multiple Overlapping Deprivation Analysis Approach (EU-MODA)." *Child Indicators Research* Vol 9 No 9: 335.

Carsten, Janet 2004. *After Kinship.* Cambridge: Cambridge University Press.

Cheney, Kristen 2017. *Crying for Our Elders: African Orphanhood in the Age of HIV and AIDS.* Chicago: University Press.

Cheney, Kristen 2016. "'Blood Always Finds a Way Home': AIDS Orphanhood and the Transformation of Kinship, Fosterage, and Children's Circulation Strategies in Uganda." In: Hunner-Kreisel, Christine, Bohne, Sabine (eds) 2016. *Childhood, Youth and Migration: Children's Well-Being, Indicators and Research.* Vol 12. Springer, Cham.

Delamonica, Enrique 2014. "Separating and Combining Child and Adult Poverty: Why? How?" *Poverty Brief.* CROP.

Deleuze, Gilles and Felix Guattari 1987. *A Thousand Plateaus: Capitalism and Schizophrenia.* Minneapolis: University of Minnesota Press.

Fassin, Didier 2013. "Children as victims: The Moral Economy of Childhood in the times of AIDS." In João, Biehl and Petryna, Adriana (eds). *When People Come First: Critical Studies in Global Health.* Princeton: Princeton University Press.

Foster Geoff, Makufa, Choice, Drew, Roger, and Etta Kralovec 1997. "Factors Leading to the Establishment of Child-Headed Households: the case of Zimbabwe." *Health Transition Review. Supplement 2 to Volume 7: 155–168.*

Gabi, Josephine 2013, *Rhizomatic Cartographies of Belonging and Identity within Early Years Education*. Thesis submitted in partial fulfilment of the requirements of the Manchester Metropolitan University for the Degree of Doctor of Philosophy.

George, Shanti 2010. "Why Children Voices are Largely Unheard in Ethnography." In Baviskar B and P. Tulsi (eds). *Understanding Indian Society Past and Present: Essays for A.M Shah*. New Delhi: Orient Blackswan: 331–351.

Gigengack, Roy 2014. "Beyond Discourse and Competence: Science and Subjugated Knowledge in Street Children Studies." *The European Journal of Development Research*. Vol 26 No 2: 264–282.

Goethals, Tina, De Schauwer Elisabeth and Geert Van Hove "Weaving Intersectionality into Disability Studies Research: Inclusion, Reflexivity and Anti-Essentialism". *Journal of Diversity and Gender Studies*. Vol. 2, No. 1–2: 75–94.

Government of Kenya and UNICEF 2014. *Situation Analysis of Children and Adolescents in Kenya: Our Children, Our Future*. Nairobi.

Government of Kenya 2012a. *Social Protection Sector Review*. Ministry for Planning, National Development and Vision 2030.

Government of Kenya 2012b. *3rd, 4th And 5th State Party Report to The UNCRC Committee*. Geneva.

Harding, Sandra 1991. *Whose Science? Whose Knowledge?* New York: Cornell University.

Honan, Eileen 2004. "(Im)plausibilities: A Rhizo-Textual Analysis of Policy Texts and Teachers' work." *Educational Philosophy and Theory*. Vol 36 No 3.

Honan, Eileen 2007. "Writing a Rhizome: An(Im)plausible Methodology." *International Journal of Qualitative Studies in Education*. Vol 20 No 5.

James, A. 2007. "Giving Voice to Children's Voices: Practices and Problems, Pitfalls and Potentials." *American Anthropologist* Vol 109 No 2.

I'Anson, John (2013). "Beyond the Child's Voice: Towards an Ethics for Children's Participation Rights." *Global Studies of Childhood*. Vol 3 No 2.

Jackson, Alecia and Lisa Mazzei 2009. "The Limits of Voice" in Jackson, Alecia and Lisa Mazzei, eds.) *Voice in Qualitative Inquiry: Challenging Conventional, Interpretive, and Critical Conceptions in Qualitative Research*. London: Routledge.

Kenya National Bureau of Statistics and UNICEF 2017. *Child Poverty in Kenya: A Multi-Dimensional Approach*. Nairobi.

Law, John 2004. *After Method: Mess in Social Science Research*. London and New York: Routledge, Taylor and Francis.

McCall, Leslie 2005. "The Complexity of Intersectionality." *Signs: Journal of Women in Culture and Society*. Vol 30 No. 3.

McDonald, Catherine 2009. "Children and Poverty: Why Their Experience of Their Lives matter for Policy." *Australian Journal of Social Issues*. Vol 44 No 1.

Martin, Adrian, and George Kamberelis 2013. "Mapping Not Tracing: Qualitative Educational Research with Political Teeth." *International Journal of Qualitative Studies in Education*. Vol 26, No 6.

Mazzei, Lisa 2007. "Inhabited Silence in Qualitative Research: Putting Post Structural Theory to Work." New York: Peter Lang Publishing.

Minh-ha, Trinh 1989. *Woman, Native, Other: Writing Post-Coloniality and Feminism.* Bloomington: Indiana University Press.

Okwany, Lilian and Elizabeth Ngutuku 2018. "Social Protection and Citizenship Rights of Vulnerable Children: A Perspective on Interventions by Non-state Actors in Western Kenya." In Awortwi, Nicholas and Gregor Walter-Drop. *Non-State Social Protection Actors and Services in Africa: Governance Below the State.* London and New York: Routledge: 55–71.

Roelen Keetie 2017. "Monetary and Multidimensional Child Poverty: A Contradiction in Terms?" *Development and Change.* Vol *48 issue 3.*

Reynolds, Vikki 2014. "A Solidarity Approach: The Rhizome and Messy Inquiry." In Simon, Gail and Alex Chard (eds). *Systemic Inquiry: Innovations in Reflexive Practice Research.* London: Everything Is Connected Books.

Milliano, Marlous and Ilze Plavgo 2018. "Analysing Child Poverty and Deprivation in Sub-Saharan Africa." *Child Indicators Research.* Vol. 11 No 3.

Spyrou, Sypiros, 2016. "Researching Children's Silences: Exploring the Fullness of Voice in Childhood Research." *Childhood.* Vol 23 No 1.

Smith, Carmel, and Sheila Greene 2015. *Key Thinkers in Childhood Studies.* Bristol: Policy Press.

St. Pierre, Elizabeth 2004. "Deleuzian Concepts for Education: The subject Undone." *Education Philosophy and Theory.* Vol 36 No 3.

Tafere, Yisak 2012. "Children's Experiences and Perceptions of Poverty in Ethiopia." Working Paper, No 85. London: Young Lives.

CHAPTER 2
Children and Young People's Experiences of Managing Poverty-Related Shame in Uganda and the UK

Grace Bantebya Kyomuhendo, Elaine Chase and Florence Kyoheirwe Muhanguzi

1. Introduction

Although ideas about how we understand and measure poverty and what constitutes development and poverty reduction are still largely dominated by economic paradigms, there is nonetheless a growing recognition of the limitations of purely economic measures of poverty assessment and alleviation. The work of Amartya Sen has been particularly influential in helping to re-conceptualise development as a process of responding to what people have cause to value rather than only considering their economic wherewithal (Sen, 1989). Sen has also been instrumental in bringing to the fore the psychosocial dimensions of poverty and how these impact on the lives of individuals as connected beings within their families and communities. Subjective perceptions of self, identity and belonging are crucial to the experience of poverty and what might or should constitute appropriate responses to it at multiple levels.

More recent work by Robert Walker and colleagues on the role of shame in the context of poverty has demonstrated how the emotional and social impacts of poverty tend to be very similar, though culturally nuanced, in countries with very different socio-economic profiles (Walker, 2014; Chase and Bantebya-Kyomuhendo, 2015). Figure 1 (below) provides an illustration of the conceptual framework, the poverty-shame nexus, emerging from this work (Walker, 2014: 65).

Figure 1.   Poverty-shame nexus

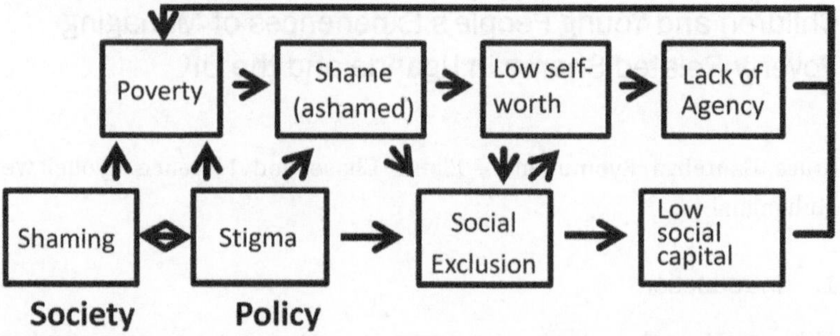

The nexus highlights how the experience of poverty often leads to an internalised sense of inadequacy or inability to achieve one's own expectations or the expectations of others (shame). This in turn can undermine people's sense of self-worth and their ability to change things or take action (agency) and as such a cycle of poverty can be perpetuated. Shame and low self-worth may result in social exclusion, either through self-exclusion or as a result of being pushed out by others in society for not meeting certain social or economic norms. This exclusion reduces people's networks, community links and lines of support (social capital), which may also make it more difficult to escape poverty. But shame is not only internally felt but can be externally imposed by society (including the media, the general public and more immediate community), making people in poverty feel inadequate; and by anti-poverty policies which are framed, designed and delivered in ways which blame people in poverty for their circumstances (shaming, stigma).

Importantly, this work by Walker et al. emphasized the commonalities of the experiences of people living in poverty across different global contexts. Participants all similarly recounted their propensity for withdrawal, self-loathing, othering, despair, depression, thoughts of suicide and reduction in personal efficacy. In some senses, therefore, these social and emotional aspects of poverty give some universality to the experience of poverty, indicating what the global policy response might and should look like (Gubrium et al., 2014).

While poverty is said to cause human suffering and negative experiences in general, poverty in childhood can last a lifetime, creating intergenerational effects (MoGLSD and UNICEF, 2014). The UNICEF and World Bank Group report (2016) emphasises the need for special attention to be paid to children in extreme poverty from the perspective that they have reduced life opportunities and limited chances to develop skills needed for life and work. Chapter 1 in this volume (written by Ngutuku) highlights the need to bring to the fore complex understandings of lived experiences of poverty, particularly for children. Much less attention has been given to the psychological and social consequences for children and young people living in poverty. Given the centrality of dignity within the United Nations Convention on the Rights of the Child (UN, 1989), understanding how such dignity might be undermined through the impacts of poverty is an important yet neglected area of research.

This said, some work to date has highlighted how poverty can impact adversely on children and young people's sense of self and identity. Hence poverty has been associated with developmental trauma when, from a young age, children experience strong feelings of shame and unworthiness that pose a threat to identity formation and instil a sense of intrinsic low self-esteem (Pitillas Salvá, 2016; Mackenzie et al., 2014 cited in Pitillas Salvá, 2016). Research has also shown that even though children's feelings of being humiliated, sad and ashamed are often hidden, these feelings can have deep emotional costs on their lives including social isolation and exclusion (Ridge, 2011; Najman et al., 2010). Although shame is seen as a self-conscious emotion, linked to self-concept and self-esteem (Tangney and Fischer, 1995), it is not always fully under one's control (Montes, 2015) and as noted earlier can be externally imposed through processes of shaming and stigmatization (Walker, 2014). Consequently, children living in poverty are exposed to verbal and symbolic messages from others indicating their failure to live up to desired social standards at a time when they are forming their own sense of self and their place in the world (Farrel, 2011; Friedman, 2015). Pitillas Salvá (2016) and others argue that shame associated with poverty in childhood can variously generate feelings of fear, anxiety, helplessness, lack of autonomy, negative or destructive mirroring, self-worthlessness, guilt, stigmatization, isolation and self-disgust.

Research demonstrates how children in poverty report having to negotiate feelings of shame and stigmatization in a range of settings including the home, school and community. According to Ridge (2010), for example, poverty penetrates deep into the heart of childhood, permeating every facet of children's lives from economic and material disadvantage, through the structuring and limiting of social relationships and social participation to the most personal often hidden aspects of disadvantage associated with shame, sadness and the fear of social difference and marginalization. (73)

In schools, children can be subjected to the indignities of being labelled as 'the poor' through policies such as free school meals (Ridge, 2012; Mathew and Pellissery, 2015). In order to mitigate such stigma, young people may use a range of strategies such as self-exclusion from activities under the pretence of non-economic reasons, obscuring signs of poverty and not asking for help when poverty impacts on their daily lives (Fernqvist, 2013; Ridge, 2010). Analysis of the Young Lives project panel data from Ethiopia, India, Peru and Vietnam (Dornan and Orgando Portlea, forthcoming) has demonstrated a consistent link between the extent of poverty experienced by children and feelings of shame at 12 years old. Furthermore, after controlling for everything else, greater feelings of shame were linked to poorer learning outcomes for children at ages 12 and again at 15 years, thus an indication of a direct impact of shame on children's learning and development (cf Evans et al., 2007, Raphael, 2011; Kim et al., 2013). Young people living in extreme poverty in rural Malawi described the negative impacts on their social networks when they did not have the resources to participate in activities with their more affluent peers, and the stigma they felt as a result of being seen to display the signs poverty (Rock et al., 2016). Similarly, children and young people living on the streets in South Africa reported the extensive stigma and discrimination imposed by other children, the general public, police and bureaucracies more broadly (Chireshe et al., 2010). Yet young people have also been shown to find ways of countering feelings of inadequacy and rationalizing their experiences of poverty. Muslim young people in Nigeria, for example, were shown to emphasize the character-enhancing virtues of endurance and stoicism associated with their faith as means of saving face and moderating feelings of inadequacy and shame in the context of poverty (Hoechner, 2015).

This chapter focuses on the psychosocial dimensions of poverty and their impact on children and young people in Uganda and the UK. It explores children's own lived experiences of poverty through narratives of their daily lives, their encounters with indignity and shame and their responses as they operate in different spatial settings (home and family, school, wider community). The chapter illustrates similarities and differences in young people's experience of the poverty-shame nexus across very different global contexts. It aims to inform the crafting of child focused anti-poverty policies and programmes that engage better with these psychosocial factors affecting children and young people living in poverty. In the process, this chapter outlines an agenda for further research to better understand the poverty-shame nexus as it impacts on children.

2. Methodology

The chapter draws on qualitative data from an Economic and Social Research Council-Department for International Development (ESRC-DfID) funded research project *Poverty, Shame, and Social Exclusion; a Study in Seven Countries* (Walker et al., 2014) conducted between 2011 and 2012. The work, which was simultaneously carried out in Uganda, UK, India, China, Pakistan, Norway and Korea, had two main objectives. Firstly, it sought to test the assertion by Amartya Sen that shame was at the universal core of the experience of poverty. The hypothesis was that if this was the case, then poverty-related shame would be experienced in contexts of very different comparative levels of material deprivation. The second objective was to consider what might be the possible implications for anti-poverty policies if shame were found to be central to the experience of poverty globally. Hence the study methodology sought to unravel the poverty-shame nexus, how it impacts on the daily lives of those living in poverty, the strategies those in poverty adopt to cope with hardship and indignity, and how they respond to state and other anti-poverty policy implementations (for further details see Chase and Bantebya-Kyomuhendo, 2015).

The current analysis focuses on children's positioning in the poverty-shame nexus in Uganda and the United Kingdom. In Uganda, children and young people were included from purposively selected households experiencing extreme hardship in a rural district in the west of the country. In total, 30 children—17 boys and 13 girls ranging from eight to eighteen years—were interviewed in their respective homes. In the UK, 22 children and young people (15 boys and 7 girls) between the ages of 5–18 years took part in the research. These were either the children of adult participants in the study or were identified via children and young people's services in the study localities, selected according to the index of multiple deprivation (Ministry of Housing, Communities and Local Government, 2011).

Young people's participation was voluntary and informed consent was given by both the children and their parents or guardians. The in-depth interviews were conducted on a one to one, face to face basis or, in the case of the UK, sometimes in pairs if young people preferred this form of participation. Importantly, the terms 'shame' and 'poverty' were not used directly in asking children and young people about their situations. Instead, children were asked about their daily lives and whether and how they perceived their economic circumstances to affect their interaction with others. Analysis of data was done using thematic content analysis. Ethical clearance was given by the University of Oxford's Central University Research Ethics Committee, as the study's hosting institution, with additional permissions secured from Makerere University, the collaborating institution in Uganda. In order to ensure anonymity, all names reported in this chapter are pseudonyms and the specific localities of the research have not been included.

3.   Study findings

3.1. The contexts

Uganda is one of the sub-Saharan countries reportedly having registered significant economic growth in recent years along with corresponding poverty reduction, although the extent to which such growth has translated into significant improvements in the wellbeing of people living in poverty remains in question (Arndt et al., 2016; Dulani et al., 2013). While overall poverty reportedly fell from 56 percent in 1992/93 to 19.7 percent in 2012/2013 (Ministry of Finance, Planning and Economic Planning [MoFPED], 2014), more recent evidence shows a reversal in the positive trend and poverty is reported to have risen to 27 percent in 2016/2017 (Uganda Bureau of Statistics, 2017). Child poverty in Uganda remains high across the different regions of the country and is estimated to affect 55 percent of children aged 0–4 years, of which 24 percent are living in extreme poverty; and 30 percent of children aged 6–17 years, with 18 percent living in extreme poverty (Ministry of Gender, Labour and Social Development and the United Nations Children Fund, 2014).

According to the Human Development Index (HDI, 2015) the UK is ranked 16th in the world, compared to Uganda at 163 out of a total of 188 countries. Yet despite its relative wealth, more than fourteen million people currently live in poverty in the UK, defined as living in households below 60 percent of median income. This includes over four million children at the time of writing, with clear indicators that child poverty is on the increase (Joseph Rowntree Foundation, 2017; Department for Work and Pensions, 2018); there are numerous current reports of how families are struggling to meet their basic household needs and to adequately provide for their children.

3.2. The spatial dynamics of shame

Children and young people's experiences of the psychological and social aspects of poverty are layered, illustrating Bronfenbrenner's (1989) social-ecological model of child development and how the different spheres of young people's lives at the family and home, school, community and wider society levels interact in complex ways. The interviews revealed that children spent most of their time either at home or at school, and to a lesser extent in the wider community. These, therefore, became the main operational spaces within which they negotiated real and anticipated exposure to stigma and indignity on a daily basis.

The home as a physical space, as well as what it represented in terms of relationships with family, was central to the narratives of all children and young people in the study.

All children and young people in Uganda narrated daily life experiences characterized by hard living conditions, and deprivation of household basic necessities. They spoke of chronic shortages of foodstuffs such as salt, sugar, flour, cooking oil and meat, combined with limited cooking facilities and basics such as kerosene. A lack of washing and toilet facilities, including no access to soap, meant that they lacked the necessities for personal hygiene and inadequate bedding and clothing were routine problems. The physical effects of such hardships were frequently described as biting hunger due to chronic food shortages, suffering the elements due to dilapidated housing and lack of bedding, exposure to soot and smoke while cooking indoors, and proneness to bouts of sickness related to poor hygiene and sanitation due to lack of latrines, solid waste and water disposal facilities. Some young people also spoke of their constant fatigue due to heavy manual work at home or frequent engagement in casual labour to help supplement household incomes.

The material shortages for children and young people in the UK were usually less extreme, although food shortages, having to skip meals and inadequate, overcrowded and poor quality housing were commonly described. Ellie, aged 16, for example reflected,

> I admit there has been times with no food on the table. We could have food but I'd rather give it to him [her brother] cos he's younger. Obviously I know I can cope till like next day or something but don't want to see them lot [her family] go without food. So I'd rather give it to them.

Similarly, in both contexts, chronic cash shortfalls including lack of money for school fees and/or school supplies such as a uniform were commonly described. Many young people spoke about the stress generated by constant lack of money to meet the family needs and how coping strategies such as borrowing money often accentuated the pressures on families. Charlie, aged 15, in the UK commented on the arrangement his mother had with a neighbour every week

> Well, like every Friday my mum borrows money off her mate ... and my mum pays him back double, because he's got to drive her to X [name of supermarket] and then drive her all the way back. So we've got to pay like 20 pound on petrol and like 20 pound that she actually borrowed... and sometimes if she's desperate, she will go to her other mate for like 20 pound.

And Harry, aged 12, spoke of witnessing his mother's fear as she anticipated the bailiffs coming to take their household goods due to her inability to pay her debts:

> There was one time I remember that, um that I'm not sure what they're called ... people that come ... oh bailiffs I think, they were meant to come round our house and take all of our stuff. But the bailiffs didn't come thankfully, but my mum was just sat on the sofa, you could see it on her face that she was just worried.

Young people in Uganda reflected on the inadequacies of their homes, often dilapidated grass thatched mud and wattle huts or lean to makeshift residential structures while young people in the UK focused more on the overcrowded conditions they lived in. However, young people in both countries expressed similar concerns about how they were perceived by others as a result. Rose, aged 14 in Uganda, for example commented,

> I live in a grass thatched makeshift structure with my mother. It is also in a poor condition. When friends come to visit I feel very ashamed.

While Katie, aged 17 in the UK and living in quite different material circumstances, similarly recalled the embarrassment of friends visiting her home,

> They've got what I would call a really nice middle class English life... and then there was me. I found it really embarrassing that in my living room is my mum's double bed because she literally had no money and had to give up her room to students.

In Uganda, children and young people's social interactions revolved around parents, siblings, and close kith or kin resident in the homestead. In making sense of their lives in poverty, there was variation in their narratives. Some tended to blame the hardship they experienced at home on their fathers who are traditionally the household heads and bread winners. Reference was sometimes made to a fathers' illiteracy and subsequent diminished opportunity in the job market; a factor they felt had entrapped their families in chronic poverty and misery or compelled them to operate in low-paid work where they could barely get by financially. A number of young people showed extreme resentment and embarrassment about their circumstances, openly castigated their fathers for not doing enough to get them out poverty and openly expressed regret at being born into their families

> I am not proud to belong to this family. My needs are mostly not met. I am mistreated, our house is poor and we don't even have a pit latrine! It is shameful. (Bernard, age 16, Uganda)
> Which father fails to build his children a decent house? Can you call this a home? Sometimes I regret why I was born here. (Godfrey, age 18, Uganda)

While young people in the UK were less likely to directly blame their parents for the economic difficulties they faced, there were, nonetheless, frequent accounts, particularly among boys, of a generalised anger about their circumstances, sometimes directed at parents, which they found difficult to contain. Alfie, aged 14, for example commented "I get angry over the like smallest of things. I don't know why, it just kind of like happens, it just snaps, literally." Similarly, in Uganda, it was noted by the research team that children frequently exhibited body language during interviews which portrayed a level of unvented frustration and pervasive anger about their lack of control over their circumstances.

Some children in Uganda, although a minority, were more optimistic in their outlook and saw their lives of hardship and indignity as transitory. They spoke of their appreciation of their parents' efforts and said that they were proud of their homes despite the hardships they faced. One girl Marion aged 15 referred to her impoverished but caring father as her role model,

> Home is home and my father is my father. I'm proud of my father, he is hard working and one day we will get money and life will improve.

Similarly, young people in the UK generally attributed their circumstances to bad luck, parental poor health, the wider economy or other systems and structures including employment agencies, social services and educational institutions which made life difficult. They spoke of parents doing their best to provide for them but struggling at times to meet their needs. They frequently reflected on how family was far more important than having money and how they felt that in the future they would be able to take on the role of supporting family and parents.

Although the home emerged as a key locus of poverty and hardship it was also a space in which children were to some extent protected from shame and embarrassment imposed by wider society.

Whereas this type of shame may appear less damaging, young people's narratives about their domestic hardship and misery were still indicative of considerable psychosocial stress and pain. Moreover, home was still a space where shame was anticipated (Goffman, 1963) as children and young people made their own assessment of themselves in relation to others and how they might be judged should their circumstances be exposed. A dilapidated home was a marker of difference between young people and their better off peers and could also become a place of self-exclusion where they would hide away and not invite others in, or of active exclusion as others did not want to visit or be associated with them.

When asked what they found most difficult about their lives, a number of young people spoke about their inability to do anything to change their circumstances. Jamila, age 13 from Uganda commented,

> If I was able, I would build a good house at home with a beautiful kitchen for my mother, but there is nothing I can do now. I have no money and I'm so young. I feel so much pain in my heart.

And similarly, Thomas age 16, also from Uganda, said:

> If I was able I would increase family income, eat good food like rice. I like rice. I would also buy a car and construct a good house with a nice compound. I feel frustrated and ashamed because I'm unable to change anything.

For young people living in poverty, the home and family created a complex space within the poverty-shame nexus. It could simultaneously offer a degree of solace and safety from the outside world while at once generating profound feelings of inadequacy and powerlessness. For some, the home, as a symbol of poverty, became the focus of their frustrations about their circumstances, sometimes directed towards parents or other adults. Others, however, tended to protect parents from such criticism by deflecting any sense of shame and instead alluding to the sense of pride they had of parental efforts to provide for them. Furthermore, despite the frustrations they felt in their current lives, children often predicted hopeful futures that would offer them happier and more successful lives.

3.2.1. School

School was a space where children in Uganda and the UK constantly saw their own circumstances reflected back at them by the relative wealth of their peers from families who did not struggle as much. Sometimes, the emotional stress or sense of inadequacy they felt stemmed from making these comparisons with others who were better off, rather than any direct teasing or taunting. At other times, however, they reported being directly stigmatized as a result of their economic situation.

In Uganda, school was frequented by all the young people participating in the study, making it a significant social setting within their daily lives. Young people valued school and saw it as a pathway to fulfilling ambitious education and career aspirations; eight girls aspired to become nurses; seven boys hoped to become medical doctors; two wanted to become accountants; two girls hoped to become teachers; two boys were determined to become civil engineers; two boys aspired to join the Catholic priest hood; and one dreamt of becoming a lawyer. One boy wanted to become a truck driver, and another a disc jockey. These aspirational goals indicate an optimism in young people's narratives and a sense that things can and will change in the future in ways to enable them to achieve their ambitions. By contrast, a number of young people in the UK study found participation in school difficult and expressed sometimes strong feelings of frustration and anger towards teachers and head teachers. However, even though some were less career orientated than others, they did similarly allude to futures where they hoped to be in positions to provide for their own children and make lives better for their parents.

Most of the Ugandan children in the study were enrolled in primary or secondary schools under the Universal Primary Education (UPE) and the Universal Secondary Education (USE) programmes. These constitute state-provided anti-poverty programmes, established since 1997, providing all school age children with free education (*bona basome*). Although UPE and USE schools have widened children's access to education, they have been increasingly associated with poor quality, inadequately-resourced education which is commonly rejected and replaced by private education by those with the financial wherewithal to pay for it. The consequence has been the association of UPE and USE schools with education for the poorest communities, and hence spaces of potential shaming for those children and young people attending them (Bantebya-Kyomuhendo, 2013).

Children in Uganda described various forms of hardship at school including going without lunch and the constant difficulties of not being able to afford the full school uniform, shoes, text books and/or other essential school equipment. They spoke of their experiences of walking long distances barefoot to school along dusty, scorching hot or muddy roads, dressed in tattered or dirty uniforms. These hardships often made children targets of taunting in school. Although education is free in Uganda, there are other hidden costs and contributions which families are expected to make, and which often prove unaffordable. Failing to make these contributions resulted in young people being subjected to being sent away from school, or the withholding of examination results or report cards (due to defaulting on supplementary payments).

In the UK, young people recounted similar experiences of having to negotiate differences between themselves and their better off peers. While children from families on low incomes are eligible to free school meals, the process of accessing meals could accentuate these differences. Anthony, aged 15 reflected on his experience,

> In a way it's like being bullied for it at school because it's like, "Anybody got free school meals?" and I go "yeah, me" and then everyone will go "oh, you've got free school meals ... oh you're poor" and "benefit bum" and stuff like that.

More generally, school was evidently a space of constant comparison. Young people reflected that while the physical effects of poverty were painfully felt, on their own they were tolerable. It was, however, the external gaze and judgement, the knowledge by others that your parents could not afford to buy you a pair of shoes, which spontaneously triggered feelings of shame and embarrassment. The same, it was noted, applied to the pangs of starvation and hunger that could be stoically endured; whereas the knowledge by others that they were going hungry because they could not afford a packed lunch immediately evoked feelings of shame and inadequacy. As one teenage girl, Jamila age 13, in Uganda observed, 'Ekikara munda tikihemura' (What remains unknown does not shame).

There were incidences described where children were laughed at, jeered or pitied out loud in reference to their deprivations. For instance, in one USE school, the students who walked barefooted described being nicknamed 'thermometers,' the reference being that they never tired of measuring the temperature of the ground. Some of the children from poor households disclosed that what they found most irksome was when their richer schoolmates appeared not to understand their plight and asked them questions whose answers were directly rooted in their hardship. As Rose aged 18 from Uganda explained:

> I always arrive at school late because my home is located 7 km away. I've pestered my father to put me in the boarding section but all in vain, he cannot afford. Then one day after being punished for late coming, my best friend asked me why I chose to commute from home instead of joining the boarding section... I just couldn't suppress tears.

Similarly, Danny, age 13 from the UK felt that others spoke about him as being "poor" just to make him angry which could have very negative consequences for him. He explained,

> They look much more minted than I am but that doesn't really bother me ... but they wanna wind me up because I get like ... when I'm wound up ... um ... it's not nice. It's not pleasant ... they just try and do it, just so that I get kicked out of school.

Some of the children from poor households pointed out that in some cases the shaming appeared to be institutionalized. They did not, for instance, understand why the school authorities withheld examination results, report cards, or even prevented the children whose parents had defaulted on school fees payment from sitting for tests and examinations. The affected children felt not only humiliated but traumatized as well. They felt that this shaming targeted their parents, but was deliberately deflected to them, the children. In this case, in the eyes of the young people, the school authorities and teachers appeared to intentionally subject them to shame and exclusion in the way described by one 16 year-old girl Irene in Uganda:

> The head teacher sent me home to remind my parents about the examination fees balance that I owed. He categorically told me not to return to school without the money. I was surprised because my father and the head teacher are close acquaintants in the village pub. I wondered why he couldn't remind him there as I continued studying for the exams that were round the corner. Anyway, I went home feeling rather low not only because my classmates remained learning, but also for being exposed as a school fees defaulter. My father gave me the money after two days but declined to escort me back to school as requested by the Head teacher. I have a feeling the purpose of summoning him was to shame him as well.

And Patrick, aged 14 in the UK, spoke of how he felt targeted by the school because his family could not afford to buy the correct uniform:

> If you don't have a piece of correct uniform, they will send you home to get changed. I decided that because I haven't got any school trousers at the minute I'm not going to come in until I get them. What they're not understanding is that I can't always go out and buy new things that I need... I don't like the teachers, I think they're cruel.

Incidences of indirect shaming of children from poor families by teachers in the classroom were also reported. In one such incident in Uganda, a child was ridiculed by other pupils in the classroom for routinely asking to borrow a mathematical set which his parents could not afford. The teacher who was aware of what was going on was said to turn a blind eye, a move that was read as giving tacit approval to those who were bullying the boy. The boy who was begging for the mathematical set said that he felt low and ashamed, and that the teacher ought to have done more to support him in the situation.

Young people described responding to these attacks on their dignity in a number of ways. Some spoke of always being on their guard and giving their richer school mates a wide berth whenever they crossed paths. Self-isolation by remaining in the classroom, even during break times or deliberate inactivity in the classroom, so as not to attract the attention of others, were common strategies. Some spoke of pestering their resource-constrained parents to let them board at school where it was presumed they would be less likely to be teased. In Uganda, perhaps surprisingly given the extent of unvented frustration and anger indicated by some children, young people appeared to resist fighting or getting angry in school. In the UK, however, a number of young people spoke of how outbursts of anger had led them to being excluded from school for periods of time or resulted in them having a reduced timetable or spending time in an alternative learning space outside of the mainstream classroom. Several spoke of how they were engaging with counselling and support therapies to help them manage their anger.

3.2.2. Community

In the context of our research the wider community referred to spaces outside of home and school such as the church, community shared spaces and events. Although such spaces were not talked about as much as children's references to home and school, the community was nonetheless an important connecting space between home and school. For many it became a setting for potential shame and one which limited their inclusion in social activities when they lacked the wherewithal to participate.

Some girls especially intimated how their lack of presentable clothing compromised their self-confidence whenever they attended social functions in the community. Rebecca age 16 from Uganda, for example, tearfully narrated an incident where her peers laughed at her when she attended a wedding dressed in a second hand (commonly known as *mivumba*) dress, her Sunday best in fact:

> I was grossly embarrassed and rudely reminded of my poverty. I sneaked away in the middle of the function and returned home crying. I've vowed never to attend any function in the community again.

And young people spoke of how their poverty was openly exposed in the community when they had to endure the indignity of providing casual labour for other families in exchange for paltry wages. Tom, age 13 in Uganda, described his frustration:

> I don't like digging and providing casual labour to other community members to supplement family income.

And Bernard, also from Uganda, explicitly referred to the shame he felt in doing the same,

> My parents' income is very low, we are always hungry and poor, I feel ashamed by engaging in casual labour to supplement family income.

In the UK, young people talked about how they were unable to join friends on outings because they didn't have enough money. Thomas, age 15 from the UK commented:

> Like my friends will ask me to go out and I am like, 'but I don't have the money'. And it does make me feel left out obviously, cos it's like you're the only one that's not going and then just the fact that everybody else seems to get more money.

4. Discussion

Although the analysis for this chapter is based on data from a study whose objectives did not primarily focus on children's positioning in the poverty-shame nexus, it does provide some compelling evidence that children's experiences of poverty, similar to those of adults, can evoke in them feelings of shame, inadequacy and frustration and that these emotions emerge early on in life. The findings from this analysis demonstrate both similarities and differences in how children and young people living in poverty in Uganda and the UK experience and respond to the psychological and social dynamics of their circumstances across different spheres of their lives.

Young people described how they experienced shame and stigma within the home and family, in school and in the wider community. They narrated examples of where they could be said to variously internalize and hide from shame and, in some cases, to channel and direct shame at others such as parents and caretakers. In some cases, particularly in the UK, there appeared to be conscious efforts by young people to reject the idea of feeling any shame or embarrassment as a result of poverty. Some young people averted potential shame by avoiding situations which might expose the degree of hardship they were living in, or by drawing on altruistic narratives to spare their parents' feelings. There was unanimity among children interviewed in Uganda that their respective lives and social status had been adversely affected by their routine experiences of hardship and that these effects were damaging both physically and emotionally. These views were less frequently articulated by young people in the UK.

Nonetheless, in both contexts, young people alluded to experiences of feeling inadequate, embarrassed, considered inferior or judged by others as a direct result of their material circumstances. The main loci for such shaming—home, school and to some extent the wider community—were difficult to avoid, and children frequently spoke of being subjected to and having to respond to shame in multiple and complex ways. The dynamics of shame in these different spaces however varied markedly. Even away from the public gaze within their own homes, young people participating in the study frequently reflected on their sense of inadequacy and low self-worth because of the poor circumstances in which they lived. They also spoke about the physical as well as psychological impacts that such poverty had on their daily lives. These findings are illustrative of what Pitillias Salvá (2016) has referred to as the 'developmental trauma' associated with the shame of poverty.

A shift from the home to the school environment brought children and young people firmly into the public realm, exposing them to different forms of direct and indirect shame. In fact, it is at school in both countries where children were most likely to report feelings of inadequacy and embarrassment about their circumstances. Moreover, young people felt that they lacked agency in being able to adequately respond to these feelings. "Mpurra ninswara kandi ndi wa hansi baitu mba ntaina kyokukora" (I feel ashamed, low and inferior but what can I do?) was a common response when the pupils in Uganda were asked how they coped with the sorts of teasing and exclusion they had reported facing in school. It is at school that children begin comparing themselves with better off children, and where they learn that they are not on equal par in terms of material possessions and social worth. Importantly, therefore, some feelings of shame can emanate from self-comparison to one's reference group, as well as from verbal exchange, provocative body language or innuendos from others. This type of internalised shame was reportedly common and described as considerably emotionally stressful. Such shame is complex and perhaps more damaging since it is difficult to both detect it or to link it to a specific coping response. These internalized feelings of shame aside, we have seen how active shaming was an integral part of the culture of schools, with the children being forced to endure indignity on a daily basis, with few options to avoid it. We still know very little about the long-term consequences on children having to endure this psychological burden of poverty. However, the indicative work by Dornan and Orgando Portela (forthcoming) suggests that aside from its social consequences, such a burden may have a direct negative impact on children's cognitive development.

A number of children and young people in the study in Uganda blamed the poverty-related indignity they experienced on their parents, especially their fathers who were considered not to be working hard enough to lift their families out of poverty and avoid its insidious effects. Other children in Uganda, and in fact most children in the UK, however, were defensive of their parents, describing them as hard working and committed to improving their families' welfare. There were also some differences observed in the extent to which children engaged with and talked about ideas relating to shame and embarrassment. These feelings appeared less explicit among children in the UK where young people rationalized their poverty with ideas such as "money is not everything," or "money can't buy you happiness." These subtleties are complex and require further research but may indicate what Scheff (2000, 2003) has referred to as the taboo surrounding shame and the difficulties of acknowledging it and its impact.

Some children and young people expressed optimism in their futures and a sense that they would be able to make things better for themselves and their families in the longer term. The extent to which such feelings of agency can be sustained over time is an area for further research, although previous work in the UK has suggested that young people with limited resources are often aware of the limits of their own agency and that this may lead to disaffection (Farthing, 2016).

As reported elsewhere in our work (see Chase and Bantebya-Kyomuhendo, 2015) parents repeatedly spoke of their own sense of shame emanating from their inability to adequately respond to and provide for the needs of their children; children themselves exacerbated these feelings of inadequacy, either through making direct demands or requests which could not be met, or equally in their resignation or lack of complaints about the hardships which they were forced to endure. In this sense, children become vectors or channels of feelings of shame on the part of parents and carers. What emerged through children and young people's narratives was a complex range of responses to shame including: internalizing feelings of shame and inadequacy; protecting parents and others from blame and accusation for their lives in poverty; and, in some cases, redirecting feelings of shame and related anger towards others whom they held responsible—hence children's engagement in what we have referred to elsewhere as the co-construction of shame in the context of poverty (Chase and Walker, 2013).

Despite the growing evidence of the pervasive effects of poverty-related shame, policy responses by governmental and non-governmental organisations and by development agencies such as the World Bank, UN agencies (with a few exceptions[1]) and DfID[2] to date have largely ignored these psychological and social dimensions of poverty in childhood. For example, Ridge (2011) in her study conducted in the UK revealed that children are rarely asked about their inner thoughts and feelings surrounding their experiences of poverty and its impact. Pitillas Salvá (2016) challenges most development practitioners' perspectives on child poverty for bypassing its psychosocial impacts on children's wellbeing and ignoring the propensity of poverty to expose children and young people to indignity. More broadly poverty reduction policies have failed to engage with issues of shame and indignity (Roelen, 2017).

5. Conclusion

Findings from this study demonstrating the negative psychological impact of poverty tally with previous work in the field (Ridge, 2010; Fernqvist, 2013; Pitillas Salvá, 2016). They highlight the negative social consequences of poverty, raise important questions about how best to enhance children's dignity in the context of poverty, and challenge the normative role of anti-poverty policies. It goes without saying that attention to the social and emotional consequences of poverty should add value to, and not detract from, broader measures to improve the economic wellbeing of millions of children living in poverty. Such policies however

---

1   For example the UN Report of the Special Rapporteur on Extreme Poverty and Human Rights (2012) states that people in poverty have a right to be protected from negative stigma (6–8).

2   These include initiatives such as cash transfers supporting nutrition, health and education programmes for children, and other programmes aimed at reforming entire healthcare, education and social systems.

need to both consider how to respond to these social as well as the material aspects of poverty, and be mindful of how interventions designed to alleviate material poverty may risk exacerbating its negative social impacts—such as, for example, modalities of delivering free school meal programmes. The starting point has to be in understanding the complex dynamics of how children and young people experience the psychological and social effects of poverty. Further research in this field might shed light on how poverty-related shame is mediated; what factors increase or lessen its incidence, degree or impact; and how it might be reduced or avoided. Applying this lens could better inform anti-poverty policies which are more conducive to reducing the impact of such shame in different settings. Given the centrality of the school in the lives of children and young people, much could be done to consider how poverty alleviation programmes targeted at schools could help reduce the negative psychological and social effects of economic hardship. The policy response, it is argued, should seek to reduce and reverse the impact of the potentially traumatic experiences and the multiple effects of shame in the context of poverty, and consider how the enhancement of children's dignity can be made more integral to poverty reduction measures.

References

Arndt, C., McKay, A. and F. Tart, eds. (2016). *Growth and Poverty in Sub-Saharan Africa.* Oxford: Oxford University Press.

Chase, E. and G. Bantebya-Kyomuhendo (2015). *Poverty and Shame: Global Experiences.* Oxford: Oxford University Press.

Chase E. and R. Walker (2013). "The Co-Construction of Shame in the Context of Poverty: Beyond a threat to the social bond." *Sociology. Vol* 47(4): 739–754.

Chireshe, R., Jadezweni, J., Cekiso, M. and C. Maphosa (2010). "Poverty: Narratives and Experiences of Street Children in Mthatha, Eastern Cape, South Africa." *Journal of Psychology in Africa.* Vol. 20 (2): 199–202.

Department of Work and Pensions (UK) (2018). *Households Below Average Income: An analysis of the UK income distribution 1994/95-2016/17.*

Dornan, P., and M.J. Orgando Portela, (Forthcoming). *Do Feelings of Shame Undermine Children's Development?* Unpublished.

Dulani, B., R. Mattes, and C. Logan (2013). "After a Decade of Growth in Africa, Little Change in Poverty at the Grassroots." *Afrobarometer Policy Brief.* No. 1: October.

Evans, G., Pilyoung, K., Ting, A., Tesher, H., and D. Shannis, (2007). "Cumulative Risk, Maternal Responsiveness, and Allostatic Load Among Young Adolescents." *Developmental Psychology* 43 (2): 341–51. doi: 10.1037/0012-1649.43.2.341.

Farrell, A. (2011). *Fat Shame: Stigma and the Fat Body in American Culture.* New York: New York University Press.

Farthing, R. (2016). "Writing in a Role for Structure: Low income young people's dual understanding of agency, choice and the welfare state." *Journal of Youth Studies.* Vol 19(6): 760–775.

Friedman, M (2015). Mother Blame, Fat Shame, and Moral Panic: 'Obesity' and Child Welfare." *Fat Studies* 4 (1): 14–27. doi: 10.1080/21604851.2014.927209.

Fernqvist, S. (2013). "Joining in on Different Terms: Dealing with Poverty in School and among 'Peers.'" *Young.* Vol. 21 (2): 155–171.

Goffman, E. (1963). *Stigma.* London: Penguin.

Gubrium, E., Pellissery, S., and I. Lødemel, eds. (2014). *The Shame of It: Global perspectives on anti-poverty policies.* Bristol: Policy Press.

Hoechner, H. (2015). "Porridge, Piety and Patience: Young Qur'anic Students Experiences of Poverty in Kano, Nigeria." *The Journal of the International African Institute.* Vol. 85(2): 269–288.

Joseph Rowntree Foundation (2017). *UK Poverty 2017.* Available at: https://www.jrf.org.uk/report/uk-poverty-2017.

Ministry of Gender, Labour and Social Development and United Nations Children Fund (2014). *Summary: Situation Analysis of Child Poverty and Deprivation in Uganda.* Republic of Uganda, Kampala.

Ministry of Housing, Communities and Local Government UK (2011). *English Indices of Deprivation 2010: Statistics on relative deprivation.*

Montes, A. "(2015). Shame and the Internalized Other". *Etica E Politica/Ethics and Politics* XVII (1): 181–200.

Najman, J M., Mohammad R., Hayatbakhsh, A., Bor, W., O'Callaghan, J., and G. Williams (2010). "Family Poverty over the Early Life Course and Recurrent Adolescent and Young Adult Anxiety and Depression: A Longitudinal Study." *American Journal of Public Health.* Vol.100 (9): 1719–23.

Pilyoung, K., Evans, G., Angstadt, M., Shaun Ho, S., Sripada, C., Wain, J., Liberzon, I. and K. Luan Phan (2013). *Effects of Childhood in Poverty and Chronic Stress on Motion Regulatory Brain Function in Adulthood: Proceedings of the National Academy of Sciences.* October 1–6.

Pitillas Salvá, C. (2016). "Child Poverty as a Potential Developmental Trauma: Shame, self-esteem and rediginifation of childhood" available at https://repositorio.comillas.edu/xmlui/bitstream/handle/11531/7184/poverty-trauma-shame.pdf?sequence=1.

Raphael, D. (2011). "Poverty in Childhood and Adverse Health Outcomes in Adulthood." *Maturitas* 69 (1): 22–26. doi:10.1016/j.maturitas.2011.02.011.

Rock, A., Barrington, C., Abdoulayi, S., Tsoka, M., Mvula, P. and S. Handa (2016). "Social Networks, Social Participation and Health among Youth Living in Extreme Poverty in Rural Malawi." *Social Science and Medicine. Vol.* 170: 55–62.

70   Bantebya Kyomuhendo et al.

Roelen, K. (2017). *Shame, Poverty and Social Protection.* Institute of Development Studies: IDS Working Paper 489. Available at: https://www.idac.uk/publication/shame-poverty-and-social-protection.

Ridge, T. (2011). "The Everyday Costs of Poverty in Childhood: A review of qualitative research exploring the lives and experiences of low-income children in the UK." *Children & Society. Vol.* 25(1): 73–84. DOI:10.1111/j.1099-0860.2010.00345.x.

Scheff, T. (2000). *Shame and the Social Bond: A Sociological Theory.* Santa Barbara: University of California at Santa Barbara.

Scheff, T. (2003). "Shame in self and society." *Symbolic Interaction.* Vol.26 (2): 239–62.

UN (2012b). *Report of the Special Rapporteur on Extreme Poverty and Human Rights.* United Nations General Assembly Sixty-seventh session, Item 70 (b) of the provisional agenda; A/67/278. New York: United Nations. http://daccess-ods.un.org/TMP/467728.637158871.html.

Walker, R. (2014). *The Shame of Poverty.* Oxford: Oxford University Press.

Walker, R., Bantebya-Kyomuhendo, G., Chase, E., Choudhry, S., Gubrium, E., Jo, Y. and I. Lødemel (2013). "Poverty in Global Perspective: Is Shame a Common Denominator?" *Journal of Social Policy.* Vol. 42(02): 215–33. doi: 10.1017/S0047279412000979.

CHAPTER 3
Poverty and Child Hunger in South Africa: A Child-Centred Analysis of Household-Level Survey Data

Winnie C. Sambu and Katherine Hall

1. Introduction

Food insecurity affects millions of people around the world. An estimated 777 million people globally were undernourished in 2015, of which 218.7 million were in Africa (FAO et al., 2017). Undernourishment, one of the indicators of food insecurity, is defined as lack of sufficient dietary energy. Conversely, food security is defined as a situation where "all people, at all times, have physical and economic access to sufficient, safe and nutritious food that meets their dietary needs and food preferences for an active and healthy life" (FAO, 1996: 1). This brings out five main principles: that food is available, accessible, always obtainable, that it is safe and nutritious, and can cater for dietary needs and food preferences. Thus, assessing the extent of household food security should not only include the quantity of food, but should also factor in the quality of diets consumed.

Access to food is dependent on the availability of financial resources, especially in cases where households primarily acquire food from markets. People living in poor households are at greatest risk of hunger and malnutrition partly because they are less able to afford adequate diets, and partly because poor living conditions and associated diseases can exacerbate undernutrition, particularly for children. Young children are especially at risk of malnutrition because they are still growing and require optimum nutrition to ensure proper growth and development. A significant proportion of young children are affected by malnutrition; globally, 155 million children aged under five years old were stunted in 2016 and 38 percent of them were in Africa (UNICEF, WHO and World Bank, 2017).

South Africa is a middle-income country with extreme inequality and high rates of poverty and malnutrition. Over a quarter of children under five years suffer from stunting (Statistics South Africa [SA], 2017a), a condition that is caused by inadequate nutrition and repeated infections, and poverty is an underlying factor. The country has various poverty alleviation programmes including the Child Support Grant, a cash transfer programme for children living in poverty. Between 2003 and 2016, the number of child beneficiaries grew from 2.6 million to 12 million (Hall and Sambu, 2017a). Numerous studies have shown the positive impacts of the grant on different aspects of child wellbeing, including improving school attendance, birth registration and child health (Grinspun, 2016).

In this chapter, we assess South Africa's progress in tackling poverty and child hunger using longitudinal data to examine national trends in child poverty and food insecurity between 2003 and 2016. In the absence of individual level data on certain variables, we use household-level data to produce child-centred estimates and highlight some of the possible underlying contributors to the persistently high and unequal levels of malnutrition in the country. In particular, we focus on dietary diversity, an indicator of dietary quality that has been found to be correlated with improved child nutritional outcomes (Hatløy et al., 2000; Hoddinott and Yohannes, 2002).

2.   Child nutrition, food insecurity and poverty: South Africa in a global context

The Food and Agriculture Organisation (FAO) derives its undernutrition estimates from national food supply data to monitor food security for individual countries and to make comparisons across countries. Using this method, average estimates for a three-year period (2015–2017) show that the proportion of population that was undernourished was 6.1 percent (FAO et al., 2018). But this approach is not sensitive to inequalities within countries, which may result in diverse nutritional outcomes across and even within households. In addition, undernourishment does not provide information on food security, including quality of diets consumed at household and individual level. Indicators used to examine food security at household level include caloric intake, dietary diversity and subjective measures like hunger and perceptions towards food standards.

Nutritional outcomes are also used as measures of food utilisation, as they show the impacts of inadequate food intake on the physical health of household members. Stunting is the most prevalent form of malnutrition and exists when children are too short for their age. Inadequate dietary intake and poor health status are the main causes of stunting, but these are in turn affected by food insecurity, inadequate health care for women and children, and exposure to unhealthy environments within and outside the home (UNICEF, 1990). Young children who suffer from stunting are unlikely to recover, and may remain stunted throughout childhood and in adulthood. Pregnant women who are stunted are more likely than those who are not stunted to give birth to infants with low birth weight and at risk of stunted growth.

Globally, there was a decrease in stunting across all regions between 2000 and 2016, except in the Oceanic region (Figure 1). Stunting rates in Africa reduced by 18 percent (seven percentage points), whereas stunting rates in Asia started at the same level but reduced by 37 percent over the same period. Despite the decreases, nearly a third of Africa's children (55 million) were stunted in 2016 (UNICEF, WHO and World Bank, 2017).

Figure 1.   Prevalence of stunting, across regions

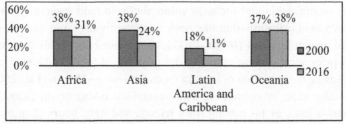

Source: UNICEF/WHO/World Bank malnutrition estimates (2017).

South Africa has high rates of malnutrition, comparable with those in many developing countries. According to recent estimates, 27 percent of children under the age of 5 years are stunted (Statistics SA, 2017a). Other indicators of undernutrition are wasting (low height for weight) and underweight (low weight for age). Overweight and obesity are indicators of overnutrition and are also caused by poor nutrition. Poverty is one of the main underlying factors of all forms of malnutrition, including stunting, overweight and obesity. While there has been a decline in wasting and underweight, the prevalence of overweight is rising and affects 13 percent of children under 5 years (Statistics SA, 2017a). Chapter 6 in this volume (Devereux, Jonah and May) offers a detailed analysis of levels of stunting in South Africa, and why they have not come down substantially since the democratic transition in 1994.

A substantial share of South Africa's population is poor and inequality is high (Barnes et al., 2017). Approximately 40 percent of households live below the upper-bound poverty line (PPP[1] $178) (Statistics SA, 2017b). The country's Gini coefficient is 0.68, making it one of the most unequal countries in the world, and 33.5 percent of people live below 50 percent of the median per capita income, highlighting the high levels of inequality (Statistics SA, 2017b). The situation is made worse by high levels of unemployment; in the first quarter of 2018, the official unemployment rate was 26.7 percent (Statistics SA, 2018).

While rural households may have been able to produce much of their own food in the past, there has been a shift away from subsistence production to a rural cash economy and dependence on the market for food (Baiphethi and Jacobs, 2009; Pereira, Cuneo, and Twine, 2014). Because of the relatively high cost of healthy foods, many households consume insufficient and poor-quality diets (Temple and Steyn, 2009, 2011; Temple et al., 2011). Food price increases make healthy diets even more unaffordable and increase vulnerability to food insecurity. South Africa's food price inflation has been consistently high and, on average, above overall inflation (NAMC, 2017). Many poor households cope with food price increases by reducing the quantity of foods consumed, and decreasing consumption of healthy foods (Oldewage-Theron et al., 2006). They also cope by consuming wild vegetables, taking credit (loans) to purchase food, or borrowing from friends and neighbours (Smith and Abrahams, 2016; Mkhawani et al., 2016).

Children living in poor households are the most likely to suffer from malnutrition because of inadequate diets and poor environments that exacerbate infections and disease (Kabubo-Mariara, Ndenge, and Mwabu, 2009; May and Timæus, 2014). Poverty has been recognised as one of the underlying factors for malnutrition (UNICEF, 1990), and poverty alleviation strategies should be included in any efforts to reduce malnutrition.

3.   Data and methods

3.1. Data sources

Goal 17 of the Sustainable Development Goals (SDGs) calls for an increase in "high-quality, timely and reliable data disaggregated by income, gender, age, race, ethnicity, migratory status, disability, geographic location and

---

1   Purchasing Power Parity

other characteristics relevant in national contexts" (UN, 2015: 27). This includes availability of regular and reliable data, collected through official surveys and administrative systems, that can be used to monitor socio-economic status of countries' populace. South Africa is a fairly data rich country compared to others in sub-Saharan Africa. The national statistical agency, Statistics South Africa, conducts various household surveys regularly, but specific data on food intake is scarce. Food consumption surveys are considered a reliable source of data on dietary intake but are expensive to undertake and can be burdensome for household members who have to keep track of their dietary intakes. Perhaps for these reasons they are not carried out regularly in South Africa, the last being in 1999. It is therefore difficult to have a comprehensive picture of dietary intake, food security patterns and malnutrition levels in the country, and especially amongst children.

The General Household Survey (GHS), is a cross-sectional survey carried out every year since 2002 and used by the government to monitor various development indicators. It is also used by the Children's Institute at the University of Cape Town to monitor the situation of children.[2] The main advantages of the GHS include the fact that it is conducted annually and has a large sample size (approximately 30,000 households every year), which allows for disaggregation—for example by province, area type and age group, although not to small area level. The survey collects a wide range of data including household demography, living conditions, education, employment and other socio-economic variables. It also collects data on subjective measures of food security, such as hunger amongst adults and children, and households' experiences with food insecurity.

We use data from the GHS to examine trends in poverty and child hunger between 2002 and 2017. The GHS is not a food consumption survey and does not provide estimates on caloric intake. Neither does it record anthropometric measurements (weight or height), which are crucial for assessing if children are growing healthily. Because the GHS is not a dedicated income and expenditure survey, it is also possible that household income may be under-reported. Nevertheless, this is the only large national survey in South Africa that is carried out every year and for this reason it is useful for examining trends in poverty, living conditions and some aspects of food security including child hunger and food poverty. We use population

---

2   www.childrencount.uct.ac.za

and household weights provided in the GHS to produce national estimates for the indicators published here. The population weights contained in the GHS are derived from a population model which is periodically recalibrated to larger and more recent population surveys. The estimates published here are based on the most recent population weights for all GHS years (2002–2017) released in 2018 by Statistics South Africa.

We also use data from the Living Conditions Survey (LCS), which is South Africa's main source of data on household income and expenditure. The survey has been conducted twice so far, in 2008/09 and 2014/15. It contains detailed data on food expenditure, based on data collected over a two-week period, thus making it possible to assess the most commonly consumed foods at household level. Both the GHS and the LCS are conducted by Statistics South Africa, using the same sample frame and many of the same questions.

To examine the anthropometric data for children under 5 years old, we also use data from the 2014/15 National Income Dynamics Study (NIDS). NIDS is a panel study that has been conducted since 2008 and has been following individuals (and their households) over time. The survey collects data on household demography, socio-economic characteristics and health, but does not contain data on food consumption.

3.2. Variables

Using the GHS data, we constructed a child hunger variable, based on subjective reporting. The GHS asks the survey respondent (usually an adult) to state how frequently children in the household went hungry over a 30-day period. Possible responses are "never", "seldom", "sometimes", "often" and "always." Children living in households where children were reported to have gone hungry "sometimes", "often," or "always" were classified as being exposed to hunger (Hall and Sambu, 2017b). Like other indicators that rely on data not collected directly from children, there are limitations associated with using this indicator, particularly the extent to which it can be used to adequately captures the levels of child hunger in the household. However, because decisions on children's dietary intake are mainly made at the household level, it is expected that the data from adult respondents will provide insight into the extent of hunger in the households.

Since 2013 the GHS has collected data on foods consumed over a 24-hour recall period, but only for one reference person per household (the primary respondent for the survey). The range of foods included in the survey are:

- Maize, rice, sorghum, millet, bread and other cereals
- Potatoes, sweet potatoes, cassava
- Beans, peas, groundnuts, cashew nuts or other nuts
- Spinach and wild green leaves
- Other vegetables, carrots, relish, tomatoes, cabbage, beetroot etc.
- Fruit
- Beef, goat, poultry (chicken), pork, fish, eggs
- Milk, yoghurt and other dairy products
- Sugar and sugar products
- Oils, fat and butter

We use these data to assess the diversity of diets consumed. In doing so we assume that the range of foods consumed by a single adult informant will also be indicative of the extent of dietary diversity for other members of the household. There are obvious limitations to this approach, as food is not necessarily evenly distributed within the household and some food may be consumed outside the household (at places of employment or through school feeding schemes, for example). We reclassified the 10 food groups into nine (staples; roots and tubers; legumes and pulses; vegetables; fruit; meat, fish and eggs; milk and dairy products; sugar; and oils), and each group allocated a score of 1 if any food in that group was consumed in the preceding 24-hour period. The scores for each respondent were then summed to give a dietary diversity score (DDS) with the highest score being 9 and the lowest 0 (no food consumed). The DDS was then divided into terciles[3] (low, medium and high dietary diversity). It is important to note that this DDS does not accurately reflect the diversity of diets consumed directly by children, as the primary informant is generally an adult. Rather the household-level score is used as a proxy indicator for the socio-economic status and food environments of the households where children live.

---

3   The terciles divide the DDS into three parts, each containing a third of the data.

We also used data from the 2014/15 LCS to assess diversity of foods acquired by households over a two-week period. Households included in the LCS keep diaries where they record all the items acquired, including food. In total, the 2014/15 LCS collected expenditure data on 303 food items that were acquired by households over a two-week period. Using FAO's Household Dietary Diversity Score (HDDS) guidelines (FAO, 2010), we reclassified the food items into 12 groups (cereals; meat; fish; milk and milk products; eggs; fruits; vegetables; legumes and pulses; roots and tubers; oils and fats; sweets; and spices and beverages). The HDDS is different from the DDS discussed above as it includes more food groups (12 instead of 9) and is a household measure rather than an individual assessment of dietary patterns.

3.3. Data limitations

In addition to the limitations of surveys discussed above, it is also important to note that these national household surveys only cover private households. They exclude children who are not household residents, including those in institutions such as child and youth care centres, boarding schools and prisons, as well as "homeless" children who live on the streets. These numbers are very small, and their exclusion is unlikely to bias the analysis, which is in any case concerned about children in the context of households. The question of institutional dietary arrangements for children could be a useful additional study in the future.

4.   Findings

The next section of this chapter presents results from our analyses of the GHS, LCS and NIDS data. We begin with analyses of trends in children's living conditions, poverty and hunger, followed by a discussion on how the three interact. Thereafter, we will present analyses on dietary diversity, food expenditure, other subjective measures of food security, and children's nutritional status. We will end with a discussion on some of the predictors of dietary diversity.

4.1. Trends in children's living conditions, poverty and hunger

Children (0–17 years of age) constitute just over a third (35 percent) of South Africa's population, out of a total population of 57 million. While two thirds (67 percent) of children live in the poorest 40 percent of households, only 8 percent live in the richest 20 percent. Just over half of children live in urban areas (57 percent in 2017), up from 48 percent in 2002. Patterns of income poverty and inequality have a strong spatial dimension: two thirds of children in the poorest income quintile are in rural households, while 90 percent of those in the wealthiest quintile are urban. Eight percent of children live in informal dwellings, and 10 percent live in traditional housing such as compounds where the dwellings are made with mud bricks and thatch, while the vast majority (82 percent) live in formal dwellings. A majority of children resident in traditional housing live in the rural areas of the country, which also tend to have poorer service infrastructure; however, these areas may provide better opportunities for small-scale agriculture and have lower living costs such as rentals, utility fees and public transport over short distances.

Table 1 illustrates differences in housing and living environments for children in urban and rural areas; the percentages represent shares within each area type. Overcrowding in households is relevant to child nutrition because diseases can spread quickly in very crowded conditions, and crowding is most common in urban informal settlements (slums) where water and sanitation points may be communal and not easily accessible for children. Nearly a fifth (18 percent) of all children live in overcrowded conditions, which we define as more than two people per room (including kitchen and living area).[4] There have been substantial improvements in water and sanitation services, both of which are important for children's nutrition and general health. Yet large numbers of children, and particularly those in rural areas, continue to live in households without adequate services.

---

4   This definition is in line with the early UN-Habitat definition (The Challenge of Slums 2003), and has been widely used in South Africa, including by the national statistics agency. In defining a composite set of measures to monitor the SDG indicator 11.1.1, UN-Habitat has used a minimum of two people per room (UN Stats SDG Metadata files, updated Feb 2018). See https://unstats.un.org/sdgs/metadata/.

Table 1.   Children's living conditions by type of area

	Urban	Rural
Number of children (weighted population)	11 115 000	8 464 000
Formal housing	86 percent (0.01)	76 percent (0.01)
Informal housing	12 percent (0.01)	3 percent (0.00)
Traditional housing	1 percent (0.00)	21 percent (0.01)
Overcrowding	20 percent (0.01)	15 percent (0.01)
Inadequate water	9 percent (0.01)	56 percent (0.01)
Inadequate sanitation	11 percent (0.01)	36 percent (0.01)

Note: Standard errors in brackets.
Source: Authors' calculations from GHS 2017.

Statistics South Africa has proposed three national poverty lines, all of which are based on a "basket of goods" approach (Statistics SA, 2015). A core component of the basket for all three lines is a basic food basket. In this way, the concept of adequate nutrition is built into the national income poverty measures. We use two of these national poverty lines to monitor child poverty trends. The food poverty line (FPL) is the minimum monetary value needed to consume a minimum acceptable energy (food) requirement of 2,100 kilocalories per person per day.[5] Children whose diets do not meet this requirement are not consuming enough calories for healthy growth and survival, and are therefore at risk of being malnourished.

The upper bound poverty line (UPBL) incorporates both food and non-food items such as basic clothing, health and transport costs, and is the value below which individuals are unable to meet both basic food and non-food items. These poverty lines were published in 2011 and are updated annually in line with inflation (Statistics SA, 2015). In 2017, the food and upper bound poverty lines were valued at R531 (PPP $87) and R1138 (PPP $187) respectively.[6]

---

5   This is based on WHO's recommendations on "Management of nutrition in major emergencies" (WHO, 2000).
6   PPP rates are expressed in United States Dollars (USD).

Poverty headcount rates are calculated from the GHS by adding individual and household income data for each household and dividing total household income by the number of household members.[7] Using this method, child poverty rates measured by the UBPL have dropped gradually but steadily from 78 percent in 2003 to 65 percent in 2017. Nevertheless, two-thirds of all children (equivalent to approximately 12.8 million children) still live below the UBPL poverty line.

Child poverty rates have declined more sharply when applying the food poverty line: the data shows a decrease from 53 percent in 2003 to 36 percent in 2017. However, this still leaves 7 million children in food poverty, and 3.2 million children (16 percent of total child population) in households where the per capita income is half the value of the food poverty line. Like other countries in sub-Saharan Africa, food poverty rates are highest in the rural areas. In 2017, 54 percent of children living in the rural areas of the country were resident in food poor households, compared to 22 percent of children in urban areas.

Figure 2.   Child poverty rates, 2003–2017

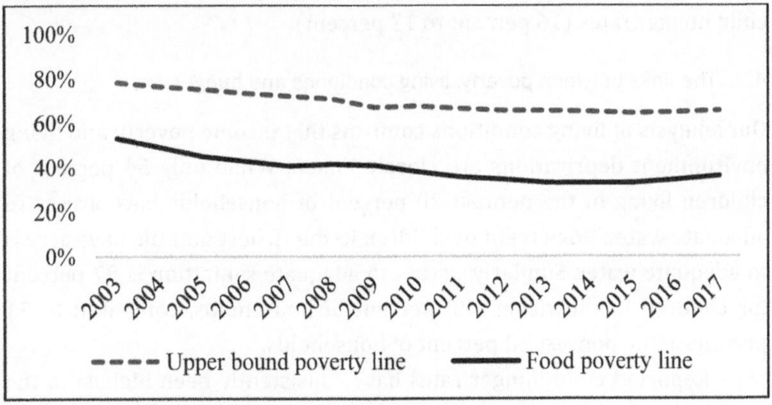

Source: Authors' calculations from GHS (2003–2017).

There has been some debate about the relative merits of using income data to calculate poverty headcounts, as opposed to expenditure data (Deaton, 1997; Budlender, Leibbrandt and Woolard, 2015). The GHS records detailed income data but not expenditure data, while the Living

---

7   While the GHS has been conducted since 2002, we report income and poverty estimates from 2003 because poverty rates for 2002 are implausibly high, possibly due to income from social grants not being adequately captured that year.

Conditions Survey (LCS) records both income and expenditure data. Recently released poverty estimates based on detailed expenditure data from the 2014/2015 LCS reveal similarly high poverty rates, particularly amongst children, and an overall reduction in child poverty over the last decade (Statistics SA, 2017b). But the reported poverty rates are higher than those seen in GHS, and they also suggest a slight increase in child poverty rates between 2011 and 2015 (from 64 percent to 67 percent), a trend that is not found in the GHS income estimates or reflected in reported rates of child hunger. In the case of the GHS, the upper bound poverty rates remained fairly stable between 2011 and 2017, declining by only one percentage point over that period.

Approximately 2.3 million children experienced hunger in 2017, equivalent to 12 percent of all children in the country. Between 2003 and 2017, there was a substantial decrease in reported child hunger, from 30 percent to 12 percent. This decrease was most pronounced in the poorest income quintile, but occurred almost entirely between 2003 and 2005, after which there was only a four-percentage point reduction in overall child hunger rates (16 percent to 12 percent).

4.2. The links between poverty, living conditions and hunger

Our analysis of living conditions confirms that income poverty and living environment deprivations are closely linked. While only 54 percent of children living in the poorest 20 percent of households have access to adequate water, 96 percent of children in the richest quintile have access to adequate water. Similarly, access to adequate sanitation is 97 percent for children in the richest 20 percent of households, compared to 71 percent in the poorest 20 percent of households.

Reported child hunger rates have consistently been highest in the poorest income quintiles, and the patterns have been fairly consistent over the last decade (Figure 3). Reported child hunger rates in the richest 20 percent of households have averaged around 1 percent between 2006 and 2017, compared to 23 percent in the poorest 20 percent of households over the same period.

Figure 3.   Child hunger rates across income quintile (2003-2017)

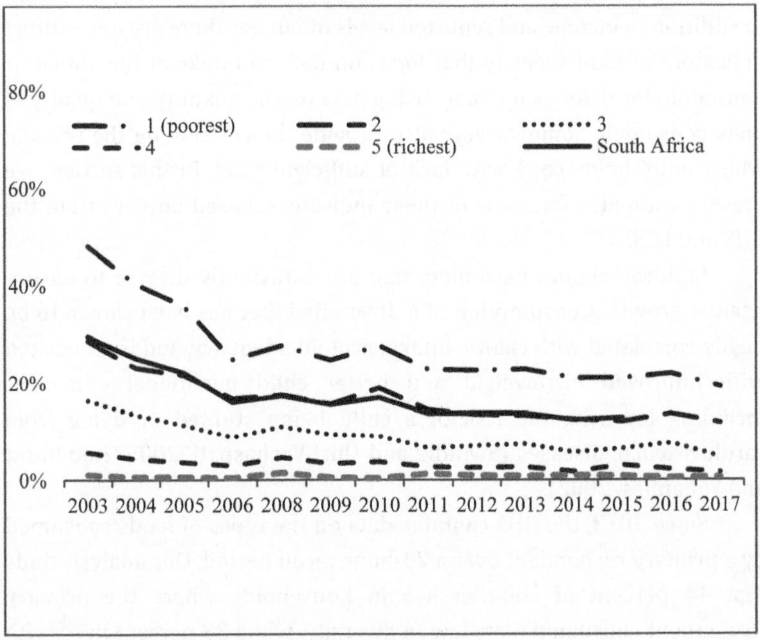

Source: Authors' calculations from GHS 2003-2017.

Subjective reporting of hunger is likely to be based on the key respondent's perception of whether there has been sufficient food in the household, and may not be a reliable indicator of actual food intake by different household members. Because the GHS does not collect data on children's dietary intake, we are unable to assess the adequacy of diets consumed amongst children who do not suffer from hunger using this source. However, our analysis shows that out of 17.3 million children who lived in households where there was no child hunger, a third (33 percent) lived below the food poverty line, while close to two-thirds (62 percent) lived below the upper bound poverty line. This suggests that the reported hunger variable alone cannot provide an adequate assessment of food insecurity. Households may not be experiencing hunger, but the foods consumed may be insufficient in quantity, quality or diversity, and might not contain enough micro-nutrients (FAO, 2008).

4.3. Beyond child hunger: assessing inequalities in dietary diversity

In addition to income and reported levels of hunger there are more direct indicators of food security that focus on dietary intake at individual or household level, for example by using data on the quantity and quality of diets consumed. Some surveys also provide information on the ways in which households cope with lack of sufficient food. In this section, we present estimates for some of these indicators, based on data from the GHS and LCS.

Children should have diets that are sufficiently diverse to ensure healthy growth. Consumption of a diversified diet has been shown to be highly correlated with caloric intake, protein adequacy, and is associated with improved birthweight and better child nutritional outcomes, including lowering the risk of a child being stunted or dying from cardiovascular diseases (Swindle and Ohri-Vachaspati, 2005; Hoddinott and Yohannes, 2002).

Since 2013, the GHS contains data on the types of foods consumed by a primary respondent over a 24-hour recall period. Our analysis finds that 44 percent of children live in households where the primary respondent consumed diets low in diversity, while 33 percent lived with those who consumed diets that were highly diversified. When reported child hunger rates were compared with the Dietary Diversity Score (DDS), we find that 71 percent of children who suffered from child hunger lived in households where the DDS was low, while 13 percent lived in households where the DDS was high. This suggests a strong association between the two measures. However, amongst children who did not suffer from hunger, 41 percent lived in households with a low DDS. This apparent contradiction might reflect adult food sacrifices in poor and food insecure households, or may be the result of reporting error. A third possibility is that cheaper staple foods such as starches are used to prevent feelings of hunger, thereby addressing the requirement of quantity but not of quality or diversity.

Forty six percent of children living in households with low DDS were also below the food poverty line, compared to a quarter (25 percent) of children in household with high DDS who were food poor. Out of 2.5 million households that participate in agricultural activities at home (such as growing of crops and livestock keeping), the majority (55 percent) have low dietary diversity and only 25 percent have high diversity. This could be due to the high levels of poverty in these predominantly rural households and the fact that, as noted above, household agriculture is seldom sufficient to provide for nutritional needs.

Figure 4.   Food group acquisition, by poorest and richest quintile

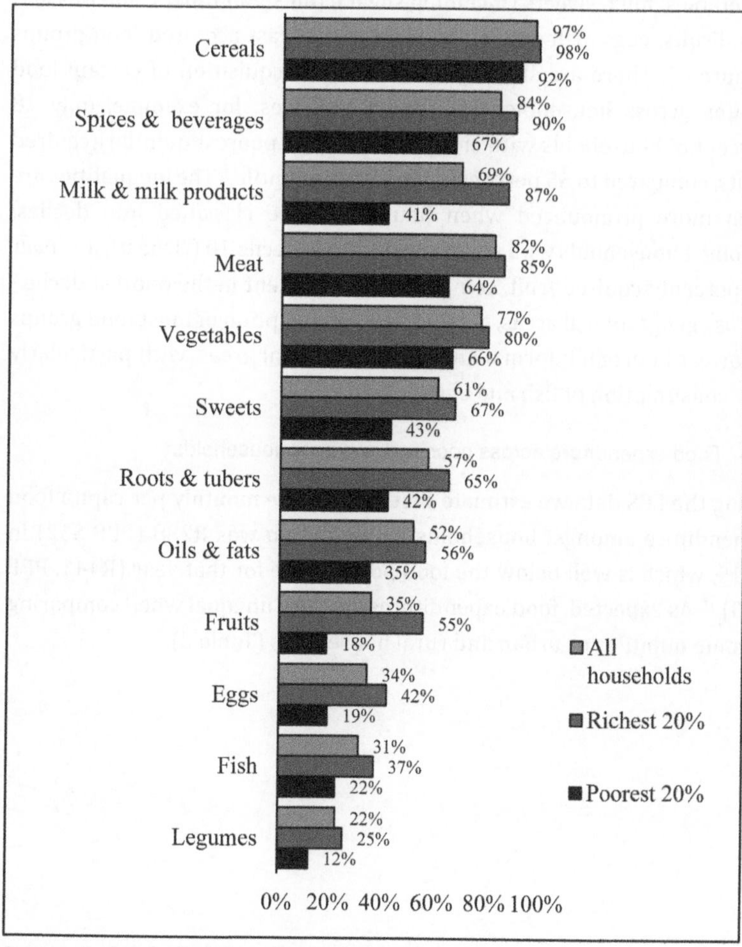

Cereals — 97% / 98% / 92%
Spices & beverages — 84% / 90% / 67%
Milk & milk products — 69% / 87% / 41%
Meat — 82% / 85% / 64%
Vegetables — 77% / 80% / 66%
Sweets — 61% / 67% / 43%
Roots & tubers — 57% / 65% / 42%
Oils & fats — 52% / 56% / 35%
Fruits — 35% / 55% / 18%
Eggs — 34% / 42% / 19%
Fish — 31% / 37% / 22%
Legumes — 22% / 25% / 12%

All households
Richest 20%
Poorest 20%

0% 20% 40% 60% 80% 100%

Source: Authors' calculations from LCS 2014/15.

Using data from the 2014/15 LCS, we also constructed a household-level dietary diversity score (HDDS) to examine the diversity of foods acquired by households with children over a two-week period. The HDDS is normally used as a measure of households' food access and socio-economic status. Households that are poor would be expected to record low diversity, as they purchase fewer and less varied items compared to non-poor households, due to budget constraints that force them to sacrifice food for other essential items. We find that at least 50 percent of households with children acquired staples, spices and beverages, meat, vegetables, milk, sweets (including sugar), roots and tubers, and oils and fats. Fruits, eggs, fish and legumes were the least acquired food groups (Figure 4). There are striking differences in acquisition of certain food groups across household expenditure quintiles: for example, only 18 percent of households with children and in the poorest quintile acquired fruits, compared to 55 percent in the richest quintile.[8] The inequalities are even more pronounced when households are classified into deciles: amongst households with children who are in decile 10 (richest), just over 60 percent acquired fruit, compared to 15 percent in the poorest decile.[9] Across geographical areas, we find that consumption of most food groups is lowest in urban informal and rural traditional areas, with particularly low consumption of fish and eggs.

4.4. Food expenditure across poor and non-poor households

Using the LCS data we estimate that the average monthly per capita food expenditure amongst households with children was R288 (PPP $52) in 2015, which is well below the food poverty line for that year (R441, PPP $79).[10] As expected, food expenditures are very unequal when comparing income quintiles or urban and rural households (Table 2).

---

8   Households are classified into quintiles and deciles using total household (food and non-food) expenditure.
9   10 groups of equal distribution.
10   This relates to expenditure in households with children. Estimates on food expenditure for all households in the country are published here: http://www.statssa.gov.za/?page_id=1854&PPN=P0310&SCH=6811.

Table 2.   Average household food expenditure, across geographical location, poor households and expenditure deciles.

	N (weighted number of households)	Mean per capita household food expenditure (monthly)	
		Rand	PPP $
Households with children	9, 198, 000	287.9 (2.4)	51.9 (0.4)
Geographical location:			
Urban	5,953,000	318.3 (3.4)	57.3 (0.6)
Rural	3,245,000	232.2 (2.8)	41.8 (0.5)
Food poverty:			
Poor	7,554,000	98.6 (1.1)	17.8 (0.2)
Non-poor	1,644,000	329.2 (2.8)	59.3 (0.5)
Food expenditure quintiles			
1	1,333,000	128.3 (1.1)	23.1 (0.2)
2	1,609,000	240.0 (2.2)	43.2 (0.4)
3	1,867,000	336.3 (4.1)	60.6 (0.7)
4	2,088,000	397.4 (6.7)	71.6 (1.1)
5	2,300,000	595.6 (14.6)	107.3 (2.6)

Note: Standard errors in brackets.
Source: Authors' calculations from LCS 2014/15.

A large share of children live in households where the monthly per capita food expenditure is below the food poverty line. Figure 5 compares the distribution of food expenditures for children in urban and rural households. The disparities are also evident across expenditure quintiles (Table 2): the average is R128 (PPP $23) in the poorest 20 percent of households with children, compared to R596 (PPP $107) in the richest 20 percent—and even this is not much higher than the food poverty line. More detailed analysis reveals the average per capita food expenditure in the poorest 10 percent is R95 (PPP $17) and R697 (PPP $125) in the richest 10 percent.

Figure 5.   Monthly per capita food expenditure

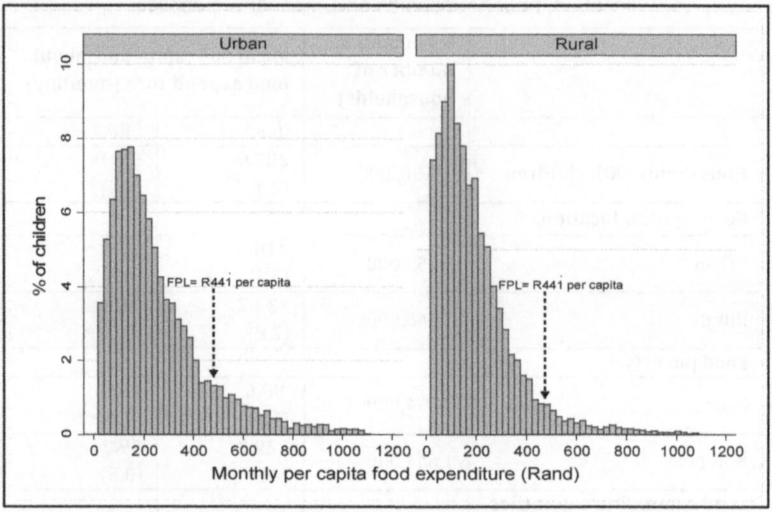

Source: Authors' calculations from LCS 2014/15.

4.5. Income and other measures of food security and nutrition

Analyses of subjective measures of food insecurity also reveal high levels of food insecurity amongst poor households. In the LCS, households are asked to rate their food consumption standards on a scale of three (below adequate, just adequate and more than adequate). We find that over a quarter (28 percent) of children live in households where the food consumption standards are considered inadequate while only 7 percent of children are in households that report their food standards as more than adequate. Poor children are more likely to live in households that run out of money to buy food, skip meals, and reduce portion size as well as eat a smaller variety of food. Eighteen percent of children (3.5 million) live in households that run out of money to buy food, another 18 percent cut the size of meals, 14 percent skip meals, and 18 percent eat a smaller variety of food and reduce the portion size. Across income quintiles, the vast majority of children who live in households that lack money to buy food cut size of meals, eat less variety or skip meals altogether, are in the poorest 40 percent of households (Table 3).

Table 3.   Food insecurity levels across income quintiles

	No money for food	Cut size of meals	Skip meals	Eat smaller portion and less variety
Quintile 1 (poorest)	64 percent	61 percent	65 percent	62 percent
Quintile 2	24 percent	24 percent	23 percent	25 percent
Quintile 3	8 percent	9 percent	8 percent	8 percent
Quintile 4	3 percent	4 percent	3 percent	4 percent
Quintile 5 (richest)	2 percent	2 percent	2 percent	2 percent
Number of children (population weighted)	3 514 000	3 455 000	2 836 000	3 561 000

Source: Authors' calculations from LCS 2014/15.

Like other indicators of food security and nutrition, stunting rates are strongly associated with poverty. Stunting rates for children under five years are 27 percent in the poorest quintile, compared to 6 percent in the richest quintile. Stunting rates are also higher amongst younger children compared to older ones (Figure 6). These differences are statistically significant.

Figure 6.   Stunting rates amongst children (6 months–9 years)

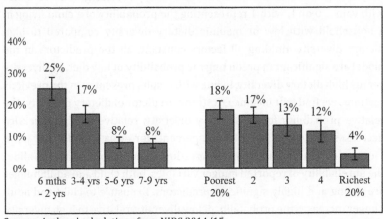

Source: Authors' calculations from NIDS 2014/15.

5.   Predictors of dietary diversity in households with children

This chapter has presented descriptive findings based on multiple indicators, most of which are proxy measures of food security. Some basic patterns of association have emerged: that income poverty, being rural, reported hunger and strategies to cope with food shortages may all be possible predictors of low dietary diversity, which in turn is linked to poor nutritional outcomes for children.

Table 4 presents results from a multinomial logistic regression that models the predictors of dietary diversity tercile level, using data from the GHS. This is the most appropriate form of regression because the dependent variable (dietary diversity score tercile) is a nominal outcome variable and contains more than two values (1=low dietary diversity, 2= medium, and 3=high). The predictor variables include geographical location, child hunger, adult hunger, household size, and whether respondents had reduced portion size of meals consumed or ran out of money to buy food. Participation in subsistence agriculture is excluded due to a fairly high correlation with geographical location, and relatively low number of households participating in agricultural activities. Household income (log) is included because of the high number of households that rely on income to purchase food.

Results presented in the table relate to low and medium dietary diversity, with high diversity being the base comparison. The outcome variables (low and medium dietary diversity) are categorical variables with values 0 or 1; with 1 representing the probability of a child living in a household with low or medium dietary diversity compared to high dietary diversity. Holding all factors constant, all the predictors in the model are significant in predicting the probability of low dietary diversity versus high dietary diversity. In line with results presented in the previous sections, we find that income is a strong predictor of dietary diversity; the relative probability for low dietary diversity, relative to high diversity, decreases by a factor of 0.681 (32 percent) for every one percent point increase in household income. Interestingly, and despite concerns about the unreliability of reported hunger variables, both child and adult hunger are strong and highly significant predictors. Exposure to child and adult hunger increases the probability of low diversity, relative to high diversity, by 60 percent. The probability is significantly higher in the case of adult hunger (more than 40 percentage points). This is not surprising given that the dietary diversity module is administered to an adult. In the case of medium diversity, only child hunger, reduction in portion size, and household income were found to be strong predictors of the probability of medium diversity versus high diversity.

Table 4.   Determinants of dietary diversity (DDS) in households with children

Outcome variable = DDS terciles (Base = high diversity)	Low diversity	Medium diversity
Rural	1.522* (0.080)	1.082 (0.065)
Child hunger (1=child hunger)	1.596** (0.279)	1.475 (0.0.286**
Adult hunger (1=adult hunger)	2.032* (0.324)	1.195 (0.213)
Household size	1.029** (0.012)	1.001 (0.013)
Reduction in portion size (1=yes)	2.655* (0.322)	1.385** (0.202)
Household income (log)	0.681* (0.017)	0.816* (0.021)

Note: Standard errors in brackets. *p<0.001, **p<0.05.
Source: Authors' calculations from GHS 2017.

6. Discussion

Our findings show that millions of children in South Africa live in poverty and suffer from various forms of food insecurity. There are stark disparities in the food security status of children across income levels: children living in the poorest households are more likely than less poor children to suffer from hunger or be exposed to diets that are relatively low in diversity. We also find that across geographical areas, children living in rural households are more likely than urban children to consume diets that are not sufficiently diversified. We find that over 80 percent purchase cereals, spices, beverages and meat, but far fewer consume fruits, legumes, fish or eggs. Consumption of fruits is particularly low, and children living in the poorest 20 percent of households are disadvantaged, with only one in every six living in households where fruits are consumed. Across other food groups, consumption is lowest in the poorest 20 percent and it is only in the case of cereals, spices, meat, milk and milk products and vegetables where at least 50 percent of children live in households that acquired these food groups. Our analysis also shows significant differences in food acquisition and dietary diversity across urban and rural areas, with children living in urban informal and rural traditional areas having access to less variety. We also found that child hunger, income and rural areas are strong predictors of low dietary diversity.

Our findings echo other studies that examined dietary patterns and found low dietary diversity levels in the country, with the poor most affected (for example Labadarios, Steyn and Nel, 2011). These studies also found that there is high consumption of starch-based, highly processed foods, partly due to the socio-economic conditions of households and lack of information on healthy consumption. Consumption of vitamin A-rich fruits and vegetables, as well as legumes and nuts, and other vegetables have been found to be particularly low while consumption of dairy products, meats and fruits are reportedly low in rural areas and in informal parts of urban areas (Labadarios, Steyn and Nel, 2011).

In addition to poverty, another factor that contributes to food access is cost of food, and food inflation that outstrips other forms of inflation. Healthy diets are more expensive (Temple and Steyn, 2011), making it difficult for poor children to access quality diversified diets. Some staple food items have been zero-rated, i.e. the value added tax payable on them is zero. These items include certain breads and grains, milk, tea and oil, legumes and pulses, and vegetables. However, these foods also record some of the highest inflation rates (Smith and Abrahams, 2016). However, because many of the staple foods are long-lasting and can be acquired in bulk, they form a significant share of poor households' food basket (Smith and Abrahams, 2016). Thus, price increases affecting these foods can lead to poor households spending a significant share of income on them, reducing financial resources available for purchase of other foods.

South Africa has a fairly comprehensive social protection package including fee waivers or rebates for education and health care, free basic services, a national school nutrition programme, and cash transfers for children, the elderly and the disabled. The Child Support Grant (CSG) is the country's largest cash transfer programme in terms of the number of beneficiaries, with about 12.3 million child beneficiaries.[11] It is an

---

11   See http://childrencount.uct.ac.za/socialgrants.php.

important source of supplementary income for poor households and at times the only source of income given the high unemployment rates in the country. However, despite rapid increase in CSG uptake since inception in 1998, child poverty is widespread, and many beneficiaries live in households that are unable to cater for their basic nutritional needs. There are strong arguments that the value of the grant is too low to substantially improve children's nutrition (Barnes et al., 2017; Delany, Jehoma, and Lake, 2016; Smith and Abrahams, 2016), especially when the money must also be used for other important households needs, such as to purchase clothes and pay for travel costs (Devereux and Waidler, 2017). These factors are discussed in more detail in Chapter 6 (Devereux et al.) in this volume. Our analysis also shows a positive association between income and dietary diversity, suggesting that a higher CSG amount would enable consumption of a wider variety of foods.

This chapter has focused on food poverty, insecurity and dietary diversity at household level in order to derive and evaluate proxy measures of children's nutrition. Because of the focus on household-level variables, it has not dealt with the important matter of early nutrition that is specific to infants. It is well established that good nutrition should start early, during and even before pregnancy, to ensure optimal nutritional and health outcomes for children. Pregnant mothers need access to high quality and diverse diets that meet their nutritional needs and that of the unborn baby. Exclusive breastfeeding is recommended for the first 6 months, after which the child should be gradually introduced to complementary diets that contain the necessary nutrients to support healthy growth and development (World Health Organization, 2003). Breastfeeding is an important source of nutrients and protects against stunting and other illnesses, but South Africa's breastfeeding rates are low: only 32 percent of infants aged 6 months and below are exclusively breastfed, while 25 percent are not breastfed at all (Statistics SA, 2017a). In addition, 77 percent of children aged between 12–23 months are not fed a minimum acceptable diet based on WHO guidelines (Statistics SA, 2017a). These early nutritional failures are thought to be contributing to the disproportionately high stunting rates for children under two years (reported above). Other factors that contribute to poor child nutritional outcomes, as highlighted by a conceptual framework published in 1990 (UNICEF, 1990), include diseases like diarrhoea which affect dietary intake of children (Nel, 2010). As discussed in Chapter 6 in this volume, access to adequate water and sanitation are important for prevention of infections which negatively affect children's physical growth (Devereux, Jonah and May, 2019).

It must be recognised however, that poverty is one of the main underlying factors of the direct causes of malnutrition. Eliminating malnutrition requires more investments in poverty eradication programmes, including those that provide income support for poor households, such as employment and access to social assistance. Considering that diets low in diversity also feature among non-poor households, it is important that households are educated and sensitised on the benefits of diverse and healthy diets.

7. Conclusion

The Sustainable Development Goals (SDGs) call for the eradication of hunger and malnutrition by 2030 (UN, 2015). Given South Africa's persistently high stunting rates, and increases in the prevalence of obesity, there is an urgent need for programmes to ensure children are adequately nourished from before they are born and continuously throughout their infancy and childhood. This requires a continuum of maternal and child health services, micro-nutrient supplementation where needed, adequate and appropriate infant feeding and transition to a sufficiently nutritious and diverse diet of solid foods. This chapter is primarily concerned with the later stages of childhood when children share in household food resources. It demonstrates the links between income poverty, food insecurity and poor nutritional outcomes for children, yet also shows that households with greater financial resources do not necessarily have adequately diverse diets. This suggests that there may be a need for greater education about nutrition and the importance of dietary diversity. Given the spatial inequalities, better strategies may be needed to ensure that the full range of food groups (especially fresh foods) are accessible to poor and rural households.

The poverty trends showed that even after substantial decreases in income poverty rates, many children remain below the food poverty line. The child support grant has been effective in targeting the poor and reaching large numbers of children, but the value of the benefit is below the food poverty line. Increasing the grant could be a relatively easy way of protecting children against food insecurity, enabling households with children to diversify their diets and improving nutritional outcomes for children. To make diverse diets more accessible, fiscal measures that make food more affordable to poor households should be also implemented, including removing value added taxes on healthy and nutritious food items that are not already zero-rated.

The use of household data has provided an important insight into child hunger and dietary diversity, but individual level data can provide more detailed information on nutrient intake and so should be more regularly conducted. This kind of information is crucial for designing interventions that can be used to improve children's dietary intake, such as micronutrient supplementation and nutrition education.

References

Baiphethi MN and PT Jacobs 2009. "The Contribution of Subsistance Farming to Food Security in South Africa" in *Agrekon*, Vol. 48 (4).

Bamford L 2016. "Leading Causes of Death in Children" In Stephen CR, ed. *Saving Chidren 2012–2013. An eighth survey of child healthcare in South Afric*a. Pretoria: Tshepesa Press.

Barnes H, Hall K, Sambu W, Wright G, and W. Zembe-Mkabile 2017. *Review of Research Evidence on Child Poverty in South Africa*. Cape Town: Southern African Social Policy Research Institute and Children's Institute, University of Cape Town.

Budlender J, Leibbrandt M and I. Woolard 2015. *South African Poverty Lines: a review and two new money-metric thresholds*. A Southern Africa Labour and Development Research Unit Working Paper Number 151. Cape Town: SALDRU, University of Cape Town.

Deaton A 1997. *The Analysis of Household Surveys. A Micro Econometric Approach to Development Policy*. Baltimore, Maryland, and London: Johns Hopkins University Press.

Delany A, Jehoma S and L Lake 2016. *South African Child Gauge 2016*. Cape Town: Children's Institute, University of Cape Town.

Devereux S and J Waidler 2017. "Why does malnutrition persist in South Africa despite social grants?" Food Security SA Working Paper Series No.001. Cape Town: DST-NRF Centre of Excellence in Food Security.

FAO 1996. *Rome Declaration on World Food Security and World Food Summit Plan of Action Rome*. http://www.fao.org/docrep/003/w3613e/w3613e00.HTM Accessed 20 September 2017.

FAO 2008. *An introduction to the Basic Concepts of Food Security*. In http://www.fao.org/docrep/013/al936e/al936e00.pdf Accessed 20 September 2017.

FAO 2010. *Guidelines for Measuring Household and Individual Dietary Diversity.* In http://www.fao.org/3/a-i1983e.pdf Accessed 15 January 2018.

FAO, IFAD, UNICEF, WFP and WHO 2017. *The State of Food Security and Nutrition in the World 2018: Building climate resilience for food security and nutrition.* Rome: FAO.

Grinspun, A 2016. "No Small Change: The multiple impacts of the Child Support Grant on child and adolescent well-being." in Aslinn Delany, Selwyn Jehoma and Lori Lake, eds. *South African Child Gauge 2016* Cape Town: Children's Institute, University of Cape Town.

Hall K, Sambu W, Berry L, Giese S, Almeleh C, and S Rosa 2017. *South African Early Childhood Review 2016.* Cape Town: Children's Institute, University of Cape Town and Ilifa Labantwana.

Hall, K and W Sambu 2017a. "Income Poverty, Unemployment and Social Grants" in: Lucy Jamieson, Lizette Berry and Lori Lake, eds. *South African Child Gauge 2017.* Cape Town: Children's Institute, University of Cape Town.

Hall K and Sambu W 2017b. "Nutrition–Child hunger" http://childrencount.uct.ac.za/indicator.php?domain=4&indicator=32 Accessed on 25 May 2018.

Hatløy A, Hallund J, Diarra MM, & Oshaug A 2000. "Food variety, socioeconomic status and nutritional status in urban and rural areas in Koutiala (Mali)" in *Public Health Nutrition,* Vol. 3 (1).

Hoddinott J & Yohannes Y 2002 "Dietary Diversity as a Food Security Indicator" https://www.fantaproject.org/sites/default/files/resources/DietaryDiversity-HH-FS-Indicator-2002.pdf Accessed 25 September 2017.

Kabubo-Mariara J, Ndenge GK, and DK Mwabu 2009. "Determinants of Children's Nutritional Status in Kenya: Evidence from Demographic and Health Surveys." *Journal of African Economie.s* Vol. 18(3).

Labadarios D, Steyn P, and J Nel 2011. "How diverse is the Diet of Adult South Africans?" *Nutrition Journal 2011.* Vol. 10: 33.

May J and IM Timæus 2014. "Inequities in Under-Five Child Nutritional Status in South Africa: What progress has been made?" *Development Southern Africa.* Vol. 31 (6).

Mkhawani K, Motadi SA, Mabapa NS, Mbhenyane XG and R Blaauw 2016. "Effects of Rising Food Prices on Household Food Security on Female Headed Households in Runnymede Village, South Africa." *South African Journal of Clinical Nutrition 2016.* Vol. 29 (2).

NAMC 2017. *Food Cost Review 2016* Pretoria: National Agricultural Marketing Council.

Nel E 2010. "Diarrhoea and Malnutrition." *South African Journal of Clinical Nutrition.* Vol. 23 (1).

Oldewage-Theron W, Emsie GD and EC Napier 2006. "Poverty, Household Food Security and Nutrition: Coping Strategies in an Informal Settlement in the Vaal Triangle, South Africa." *Public Health.* Vol. 120 (9).

Pereira LM, Cuneo CN and WC Twine 2014. "Food and Cash: Understanding the role of the retail sector in rural food security in South Africa."*Food Security.* Vol. 6 (3).

Smith J and M Abrahams 2016. *PACSA Food Price Barometer Annual Report.* Pietermaritzburg: Pietermaritzburg Agency for Community Social Action.

Southern Africa Labour and Development Research Unit 2016. *National Income Dynamics Study 2014-2015, Wave 4 [dataset].* Version 1.1. Cape Town and Pretoria: Southern Africa Labour and Development Research Unit, DataFirst and Department of Planning Monitoring and Evaluation.

Statistics South Africa 2015. *Methodological report on rebasing of national poverty lines and development on pilot provincial poverty lines—Technical Report.* Pretoria: Statistics South Africa.

Statistics South Africa 2017a. *South Africa Demographic and Health Survey 2016: Key Indicator Report.* Pretoria: Statistics South Africa.

Statistics South Africa 2017b. *Poverty Trends in South Africa: An examination of absolute poverty between 2006 and 2015* Pretoria: Statistics South Africa.

Statistics South Africa 2003; 2017c. *General Household Survey 2002-2016.* Pretoria: Statistics South Africa.

Statistics South Africa 2017d. *Living Conditions Survey 2014/2015.* Pretoria: Statistics South Africa.

Statistics South Africa 2018. *Quarterly Labour Force Survey. Quarter 1: 2018.* Pretoria: Statistics South Africa.

Steyn NP and R Ochse 2013. "'Enjoy a variety of foods': as a food-based dietary guideline for South Africa". *South African Journal of Clinical Nutrition* Vol. 26 (3).

Swindle A and P. Ohri-Vachaspati 2005. *Measuring household food consumption: a technical guide* Washington, D.C: Food and Nutrition Technical Assistance (FANTA) Project, Academy for Educational Development (AED).

Temple NJ and NP Steyn 2009. "Food Prices and Energy Density as Barriers to Healthy Food Patterns in Cape Town South Africa." *Journal of Hunger & Environmental Nutrition.* Vol. 4 (2).

Temple N and NP Steyn 2011. "The Cost of a Healthy Diet: A South African perspective." *Nutrition* Vol. 27(5).

Temple NJ, Steyn NP, Fourie J and A De Villiers 2011. "Price and Availability of Healthy Food: A study in rural South Africa." *Nutrition.* Vol. 27 (1).

UN General Assembly 2015. *Resolution adopted by the General Assembly on 25 September 2015* in http://www.un.org/ga/search/view_doc.asp?symbol=A/RES/70/1&Lang=E Accessed 25 September 2017.

UNICEF 1990. *Strategy for improved nutrition of children and women in developing countries.* New York: UNICEF.

World Health Organization 2000. *The Management of Nutrition in Major Emergencies.* Geneva: WHO.

World Health Organization 2003. *Global Strategy for Infant and Young Child Feeding.* Geneva: WHO.

CHAPTER 4
Child Stunting in Sub-Saharan Africa: The Interrelated Effects of Neighbourhoods and Families

Oluwaseyi Dolapo Somefun, Joshua Odunayo Akinyemi and Clifford Odimegwu[1]

1. Background

Globally almost half of under-5 mortality is the result of undernutrition, and a large number of nutritionally troubled children reside in sub-Saharan Africa (SSA) (Black et al., 2013). Childhood nutrition, which requires that a child's energy and nutrient needs are met, is fundamental for physical and cognitive development as well as future economic productivity (Remans et al., 2011). A recent report states that roughly three million lives are lost per year as a result of undernutrition (UNICEF, 2018). Although countries in SSA have achieved reductions in child mortality and gains in child survival, regions such as West and Central Africa have been documented to be making slow progress (Kassebaum et al., 2014) and the region is still plagued with the highest levels of child malnutrition globally (Akombi, Agho, Merom, Renzaho, and Hall, 2017; Danaei et al., 2016).

A child is considered to be stunted if his/her height-for-age standard score is below minus 2 standard deviations from the WHO length or height-for-age standards median (Onis and Branca, 2016). Socio-economic variables such as educational status of the mother have been documented to be associated with stunting (Gewa, 2010; Kimani-Murage et al., 2015). Some studies (Fox and Heaton, 2012; Kravdal and Kodzi,

---

1   We acknowledge the ICF Macro International and other implementing partners for granting access to the DHS data. This research was supported by the Consortium for Advanced Research Training in Africa (CARTA). CARTA is jointly led by the African Population and Health Research Center and the University of the Witwatersrand and funded by the Wellcome Trust (UK) (Grant no. 087547/Z/08/Z), the Carnegie Corporation of New York (Grant no. B8606.R02), and Sida (Grant no. 4100029). The statements made and views expressed are solely the responsibility of the authors. We acknowledge Prof Devayani Tirthali of AuthorAid for assisting with editorial aspects of the manuscript and Tom Pullum for his help in deriving the family structure variable.

2011) have also found a positive relationship between residing in a rural area and child stunting, although Fotso (2007) found a narrow difference in stunting of children in urban areas and rural areas. Children living in large households (Cruz et al., 2017; Fikadu, Assegid, and Dube, 2014) have also been shown to have higher odds of stunting compared to their counterparts in smaller households. At the household level, wealth status has been shown to have a negative relationship with child stunting (Darteh, Acquah, and Kumi-Kyereme, 2014; Keino, Plasqui, Ettyang, and van den Borne, 2014) and some other authors have highlighted the relationship between structural factors such as access to healthcare services and child stunting (Aoun, Matsuda, and Sekiyama, 2015).

There are notable changes in the structure of families in sub-Saharan Africa (SSA) as the region is witnessing a change in the traditional family pattern due to globalization and urbanization (Odimegwu, Somefun, and De Wet, 2017). A large number of studies have shown the association between these changing family structures and various child health outcomes. For instance, numerous studies have documented the advantages that children living with both parents have compared to their counterparts living with single parents (Clark and Hamplová, 2013; McLanahan and Sandefur, 1994; Muniagurria and Novak, 2014; Ntoimo and Odimegwu, 2014).

While there is evidence on the influence family structure has on educational (Davids and Roman, 2013; Davids, Ryan, Yassin, Hendrickse, and Roman, 2016) and behavioural outcomes of children, few authors have documented these associations with regard to stunting, which is a precise measure of social inequalities (Onis and Branca, 2016). Although there is extensive literature on factors associated with stunting, most of them focus on the individual and household level determinants and literature on the effect of communities in which these individuals reside is scarce.

We find one study considering the link between family status and malnutrition from a pooled analysis of 21 countries in SSA and found no association between single motherhood and marasmus[2] among under-five children (Olamijuwon, Odimegwu, Gumbo, and Chisumpa, 2017). A few more studies have considered the role of community factors. Using

---

2   A severe form of malnutrition that is characterised by energy deficiency following inadequate energy intake, including protein.

data from the 2008 Nigeria Demographic and Health Survey (NDHS), Adekanmbi, Kayode, and Uthman (2013) showed that literacy level at the community level was an important predictor of child stunting. Other studies in Ethiopia (Haile, Azage, Mola, and Rainey, 2016), Ghana (Aheto, Keegan, Taylor, and Diggle, 2015) and Malawi (Chikhungu, Madise, and Padmadas, 2014) have also shown the importance of community factors for child stunting. However, these studies have focused on one country only, and there is scarce literature on factors associated with stunting for multiple countries which may help show contextual differences. While international comparative research is a developing area in population studies, there are not enough studies comparing child stunting of different countries in SSA. Examining child stunting in different countries in SSA can inform existing and new policies about initiatives that would help attain the sustainable development goals (Akombi et al., 2017).

Given this lack of evidence, there is a need to go beyond individual or common family level characteristics when examining child stunting, to include family structure and community factors. Community factors can mediate the relationship between family structure and child stunting in SSA regardless of the different family types. This holds especially true because the social environments that mothers reside in are important for children's developmental outcomes (Pickett and Pearl, 2001). At the basic level, it is believed that mothers play a critical role in determining the nutritional outcomes of their children and the UNICEF's conceptual framework labels "the mother" as an underlying factor in child nutritional status (Carlson, Kordas, and Murray-Kolb, 2015). It is also possible that the environment where the mother resides influences the child's health outcomes because of practices in that environment or access to information and services in the particular environment. For instance, neighbourhoods with a higher percentage of working women may be more likely to have access to healthcare and information that may prevent their children from being stunted. This has been supported by (Brooks-Gunn and Duncan, 1997; Wilson, 1987) who argue that the combination of individuals and family units within a particular neighbourhood forms a "context" that influences child developmental outcomes.

Although a number of theories have been used to explain stunting among children, we use the UNICEF conceptual framework (Unicef, 1990). This is because the framework takes into account multiple causes of child stunting and accounts for the individual, household and community level determinants (Pridmore and Carr-Hill, 2009, 2011). This approach not only substantiates the complex, multi-level determinants of child stunting but also calls for the need for a multifaceted approach to reduce child stunting and sustain improvements that have been made before. This framework also underpins the analysis in Chapters 3 (by Sambu and Hall) and 6 (by Devereux et al.) in this volume.

Adapting this framework, we examine the interplay between family structure, community characteristics and child stunting. We hypothesize that family structure has a strong effect on child stunting in the presence of community factors in all the countries studied. To summarise, the impact of family structure on child stunting remains unclear. Is it a direct relationship or can the relationship be better explained by the presence of community factors and are these associations context specific? Also, often due to data limitations, the available studies on family structure have focused on a limited measure of family forms, by ignoring or combining the less common forms. Our study improves on this by using a nationally representative dataset measuring a broad range of family types in SSA. In addition, most previous studies on family structure and child stunting in SSA have used marital status of the mother as an indicator of family structure. This chapter brings other dimensions which could also affect child health and development, especially, living with father alone and living with neither parent.

2. Data and methods

This study was based on secondary data that was obtained from 10 purposefully selected countries' national surveys: Demographic and Health Surveys (DHSs). The countries which were selected for the analysis belong to different geographical regions of sub-Saharan Africa and differ from each other in historical experience, present degree of economic and social development and demographic conditions. Although they may not represent the whole sub-Saharan area, they undoubtedly give an effective picture of the factors associated with child stunting in different settings. Although the study countries have slightly different survey years, we selected countries that have surveys ranging from 2011–2015 and analysed data for each country instead of a pooled analysis. The aim of the chapter is to provide a cross-sectional perspective on child stunting. More importantly, we selected countries in the East, West, Central and Southern regions which had similar child stunting prevalence rates. The selected countries, survey year and sample size have been presented in Appendix 1 of this chapter.

The DHS employs a similar methodology in data collection across countries, and this permits comparative analysis and comparability of findings across countries. The data which was used for this analysis has one record for every household member and includes the characteristics of the households where the individual lives or was visiting. The present analysis is based on data from children born in the last five years whose anthropometric data were collected. Following DHS measurement procedures, all children of selected mothers are included for anthropometric measurements (Corsi, Perkins, and Subramanian, 2017).

3. Variables

3.1. Outcome variable

The outcome variable for this study is child nutritional status measured as stunting. Although there are various forms of malnutrition, we focus on stunting because stunting occurs over a long period of time and has more long-lasting consequences that become irreversible with age (Unicef, 2007). It has also been documented to be the most prevalent form of child malnutrition (Onis and Branca, 2016). New evidence on stunting will contribute to the achievement of the Sustainable Development Goal 2 by 2030 and the World Health Assembly global nutrition targets which aim to reduce the number of stunted children globally by 40 percent in 2025. A child is regarded as stunted if height-for-age is less than minus 2 standard deviations of the World Health Organisation (WHO) height-for-age or length-for-age standard median. This variable was coded as: 0— Not stunted; and 1—stunted.

3.2. Independent variables

The key independent variable for this study is family structure measured as the living arrangement of the child. Family structure was categorized as: living with both parents; living with mother alone; living with father alone; and living with neither parent. The selected control variables at the individual level included: sex of the child; place of residence; number of children; household wealth status; mother's education; sex of household head; and birth order of the child. The community variables considered are community-level education and community poverty. The community level variables were created by aggregating the individual and household-level variables at the level of primary sampling units and the newly created variables were divided into proportions. These variables are grounded in the theoretical framework and existing literature (Davenport, Grace, Funk, and Shukla, 2017; Haile et al., 2016).

3.3. Statistical analysis

Our data and analysis are cross-sectional in nature. The analysis is divided into three parts. The first part includes descriptive statistics that are used to summarise the background characteristics of the sample. The bivariate analysis presents the independent association between family structure and child stunting, and logistic regression is used due to the binary nature of the outcome variable. The multivariate analysis fits regression models to estimate the main and random effects of family structure and stunting while controlling for other variables. A two-level model is specified for the outcome where level 1 is the individual level and level 2 is the community level.

A total of five models are estimated: (i) null model without independent variables; (ii) model including individual-level variables; (iii) model including community-level variables; (iv) model including all of the variables; and (v) the final model including adjusted interaction effects between family structure, community characteristics and child stunting.

Fixed effects are reported as odds ratios with their confidence intervals (CIs) while the random effects are reported as variance, intra-class correlation and proportional change in variance. Sampling weights are applied to adjust for differences in probability of selection and to adjust for non-response in order to produce the proper representation. Individual weights are used for descriptive statistics in this study, using Stata 14 for Windows.

4.   Results

4.1. Descriptive statistics

The results in Figure 1 show stunting status by country. The highest prevalence of stunting is found among children in countries in East Africa and Central Africa with more than half of all children being stunted in Burundi. Zimbabwe and Cameroon have the lowest stunting rates among the countries studied (27 percent and 33 percent respectively).

Figure 1.   Child stunting by country

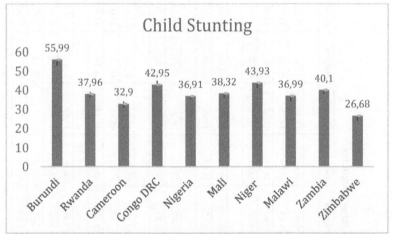

Table 1 shows the percentage distribution of stunting by selected characteristics. The distribution of stunting by family structure differs by country. For instance, stunting rates are highest among children living with neither parent compared to their counterparts living with mother alone or with father alone in Burundi, Congo DRC, Mali, Niger and Zimbabwe. In Cameroon, Nigeria and Zambia, children living with their father alone are more likely to be stunted compared to their counterparts living with neither parent. Stunting rates are higher among boys compared to girls in all the studied countries. In terms of place of residence, rural areas have the highest prevalence of child stunting, but the gap differs per country. For example, in Burundi, the number of children stunted in rural was more than twice the number of children stunted in the urban areas. Stunting rates are higher among children in poorer households. Across all countries, more than 40 percent of children in poor households were stunted, with the exception of Zimbabwe, where 31 percent of the children in poor households were stunted. Stunting rates among children in non-poor households ranged from 18 percent in Cameroon to 41 percent in Burundi and Niger. Stunting rates among children with educated (secondary or higher education) mothers are lower compared to children with mothers that have no or little education.

Table 1.   Percentage distribution of stunting by family structure and other covariates

	Burundi	Cameroon	Congo DRC	Rwanda	Nigeria	Mali	Niger	Malawi	Zambia	Zimbabwe
Family Structure										
Living with both parents	56.34	33.1	43.81	36.86	38.07	38.63	43.47	35.91	39.76	25.54
Living with mother alone	53.31	29.69	39.9	40.78	28.25	33.54	44.55	38.12	41.01	27.4
Living with father alone	61.92	42.89	43.84	40.9	40.83	34.41	45.85	40.9	43.54	28.17
Living with neither parent	65.71	37.24	46.8	40.94	36.52	44.57	49.12	41.58	40.46	29.44
Child Sex										
Male	59.41	35.41	45.71	42.67	38.67	39.86	45.86	38.69	42.61	29.54
Female	52.54	30.49	40.17	33.16	35.15	36.69	41.99	35.38	37.57	23.88
Place of Residence										
Urban	27.82	21.88	32.55	24.04	26.02	23.13	29.58	24.17	36.13	21.11
Rural	58.79	41.19	47.38	40.59	43.33	41.95	45.96	38.82	42.11	28.74
Wealth Status										
Poor	66.27	46.01	48.99	46.96	49.91	45.39	47.55	43.21	44.63	31.16
Middle	60.58	31.66	46.44	37.11	35.17	42.41	41.96	36.51	39.99	25.94
Rich	41.31	17.72	32.96	25.81	22.32	28.05	41.24	28.54	33.55	21.36
Education of the Mother										
No education	61.29	45.71	51.19	47.53	49.69	40.06	44.97	42.66	44.63	44.79
Primary	55.55	33.7	47.24	39.09	33.18	31.99	40.31	38.28	42.07	31.47
Secondary	33.48	20.09	33.28	22.01	22.65	25.63	25.14	29.23	36.95	24.33
Higher	5.64	7.37	12.59	5.27	13.16	12.04	7.44	9.08	18.13	8.2

4.2. Bivariate associations

Bivariate results in Table 2 show the unadjusted association between family structure and stunting. We also show the unadjusted association between control variables and stunting and the interaction effects between family structure, community variables and child stunting.

Associations between family structure and stunting differ across countries. Living with neither parent is associated with higher odds of stunting compared to living with both parents in Burundi (OR, 1.45), Cameroon (OR, 1.41), Congo DRC (OR, 1.22), Niger (OR, 1.40) and Zimbabwe (OR, 1.20). In Cameroon, children living with their father alone are about twice more likely to be stunted compared to their counterparts living with both parents. The results of living with the mother alone are mixed. In Burundi (OR, 0.88) and Nigeria (OR, 0.65), children living with their mother alone have lower odds of being stunted compared to their counterparts with both parents. In Rwanda (OR, 1.18) children living with their mother alone have higher odds of being stunted compared to their counterparts living with both parents.

The association between stunting and control variables such as child sex, place of residence, wealth status, and education of the mother were similar in all the countries. For instance, girls have significantly lower odds of being stunted compared to boys, and children from rural areas have significantly higher odds of being stunted compared to their counterparts in urban areas. Children of women who belong to the richest quintile and who have obtained secondary and higher level of education have lower odds of being stunted compared to their counterparts with mothers in the poorest quintile and who have not obtained an education.

With respect to community level characteristics, children in communities with high levels of poverty have significantly higher odds of being stunted in all countries. Children who were staying in communities with high levels of education are significantly less likely to be stunted, except in Niger where the association is not significant.

Table 2.   Unadjusted association between family structure, covariates, interaction terms and child stunting

	Burundi	Cameroon	Congo DRC	Rwanda	Nigeria	Mali	Niger	Malawi	Zambia	Zimbabwe
Family Structure										
Living with both parents										
Living with mother alone	0.88 (0.78-0.99) *	0.89 (0.78-1.02)	0.92 (0.83-1.01)	1.18 (1.01-1.38) *	0.65 (0.60-0.70) ***	0.83 (0.69-1.01)	1.03 (0.88-1.20)	1.06 (0.94-1.19)	1.02 (0.94-1.11)	1.12 (0.98-1.28)
Living with father alone	1.07 (0.61-1.87)	1.62 (1.14-2.32) ***	1.17 (0.87-1.56)	1.10 (0.56-2.17)	1.16 (0.97-1.38)	0.87 (0.55-1.37)	0.93 (0.51-1.67)	0.89 (0.49-1.59)	0.89 (0.57-1.42)	0.99 (0.58-1.67)
Living with neither parent	1.45 (1.07-1.97) *	1.41 (1.16-1.70) ***	1.22 (1.02-1.46) *	1.17 (0.86-1.58)	0.95 (0.84-1.09)	1.09 (0.83-1.41)	1.40 (1.05-1.86) *	1.21 (0.98-1.51)	0.92 (0.78-1.09)	1.20 (1.02-1.42) *
Child Sex										
Male										
Female	0.77 (0.69-0.85) ***	0.82 (0.73-0.91) ***	0.77 (1.55-1.87) ***	0.67 (0.58-0.76) ***	0.86 (0.82-0.90) ***	0.88 (0.78-0.99) *	0.84 (0.76-0.94) ***	0.86 (0.77-0.96) ***	0.80 (0.74-0.86) ***	0.74 (0.66-0.83) ***
Place of Residence										
Urban										
Rural	3.17 (2.75-3.67) ***	2.34 (2.07-2.63) ***	1.70 (1.55-1.87) ***	2.13 (1.78-2.54) ***	2.17 (2.05-2.29) ***	2.44 (2.10-2.84) ***	1.97 (1.71-2.28) ***	1.73 (1.47-2.04) ***	1.32 (1.22-1.42) ***	1.56 (1.37-1.77) ***
Wealth Status										
Poor										
Middle	0.79 (0.69-0.91) ***	0.54 (0.47-0.63) ***	0.90 (0.81-1.00)	0.68 (0.56-0.81) ***	0.55 (0.51-0.58) ***	0.95 (0.81-1.11)	0.83 (0.71-0.97) *	0.77 (0.67-0.90) ***	0.77 (0.71-0.85) ***	0.81 (0.68-0.95) *
Rich	0.33 (0.30-0.37) ***	0.27 (0.23-0.31) ***	0.54 (0.49-0.59) ***	0.38 (0.32-0.44) ***	0.27 (0.25-0.28) ***	0.45 (0.39-0.51) ***	0.69 (0.61-0.78) ***	0.55 (0.49-0.63) ***	0.58 (0.53-0.63) ***	0.58 (0.51-0.66) ***

Education of the Mother										
No education										
Primary	0.78 (0.70–0.87) ***	0.62 (0.54–0.72) ***	0.87 (0.78–0.97) *	0.70 (0.58–0.85) ***	0.50 (0.46–0.53) ***	0.69 (0.55–0.85) ***	0.70 (0.58–0.85) ***	0.80 (0.68–0.95) *	0.94 (0.83–1.06)	0.62 (0.37–1.03)
Secondary	0.27 (0.23–0.33) ***	0.31 (0.26–0.37) ***	0.54 (0.48–0.61) ***	0.31 (0.23–0.41) ***	0.27 (0.25–0.29) ***	0.45 (0.35–0.58) ***	0.41 (0.30–0.55) ***	0.54 (0.44–0.66) ***	0.72 (0.63–0.82) ***	0.43 (0.26–0.72) ***
Higher	0.07 (0.03–0.17) ***	0.09 (0.05–0.17) ***	0.22 (0.12–0.41) ***	0.06 (0.02–0.16) ***	0.13 (0.11–0.16) ***	0.27 (0.10–0.70) **	0.12 (0.03–0.42) ***	0.19 (0.09–0.37) ***	0.28 (0.21–0.36) ***	0.13 (0.06–0.24) ***
Community Poverty	1.65 (1.52–1.79) ***	2.00 (1.83–2.19)	1.25 (1.16–1.34) ***	1.49 (1.35–1.64) ***	2.06–2.35 ***	1.61 (1.45–1.79) ***	1.29 (1.16–1.43) ***	1.32 (1.23–1.42) ***	1.25 (1.18–1.32) ***	1.27 (1.16–1.38) ***
Variance (SE)	0.25 (0.04)	0.21 (0.04)	0.21 (0.03)	0.18 (0.05)	0.45 (0.03)	0.35 (0.06)	0.41 (0.16)	0.07 (0.03)	0.15 (0.02)	0.14 (0.03)
Model fit statistics										
AIC	8460.59	6797.52	12067.53	4903.06	31277.41	6137.16	6866.78	7328.06	16255.17	6791.78
BIC	8480.86	6817.44	12088.8	4921.77	31301.93	6156.6	6886.43	7347.99	16277.41	6811.86
Community Education	0.67 (0.61–0.73) ***	0.59 (0.53–0.65) ***	0.73 (0.68–0.79) ***	0.83 (0.75–0.93) ***	0.43 (0.40–0.45) ***	0.82 (0.73–0.92) ***	0.93 (0.83–1.03)	0.85 (0.79–0.92) ***	0.78 (0.74–0.83) ***	0.81 (0.74–0.88) ***
Variance (SE)	0.32 (0.04)	0.35 (0.06)	0.21 (0.03)	0.27 (0.06)	0.37 (0.03)	0.49 (0.07)	0.43 (0.06)	0.10 (0.04)	0.14 (0.02)	0.15 (0.03)
Model fit statistics										
AIC	8517.35	6904.01	12036.01	4954.85	31180.81	6199.522	6888.74	7370.37	16246.81	6799.61
BIC	8537.62	6923.98	12057.28	4973.56	31205.33	6218.959	6908.38	7390.31	16269.05	6819.69

*p < 0.05; **p < 0.01; ***p < 0.001; OR refers to Odds Ratio.

When estimating associations adjusting for control variables[1], results in relation to family structure mirror country differences reported for the unadjusted bivariate associations. Children living with neither parent in Burundi, Cameroon, Congo DRC and Niger have significantly higher odds of being stunted compared to their counterparts that are living with both parents. In Cameroon, living with a father alone is significantly associated with higher odds of stunting compared with children living with both parents. Also, living with a mother alone is associated with higher odds of stunting among children in Rwanda and lower odds of stunting among children in Nigeria.

The results regarding the association between a child's sex and stunting remains unchanged in the adjusted model. Also, children of women in the richest quintile have lower odds of being stunted in all the countries studied compared to the counterparts in the poorest quintile. However, we no longer find significant association between the place of residence and child stunting in Cameroon, Zambia and Zimbabwe.

4.3. Multivariate associations

Table 3 shows the association between family structure and child stunting, while controlling for community characteristics alone. Results remain unchanged except for Nigeria. Children living with neither parent have higher odds of being stunted in Burundi, Cameroon, Congo DRC and Niger as seen in the unadjusted model. Taking community variables into account, children living with neither parent (OR, 1.36) and a father alone (OR, 1.27) have significantly higher odds of being stunted compared to their counterparts living with both parents in Nigeria. Community poverty remains significantly associated with higher levels of stunting among children in all countries. Community education is also significantly associated with lower level of stunting among children except for children in Rwanda, Mali, Niger, Malawi and Zimbabwe.

When adding control variables and community characteristics to the model, the association between family structure and child stunting remains the same. The effect of community poverty on stunting differs by country in this model; children residing in communities with a higher percentage of poor women have higher odds of being stunted in Burundi,

---

1   These and other results that are not presented in this chapter can be made available upon request.

Cameroon, Rwanda, Nigeria, Mali and Malawi. In Congo DRC, Niger and Zimbabwe, children residing in communities with a higher percentage of poor women have lower odds of being stunted, but this association was only significant in Congo DRC.

Analyses of the interaction effects show that children living with neither parent residing in communities with high levels of poverty have significantly higher odds of being stunted compared to their counterparts living with both parents in Cameroon, Nigeria, and Mali. In Congo DRC, Nigeria and Zimbabwe, children living with their mother alone, residing in communities with a higher percentage of poor women, have significantly lower odds of being stunted.

In terms of community education, living with both parents and residing in communities with a high level of education was associated with lower levels of stunting among children in Burundi, Cameroon, Congo DRC, Nigeria and Zambia.

Table 3.   Adjusted association between family structure, community characteristics and child stunting

	Burundi	Cameroon	Congo DRC	Rwanda	Nigeria	Mali	Niger	Malawi	Zambia	Zimbabwe
Family Structure										
Living with both parents										
Living with mother alone	0.96 (0.85–1.10)	1.07 (0.92–1.25)	0.95 (0.86–1.05)	1.23 (1.04–1.46)*	0.98 (0.90–1.08)	0.88 (0.71–1.09)	1.06 (0.89–1.26)	1.06 (0.93–1.19)	1.08 (0.98–1.18)	1.10 (0.96–1.26)
Living with father alone	1.24 (0.68–2.26)	1.79 (1.22–2.63)***	1.19 (0.88–1.62)	1.23 (0.60–2.51)	1.27 (1.05–1.54)*	0.84 (0.51–1.36)	1.04 (0.55–1.96)	0.87 (0.48–1.59)	0.98 (0.61–1.55)	1.01 (0.59–1.74)
Living with neither parent	1.82 (1.31–2.52)***	1.84 (1.49–2.27)***	1.35 (1.11–1.64)***	1.19 (0.86–1.65)	1.36 (1.18–1.58)***	0.99 (0.73–1.33)	1.46 (1.07–1.99)*	1.24 (0.99–1.55)	1.02 (0.86–1.21)	1.16 (0.98–1.39)
Community Poverty	1.51 (1.38–1.65)***	1.79 (1.61–1.98)***	1.09 (1.01–1.18)*	1.46 (1.32–1.62)***	1.41 (1.29–1.54)***	1.58 (1.42–1.77)***	1.28 (1.15–1.42)***	1.30 (1.20–1.41)***	1.13 (1.05–1.21)**	1.18 (1.05–1.32)***
Community Education	0.79 (0.73–0.87)***	0.78 (0.70–0.87)***	0.77 (0.71–0.83)***	0.90 (0.82–1.00)	0.55 (0.50–0.60)***	0.95 (0.85–1.06)	0.96 (0.88–1.06)	0.96 (0.88–1.04)	0.84 (0.78–0.90)***	0.89 (0.80–1.00)
Variance (SE)	0.23 (0.04)	0.19 (0.04)	0.18 (0.02)	0.18 (0.05)	0.33 (0.02)	0.35 (0.06)	0.41 (0.06)	0.06 (0.03)	0.14 (0.02)	0.14 (0.03)
Model fit statistics										
AIC	8430356	6752.36	12026.34	4901.46	31106.29	6142.67	6868.25	7330.96	16240.76	6793.21
BIC	8477.86	6798.85	12075.99	4945.12	31163.5	6188.02	6914.09	7377.48	16292.65	6840.07

*p < 0.05; **p < 0.01; ***p < 0.001; OR refers to Odds Ratio.

5.   Discussion and conclusion

This study examined the association between family structure, community characteristics and child stunting in SSA. The region is witnessing an increasing change in family forms, and a number of studies have documented the effects of these changing family dynamics on various health outcomes. Some of these studies have also explored the influence of different family types on stunting but literature on the role of communities in this relationship is scarce. This study was carried out to explore the mediating effect that communities have on child stunting. We consider child stunting because SSA has one of the highest levels of child stunting globally, and understanding the factors associated with these high levels in different context would be useful for designing specific interventions for each country.

Although more than a quarter of children in all the countries studied were stunted, stunting levels varied by country and were seen to be highest in Burundi, Niger, Congo DRC and Zambia. These results are similar to what other studies (Kismul, Acharya, Mapatano, and Hatløy, 2018; Nkurunziza, Meessen, and Korachais, 2017) have found.

The unadjusted results showed significant variations in the association between family structure and stunting. Children living with neither parent were more likely to be stunted in all the countries studied. This is not surprising as the consequences of living outside of families with two biological parents have been well documented (Campbell, Handa, Moroni, Odongo, and Palermo, 2010; Finlay et al., 2016). Another expected finding was our result in Cameroon where children living with a father alone were found to be at higher odds of being stunted. This could be based on the fact that mothers are usually the primary care givers, and are more likely to have information about the nutritional requirements for children's health. One reason for this could be because the majority of the health education messages on child nutrition is usually targeted at mothers alone, and interventions such as engaging males into nutrition programmes have not been at the forefront of nutrition education communication.

The association between living with a mother alone and child stunting differed by countries. For instance, children living with a mother alone in Burundi and Nigeria were less likely to be stunted while children living with a mother alone in Rwanda were more likely to be stunted (compared to living with both parents). The different effects of living with a mother alone on child stunting in Burundi and Rwanda are a bit surprising as both countries have similar ethnicities (Vandeginste, 2014) and natural resources compared to Nigeria in West Africa. However, the results highlight the fact that factors associated with child stunting may differ within regions. We link the protective effect of living with mother alone in Burundi and Nigeria to parental presence. Parental presence, especially the presence of mothers, has been linked with positive outcomes among children. The effect of single motherhood on stunting may also be influenced by the marital status of the mother and the socio-economic status of the household. These factors may explain the differences across countries. The results in Burundi and Nigeria could also be explained by the increase in female bargaining power inside the household (Agarwal, 1997) which differs from Becker's Unitary model (Martínez A, 2013). It is possible that women in Burundi and Nigeria have some sort of autonomy which may be in the form of good income or land which allows them control the household budget to a large extent and spend more on resources useful for child health.

In all the countries studied, community poverty was associated with higher levels of stunting. This is not unexpected as poverty deprives people of the capability to be healthy and well nourished. Poverty could mean that mothers do not have access to different types of resources which could be economic, social and environmental which may be beneficial for their well-being. This definition is captured by the DHS measure of poverty, which measures household ownership of consumer goods, resources such as electricity and water (Booysen, 2002). Community education was a protective factor for child stunting in all the countries studied which is in line with the literature (Adekanmbi et al., 2013).

Living with neither parent remained significantly associated with child stunting even in the presence of the community characteristics. It is possible that children who are living with neither parent may be living with relatives or unrelated adults, but the data was unable to confirm that. Although research on the health outcomes of these children is quite scarce, it is possible that they may not be given as much attention than if they would if they stayed with their biological parents. This is because care-givers may be more inclined to invest in their own children based on affinity (Case 2004) or the low socio-economic status of the care giver. With respect to community characteristics, children of mothers residing in poor communities in Burundi, Cameroon, Rwanda, Nigeria and Mali were more likely to be stunted but the results were different for children of mothers in Congo DRC. This ambiguous effect of community poverty has been established in a number of other studies in the region (Kayode et al., 2014; Ntenda and Chuang, 2018). However, community poverty was shown to be a protective factor for stunting among children in Congo DRC. This was unexpected, and we suspect that mothers in Congo DRC may benefit from social capital that may be available in their networks. Sometimes, the effect of social capital is stronger in poorer communities which has been explained by bonding. Our results could also be partly explained by a qualitative study in Congo which aimed to describe the social context of malnutrition in a rural part of the DRC, and to understand how some households succeed in ensuring that their children are well-nourished while others do not. They concluded that through neighbour cooperation, in the form of *"gbisa"*[1], residents were able to organise capital which helped them avoid seasonal shortages. They were also supported by the local authorities and non-governmental organisations (NGOs) which helped provide access to social services (Kismul et al., 2015). This result also draws support from a study that examined geographical disparities in stunting rates in Congo DRC. They explained that regardless of the high state of poverty in the country, some regions enjoy better access to food products due to higher incomes, and having more educated mothers, which may allow for better nutritional practices (Kandala, Madungu, Emina, Nzita, and Cappuccio, 2011). We also suggest that some mothers may exhibit resilience based on the presence of extended family in the household, which is common in a number of African settings.

The interaction effects showed that community poverty was a risk factor for children living with both parents in Cameroon and Nigeria. This reiterates the deleterious effect of poverty on child stunting regardless of the protective effect of living with both parents.

---

1   These are interdependent groups of people that come together to solve tasks that the household unit cannot solve alone such as land clearing and timely weeding.

6. Policy implications

We can draw a number of lessons for policy making from our results. Firstly, children living with neither parent were found to be the most vulnerable. Although there are policies targeted at orphans, it is important that they are strengthened in order to target extended family members to be assisted with resources or programmes that could boost the human capital of the care-givers for children not living with either parent. Secondly, policies must also target fathers raising their children alone. They should be educated on healthy nutritional practices (sensitisation) and lone fatherhood should not be stigmatised. This kind of support may encourage single fathers to seek help from their extended families, communities and health providers which may improve the health of their children. This can be achieved through public health campaigns and designing effective communication strategies. This is because fathers in the rural areas or low level of education may not have access to information that can usually be accessed on the internet.

Our discussion of findings in Congo DRC suggest the importance of social capital. We propose that interventions in disadvantaged neighbourhoods should aim at improving social capital at the community level by encouraging women to form associations where they can share information and help each other achieve positive health outcomes for themselves and their children. This can help buffer the detrimental effect that community poverty has on child health outcomes.

Finally, the results in this chapter show that determinants of stunting are context specific and interventions should differ by country. This is because the effects of family structure and community variables differed among some countries in the same region. Therefore, there is need for taking specific socio-cultural factors into account when designing interventions considering the different results for study countries.

Some limitations should be noted. The DHS is a cross-sectional survey thus we are not able to draw causal inferences. The analysis is also limited as we cannot account for timing of the changes in family structure. The presence of extended family members in the household may influence the effect of lone motherhood or fatherhood on child stunting, but the present data could not control for that. In addition, there is no information on the migration status of the parents. Some parents may be living elsewhere and sending remittances which may influence child stunting.

Further studies must examine the child developmental outcomes of fostered children and explore how geographical factors such as living in high drought areas, may influence child stunting. In spite of these limitations our analysis has some important implications for policy makers.

Appendix 1.   Selected countries, survey countries and sample size

Country	Survey Year	Sample Size
Burundi	2016/17	6,434
Rwanda	2014/15	5,710
Cameroon	2011	9,059
Congo DRC	2013/14	3,812
Nigeria	2013	26,104
Mali	2012/13	4,866
Niger	2012	5,501
Malawi	2015/16	5,704
Zambia	2013/14	12,167
Zimbabwe	2015	6,214

References

Adekanmbi, V. T., Kayode, G. A., and Uthman, O. A. (2013). Individual and contextual factors associated with childhood stunting in Nigeria: a multilevel analysis. *Maternal & child nutrition, 9*(2), 244–259.

Agarwal, B. (1997). "Bargaining" and gender relations: Within and beyond the household. *Feminist economics, 3*(1), 1–51.

Aheto, J. M. K., Keegan, T. J., Taylor, B. M., and Diggle, P. J. (2015). Childhood Malnutrition and Its Determinants among Under-Five Children in Ghana. *Paediatric and perinatal epidemiology, 29*(6), 552–561.

Akombi, B. J., Agho, K. E., Merom, D., Renzaho, A. M., and Hall, J. J. (2017). Child malnutrition in sub-Saharan Africa: A meta-analysis of demographic and health surveys (2006–2016). *PloS one, 12*(5), e0177338.

Aoun, N., Matsuda, H., and Sekiyama, M. (2015). Geographical accessibility to healthcare and malnutrition in Rwanda. *Social Science & Medicine, 130*, 135–145.

Black, R. E., Victora, C. G., Walker, S. P., Bhutta, Z. A., Christian, P., De Onis, M., ... Martorell, R. (2013). Maternal and child undernutrition and overweight in low-income and middle-income countries. *The Lancet, 382*(9890), 427–451.

Booysen, L. R. (2002). Poverty and Health in Southern Africa: Evidence from the Demographic and Health Survey (DHS). *South African Journal of Economics, 70*(2), 181–192.

Brooks-Gunn, J., and Duncan, G. J. (1997). The effects of poverty on children. *The future of children*, 55–71.

Campbell, P., Handa, S., Moroni, M., Odongo, S., and Palermo, T. (2010). Assessing the "orphan effect" in determining development outcomes for children in 11 eastern and southern African countries. *Vulnerable Children and Youth Studies, 5*(1), 12–32.

Carlson, G. J., Kordas, K., and Murray-Kolb, L. E. (2015). Associations between women's autonomy and child nutritional status: a review of the literature. *Maternal & child nutrition, 11*(4), 452–482.

Chikhungu, L. C., Madise, N. J., and Padmadas, S. S. (2014). How important are community characteristics in influencing children's nutritional status? Evidence from Malawi population-based household and community surveys. *Health & Place, 30*, 187–195. doi: https://doi.org/10.1016/j.healthplace.2014.09.006.

Clark, S., and Hamplová, D. (2013). Single motherhood and child mortality in sub-Saharan Africa: a life course perspective. *Demography, 50*(5), 1521–1549.

Corsi, D. J., Perkins, J. M., and Subramanian, S. (2017). Child anthropometry data quality from Demographic and Health Surveys, Multiple Indicator Cluster Surveys, and National Nutrition Surveys in the West Central Africa region: are we comparing apples and oranges? *Global health action, 10*(1), 1328185.

Cruz, L. M. G., Azpeitia, G. G., Súarez, D. R., Rodríguez, A. S., Ferrer, J. F. L., and Serra-Majem, L. (2017). Factors Associated with Stunting among Children Aged 0 to 59 Months from the Central Region of Mozambique. *Nutrients, 9*(5), 491.

Danaei, G., Andrews, K. G., Sudfeld, C. R., Fink, G., McCoy, D. C., Peet, E., ... Fawzi, W. W. (2016). Risk Factors for Childhood Stunting in 137 Developing Countries: A Comparative Risk Assessment Analysis at Global, Regional, and Country Levels. *PLoS Medicine, 13*(11), e1002164.

Darteh, E. K. M., Acquah, E., and Kumi-Kyereme, A. (2014). Correlates of stunting among children in Ghana. *BMC public health, 14*(1), 504.

Davenport, F., Grace, K., Funk, C., and Shukla, S. (2017). Child health outcomes in sub-saharan africa: A comparison of changes in climate and socio-economic factors. *Global Environmental Change, 46*, 72–87.

Davids, E. L., and Roman, N. V. (2013). Does family structure matter? Comparing the life goals and aspirations of learners in secondary schools. *South African Journal of Education, 33*(3).

Davids, E. L., Ryan, J., Yassin, Z., Hendrickse, S., and Roman, N. V. (2016). Family structure and functioning: Influences on adolescents psychological needs, goals and aspirations in a South African setting. *Journal of Psychology in Africa, 26*(4), 351–356.

Fikadu, T., Assegid, S., and Dube, L. (2014). Factors associated with stunting among children of age 24 to 59 months in Meskan district, Gurage Zone, South Ethiopia: a case-control study. *BMC public health, 14*(1), 800.

Finlay, J. E., Fink, G., McCoy, D. C., Tavárez, L. C., Chai, J., Danaei, G., ... Fawzi, M. C. S. (2016). Stunting risk of orphans by caregiver and living arrangement in low-income and middle-income countries. *Journal of epidemiology and community health*, jech-2015.

Fotso, J.-C. (2007). Urban-rural differentials in child malnutrition: Trends and socioeconomic correlates in sub-Saharan Africa. *Health & Place, 13*(1), 205–223. doi: https://doi.org/10.1016/j.healthplace.2006.01.004.

Fox, K., and Heaton, T. B. (2012). Child Nutritional Status by Rural/Urban Residence: A Cross-National Analysis. *The Journal of rural health, 28*(4), 380–391.

Gewa, C. A. (2010). Childhood overweight and obesity among Kenyan pre-school children: association with maternal and early child nutritional factors. *Public health nutrition, 13*(04), 496–503.

Haile, D., Azage, M., Mola, T., and Rainey, R. (2016). Exploring spatial variations and factors associated with childhood stunting in Ethiopia: spatial and multilevel analysis. *BMC pediatrics, 16*(1), 49.

Kandala, N.-B., Madungu, T. P., Emina, J. B. O., Nzita, K. P. D., and Cappuccio, F. P. (2011). Malnutrition among children under the age of five in the Democratic Republic of Congo (DRC): does geographic location matter? *BMC public health, 11*(1), 261.

Kassebaum, N. J., Bertozzi-Villa, A., Coggeshall, M. S., Shackelford, K. A., Steiner, C., Heuton, K. R., ... Dicker, D. (2014). Global, regional, and national levels and causes of maternal mortality during 1990–2013: a systematic analysis for the Global Burden of Disease Study 2013. *The Lancet, 384* (9947), 980–1004.

Kayode, G. A., Amoakoh-Coleman, M., Agyepong, I. A., Ansah, E., Grobbee, D. E., and Klipstein-Grobusch, K. (2014). Contextual risk factors for low birth weight: a multilevel analysis. *PloS one, 9*(10), e109333.

Keino, S., Plasqui, G., Ettyang, G., and van den Borne, B. (2014). Determinants of stunting and overweight among young children and adolescents in sub-Saharan Africa. *Food and Nutrition Bulletin, 35*(2), 167–178.

Kimani-Murage, E. W., Muthuri, S. K., Oti, S. O., Mutua, M. K., van de Vijver, S., and Kyobutungi, C. (2015). Evidence of a double burden of malnutrition in urban poor settings in Nairobi, Kenya. *PloS one, 10*(6), e0129943.

Kismul, H., Acharya, P., Mapatano, M. A., and Hatløy, A. (2018). Determinants of childhood stunting in the Democratic Republic of Congo: further analysis of Demographic and Health Survey 2013–14. *BMC public health, 18*(1), 74.

Kismul, H., Hatløy, A., Andersen, P., Mapatano, M., Van den Broeck, J., and Moland, K. M. (2015). The social context of severe child malnutrition: a qualitative household case study from a rural area of the Democratic Republic of Congo. *International journal for equity in health, 14*(1), 47.

Kravdal, Ø., and Kodzi, I. (2011). Children's stunting in sub-Saharan Africa: Is there an externality effect of high fertility? *Demographic Research, 25*, 565.

Martínez A, C. (2013). Intrahousehold allocation and bargaining power: Evidence from Chile. *Economic Development and Cultural Change, 61*(3), 577–605.

McLanahan, S., and Sandefur, G. (1994). *Growing Up with a Single Parent. What Hurts, What Helps*: ERIC.

Muniagurria, M., and Novak, B. (2014). Family Structure and Child Health in Argentina. *International Journal of Sociology of the Family, 40*(2).

Nkurunziza, S., Meessen, B., and Korachais, C. (2017). Determinants of stunting and severe stunting among Burundian children aged 6–23 months: evidence from a national cross-sectional household survey, 2014. *BMC pediatrics, 17*(1), 176.

Ntenda, P. A. M., and Chuang, Y.-C. (2018). Analysis of individual-level and community-level effects on childhood undernutrition in Malawi. *Pediatrics and Neonatology, 59*(4), 380–389.

Ntoimo, L. F. C., and Odimegwu, C. O. (2014). Health effects of single motherhood on children in sub-Saharan Africa: a cross-sectional study. *BMC public health, 14*(1), 1145.

Odimegwu, C., Somefun, O. D., and De Wet, N. (2017). Contextual determinants of family dissolution in sub-Saharan Africa. *Development Southern Africa*, 1–17.

Olamijuwon, E. O., Odimegwu, C. O., Gumbo, J., and Chisumpa, V. H. (2017). Single motherhood and marasmus among under-five children in Sub-Saharan Africa: a regional analysis of prevalence and correlates. *African Population Studies, 31*(1).

Onis, M., and Branca, F. (2016). Childhood stunting: a global perspective. *Maternal & child nutrition, 12*(S1), 12–26.

Pickett, K. E., and Pearl, M. (2001). Multilevel analyses of neighbourhood socioeconomic context and health outcomes: a critical review. *Journal of epidemiology and community health, 55*(2), 111–122.

Pridmore, P., and Carr-Hill, R. (2011). Tackling the drivers of child undernutrition in developing countries: what works and how should interventions be designed? *Public health nutrition, 14*(4), 688–693.

Remans, R., Pronyk, P. M., Fanzo, J. C., Chen, J., Palm, C. A., Nemser, B., ... Coulibaly, M. (2011). Multisector intervention to accelerate reductions in child stunting: an observational study from 9 sub-Saharan African countries. *The American journal of clinical nutrition, 94*(6), 1632–1642.

Unicef. (1990). Strategy for improved nutrition of women and children in developing countries. *A UNICEF Policy Review. New York: UNICEF.*

Unicef. (2007). *Progress for children: a world fit for children statistical review*: Unicef.

UNICEF. (2018). *Malnutrition rates remain alarming: stunting is declining too slowly while wasting still impacts the lives of far too many young children.* Retrieved from

Vandeginste, S. (2014). Governing ethnicity after genocide: ethnic amnesia in Rwanda versus ethnic power-sharing in Burundi. *Journal of Eastern African Studies, 8*(2), 263–277.

Wilson, W. J. (1987). The truly disadvantaged Chicago. *IL: University of Chicago.*

CHAPTER 5
Dynamics of Child Poverty in Ethiopia[1]

Tassew Woldehanna, Yisak Tafere, Mesele Araya and Adiam Hagos

1. Background and empirical evidence

1.1. Background

Ethiopia experienced a substantial reduction in poverty rates between the years of 2000 and 2015 (UNDP, 2015). The proportion of the population living below US$ 1.25 purchasing power parity (PPP) fell from 56 percent in 2000 to 31 percent in 2011. However, the reduction is not equally distributed between adults and children. The share of children that are poor is greater than that of adults (UNICEF and MOFEC, 2015). While the national average poverty rate was 30 percent, based on the national poverty line, it was 32 percent for children below the age of 14. On the other hand, a significant gain in school enrolment has been achieved within this period. Between 2005 and 2011, the proportion of primary school age children not enrolled in school declined from 83 percent to 58 percent in rural areas and from 26 percent to 16 percent in urban areas. The same trend is observed in the dimension of child health. The number of under-five children that have had episodes of acute respiratory infection, fever and diarrhoea decreased from 45 percent to 27 percent (UNICEF and MOFEC, 2015). Given the variation in improvements of different dimensions of child well-being, it is crucial to take a multidimensional approach to studying childhood poverty. Cognisant of this, the current study takes a multidimensional approach—mainly the Multiple Overlapping Deprivations Analysis (MODA)—to identify the determinants of child well-being and the dynamics of childhood poverty in Ethiopia.

1.2. Multidimensional approach towards the dynamics of child poverty

Although income deprivation has long been used as the primary indicator of poverty, there is growing emphasis that poverty is essentially a complex phenomenon requiring multidimensional approaches. Therefore, the

---

1   This chapter is based on earlier analysis with a financial support from UNICEF Ethiopia Office.

traditional poverty assessment that mainly uses income-based measures is deemed incomplete, as it disregards some non-income measures that are equally vital for improving the design and effectiveness of poverty reduction policies (Ballon and Krishnakumar, 2010). This is also evident in the works of Singh and Sakar (2014) and Roelen (2014). The capabilities approach by Amartya Sen is a main contributor to the theoretical basis for multidimensional poverty analysis (Sen, 1980, 1985a, 1985b, 1992 and 1999). Sen (2000) stresses that this approach is not a theory to explain poverty, inequality, or well-being, but it provides concepts and frameworks within which to conceptualize, measure, and evaluate poverty as well as the institutions and policies that affect it (Sen, 2000; Robeyns, 2003; Crocker and Robeyns, 2010).

This study employs MODA, developed with a focus on childhood deprivations and adopting the child as the main unit of analysis, typically children aged 0–4 and 5–17 (De Neubourg et al., 2012; Bitew et al., 2013). This method of analysis is an extended part of the Multi-Dimensional Poverty Index (MDPI) designed by the Oxford Poverty and Human Development Initiative (OPHI). The MDPI has three dimensions with sub-indicators selected on the basis of targets set in the MDGs. The dimensions are health, education and living conditions (Alkire and Foster, 2010; Calderon and Kovacevic, 2015). Building on the MDPI, the MODA was developed by UNICEF in a way that sheds more light on children's deprivations. It has four broad dimensions, namely: survival, development, protection and participation (De Neubourg et al., 2012a). The dimensions of the MODA and the targets of the sub-indicators are based on international standards such as the Convention of the Rights of the Child (1989), World Summit on Social Development (1995) and the Millennium Development Goals (De Neubourg et al., 2012a), and can be modified based on country specificities.

Adopting MODA for analysis of child well-being is useful in four ways. First, given the fact that children experience poverty differently from adults, MODA takes the child as the unit of analysis instead of the household. Second, MODA addresses the heterogeneity of children's needs across age groups and adopts a life-cycle approach. Third, MODA illuminates child poverty by accounting for deprivations experienced simultaneously across sectors. Last, but not least, MODA allows one to capture the extent of the deprivations in different social and geographical profiles. This gives an insight on the variation in the extent of deprivations across groups' socio-economic profiles (De Neubourg et al., 2012). Table 1 reports the different dimensions used to compute MODA for different age groups.

Table 1.   Dimensions of the lifecycle approach

Age (0–4)	Age (5–17)
Nutrition	Education
Health	Information
Water	Water
Sanitation	Sanitation
Housing	Housing
Protection from Violence	Protection from Violence

Source: De Neubourg et al. 2012

After accounting for the multidimensionality of children's deprivations using MODA, the study builds on literature on chronic child poverty to investigate its persistence and dynamics. The work conducted by Chronic Poverty Research (CPR) highlighted the need to conduct poverty analysis that focuses on the duration and dynamics of chronic poverty (CPRC, 2008; Brown and Teshome, 2007). Research shows the need for analysis that disaggregates the severity and duration of poverty by age, gender and family socio-economic status such as parental educational level. This need is even stronger for children as the effects of poverty at a young age are long-lasting. In particular, the deprivation of education, nutrition and health can have a strong negative effect in their human capital endowment, significantly reducing their lifetime earning capacity (Moore, 2005).

1.3. Empirical evidence from Ethiopia

A few studies have adopted a multidimensional approach to poverty in exploring the status of deprivation in Ethiopia. Among these is OPHI (2013), which found about 87 percent deprivation rate in MDPI[2], while

---

2   The MDPI identifies deprivations across health, education and living standards. Each dimension is equally weighted, and each indicator within each dimension is equally weighted. A person is identified as multidimensionally poor if he or she is deprived in at least one third of the weighted indicators (OPHI, 2017).

the average intensity[3] of deprivation was 64.6 percent. This was mainly driven by the living standards dimension. Similarly, Ambel, Mehta and Yigezu (2015) looked into multidimensional poverty and the extent to which dimensions overlap. Results showed that despite the high MDPI, the number of overlapping deprivations declined. In addition, making use of Demographic Health Survey (DHS) data from 2000 to 2011, Bitew et al. (2013) examined the incidence of overlapping deprivations among children in Ethiopia and found a significant decline in the incidence of overall deprivations. Our study therefore builds on the existing literature on multiple overlapping deprivations analysis in Ethiopia, particularly on Bitew et al. (2013) who also adopted the MODA.

Drawing on the MODA to identify the deprivation status of children and applying the Alkire and Foster (2010) framework for establishing poverty thresholds, we categorise children as never poor, poor only once in four rounds, transient poor (poor in two or three rounds) and chronically poor (poor in all four rounds). This assists us in investigating the dynamics and transition of childhood deprivations across the four survey rounds. Following Alkire and Foster (2010), children that are deprived in more than 30 percent of the dimensions are considered moderately poor (MOD poor) while children deprived in more than 50 percent of the dimensions are considered severely MOD poor.

All in all, in this study we aim to: (i) Construct a multidimensional deprivation index based on the application of the capability approach; (ii) Conduct a dimensional analysis of deprivations; (iii) Divide children for each period into MOD non-poor, MOD moderately poor and MOD severely poor; (iv) Identify the transition of children across the poverty categories (chronically poor, transient poor and never poor) and explore the determinants of poverty dynamics; (v) Analyse poverty trajectories of children (the different types of poverty and movement between categories) through the gender of child and location-based disaggregation.

---

3   Intensity of poverty is the average number of deprivations poor people face (OPHI, 2017).

2.   Data and model specification

2.1 Data

We use a unique mixed methods panel dataset of the Young Lives study that follows 3,000 children (with 2,000 younger cohort children that were aged 1 in 2002 and 1,000 older cohort children that were aged 8 in 2002). The longitudinal nature of the data allows for tracking changes in the number of deprivations over the study period 2001–2013; it also reduces the variability that may have otherwise been caused by using data from different pools of children over survey rounds. This allows us to capture both nutrition and health dimensions of children under five, and education and information variables for children aged 5–17 (see Table 1 for the dimensions and age groups).

2.1.1. Quantitative data

The quantitative survey covers 20 sentinel sites located in Addis Ababa, Oromia, Amhara, Tigray and Southern Nations, Nationalities and Peoples' Region (SNNPR). The regions were selected because 90 percent of the population lived in these areas at the beginning of the first round in 2002. The selection of the sample is gender balanced. While 60 percent of the children live in rural areas, the remaining 40 percent live in urban areas. Data was conducted for four rounds, in the years 2002, 2006, 2009 and 2013. The total attrition rate[4] up to the fourth round is 2.2 percent for the younger cohort and 8.4 percent for the older cohort. The main reasons for attrition are migration (internal or abroad), household moves and refusal, but the attrition rate is still low compared to the other Young Lives study countries (Peru, India and Vietnam) (Young Lives, 2014).

In the quantitative survey, there are three types of questionnaires that belong to the sample children, their households and communities. Using these questionnaires, data has been collected on children's physical and mental growth over time, their school enrolment, progress and time use, their food consumption and health conditions, household assets and socio-economic conditions as well as access to services, access to social protection programmes and experience of socio-economic shocks such as drought, crop failure, flooding and food price shocks.

---

4   Attrition rate is defined as the number of children who were untraceable or refused to answer the questionnaire divided by the total number of children. Attrition rate does not include death as death by itself is an outcome.

2.1.2. Qualitative data

The qualitative study was conducted in five (two urban and three rural) of the 20 Young Lives study sites involving 60 children and their households. The sample comprised equal percentages of children in each cohort and gender group. The urban sites are: Bertukan from Addis Ababa and Leku from Hawassa, the capital city of SNNPR. Both are very poor neighbourhoods, characterized by poor housing and inadequate services. Tach-Meret from Amhara region, Leki from Oromia and Zeytuni from Tigray constitute the rural study sites. All the rural communities are prone to poor economic situations and many of the households are dependent on productive safety net transfers[5].

The qualitative study began in 2007 and continued in 2008, 2011 and 2014 involving four rounds of data collections. For this chapter, we drew on data from the older cohort children and their households. Data was collected using child-focused exercises such as: the Poverty Tree (drawing a tree showing three parts; namely, the roots representing the causes, the stem signifying the indicators and the fruits demonstrating the consequences of poverty); group discussions; and individual interviews. Throughout the data collection rounds, children and their caregivers were asked about their real-life experiences, including their economic situation, schooling, and activities including paid and unpaid work, aspirations, life opportunities and challenges.

2.2. Model specification and estimation methods

The literature directs to a set of explanatory variables that may affect children's deprivation status. These include education level of household heads (Alisjahbana and Yusuf, 2003; Hagos and Holden, 2003; and Quisumbing, 2007) and of household members (Contreras et al., 2004; Dercon et al., 2011; Mills et al., 2004) and gender of household head and child (Bane and Ellwood, 1986; McKernan and Ratcliffe, 2005; Naifeh, 1998; Stevens, 1994). Studies such as Bigsten and Shimeles (2007) and Contreras et al. (2004) also show that where children live affects the deprivation levels. Similarly, shocks at household level such as illness or crop failure are found to deteriorate child well-being (Contreras et al.,

---

5   The Ethiopian Government has launched a productive safety net program since 2005 to support food insecure households by providing food and cash.

2004; Dercon, 2002; Dercon, Hoddinott, and Woldehanna, 2005; Quisumbing, 2007; Woldehanna and Hagos, 2014).

As such, we include the following variables in our model for studying childhood deprivation: average and maximum level of education within the household; the gender of household head; household size; a set of household composition variables; and regional differences and variation in type of residence (rural/urban).

Accordingly, the underlying model is

$$D_i = \alpha + b_1H_i + b_2E_i + b_3G_i + b_4S_i + b_5L_i + e_i \dots\dots\dots (1)$$

Where D is multiple overlapping deprivations, H is the vector of household composition variables, E is the vector of education variables, G is a vector of child gender and the gender of the household head, S is the vector of socio-economic shocks experienced by the household and L is the vector of location variables (type of residence and regional dummies), the subscript i denotes the individuals, which in our case are children.

The study further extends this model to explore the effect of policy variables such as access to credit, land, and irrigation and extension services on the dynamics of poverty. The extended model is

$$DP_i = a + b_1H_i + b_2E_i + b_3G_i + b_4S_i + b_5L_i + b_6P_i + e_i \dots\dots\dots (2)$$

Where DP_i is a categorical variable[6] capturing poverty transitions and P is a vector of policy variables mentioned above.

We employ several econometric techniques for analysis. Firstly, we conduct a Poisson[7] estimation using the pooled dataset from the four rounds of surveys to identify the determinants of multiple overlapping deprivations across children. Poisson is chosen as an estimation model since the MODA is a count variable that only takes on values ranging from zero to five; and hence the ordinary distributional assumptions of the Ordinary Least Square (OLS) do not apply (Wooldridge, 2000). Secondly,

---

6   The variable takes on the value 0 if the child has never had deprivations in more than 30 percent of the dimensions; 1 if the child experienced deprivations in more than 30 percent of the dimensions in only one round; 2 if the child experienced deprivations in more than 30 percent of the dimensions in two or three rounds and 4 if the child has experienced deprivations in more than 30 percent of the dimensions in all 4 rounds.

7   Poisson estimation is a generalized linear method that assumes count data in its regression analysis.

we conduct a Poisson fixed effects estimation over the number of deprivations experienced by children. This allows for controlling for time invariant unobservable characteristics across survey rounds, and therefore provides more reliable results (Verbeek, 2004). Thirdly, a Poisson estimation with lagged MOD is conducted to explore if there is a link between current levels of MOD and past levels of MOD, pointing at the existence of convergence in the long run. In addition, this helps control for any autocorrelation effect across survey rounds in the case of the pooled sample, and increases the robustness of results. Finally, we also conduct a multinomial logit estimation of the dynamics of multiple overlapping deprivations, grouping the children into chronic poor, transient poor, poor once and never poor.

3.   Results

We start by presenting a detailed discussion of the trend in dimensional deprivations as experienced by the children. Results from the quantitative data are presented as the proportion of children in any of the six possible categories of deprivation counts ranging from zero to five. Children that are not deprived in any of the dimensions would be in the first category, while those that are deprived in all dimensions would fall in the last category.

3.1. Deprivation by dimension among all children

Table 2 below reports the extent of overlapping deprivations experienced by both cohorts of children. For the younger cohort the percentage of children who are deprived in the health dimension declined significantly in Round 2. In contrast, the nutrition dimension saw a sharp increase.[8] Similarly, the percentage of children in the younger cohort who are deprived in the education dimension declined from Round 3 to Round 4. The same was found to be true for the information dimension, although

---

8   The rise is triggered by the introduction of the dietary diversity indicator to the nutrition dimension, which was not included in Round 1 because the children in the younger cohort were only one year old at that time and hence the dietary diversity indicator did not apply to them. While the requirements for a child to be deprived in the nutrition dimension were either weight for age or weight for height z-scores being two standard deviations below the sample mean in Round 1, we added the requirement of having at least three meals a day and having at least three food items per day in Round 2.

the reduction is modest when compared to the education dimension. Moreover, the proportion of children who are deprived in their access to safe water declined progressively across the four rounds from 53 per cent in the first round to 11 per cent in the final round.

For the shelter dimension, the percentage of children who are deprived fluctuated across survey rounds. The percentage of younger cohort children who are deprived in the shelter dimension decreased across the first three rounds while it increased by five percent in Round 4. This can be explained by the increase in household size in Round 4, increasing the number of children that are living in overcrowded households, which is one of the components determining the shelter dimension. The proportion of children in the younger cohort who are deprived in the sanitation dimension decreased progressively across the four rounds.

In the first round the children in the older cohort were eight years old. Hence, unlike the younger cohort, we do not need to substitute the health and nutrition dimensions with the education and information dimensions. Given their age, we use the education and information dimensions in all four rounds. The percentage of children who are deprived in the education dimension declined from the first round to the second. However, when we include the criterion of primary school completion it increased significantly in Round 3, even beyond the level in Round 1. Although it declined in Round 4, it remained above the percentage of children who were deprived in education in Round 1. The substantial increase in the percentage of children who are deprived in the education dimension can therefore be explained by the introduction of a primary education completion requirement. The children in the older cohort were fifteen years old in Round 3, which is beyond the primary school age designated by the Ministry of Education (between 7–14 years old). The addition of the primary education completion component in Round 3 to school enrolment was the only indicator used to designate children as deprived in education below 14 years of age. Since the substantial rise in the percentage of children who are deprived in this dimension can be explained by the large number of children beyond primary school age that have not completed primary school, caution is required in interpreting the results and comparing children across the rounds.

Unlike the education dimension, the percentage of children in the older cohort who are deprived in the information dimension declined consistently across the four survey rounds. A similar trend is observed for the access to safe water and sanitation dimensions. This trend resonates with that of the younger cohort, which also showed a consistent decline in the proportion of children deprived in access to safe water. In contrast, a fluctuation was observed in the percentage of children deprived in the shelter dimension. Despite the consistent decline in the first three rounds, a rise was observed in the last round. The same trend was observed for the younger cohort. The increase in Round 4 is likely to have resulted from the rise in household size leading to an increase in the incidence of overcrowding in children's households.

Table 2.   Percentage of children deprived by dimension among all children

Dimensions	Younger Cohort				Older Cohort			
	Round 1	Round 2	Round 3	Round 4	Round 1	Round 2	Round 3	Round 4
	2002	2006	2009	2013	2002	2006	2009	2013
Health	48.0	17.1						
Nutrition	0.3	22.1						
Education			23.3	5.4	34.4	5.2	83.0	56.3
Information			36.9	25.2	57.8	40.1	33.9	13.1
Shelter	73.5	59.8	53.9	58.9	72.1	55.6	49.4	60.4
Safe water	53.4	24.1	16.2	11.1	55.6	24.1	16.8	10.8
Sanitation	62.1	45.3	27.0	22.6	63.1	44.1	24.7	23.3
N	1,998	1,912	1,884	1,873	1000	980	973	907

Source: Young Lives (2018)

3.2. Number of deprivations among all children

We examine the number of deprivations that children experience by cohort (see Figure 1). The proportion of younger cohort children facing multiple deprivations decreased over time. There has been a considerable increase in the proportion of children facing no deprivations in any of the dimension to over a quarter by Round 4. In the first two rounds, most children faced two or three deprivations but by Round 4 most children faced only one or no deprivations. A similar pattern can be seen for the older cohort, with a substantial increase in the proportions facing no deprivations over the four rounds, and most children in Round 1 facing three or four deprivations, whereas by Round 4 most faced two or three deprivations.

Figure 1.   Percentage trends in number of deprivations among all children

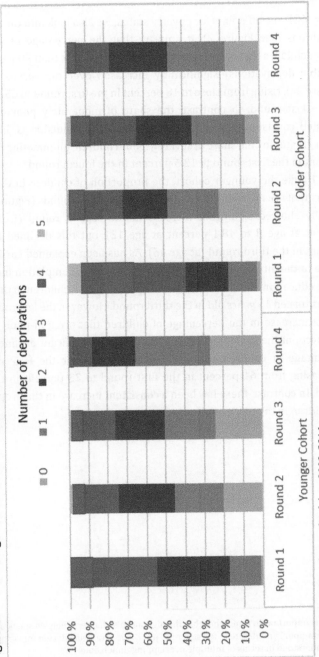

Source: Young Lives longitudinal data, 2002–2016.

3.3. Multidimensional poverty status

Using MOD cut-off points for poverty status, we also look into the poverty transitions (see Figure 2). It appears that the percentage of younger cohort children that are not poor[1] (i.e. experience less than 30 percent of possible deprivations) significantly increased over the survey rounds (Figure 2a), rising from close to 18 percent in the first round to 65 percent in the last round. In contrast, the share of moderately poor children declined consistently over the four rounds. The reduction is, however, much greater for the share of severely poor children, plummeting from 45 percent in the first round to 12.5 percent in the fourth round.

Unlike the younger cohort, the proportion of children in the older cohort that are non-poor fluctuated over the survey rounds (Figure 2b). It initially showed significant increase in the second round (from 17.2 percent at age 8 to 48.1 percent at age 12), but this declined to 35.3 percent in the third round (at age 15). As has been explained earlier, this is due to the introduction of the primary education completion indicator to the education dimension, triggered by the fact that children in the older cohort turned 15 years old in the third round. However, the last round did see an increase in the percentage of children that are non-poor. Taking into account the same fluctuations, there was a significant decline in the percentage of children that are severely poor over the four rounds, decreasing from 61 percent in the first round to 23 percent in the last round. In contrast, there has been a consistent increase in the proportion of children in the moderately poor category.

---

1   It is important to remember that throughout this chapter when we speak of 'poor', 'non-poor', 'moderately or severely poor' we are considering poverty to be understood in terms of multiple overlapping dimensions.

Figure 2.   Status of poverty as measured by Multiple Overlapping Deprivations Analysis (MODA)

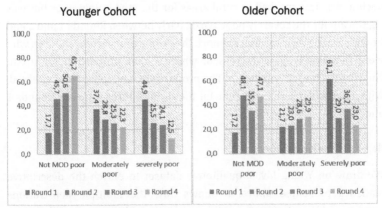

Source: Authors' calculation from Young Lives longitudinal data.

3.4   Poverty status disaggregated

Gender disaggregated results[2] show that although the proportion of boys in the younger cohort that are not MOD poor was greater than girls in the first two rounds, the reverse was found in the third and fourth rounds. For the moderately poor and severely poor categories, however, the proportions are evenly distributed between the two gender groups and the different categories of poverty status. With regards to the older cohort, the proportion of girls that are not MOD poor are much greater than boys in the first round. However, the situation was reversed in the following rounds, where the percentage of boys was larger than girls in rounds two, three and four. In contrast, the proportion of girls that are severely poor was smaller than their boy counterparts in the first round. Nonetheless, the opposite was true for following two rounds. As for the moderately poor category, the proportion of male children was consistently greater than the proportion of female children in all rounds except for the third round.

When disaggregated by residence,[3] the proportion of non-poor is greater in urban areas for both cohorts, whereas larger numbers of the severely poor are found in rural areas. For the younger cohort, the decline

---

2   The disaggregated data can be made available upon request.
3   The disaggregated data can be made available upon request.

in the proportions of moderately poor and severely poor was marked for the urban children, particularly from Round 1 to Round 2, whereas the decline was less marked in rural areas for the moderately poor but was significant for the severely poor, particularly between Rounds 1 and 2 and Rounds 3 and 4. For the older cohort, the proportion of rural children who were moderately poor increased, whereas that proportion for urban children decreased somewhat. The proportions severely poor decreased, with a particularly sharp decline for the rural children between Rounds 1 and 2.

4.   Qualitative evidence

We draw on Young Lives' qualitative dataset to enrich the descriptive statistics presented above. It shows how the multiple deprivations overlap and thereby deepen child poverty. In addition, it provides some qualitative evidence on the exploitation and participation categories of the MODA which could not be analysed quantitatively due to the lack of data. This section will also present a case study on the intergenerational nature of poverty.

4.1. Children's perception of poverty

Children in the older cohort were asked to list what it means for them to be living in poverty, in order to understand how they perceive of their situation. Using Poverty Tree methodology, children drew the poverty indicators, the causes and the consequences of poverty, and discussed what poverty means to them. Table 3 provides an overview of findings.

Table 3.   Children's perception of poverty, Focus Group Discussions (FGD), 2011

	Poverty indicators		
Urban boys	Not enough food Wearing torn clothes Living in crowded housing Earning a living with aid No materials for learning, and not going to school at all Very low income Working as wage labourer	Unemployment Lack of available jobs Poor income management (extravagance/lack of saving habits) Laziness Lack of start-up capital for business Being uneducated (to work or run business) Having large family size (many children)	Poor health Quit school to work Family conflict Hopelessness Become street child and addicted to bad habits Becoming a burden to a nation Having a worse future
Urban girls	Not enough food Wearing tattered clothes Living in confined and rented houses Not going to school or not having necessary school materials Lack of regular income/unemployed	Lack of job opportunities Illiteracy/not being educated Lack of interest to do any kind of work Extravagance—poor management Family conflict	Not going to school Being worried about life Feeling inferiority or low self-esteem Exclusion Growing to be poor adult
Rural boys	Not having enough food Not having enough clothes Living in poor housing Lacking school materials Not having enough farm/irrigation land and livestock Working as wage labourer	Lack of preferred job opportunities/laziness/dependency on aid Having many children—big family size Extravagance (fathers) Shocks (drought, death of animals) Lack of farmland/irrigation and livestock	Hunger Drop out of school to work Always worried Being insulted/seen inferior Hopelessness/stress Poor school performance Being unhealthy Migration No time for play
Rural girls	Lack of enough/variety of food Wearing torn clothes/no shoes Not having enough farmland/livestock Living in poor housing Not attending school or lack of necessary school materials Poor health/skinny	Early marriage Not being educated Poor job opportunities Big family (many children) Landlessness Laziness Extravagance Shocks (illness/death of family head, drought, death of livestock)	Hunger Early marriage/divorce Inferiority Stress Physically weaker Behaving badly (thefts, conflict, etc.) School dropout Migration

Source: FGD (2011).

Although they differ by gender and location, the indicators of poverty as identified by the children themselves could be summarized as follows:

- Food: insufficient amount or variety of food
- Housing: living in an overcrowded house or poorly constructed house; living in rented house
- Clothing: wearing tattered clothes
- Education: not attending school, attending irregularly, quitting school, not having school materials
- Lack of resources: lack of regular income (urban) or lack of farmland or livestock (rural).

The poverty indicators identified by children resemble the dimensions identified for the MODA. The children also relate these indicators to a wider notion of well-being, including their physical well-being, developmental needs, migration, family conflict, early marriage (for girls), experiences of bad habits and social exclusions. Most children included in this study have experienced many of these, and some illustrative examples are presented below. These findings speak to the discussion in Chapter 1 of this volume by Ngutuku, regarding the need to look at child poverty and children's lives from a broader perspective.

4.2. Exploitation and participation

The following sections discuss how children living in poverty in certain communities faced child labour and exclusion.

4.2.1. Child labour

Many children who find it hard to attend school without food, and who don't have enough school materials, opt for paid work to survive. As a result, school attendance for these children becomes irregular, impacting their progress. Except for one rural boy, all children included in the qualitative study attended some school at various grade levels. Owing to late entry, interruptions, repetitions and dropouts, by age 17 only four children (all girls) were able to finish primary school. Those in school were attending grades between two and eight. This suggests that the educational outcomes were extremely low, demonstrating one dimension of child poverty.

The reasons given for dropping out of school included economic problems, paid work and marriage (for girls). All children reported to have been engaged in some type of non-school activities, with half of them doing paid work to subsidize their families and earn a living. In rural areas, poverty forced them to work for wages in stone crushing plants and haricot bean picking, while urban children washed cars, tended shops, worked as taxi attendants or street vendors.

Child labour disrupts their schooling and affects their health. Defar, a boy who dropped out of fifth grade, explained how poverty forced him to leave school and exposed him to hunger and health problems:

> When my poor parents failed to provide me with school materials and enough food, I discontinued my education and I moved to a nearby town and began earning a living by carrying things for people at the bus station... I sleep on the veranda and am cold which makes me very thin... I feel inferior to my friends who are attending school. (Tach-Meret, Amhara, 2011)

Beletech, a 17 year-old girl from Leki, was in just fifth grade, as she had experienced school interruptions to do paid work in irrigation fields in her community. She had to sponsor her schooling through paid work. She said, "as I am poor, I do paid work for half-day to earn money for basic needs and school materials."

Tufa, 17, a girl from the same community said:

> I am just in grade two. Every year, I get enrolled but it is soon interrupted because my family is too poor to afford my schooling ... My family sharecropped our farmland because we do not have oxen. I catch fish in the nearby lake for sale and do paid work to subsidize my poor family. (Leki, 2011)

Bereket, a boy from Bertukan, had been washing cars since the age 11, when he was injured when fixing a flat tire in 2009 and had to be hospitalized for some weeks. The injury not only affected him economically, requiring high medical costs and preventing him from working, but it also meant he had to interrupt his education for one year.

All of these specific cases illustrate how the different dimensions of children's lives including education, health, nutrition and child labour are strongly interlinked and related to poverty.

4.2.2 Social exclusion

The data also strongly indicates that poverty exposes children to psycho-social problems and exclusions, which is in line with findings in Chapter 2 by Bantebya et al. in this volume. Children who experienced generally lower self-perceptions felt excluded by their peers and communities at large. Across the sites of the Young Lives survey, children stated that poor children felt lower self-esteem and self-efficacy. Poor children "feel shy in front of their [non-poor] friends because they don't wear clothes and shoes like them" (Girls FGD, Bertukan, 2011). Children from poor families segregate themselves from others since they "lack self-confidence" (Denbel, Leku, 2011). According to Tsega, one of the children interviewed in Leku area, "being poor results in undermining oneself or feeling inferior, getting mad!" (Leku, 2011). Poverty is so stressful, as Fatuma from Bertunkan puts it: "poverty kills *hilina*" (conscience). Low self-perception forces poor children to distance themselves from non-poor peers. As the boys from Tach-meret described it:

> Nobody looks at the poor child as equal to the rich child. Nobody may care about the poor child. Thus, the poor child thinks that he is not an equal person to the other children. (Boys FGD, Tach-meret, 2011)

Exclusion is not just a social phenomenon but it also entails economic consequences. Children from Bertukan, Addis said:

> A boy's clothing condition makes him appear like a thief. If he is not dressed well, the people would not trust the man. Even when they hire him, they tell others to have a good look over him, because they do not trust him. (Boys FGD of Bertukan, 2011)

Among the FGD participants, Bereket, who washes cars, said:

> If he is not dressed well, they will suspect him. They might say that he has come to spy or to steal. I take this as one obstacle for work. (Bertukan 2011)

Bereket's perception was based on his real experience while working for others. This suggests that lack of clothing is not just a material deprivation that affects health or schooling but contributes to social exclusion and so creates an obstacle to employment. The key issue worth noting is that poor children who do not wear proper clothing find it hard to obtain work to gain income to change their life because of the stigma associated with their dress.

4.3. Intergenerational poverty—the case of a child named Haymanot

The qualitative data also reflects intergenerational aspects of poverty. There are many children whose developmental needs are not being met as they lack resources to carry them through to adulthood. For instance, uneducated children are more likely to end up poor as adults with a contribution to the overall national poverty. The qualitative data, although based on fewer cases, illustrates this.

The same applies to overlapping deprivation. It all starts from childhood and continues through young adulthood. One of the many cases is presented below. It is a story of a girl named Haymanot from Zeytuni, Tigray, who grew up in poor households facing multiple shocks that dictated the course of her life.

Haymanot's parents divorced when she was just seven years old. Since her mother was unable to afford to raise her, Haymanot had to move to her aunt's house to attend school. After three years, she had to return home to care for her ailing mother. She attended school with the social safety net support her mother obtained. However, the food support became increasingly insufficient mainly due to a drought affecting the crop yields from their small farms. Haymanot quit school in fifth grade and began working in a stone crushing plant for wages. She faced multiple injuries at work and the job was very difficult for her. Pressured by her mother, she married at 16, ending her educational hopes because she found it difficult to combine marriage life with schooling. Unfortunately, the poor economic situation of her husband led to their divorce after a year. Haymanot returned to her mother's house with her baby girl and resumed working as a daily labourer. Below is a figure that presents the timeline of the major incidents in Haymanot's life reflecting the intergenerational aspects of poverty.

Figure 3.   Timeline of Haymanot's family events and her experiences

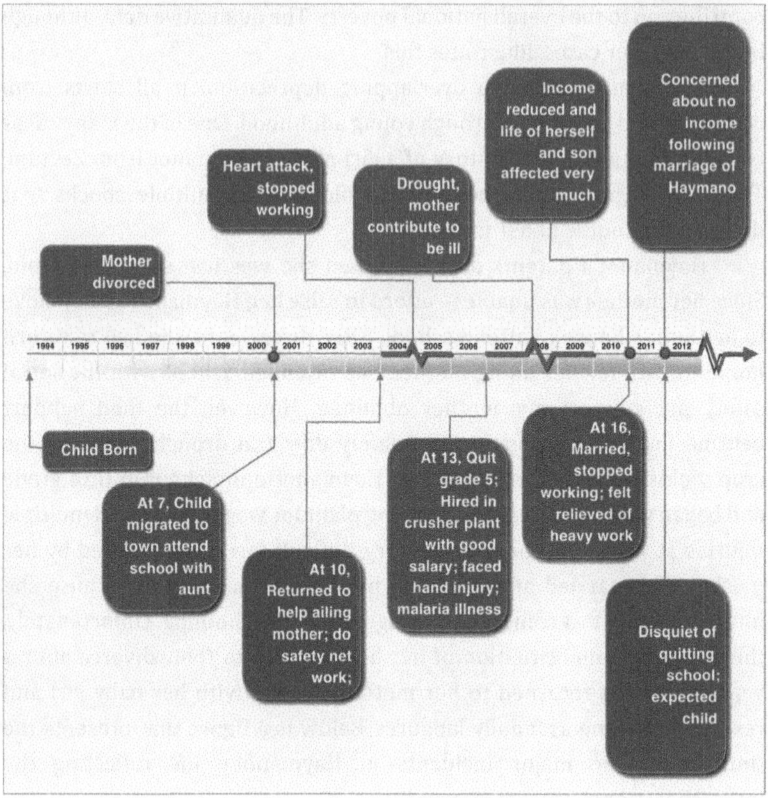

Source: Tafere 2014

This case illustrates two points. First, various aspects of child poverty not only overlap but also reveal themselves more significantly at certain stages of a child's life. This is in line with the lifecycle approach followed by the MODA to address the varying needs of children at different points of their childhood. Second, child poverty does not end at childhood. It is lasting and has intergenerational effects.

5. Quantitative regression results

We move on to gain insight into determinants of overlapping deprivations of children from a quantitative perspective, using regression modelling.

5.1. Determinants of multiple overlapping deprivations of children

To identify the determinants of multiple overlapping deprivations among children, the study conducted Poisson estimations on the pooled sample without accounting for the rounds of the surveys. The pooled regressions were conducted on two estimation models with the first one not accounting for the lagged value of MOD in contrast to the second which controls for lagged effects. In addition, fixed effects Poisson estimation was conducted to control for time invariant unobservable characteristics that affect multiple overlapping deprivations by accounting for the survey rounds. The results are discussed in the following subsections.

5.1.1. Pooled regressions

Table 4 presents the Poisson estimation results conducted using the pooled data from the four rounds of the Young Lives data and included household characteristics.

The number of boys and girls below the age of seven in the same household has a positive relationship with the number of deprivations experienced by children. Similarly, the number of male household members above the age of 65 was found to have an increasing effect on being deprived. This relationship can be explained by the contribution of children and elderly to the consumption needs of the household, while not being able to contribute as much to the household income. On the other hand, the number of female household members between the age of 17 and 65 was found to reduce the number of deprivations experienced by children. The results also show that household members' average education correlates negatively with the number of deprivations experienced by children. This aligns with the premise that higher human capital endowment increases earning capacity for the household and, thus, enables households to protect children from different sources of deprivation.

A set of dummy[4] variables that represent households' experience of socio-economic shocks were accounted for in the estimation. One of the shocks, a household's experience of employment loss, has a positive relationship with the number of deprivations experienced by children. Children that live in a household that has faced job loss experience deprivations in more dimensions than other children. Similarly, households' experience of death of livestock increased number of deprivations. Given the reduction in income resulting from the job loss or the loss of productive asset such as livestock, the higher number of deprivations associated with the experience of these shocks is expected. The same applies for households' experience of crop failure.

Children that live in rural households experience deprivations in more dimensions than in urban households. There is also regional variation with the number of deprivations. Children coming from Oromia region were found to have smaller number of deprivations MOD than children coming from other regions, showing that location plays a key role in determining the extent of children's exposure to overlapping deprivations, might be due to fewer shocks in this region than in the others.

To test for the existence of state dependence in overlapping deprivations across rounds, an alternative model was estimated with all the explanatory variables in the original model and the lagged value of overlapping deprivations. Controlling for lagged value of MOD also contributes to the robustness of results as it deals with the bias that may be introduced due to autocorrelation. The coefficient of lagged MOD is however statistically insignificant, showing the absence of state dependence. All of the variables that were found to be statistically significant in the original model specification, however, remained significant in the estimation that accounted for lagged dependent variables.

---

4   A dummy variable is a numerical variable used in regression analysis to represent subgroups of the sample that takes the value 0 or 1 to indicate the absence or presence of an expected categorical effect

Table 4. Determinants of MOD among children (Pooled Sample—Poisson Estimates) and fixed effects estimates

	Poisson Estimates	Poisson Estimates	Fixed Effects
	Model 1	Model 2	Model 3
	Coef./t	Coef./t	Coef./t
Lagged MOD		0.003	
		0.479	
Household characteristic variables			
Number of boys below 7	0.044***	0.044***	-0.006
	-3.728	-3.745	(-0.498)
Number of boys between 7 and 17 years	0.005	0.005	0.01
	-0.558	-0.552	-1.044
Number of male household members between 17 and 65 years-old	-0.008	-0.008	-0.007
	(-0.952)	(-0.924)	(-0.614)
Number of male elderly above 65 years	0.118***	0.118***	0.052
	-3.388	-3.391	-1.192
Number of girls below 7	0.041***	0.041***	-0.001
	-3.549	-3.518	(-0.096)
Number of girls between 7 and 17 years	-0.005	-0.005	0.003
	(-0.517)	(-0.533)	-0.343
Number of female household members between 17 and 65 years-old	-0.019**	-0.020**	-0.018
	(-2.050)	(-2.068)	(-1.304)
Number of female elderly above 65 years	-0.081**	-0.080**	-0.056
	(-2.189)	(-2.179)	(-1.281)
Sex of head of household	-0.032	-0.033	-0.122***
	(-1.481)	(-1.518)	(-4.174)
Household's average education	-0.035***	-0.036***	-0.040***
	(-14.456)	(-14.459)	(-8.165)
Land Size	-0.012	-0.012	-0.014
	(-1.129)	(-1.131)	(-1.036)

Socio-economic shocks			
Dummy for household's experience of death or illness	0.009	0.009	–0.023
	–0.497	–0.506	(–1.115)
Dummy for household's experience of crop failure	0.044**	0.044**	0.042*
	–2.251	–2.23	–1.859
Dummy for household's experience of job loss	0.199***	0.199***	0.197***
	–8.766	–8.773	–7.895
Dummy for death of livestock	0.095***	0.094***	0.085***
	–4.436	–4.399	–3.44
Sampling components			
Dummy for younger cohort	–0.237***	–0.236***	
	(–12.177)	(–12.022)	
Dummy for urban household	–0.473***	–0.473***	
	(–18.966)	(–18.969)	
Dummy for male child	–0.018	–0.019	
	(–0.892)	(–0.925)	
Region Dummies			
Dummy for Amhara region	0.502***	0.503***	
	–8.467	–8.475	
Dummy for Oromia region	0.239***	0.239***	
	–3.965	–3.967	
Dummy for SNNP region	0.351***	0.351***	
	–5.997	–6.004	
Dummy for Tigray region	0.442***	0.443***	
	–7.474	–7.483	
Constant	0.567***	0.562***	
	–7.881	–7.643	
Number of Observations	7,772	7,768	5621

Note: *p-value = 0.1, **p-value=0.05, ***p-value=0.01

5.1.2. Fixed Effects estimation results

To control for time invariant child specific unobservable factors, the study conducted a Fixed Effects Poisson estimation using the variables that were found to vary over time (Model 3 of Table 4 above). The results are in alignment with the results from the pooled estimation for many of the explanatory variables. However, the Fixed Effects estimation results show that children from female-headed households experience deprivations in more dimensions than children in male-headed households. This resonates with the literature on gender gaps that show that female-headed households have less access to productive resources and information, leading to a more severe experience of poverty among household members (De Neubourg et al., 2012a).

5.2. Longitudinal patterns of poverty

In this section, the determinants of child poverty transitions are discussed. We adopted multinomial logit which shows the change in the probability of being in one category in comparison to the base outcome category. Table 5 presents the multinomial logit estimates of determinants of poverty transitions. The poverty transition variable has four categories with a base outcome of being never MOD poor, and three alternative outcomes of being in chronic poverty (MOD poor in all four rounds), in transient poverty (MOD poor in two or three rounds) and MOD poor in just one round.

Among the socio-economic shock variables, the illness of a household member is found to have a statistically significant effect. Children who come from a household that has experienced illness of a member are found to have a greater probability of being in transient poverty or chronic poverty than children in a household that has not experienced such a shock.

In this multinomial model, we have added three more policy variables in our analysis. These variables are access to credit, size of irrigated land and access to extension. The results of the estimations show that access to credit has a negative effect on the probability of being in transient poverty or the chronic poverty category, albeit a small effect. The size of land owned by households is also found to have a negative effect on the probability of being in chronic poverty.

Some of the location variables were also found to have statistically significant effect on the probability of being in different statuses of poverty. Children coming from urban households were found to have smaller probability of being in either transient or chronic poverty in contrast to their rural counterparts. In addition, children coming from

Oromia region have smaller probability of being in transient poverty in contrast to children in other regions. The relationship of the location variables with the poverty status indicators resonate with the results found from the estimation of the determinants of the MOD.

Table 5.   Determinants of poverty transition (Multinomial Logit Estimates)

	Poor once over four rounds	Transient Poor (two or three times)	Chronic Poor (Poor in all four rounds)
Household characteristic variables			
Number of boys below 7	0.332	0.038	0.120
	(1.555)	(0.181)	(0.545)
Number of boys between 7 and 17 years	0.122	0.127	0.139
	(0.703)	(0.764)	(0.798)
Number of male household members between 17 and 65 years-old	0.145	0.148	0.084
	(1.336)	(1.446)	(0.766)
Number of male elderly above 65 years	0.484	0.681	0.898
	(0.753)	(1.120)	(1.435)
Number of girls below 7	−0.009	0.163	0.065
	(−0.043)	(0.818)	(0.310)
Number of girls between 7 and 17 years	0.247	0.259	0.127
	(1.421)	(1.573)	(0.725)
Number of female household members between 17 and 65 years-old	−0.020	−0.019	−0.039
	(−0.188)	(−0.191)	(−0.366)
Number of female elderly above 65 years	0.132	0.359	−0.125
	(0.234)	(0.673)	(−0.218)
Sex of head of household	−0.221	−0.528	−0.595
	(−0.580)	(−1.460)	(−1.529)

	Poor once over four rounds	Transient Poor (two or three times)	Chronic Poor
Household's average education	0.040	0.014	−0.008
	(1.350)	(0.497)	(−0.256)
Socio-economic shocks			
Dummy for household's experience of death or illness	0.603	0.737**	0.726*
	(1.606)	(2.047)	(1.933)
Dummy for household's experience of crop failure	0.222	0.347	0.392
	(0.448)	(0.739)	(0.817)
Dummy for household's experience of job loss	−0.465	−0.221	−0.239
	(−0.953)	(−0.482)	(−0.481)
Dummy for death of livestock	0.171	−0.063	−0.035
	(0.424)	(−0.164)	(−0.088)
Policy variables			
Land size	−0.261	−0.257	−0.491***
	(−1.440)	(−1.490)	(−2.590)
Credit	0.760	1.260***	1.416***
	(1.607)	(2.842)	(3.075)
Irrigated land	−0.000**	−0.000***	−0.000***
	(−2.055)	(−2.771)	(−3.761)
Dummy for extension services	1.535	2.220	2.992
	(0.563)	(0.837)	(1.125)
Sampling variables			
Dummy for younger cohort	0.273	−0.593	−1.215***
	(0.680)	(−1.557)	(−2.947)
Dummy for urban household	−0.592	−2.157***	−2.936***
	(−1.380)	(−5.323)	(−6.674)
Dummy for male child	0.212	−0.019	−0.081
	(0.656)	(−0.063)	(−0.250)
Region dummies			
Dummy for Amhara region	−1.156	−0.595	13.955
	(−1.160)	(−0.586)	(0.019)

	Poor once over four rounds	Transient Poor (two or three times)	Chronic Poor
Dummy for Oromia region	−1.614*	−1.530*	12.001
	(−1.918)	(−1.734)	(0.016)
Dummy for SNNP region	−1.725**	−0.927	13.119
	(−2.118)	(−1.089)	(0.017)
Dummy for Tigray region	−1.299	0.066	14.356
	(−1.498)	(0.074)	(0.019)
Constant	1.388	3.328***	−9.924
Number of observations	(1.275)	(3.049)	(−0.013)
		1,242	

Note: *p-value = 0.1, **p-value=0.05, ***p-value=0.01

6. Conclusion

This chapter's study of multiple overlapping deprivations of children in Ethiopia reveals substantial improvements in all dimensions. However, the extent of progress has not been equal; biggest gains were made in health, education, and access to safe water and sanitation, and lesser improvements and fluctuations were observed for the information and shelter dimensions. In terms of experiencing multiple overlapping deprivations, the proportion of children not facing any deprivations increased over time, while proportions facing several deprivations reduced. When we distinguish between the moderately and severely poor, we find the latter concentrated in rural areas, and we see a movement over the rounds from severe poverty to moderate poverty and from moderate poverty to the non-poverty.

The most important factors that are associated with poverty were found to be: high dependency ratio; lower education level of household members; and socio-economic shocks such as illness of a household member, loss of employment, or livestock deaths. Factors that are associated with reducing the likelihood of poverty also include: the presence of women working outside the home; access to credit and irrigated land; and living in urban areas within households headed by men. Boys in urban sites were less likely to face chronic poverty than girls.

The results emphasise the need for more household human capital endowment, particularly education, which is found to reduce children's experience of overlapping deprivations and the persistence of poverty. A long-term plan to increase the education endowment of households will help improve children's well-being. Also, it is important to note that children from family with more dependents face greater transient or chronic poverty, implying the need for continued attention to promoting family planning. The effect of socio-economic shocks on children's deprivations and poverty transitions also call for increased access to insurance schemes to shield children from worsening well-being.

References

Alkire, S. and Foster, J. (2011) "Counting and multidimensional poverty measurement." *Journal of Public Economics*. Vol. 95: 476–487.

Alkire, S. and Santos, M. (2010) "Acute Multidimensional Poverty: A New Index for Developing Countries." *UNDP Human Development Research Paper 2010/11.*

Alisjahbana, A. and Yusuf, A.A. (2003). *Poverty dynamics in Indonesia: Panel data evidence.* Working paper in Economics and Development Studies No. 200303.

Apablaz, M.; and G. Yalonetzky (2011). *Measuring the Dynamics of Multiple Deprivations Among Children: The cases of Andhra Pradesh, Ethiopia, Peru and Vietnam.* Paper submitted to CSAE conference, March 2011.

Atkinson, A. B. (2003). "Multidimensional deprivation: contrasting social welfare and counting approaches." *Journal of Economic Inequality.* Vol. 1: 51–65.

Ballon, P. and Krishnakumar, J. (2008). *A Model-Based Multidimensional Capability Deprivation Index.* Paper Presented at the 30th General Conference of The International Association for Research in Income and Wealth. Portoroz, Slovenia.

Belhadj, B. (2012). "New weighting scheme for the dimensions in multidimensional poverty indices." *Economics Letters*, 116: 304–307.

Bane, M. J. and Ellwood, D. (1986). "Slipping Into and Out of Poverty: The dynamics of spells." *Journal of Human Resources.* Vol. 21(1): 1–23.

Baulch, B. and Mccullonch N. (1998). *Being Poor and Becoming Poor: Poverty Status and Poverty Transitions in Rural Pakistan.* Working paper 79, Institute of Development studies.

Betti, G. and Verma, V. K. (1998). *Measuring the Degree of Poverty in a Dynamic and Comparative Context: A multi-dimensional approach using fuzzy set theory. Working Paper 22.* Department di Metodi Quantitativi, Università di Siena.

Betti, G., Cheli, B., Lemmi, A. and Verma, V. K. (2008). "The Fuzzy Set Approach to the Multidimensional Poverty: The case of Italy in the 1990s." In *Quantitative Approaches to Multidimensional Poverty Measurement,* edited by N. Kakwani and J. Silber. New York: Palgrave Mac Millan: 30–48.

150   Woldehanna et al.

Bigsten, A., Kebede, B., Shimeles, A. and Taddesse M. (2003). "Growth and Poverty Reduction in Ethiopia: Evidence from Household Panel Surveys." *World Development*, Vol. 31 (1): 87–106.

Bitew, M., Gebreselassie, T., Kibur, M., Matsuda, Y., Pearson, R. and Plavgo, ILZE (2013). "Multidimensional Child Deprivation Trend Analysis in Ethiopia." *DHS Further Analysis Reports No. 83*. Calverton, MD: ICF International.

Bourguignon, F. and Chakravarty, S. R. (2003). "The Measurement of Multidimensional Poverty." *Journal of Economic Inequality*. Vol. 1, 25–49.

Boyden, J., Hardgrove, J., and Knowles, C. (2012). 'Continuity and change in poor children's lives: evidence from young lives'. *Global child poverty and well-being*, 475.

Brandolini, A. and D'alessio, G. (1998). *Measuring Well-being in the Functioning space*. Rome: Bank of Italy.

Brown, T., and Teshome, A. (2007). *Implementing Policies for Chronic Poverty Reduction in Ethiopia*. Chronic Poverty Research Centre Working Paper No. 2008-09. Available at SSRN: https://ssrn.com/abstract=1755077 or http://dx.doi.org/10.2139/ssrn.1755077

Camfield, L. and Tafere, Y. (2011). 'Good for children? Local Understandings Versus Universal prescriptions: Evidence from Three Ethiopian Communities.' In: Children and the Capability Approach. Biggeri M, Ballet J, Comim F (eds). Palgrave.

Chakravarty, S. R. and D'Ambrossio, C. (2006). "The Measurement of Social Exclusion." *Review of Income and Wealth*. Vol. 523: 377–398.

Chakravarty, S. R., Deutsch, J. and Silber, J. (2008). "On the Watts Multidimensional Poverty Index and its Decomposition." *World Development*. Vol. 36: 1067–1077.

Chakravarty, S. R., Mukherjee, D. and Ranade, R. R. (1998). "On the Family of Subgroup and Factor Decomposable Measures of Multidimensional Poverty." *Research on Economic Inequality*. Vol. 8: 175–194.

Comin, F. and Carey, F. (2001). "Social Capital and the Capability Approach: Are Putnam and Sen Incompatible Bedfellows?" *Paper presented at the European Association for Evolutionary Political Economy Conference*, Siena.

Contreras, D., Cooper, R., Hermann, J. and Neilson, C. (2008). "The Dynamics of Poverty in Chile." *Journal of Latin American Studies*. Vol. 40: 251–273. Cambridge University Press.

Crocker, D. A. and Robeyns, I. (2010). "Capability and Agency." In MORRIS, C. W., ed. *Amartya Sen*. New York: Cambridge University Press.

CPRC. (2008). *Chronic Poverty Report: 2008-2009*. Manchester: Chronic Poverty Research Centre.

De Neubourg, C., J. Chai, M. De Milliano, I. Plavgo, Z. Wee (2012). *Step-by-Step Guidelines to the Multiple Overlapping Deprivation Analysis (MODA)*. Working Paper 2012-10. Florence: UNICEF Office of Research.

De Neubourg, C., J. Chai, M. De Milliano, I. Plavgo, Z. Wei (2012). *Cross-Country MODA Study.* Office of Research Working Paper—WP-2012-05. Florence: UNICEF Office of Research.

De La Vegal, L., Urrutia, A. and Diez, H. (2009). *The Bourguignon and Chakravarty Multidimensional Poverty Family: A Characterization.* ECINEQ Working Paper 2009-109.

Dercon, S. (2002) *Growth, Shocks and Poverty During Economic Reform: Evidence from Rural Ethiopia.* International Monetary Fund.

Dercon, S., Hoddinott, J. and Woldehanna, T. (2011). *Growth and chronic poverty: Evidence from rural communities in Ethiopia.* CSAE working paper, WPS/2011-18. Oxford: Centre for the Study of African Economies, Department of Economics, University of Oxford.

Dercon, S., Hoddinott, H. and Woldehanna, T. (2005). "Shocks and Consumption in 15 Ethiopian Villages, 1999–2004." *Journal of African Economies.* Vol. 14(4): 559–585.

Devicienti and Poggi (2007). *Poverty and Social Exclusion: Two sides of the same coin or dynamically interrelated processes?* Working paper no 62. Laboratorio R. Revelli-Collegio Carlo Alberto Center for Employment Studies.

Fleurbaey, M., (2006). "Social welfare, priority to the worst-off and the dimensions of individual well-being." In *Inequality and Economic Integration,* edited by Farina, F. and E. Savaglio. London: Routledge.

Foster, J., Greer, J. and Thorbecke, E. (1984). "A Class of Decomposable Poverty Measures." *Econometrica.* Vol. 52 (3): 761–6.

Gasper, D. (2007). "What is the Capability Approach? Its Core, Rationale, Partners and Dangers." *Journal of Socio-Economics.* Vol. 36(3):335–359.

Hago, F. and Holden, S. (2003). *Rural Household Poverty Dynamics in Northern Ethiopia 1997–2000: Analysis of determinants of poverty.* Research for Development, Department for International Development (DFID).

Kedir, A. M. and Mckay, A. (2003). "Chronic Poverty in Urban Ethiopia: Panel data evidence." A Paper prepared for International Conference *Staying Poor: Chronic Poverty and Development Policy.* University of Manchester, UK, 7–9 April 2003.

Krishankurmar, J. (2007). "Going Beyond Functionings to Capabilities: An econometric model to explain and estimate capabilities." *Journal of Human Development.* Vol. 8(1):39–63.

Lee, P. and A. Murie (1999). "Spatial and Social Division within British Cities: Beyond Residualisation." *Housing Studies.* Vol. 14(5): 625–640.

Maasoumie, E., and Lugo, M. A. (2008). The information basis of multivariate poverty assessments. In Quantitative approaches to multidimensional poverty measurement (pp. 1–29). Palgrave Macmillan, London.

Mckernan, S. M. and Ratcliffe, C. (2002). *Transition Events in the Ddynamics of Poverty* (Department of Health and Human Services report). Washington, D.C.

Mckernan, S. M. and Ratcliffe, C. (2005). "Events that trigger poverty entries and exits." *Social Science Quarterly*. Vol. 86 (s1): 1146–1169.

Mills, B., Del Ninno, C. and Rajemsion, H. (2004). *Commune Shocks, Household Assets, and Economic Wellbeing in Madagascar.* American Agricultural Economics Association, 2004 Annual meeting, August 1–4, Denver, CO, No. 19956.

MOFED (2008). *Dynamics of Growth and Poverty in Ethiopia (1995/96–2004/05).* Addis Ababa: Ministry of Finance and Economic Development. April, 2008.

Moor, K. (2005). *Thinking About Youth Poverty Through the Lenses of Chronic Poverty, Life-Course Poverty and Intergenerational Poverty* (July 1, 2005). Chronic Poverty Research Centre Working Paper No. 57.

Naifeh, M. (1998). "Trap door? Revolving door? Or both?" Current Population Reports. *Dynamics of Economic Well-Being: Poverty 1992–1993*: 70–63. Washington, D.C.: Census Bureau.

Nussbaum, M. (2000). *Women and Human Development: The Capability Approach.* Cambridge: Cambridge University Press.

Nussbaum, M. (2003). "Capabilities as Fundamental Entitlements: Sen and Social Justice." *Feminist Economics*. Vol. 9: 33–59.

OPHI (2017). *OPHI Country Briefing 2017: Ethiopia.* Oxford Department of International Development.

Poggi, A. (2003). *Measuring Social Exclusion Using the Capability Approach.* Barcelona: Department of Applied Economics, Universitat Autonoma de Barcelona.

Poggi, A. (2007). "Does Persistence of Social Exclusion Exist in Spain?" *Journal of Economic Inequality*. Vol. 5: 53–72.

Quisumbing, A. R. (2007). *Poverty Transitions, Shocks and Consumption in Rural Bangladesh: Preliminary Results from a Longitudinal Household Survey.* CPRC Working Paper No. 105. International Food Policy Research Institute, Washington D.C.

Robeyns, I. (2003). "Sen's Capability Approach and Gender Inequality: Selecting Relevant Capabilities." *Feminist Economics*. Vol. 9: 61–92.

Roelen, K. (2017). "Monetary and Multidimensional Child Poverty: A Contradiction in Terms?" *Development and Change*. Vol. 48(3): 502–533.

Sen A.K. (2000). "Social Exclusion: Concept, application, and scrutiny." *Social Development Papers*, No. 1. Office of Environment and Social Development, Asian Development Bank, January.

Sen, A. (1980). Equality of What? In S. McMurrin (ed.) Tanner Lectures on Human Values, Cambridge: Cambridge University Press.

Sen, A. (1985a). *Commodities and Capabilities.* Amsterdam: North Holland.

Sen, A. (1985b). Well-being and freedom. *The Journal of Philosophy*, 82(4), 185–203.

Sen, A. (1992). *Inequality Re-examined.* Oxford: Clarendon Press.

Sen, A. (1993). "Capability and Well-being." In *The Quality of Life* edited by Nussbaum, M. and Sen, A. Oxford: Clarendon Press.

Sen, A. (1998). "Mortality as an Indicator of Economic Success and Failure." *Economic Journal.* Vol. 108: 1–25.

Sen, A. (1999). *Development as Freedom.* Oxford: Oxford University Press.

Shahateet, M. (2007). "The Determinants of Deprivation in Jordan: An Empirical Study." *Journal of Social Sciences.* Vol. 3 (1): 36–42.

Shepherd, A. (2011). *Tackling Chronic Poverty: The policy implications of research on chronic poverty and poverty dynamics.* Chronic Poverty Research Centre.

Singh, R. and Sakar, S. (2014). *The Relationship of Household Monetary Poverty and Multidimensional Child Deprivation: A Longitudinal Study of Children Growing Up in India.* Young Lives Working Paper 121.

Stevens, A. H. (1994). "The Dynamics of Poverty Spells: Updating Bane and Ellwood." *AEA Papers and Proceedings.* 84(2):34–37.

Thomas, A. (2009). *The Impact of Agricultural Shocks on Household Growth Performance in Rural Madagascar.* Document de Travail, DT/2009-05, Development Institutions and Analyses de Long Term.

Tsui, K. (2002). "Multidimensional Poverty Indices." *Social Choice and Welfare.* Vol. 19: 69–93.

UNDP (2015). *Sustainable Development Goals* (booklet). New York: United Nations Development Program.

UNICEF and MOFEC (2015). *Updated National Equity Situation Analysis on Children and Women in Ethiopia.* Addis Ababa, Ethiopia: United Nations Children's Fund and the Ministry of Finance and Economic Cooperation. Accessed from https://www.unicef.org/ethiopia/ECO_UNICEF_Ethiopia_SitAn_Full_report.pdf, on 09 April 2017.

Young Lives (2014). *Survey Design and Sampling in Ethiopia: Preliminary Findings from the 2013 Young Lives Survey (Round 4).* Young Lives, Oxford: The University of Oxford.

Wagle, U. (2005). "Multidimensional Poverty Measurement with Economic Well-Being, Capability and Social Inclusion: A Case from Kathmandu, Nepal." *Journal of Human Development.* Vol. 6: 301–328.

Wagle, U. (2008). "Multidimensional Poverty: An alternative measurement approach for the United States?" *Social Science Research.* Vol. 37: 559–580.

Woldehanna, T., R. Gudisa, Y. Tafere and A. Pankhurst (2011). *Understanding Changes in the Lives of Poor Children: Initial Findings from Ethiopia Round 3 Survey.* Young Lives, Oxford: Oxford University.

World Bank (2015). *National Poverty Assessment Report: Report No. AUS6744.* Washington D.C: World Bank Poverty Global Practice, Africa Region.

PART TWO
Child-Sensitive Social Protection

PART TWO
Child-Sensitive Social Protection

CHAPTER 6
How Many Malnourished Children Are There in South Africa? What Can Be Done?

Stephen Devereux, Coretta Jonah and Julian May

1. Introduction

Child stunting rates in South Africa are high at around 25 percent, which is inconsistent with South Africa's status as an upper-middle-income country (May and Timæus, 2014). More concerning than this high figure is its persistence over time (Devereux and Waidler, 2017), along with the persistence of the underlying determinants of stunting (May and Jonah, 2017). As this chapter will show, evidence that the prevalence of child stunting has declined significantly since the transition to democracy in 1994 is inconstant. This is despite the fact that there is more than enough food in South Africa at the national level, and notwithstanding the introduction since the late 1990s of the most comprehensive social protection system in Africa.

The drivers of child malnutrition can be understood by drawing on UNICEF's conceptual framework, which identifies four underlying causes: inadequate access to food; inadequate care for children and women; insufficient health services and unhealthy environment; and inadequate education (UNICEF, 1990). We examine these four determinants in an attempt to understand what we call South Africa's "food security paradox." South Africa achieves "national food sufficiency through a combination of own production and food imports" (FAO, 2015: 10), the prevalence of child hunger is falling, but millions of children remain malnourished. Explaining this paradox is important both theoretically, to better understand the difference between food security and nutrition security, and for public policy, because existing interventions clearly are not addressing the malnutrition problem in South Africa.

This chapter is divided into three substantive sections. Section 2 answers the empirical question: "How many malnourished children are there in South Africa?" Section 3 addresses the analytical question: "Why are 1 in 4 children in South Africa stunted?" Section 4 tackles the perennial policy question: "What can be done?"

2.   How many malnourished children are there in South Africa?

Although South Africa is a data-rich country, the trends for several basic statistical indicators are contested, not least the number of malnourished children. Globally, the under-five stunting rate is a robust indicator of child poverty, but there is no consensus on whether this figure is rising or falling over time in South Africa. This has implications for the design, targeting and evaluation of social protection and other interventions intended to improve the wellbeing of children.

Several nutrition surveys have been undertaken in South Africa since the democratic transition in 1994, but analyses of trends in these data have reached diametrically opposed conclusions. May and Timæus (2014: 771) conclude that "stunting among young children has fallen," and Save the Children (2016: 5) applauds South Africa's "exceptional progress" in reducing child stunting from 33 percent to 24 percent between 2004 and 2008.[1] Conversely, a systematic review of nutrition surveys in South Africa suggests a 6.8 percent increase in stunting between 2005 and 2008, from 23.2 percent to 30 percent (Said-Mohamed et al., 2015: 5). Similarly, Hendriks (2014: 18) asserts that "aggregate levels of children's nutrition have deteriorated" in South Africa, and that child stunting rates have increased. An intermediate position is reported by Devereux and Waidler (2017: 1) who conclude that "the nutrition status of children has stagnated or improved only marginally" since 1994.

One of these interpretations of the available data sources must be correct, but which one, and why do different sources disagree? This section reviews the evidence from nutrition surveys conducted since 1993, conducts a meta-analysis of published reviews, and attempts to draw a line underneath this debate, by definitively answering the question: how many children in South Africa are stunted?

We start by introducing a confounding factor: evidence from a subjective indicator that the numbers of "hungry children" in South Africa have fallen rapidly over the period under consideration.

---

1   These figures are derived from joint child malnutrition estimates produced by UNICEF, WHO and the World Bank (http://www.who.int/nutrition/publica tions/jointchildmalnutrition_2015_estimates/en/).

2.1. Trends in child hunger

Although the nutrition data are ambiguous, there is a subjective indicator of food security that suggests significant improvements in food insecurity among children in South Africa. In its annual General Household Survey (GHS), Statistics South Africa (Stats SA) asks this question about hunger: "In the past 12 months, did any child (17 years or younger) in this household go hungry because there wasn't enough food?" This question has been asked every year since 2002, except in 2009, which means that trends in this subjective indicator can be observed over 15 years, until the most recently published GHS report of 2016.

The GHS indicator more than halved in just five years, from 29.3 percent in 2002 to 13.7 percent in 2007, indicating a significant reduction in the prevalence of child hunger in the early 2000s. This sharp downward trend reversed slightly in 2008 and remained at 15.9 percent in 2010 before falling again; it has plateaued at around 13 percent since 2011 (Figure 1). By this subjective indicator, the number of children in South Africa who experience hunger has more than halved since the turn of the millennium.

Figure 1.   Children experiencing hunger in South Africa, 2002 to 2016

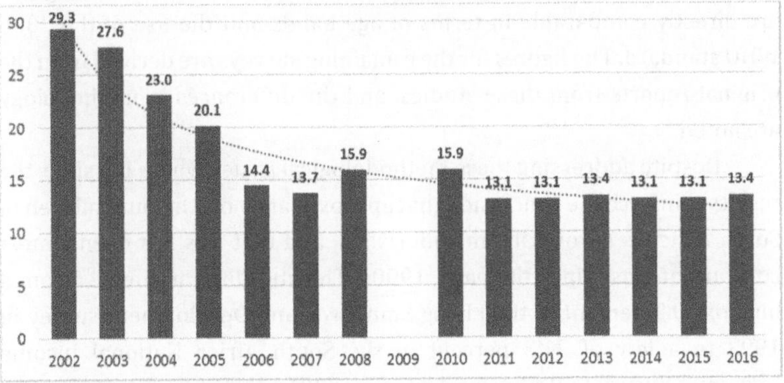

Source: Stats SA (2017: 59)
Note: Questions on hunger were not asked in the 2009 GHS

2.2. Child stunting rates

Our review of available sources of anthropometric data on child nutrition in South Africa reveals that there has been very little improvement in the 20 years since the transition to democracy in 1994. Specifically, child stunting rates have been more or less constant, fluctuating around 25 percent since 1993—never above 30 percent, never below 20 percent. However, the surveys vary in sample size, sampling frame, and for some, even in the age range of children measured. As a result, attempts to determine trends that make use of the prevalence of stunting as originally reported are unreliable.

Stunting rates of children older than 5 months and younger than 60 months are preferred in the food security and nutrition literature. When correctly reported, and accompanied by careful measurement of the height of children using properly calibrated stadiometers, this is accepted as an objectively measured indicator of chronic undernutrition or long-term food insecurity (Barrett, 2010).[2] To determine the prevalence of stunting, this indicator must be compared to a reference child. In earlier surveys, the US National Center for Health Statistics (NCHS) was used, but since 2006, the World Health Organization's Child Growth Standards are preferred (WHO, 2016).

Figure 2 presents the child stunting rates reported in 10 studies between 1993 and 2016. Error bars are provided for those figures for which the primary data are in the public domain and have been accessed by the authors in order to re-calculate stunting prevalence. These figures are directly comparable in terms of age bands and the use of the 2006 WHO standard. The figures for the remaining surveys are derived from the original reports from these studies, and the differences in methodology are noted.

Despite addressing these methodological issues where possible, the results reinforce the conclusion that approximately one in four children in South Africa is chronically malnourished, and that this has been almost constant at least since the early 1990s. The stunting rate ranges from a high of 30.2 percent in the Living Standards and Development survey in 1993 to a low of 21.3 percent in the South Africa National Income Dynamics Survey (NIDS) wave 4 survey of 2014.[3]

---

2   Stunting is an anthropometric measure of height-for-age (HAZ). A child is characterised as having stunted growth if her or his height is less than 2 standard deviations below the height of a child the same age in a reference population.

3   Note that NIDS wave 2 (2010) is omitted from this compilation of nutrition surveys, since there are concerns about the credibility of this dataset. NIDS-2 reported a stunting rate of 33.8 percent which is an outlier in this series.

Figure 2 shows that the confidence intervals of most surveys are wide, in most cases overlapping with each other so that there are no statistically significant differences between most of the stunting estimates, and there is not a statistically significant decline in stunting prevalence between 1993 and 2016, the earliest and most recent years for which primary data could be accessed. The most recent estimate, the 2016 South African Demographic and Health Survey (SADHS) suggests a less promising trend, reporting that 27 percent of children in the same age band were stunted (NDoH et al., 2017). These data are not yet in the public domain.

Figure 2.   Child stunting rates in South Africa, 1993–2016

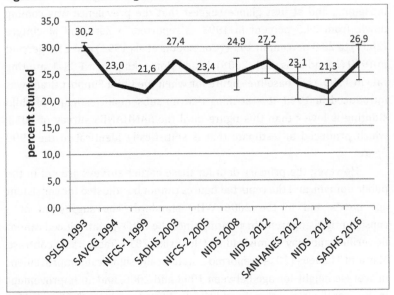

Sources:
1993: data from the national Project for Statistics on Living Standards and Development (PSLSD) survey; n=3,765 children aged 6–59 months, authors' calculation.
1994: data from the South African Vitamin A Consultative Group (SAVACG); n=4,788 children aged 6–71 months (Coutsoudis et al., 1994: 355).
1999: data from the first National Food Consumption Survey (NFCS); n=2,894 children aged 1–9 years (Labadarios et al., 2005).
2003: data from the first South African Demographic and Health Survey (DHS-1); n=1,159 children under 5 years old (Department of Health et al., 2007, Table 8.6).
2005: data from the second National Food Consumption Survey (NFCS); n=2,413 children aged 1–9 years (Labadarios, Steyn and Nel, 2011: 893).

2008: data from National Income Dynamics Study (NIDS) wave 1; n=1,970 children aged 6–59 months, authors' calculation.[4]
2012: data from South African National Health and Nutrition Examination Survey (SANHANES-1); n=2,044 children aged 0–6 years, data are for children aged 0–5 years (Shisana et al., 2013: 210), recalculated by Ronel Sewpaul for children aged 6–59 months [28 September 2017].
2012b: data from National Income Dynamics Study (NIDS) wave 3 for children aged 6–59 months, authors' calculation.
2014: data from National Income Dynamics Study (NIDS) wave 4 for children aged 6–59 months authors' calculation.
2016: data from the second South African Demographic and Health Survey (DHS-2); n=1,404 authors' calculation from report for children aged 6–59 months (NDoH et al., 2017: 28, Table 12).

Possible trends in child stunting prevalence during the 1990s are intriguing, and at first glance suggest that the prevalence was coming down, from 24.5 percent in 1993 as reported in Zere and MacIntyre (2003) to 23.0 percent in 1994 (Coutsoudis et al., 1994) and 21.6 percent in 1999 (Labadarios et al., 2005). In addition, taking the NFCS–1 stunting rate in 1999 as a "baseline" figure for when the Child Support Grant was introduced in 1998, it is striking that no subsequent estimate of child stunting is lower than this figure until the SANHANES survey of 2012, which produced an estimate that is statistically identical to the 1999 figure.

However, the primary data for these earlier surveys are not in the public domain, and the reported figures cannot be adjusted for consistent age bands and to the 2006 WHO standard. The suggestion of a consistently rising trend in stunting since the CSG was introduced cannot be verified and may be misleading (Hendriks, 2014, Table 3). By contrast, May and Timaeus (2014) reported a statistically significant improvement in average height-for-age between 1993 and 2008, and an improvement in the overall distribution. In addition to differences in methodology, May and Timæus (2014: 5) suggest that sample bias may mean that child malnutrition was overestimated in the 1993 PSLSD survey and underestimated in each successive wave of the NIDS survey. If this is true, it follows that the trend over the past two decades has been flat. On the

---

4   The sample size of 1,970 derives from May and Timæus (2014: 5): "NIDS surveyed 2925 children aged 6–59 months and measured the heights and weights of 74 percent of them. When they were compared to the reference population, the data on up to 9 percent of those measured in 2008 had to be excluded as being implausible."

other hand, a systematic review found a mixed trend—a 5 percent increase in child stunting prevalence between 1993 and 2008, followed by a 10 percent decrease by 2013—or a net decline of 5 percent in 20 years, from 24.5 percent to 19.5 percent (Said-Mohamed et al., 2015: 6).

This uncertainty about trends is unsurprising given both the cost and methodological rigour required for anthropometric measurement without reporting error (Ulijaszek and Kerr, 1999), and the use of differing age bands and reference children. The task is made more complex when critical data sets are not placed in the public domain so that results can be replicated. However from the data that can be verified, it is evident that for more than two decades at least one in four South African children below the age of 5 has been stunted, which is incongruous with South Africa's position as an upper middle-income country.

3.   Why are one in four children in South Africa stunted?

Food security exists when all people at all times have physical and economic access to sufficient, safe and nutritious food to meet their dietary needs and food preferences for an active and healthy life (CFS, 2012). Nutrition security exists when secure access to an appropriately nutritious diet is coupled with a sanitary environment, adequate health services and care, in order to ensure a healthy and active life for all household members. Nutrition security differs from food security in that it also considers the aspects of adequate caring practices, health and hygiene in addition to dietary adequacy (FAO, IFAD and WFP, 2015).

Food security is analysed mainly in terms of availability of food and access to food, measured by "entitlements to food" and food intake, or by proxy indicators such as self-reported hunger or the Household Food Insecurity Access Score (HFIAS). Nutrition security is better understood as a biological outcome that is determined by individual health, and is measured anthropometrically. This distinction can be seen by referring to UNICEF's conceptual framework for the causes of child malnutrition (Figure 3), which identifies four underlying causes: inadequate access to food; inadequate care for children and women; insufficient health services and unhealthy environment; and inadequate education.

Figure 3.   UNICEF conceptual framework for causes of child malnutrition

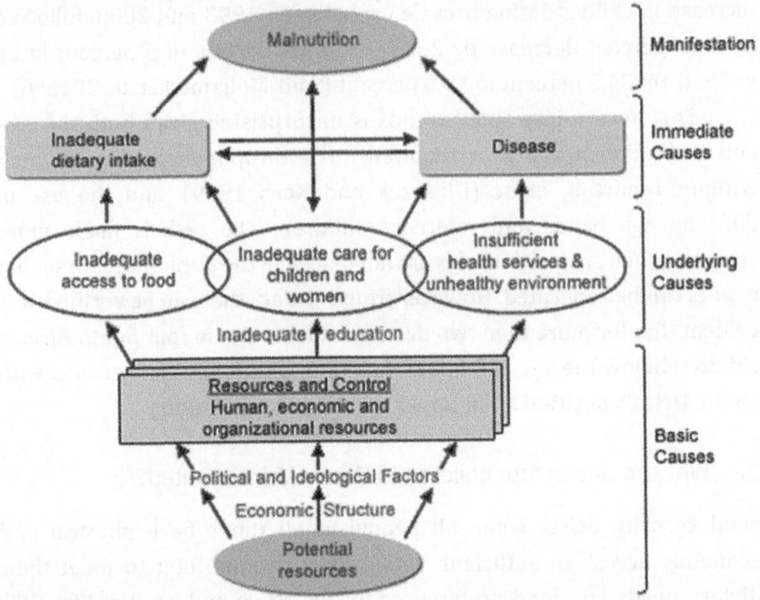

Source: UNICEF, 1990

3.1. Inadequate access to food

An inability to access adequate food can be caused by problems on the supply side (not enough food produced, or not enough food in the market) or on the demand side (not enough money to buy the food needed, because of income poverty and/or high food prices). A separate problem relates to not accessing the right kind of food that provides adequate nutrition to mothers and to infants (poor food quality due to inappropriate or constrained dietary choices). All three issues are discussed here.

3.1.1. Not enough food availability

In terms of national food availability, South Africa has enough food to feed all of its population, currently around 55m people. Data compiled by the Food and Agriculture Organisation (FAO) shows that aggregate food supplies have been steadily rising for the past 25 years, not only in absolute terms but faster than population growth, from around 2,800 kilocalories per person per day in the early 1990s to 3,000 kcal/capita/day by 2011 (Figure 4).

Figure 4.   Food supply in South Africa, 1991–2011 (kcal/capita/day)

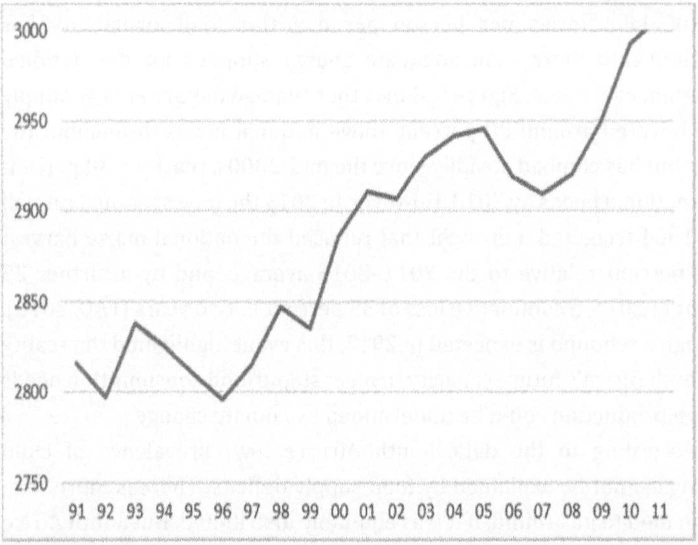

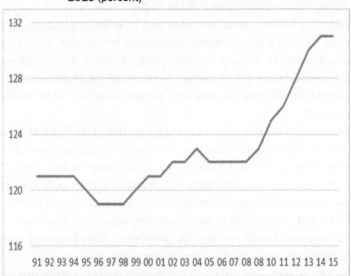

Figure 4: data from FAOSTAT (http://faostat3.fao.org/browse/FB/*/E) downloaded 15 July 2016

Figure 5.   Dietary energy supply (DES) adequacy in South Africa, 1991–2015 (percent)

Figure 5: data from FAOSTAT (http://faostat3.fao.org/browse/D/FS/E) downloaded 15 July 2016.

Even assuming a relatively generous average energy intake requirement of 2,300 kilocalories per person per day, this food availability has translated into more than adequate energy supplies for the national population every year. Figure 5 shows that average dietary energy supply (DES) hovered around 20 percent above national needs throughout the 1990s, but has climbed steadily since the mid-2000s, reaching 30 percent above national needs by 2013. However, in 2015 the lowest annual rainfall since 1904 triggered a drought that reduced the national maize harvest by 14 percent relative to the 2011–2015 average, and by a further 25 percent in 2016, a cumulative loss of 35 percent in two years (FAO, 2016). Although a rebound is expected in 2017, this event highlighted the reality that South Africa's future capacity to meet staple food consumption needs through production could be undermined by climate change.

According to the data, South Africa's high prevalence of child stunting cannot be explained by food supply deficits. There is more than enough food to go around, if it was equitably distributed. But South Africa is one of the most unequal societies in the world, so wealth, income and food are not distributed equitably among all of South Africa's citizens and residents.

3.1.2. Not enough purchasing power to buy food

Food security is not only about how much food is available, it is about who has access to that food. In market-dependent households, access is determined mainly by poverty and affordability. In South Africa millions of poor households and individuals are recipients of social grants, which are intended to alleviate poverty and ensure access to basic needs including food.

According to Stats SA (2017: 14), the proportion of the South African population living below the food poverty line has fluctuated, from 28.4 percent in 2006 to 33.5 percent in 2009 to 21.4 percent in 2011 to 25.2 percent in 2015. It is no coincidence that this corresponds quite closely with the proportion of stunted children. Studies from across the world have found that poverty and child malnutrition are closely correlated— when poverty rises or falls, so does the prevalence of child stunting (see Headey, Hoddinott and Park, 2016 for evidence from South Asia).

Income poverty and economic deprivation explain a large part of malnutrition. Jonah and May (2017) conducted a multivariate regression analysis of the four waves of South Africa's NIDS. Their analysis found that, at household level, household expenditures and a durable asset index were both associated with stunting, suggesting that better-off households were less likely to have stunted children than poorer households in terms of both money-metric and asset-based measures. Several studies have noted the association between family income and malnutrition in general, and stunting specifically (Victora et al., 1986; Christiaensen and Alderman, 2004; Alderman, Hoogeveen and Rossi, 2006). Using DHS data (Bwalya et al., 2015; Ikeda et al., 2013), other studies have pointed to the association between household assets scores and stunting in children, confirming the effect of socioeconomic status on child malnutrition. An index of durable household assets that replicates the durable asset index used in May and Timaeus (2014) confirms that scoring higher on an index of durable household goods is associated with lower levels of stunting in children.

For 20 years social grants have been provided to rising numbers of poor households, and the Child Support Grant (CSG) now reaches two-thirds of all children in South Africa. The failure of these grants to reduce child stunting at aggregate level suggests either that the value of these transfers is too low or that income poverty is not the only driver of malnutrition. This mirrors findings elsewhere in this volume, namely in Chapter 3 in relation to South Africa (Sambu and Hall) and in Chapter 7 in reference to cash transfer programming across Africa (Hypher et al).

On the other hand, it must be noted that several empirical studies have found robust evidence that receiving social grants—especially the Old Age Grant and the Child Support Grant—has positive impacts on household food security indicators and on individual nutritional status, at least among grant recipients. The "Langeberg survey" of 1,300 racially stratified individuals in the Western Cape in 1999 generated evidence that the Old Age Grant reduces the probability of adults skipping meals (due to not having enough money for food) by approximately 25 percent, in households where these grants are pooled with other income. Recipients reported that they could now buy enough food, thanks to the Old Age Grant. The same study found that children living in households with Old Age Grant recipients were about five centimetres taller. "This effect is roughly equal to a half-year's growth for Black and Coloured children aged 0 to 6 in the Langeberg data, and is roughly one standard deviation increase in height for age" (Case, 2001: 15).

A study by Duflo (2003), based on a 1993 national survey of 9,000 randomly selected households, also found that children's nutritional status improved if they lived with an older person who was an Old Age Grant recipient, but this effect was highly gendered in two ways. Firstly, Old Age Grants received by women had a bigger impact on children's nutritional status (height-for-age and weight-for-height z-scores) than did Old Age Grants received by men. Secondly, Old Age Grants had a bigger impact on the nutrition status of girls than boys. Specifically, Duflo (2003: 18) found that Old Age Grants "received by women led to an increase of at least 1.16 standard deviations in the height of girls and to a much smaller (and insignificant) effect (0.28 standard deviation) on the height of boys. Pensions received by men appear to have had no effect on the height of boys or girls."

An analysis of the KwaZulu-Natal Income Dynamics Study (KIDS) panel dataset by Agüero, Carter and Woolard (2007) found that the Child Support Grant significantly reduces the incidence of child stunting. Specifically, boys who started receiving the CSG before their first birthday gained 0.40 in height-for-age z-scores by three years of age, compared to boys in the control group. This translates into an estimated gain of 3.5cm (2.1 percent) in height as adults, compared to other 25–35 year-old men.

Coetzee (2013) estimated the impacts of the CSG on child well-being by analysing the first wave of the NIDS panel data and found small but significant effects on children's height-for-age (4 percent of a standard deviation) and household expenditure on food items (3 percent per person). The anthropometric impact translates into children growing approximately one centimetre taller than non-beneficiaries (Coetzee, 2014: 5), which is less than the finding by Agüero et al. (2007). "These effect sizes are much smaller than expected, given the relative size of the transfer in relation to the mean per capita household expenditure of households in the sample" (Coetzee, 2013: 429).

A rigorous evaluation of the CSG conducted in 2010/11 found no impact of the CSG on stunting in the full sample of 665 children who were enrolled early (during their first two years of life), but a significant positive impact on children in the sample with educated mothers (DSD, SASSA and UNICEF, 2012: 50).

In their analysis of NIDS-1 data, Devereux and Waidler (2017: 23) found "no relationship between receiving social grants and certain nutrition outcomes. Children (under 5 years old) in households receiving only the CSG are slightly more likely to be stunted (24.4 percent) than children in households receiving no social grants (22.7 percent). However, these differences are not statistically significant."

One possible explanation for these disappointing findings is that the CSG is inadequate to meet the nutritional needs of the child receiving the grant. PACSA (2016) estimates that the cost of a nutritionally adequate diet for a young child (aged 3–9 years) in May 2016 was R557, and for an older child (10–13 years) it was R604. This means that even if all the CSG cash is spent only on nutritious food (no non-food spending) and even if all this food is given to the designated beneficiary (not shared with other household members), the CSG of R350 can cover less than two-thirds of the minimum food needs of a young child (63 percent) or an older child (58 percent). But we know that only a proportion of the CSG will be spent on food for the child, because this cash is also needed for other household expenses. In effect, the CSG cash is "diluted" among many users (other household members) and many uses (non-food household needs). Inadequate and "diluted" social grants might explain the puzzle of little observed improvement in children's nutrition status over 20 years, "despite significant increases in the participation of the food insecure in the social security system" (Hendriks, 2014: 18).

3.1.3. Poor quality diet
Even if there is enough food in the market, and even if people have enough money to buy the food they need, they could still become malnourished if they purchase and consume a poor quality diet. Food security is not only having enough food to eat, but accessing the right kinds of food.

There is a well-established relationship between dietary diversity (the number of discrete food groups consumed in the daily diet) and household income: wealthier people consume a wider variety of food items than poor people (Hoddinott and Yohannes, 2002). Indeed, analysis in Chapter 3 of this volume by Sambu and Hall finds that income poverty is a strong predictor of low dietary diversity in South Africa. This is in line with previous studies: analysing food consumption data from the 2005/06 Income and Expenditure Survey (IES), Aliber (2009) confirms that this relationship holds in South Africa. The poorest rural households consume, on average, 5.5 discrete food groups, while the richest urban and rural households consume 10 food groups, out of a possible 12

(Aliber, 2009: 404). Labadarios, Steyn and Nel (2011: 894) found that "dietary diversity score was positively related with z-scores for underweight, stunting and wasting among children included in the 1999 NFCS". Average height-for-age was above the mean only when the dietary diversity score reached 8 out of 12.

Poor diets are of particular concern when experienced by pregnant women. Studies have revealed some worrying trends, with over 16 percent of mothers reporting that they had experienced a depletion of food in the 12 months prior to visiting a neonatal clinic (Goga et al., 2012). Pregnant women also face the risk of micronutrient deficiencies, and NFCS-FB reported that in 2005, 27.2 percent of females of reproductive age were Vitamin A deficient (VAD). This has improved and in 2011, the SANHANES reports a prevalence of VAD for 13.3 percent females in the reproductive age group (16–35 years). SANHANES reports that the prevalence of anaemia in female participants being almost twice the prevalence (22.0 percent) when compared with males (12.2 percent). The prevalence of iron deficiency anaemia (IDA) was 9.7 percent of women of reproductive age. However, it appears that anaemia in women of reproductive age may have improved, and the prevalence reported by SANHANES-1 in 2013 (16–25 years) was lower than that found in NFCS-2005 (Labadarios et al., 2005), at 23.1 percent compared to 29.4 percent.

Black et al. (2008) report on studies in developing countries that have established a link between short stature and anaemia and an increased risk of maternal death during childbirth. The link between maternal undernutrition and perinatal or neonatal conditions is less clear, but some evidence does associate intrauterine growth restriction with mothers who have a low body mass. In South Africa, analysis of the 1999 National Food Consumption Survey found that 3.5 percent of the burden of low birthweight can be attributed to maternal undernourishment (Nannan et al., 2007). Diets provide a partial explanation for these trends. Especially in poor households, meals are predominantly cereal-based and are low in animal foods, vegetables and fruit. One study found that poor South Africans have "bad access to good food and good access to bad food" (Oxfam, 2014: 4).

SANHANES reports that 39.7 percent of adults had Dietary Diversity Scores (DDS) of less than 4 in 2012, meaning that less than 4 of the major food groups were consumed in the previous day. There was little variation by age group but respondents in rural informal areas were most likely to have a low dietary diversity (59.7 percent) followed by those in urban informal areas (46.6 percent). This has not changed since 2009 when Labadarios, Steyn and Nel (2011) found that 38 percent of the population had DDS less than 4. A higher DDS has been associated with better nutrient quality (Oldewage-Theron and Kruger, 2008). One component of such a diet relates to the intake of fruit and vegetables that is around 200 grams per person per day in South Africa (Nel and Steyn, 2002). This is half the WHO recommendation of 400 grams per day (WHO, 2003).

3.2. Inadequate care for children and women

One indicator of inadequate care for women is low birthweight babies, which is a reflection of undernourished mothers. The prevalence of low birthweight children is generally higher in developing countries (Black et al., 2013; Qadir and Bhutta, 2008; Rahman et al., 2016) and these children tend to have poorer levels of development than children born in the normal birthweight range. In line with results from other countries (Aryastami and Shankar, 2017; Bwalya et al., 2015; Jiang et al., 2015), our analysis shows that in South Africa a child born with low birthweight has a higher likelihood of being stunted (Figure 6).

Another possible explanation for the persistence of high levels of child malnutrition may lie in the ongoing effects of South Africa's HIV/AIDs pandemic. Although mother-to-child transmission has fallen dramatically, HIV-positive mothers have an increased risk of infection, and infection has been found to be an influence on child health and thus on child linear growth. The results of earlier studies that found no impact of anti-retroviral drugs (ARVs) on birthweight are being challenged in the context of resource-poor environments, and depending upon the maternal HIV stage (Li et al., 2015; Young et al., 2012).

Figure 6.   Stunting levels for normal and low birthweight children

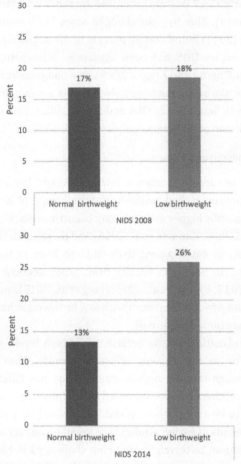

Note: Low birthweight is defined by the WHO as a 2,499g or less; normal birthweight at term delivery is defined as 2,500–4,200g.
Source: derived from NIDS 2014.

One indicator of inadequate care for children is infant feeding practices. Exclusive breastfeeding is recommended for infants up to six months old, but South Africa performs very poorly on this indicator. According to the first DHS, only 6.8 percent of infants were exclusively breastfed for their first six months in 1998—one of the lowest rates in Africa—and this improved only marginally to 8.3 percent in 2003 (Department of Health et al., 2007: xvi). The 2016 DHS reported an "extremely encouraging" improvement to 31.6 percent (NDoH et al., 2017: xiii, 29), but this is still less than one in three infants, 25 percent of whom are not breastfed at all.

3.3. Insufficient health services and unhealthy environment

Child malnutrition is also linked to the physical environment in which children live. Illness, specifically diarrhoeal diseases, inhibits the body's capacity to absorb nutrients from food that has been ingested, and can lead to stunted growth. In terms of access to services and to health care facilities, 45 percent of all children in South Africa (8.5 million) live in rural areas, most in traditional housing; nine percent of all children (1.6 million) live in informal settlements or backyard shacks, and 32 percent and 31 percent, respectively, live in households that do not have adequate water on site or adequate sanitation (Hall et al., 2014). This means that between 5 and 6 million children are exposed to a significant risk of gastro-intestinal infection in relation to hand and food hygiene, sanitation and water supply. Chambers and Mendoza (2014) refer to this as undernutrition's "blind spot."

In a review of international evidence, Ngure et al. (2014) link poor water, sanitation, and hygiene (WASH) to anaemia and child growth and note that studies have argued that poor WASH may account for as much as 50 percent of maternal and childhood underweight. The 2015 GHS reports that less than half (46 percent) of households in South Africa have access to piped water in their dwelling (Stats SA, 2016). Similarly, while 80 percent of the population is described as having access to improved sanitation, only 37 percent of households with children under five have a flush toilet in their dwelling (Stats SA, 2016).

3.4. Inadequate education

Several studies have examined the linkages between mother's education and childhood malnutrition. A review of time series data from 63 countries found that 43 percent of reductions in child malnutrition over time can be attributed to women's education, while improvements in food availability contributed only 26 percent (Smith and Haddad 1999). This is not only because education is usually associated with higher income. Educated mothers are less likely to have malnourished children through beneficial effects on child care practices, access to health care and dietary choices (Hasan and Magalhaes, 2015; Makoka and Masibo, 2015). UNICEF's conceptual framework (Figure 3 above) shows that inadequate education lies behind the three other underlying causes of child malnutrition. Studies have confirmed that caring practices in childhood, including feeding and health-care, are positively associated with maternal education (Jiang et al., 2015). Other researchers have found that higher educated mothers participate more in health decision-making at home, which leads to better outcomes for children (Barrios and Hoffman 2013; Hasan et al., 2016; Makoka, 2013).

In South Africa, analysis of all four waves of the NIDS panel confirmed that mothers' education is negatively associated with childhood stunting, as the higher the education of the mother the less likely the child is to be stunted. Similarly, as noted above, an evaluation of the Child Support Grant found no impact of the CSG on child stunting across the full sample, but a significant fall in the prevalence of stunting among children who were enrolled before the age of two and those whose mothers have 8 or more grades of schooling. For these children, receiving the CSG early improved their height-for-age z-score by 0.19 standard deviations (DSD, SASSA and UNICEF, 2012: 50).

4.   What can be done?

The co-existence of falling food insecurity but persistently high malnutrition in South Africa suggests that the drivers of food security are not the same as the drivers of malnutrition. Social grants are important because they enhance access to food. But the grants are not enough, because they are not adequate to meet all the food and non-food needs of the families that receive them, and because access to food is not the only determinant of nutrition outcomes. Nutrition-sensitive social protection requires more than social grants, it also requires linkages to complementary services, such as nutrition education, antenatal and post-natal health care, and maternal health and nutrition.

4.1. "Cash plus" programming

The fact that South African diets tend to lack diversity, and the evidence that behaviour change communication (BCC) can contribute to improved nutrition outcomes for children, suggest that nutrition education could play an important positive role in South Africa.

Evidence is accumulating that cash transfers can achieve significantly greater impacts on wellbeing outcomes when combined with linkages to other services, instead of delivering cash transfers alone (Banerjee et al., 2015; Roelen et al., 2017). In particular, maternal health and children's nutritional status can be improved by offering access to relevant services and information. For example, conditional cash transfer programmes (CCTs) typically require recipients of cash transfers to send their children for immunisation and growth monitoring, and sometimes require mothers to attend mother-child health education sessions. Similarly, "graduation model" programmes include BCC—messages about dietary diversity, appropriate child feeding and hygiene and sanitation practices—among the package of support delivered to participants during the programme cycle, in addition to regular cash transfers (de Montesquiou and Sheldon, 2014).

An evaluation of Zambia's Child Grant Programme found that child stunting rates fell in recipient households that had a protected water source (Seidenfeld et al., 2014), which highlights the importance of access to clean water—reducing the risk of diarrhoea—as well as purchasing power to buy food in tackling malnutrition. In Niger, households that received cash transfers plus nutrition supplements registered higher reductions in acute malnutrition than households that received either cash or supplements, but not both (Langendorf et al., 2014).

A pilot project from Bangladesh confirms that when cash transfers are disbursed in conjunction with nutrition-related BCC—giving messages about dietary diversity, health eating choices and appropriate child feeding practices—impacts on child nutrition outcomes are significantly enhanced. The Transfer Modality Research Initiative (TMRI) delivered combinations of food, cash and BCC to 4,000 households in Bangladesh for 24 months. BCC sessions included: nutrition awareness, dietary diversity, hygiene and hand-washing, micronutrients (Vitamin A, iron, iodine and zinc), breastfeeding, complementary feeding, and maternal nutrition. The endline evaluation found no noticeable improvement in child nutrition outcomes for households that received "cash only" or "food only," while a statistically insignificant improvement was found for households that received "cash + food." However, a statistically significant reduction in stunting and a height gain of almost one centimetre was found for children in households that received "cash

+ BCC" (Figure 7). Ahmed et al. (2016: 107) conclude that "combining transfers with nutrition behaviour change communication (BCC) trainings consistently causes considerably larger improvements than transfers alone."

Figure 7.   TMRI impacts on child stunting, Bangladesh

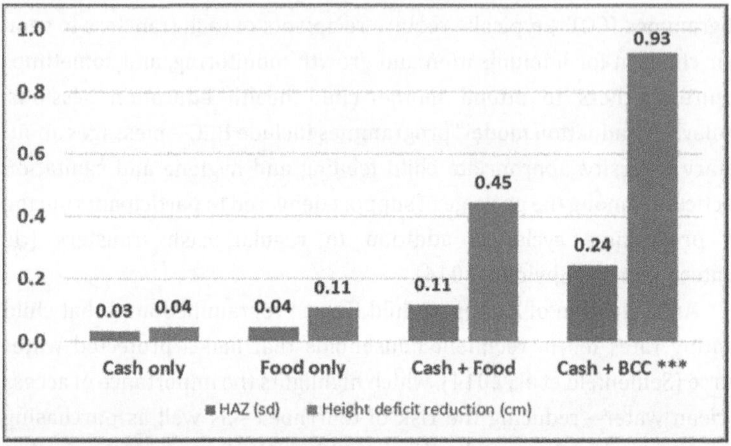

Source: derived from Ahmed et al., 2016.

The potential of so-called "cash plus" programming to address the multiple drivers of undernutrition is also explored at length in Chapter 7 in this volume (by Hypher et al.).

4.2. Antenatal and post-natal health care

The South African government aimed to ensure that more than 60 percent of pregnant women and girls access antenatal care before 20 weeks of pregnancy by 2016. Antenatal care is free in South Africa's public health system and is accompanied by vitamin supplementation for those who attend. Although nearly all pregnant women and girls attend an antenatal clinic at least once while pregnant, less than half seek antenatal care before 20 weeks of pregnancy (Health Systems Trust, 2013). Adequate antenatal care is associated with healthy birthweight (Branco da Fonseca et al., 2014) and studies in three Latin American countries show an association between antenatal care and malnutrition in children (Forero Ramirez et al., 2014). Although a policy already exists in South Africa to improve access to antenatal care that pregnant women have responded to, it is possible that attendance is irregular and that health care messages may need to be reviewed to be tailored to the specific context of those making sporadic use of these facilities. In addition, the role of confounding factors such as maternal ill-health should also be taken into account.

4.3. Maternal nutrition

Studies provide evidence that beyond two years of age little may be done to improve stunting in children (Ruel, 2010; Sudfeld et al., 2015). This means early intervention is needed if an infant has been exposed to an extended period of undernutrition, including prior to being born. As shown in Figure 6 above, in South Africa as elsewhere low birthweight babies face a higher risk of stunting (Jonah and May 2017; Bwalya et al., 2015). Low birthweight babies are a reflection of undernourished mothers and inadequate care received during pregnancy.

Breaking the intergenerational transmission of malnutrition requires investing in the nutrition of adolescent girls and pregnant and lactating women (PLW). Currently, the South African Child Support Grant is provided only to infants after they are born, and thus does not improve the health and nutrition of pregnant women or their in-utero babies. However, cash transfers have been found to be an important option for improved family's health, nutrition and food security (Fernald, Gertler and Neufeld, 2008; Soares, Ribas and Osório, 2010). As such, the current social protection scheme could be expanded to include pregnant women. An alternative would be increasing the levels of cash transfers which are provided in combination with micronutrient supplements such as iron and vitamin A to pregnant and lactating women.

4.4. A holistic approach

South Africa could learn from the experience of countries that have adopted a holistic approach to tackling hunger and malnutrition that focused on policy objectives (e.g. zero hunger) rather than policy instruments (e.g. cash transfers). Two examples are Peru and Brazil.

Child stunting in Peru halved in just 10 years, from 30 percent in 2004 to 15 percent in 2014. This was achieved through a combination of ambitious programmes and focused efforts by government. The main programmes included the National Nutrition Assistance Programme for children under 3 years old; the *Juntos* conditional cash transfer that linked cash transfers to health and education services; and *Crecer* (to grow) which delivered complementary foods to children as well as ensuring access to clean water and sanitation. These interventions succeeded because of effective multi-sectoral and multi-level cooperation between national government, regional government and civil society, and because of strong and credible accountability mechanisms, from the national political level to local budgets. Probably the most important factor was political commitment. The government prioritised tackling undernutrition and demonstrated its intentions by investing in a "5 by 5 by 5" goal—to reduce stunting among children under-5 by 5 percent in 5 years—which was achieved (Gillespie et al., 2016).

While South Africa has achieved no significant reduction in chronic child malnutrition despite a substantial expansion in social grants during the past 20 years, Brazil reduced child stunting from about 25 percent in 1985 to just 7 percent by 2007. In their analysis of this trend in Brazil, Monteiro et al. (2010: 308) identified four factors that were responsible for two-thirds of the improvements:

1. Better educated mothers, due to rising access and quality of education services;

2. Rising incomes of poor families, due to economic growth, rising minimum wages, the Family Agriculture Programme and cash transfers such as *Bolsa Familia* linked to social services;

3. Improving maternal and child health care, due to free health services and the Family Health Strategy; and

4. Wider coverage of water supply and sanitation services, as measured by the numbers of households served by the public water supply and the public sewage system.

A holistic approach to tackling child malnutrition that addresses all its drivers simultaneously—like Brazil's "Zero Hunger Programme"—is likely to achieve better results than the uncoordinated approach to food and nutrition security, dominated by social grants, that South Africa has pursued to date.

5. Conclusions

South Africa's incongruously high prevalence of child stunting is a reflection of widespread multidimensional poverty and is an indictment of the failure of economic and social policies over many decades, notwithstanding several pro-poor interventions since the ANC took power in 1994, notably the expansion of social grants to reach millions of children and poor families. South Africa remains one of the most unequal countries in the world in terms of income distribution, and the social grants have made little difference to that dubious status.

It must be acknowledged that the Child Support Grant has protected children and their families from falling further into deprivation and destitution. But the value of the grant is not enough to meet the nutritional needs of the child. Moreover, the CSG is spent on food as well as non-food needs, and on other household members, which dilutes its potential impact on the child's nutritional status. One obvious remedy would be to raise the value of the grant substantially, but this will inevitably raise government concerns about fiscal sustainability and public concerns about "dependency syndrome." A more sustainable trajectory would be to invest in job creation to eradicate the high levels of unemployment that have trapped millions of families in structural poverty, dependent on social grants because they lack earned income to purchase adequate food. Across the world, poverty reduction has consistently emerged as one of the strongest drivers of improved nutrition.

Aside from income poverty, the literature identifies several non-income drivers of malnutrition outcomes, including undiversified diets, maternal undernourishment and illiteracy, failure to exclusively breastfeed infants, and no access to clean water or improved sanitation facilities. All these drivers are identified in this chapter as prevalent among low-income households in South Africa, confirming that child stunting is a complex outcome of multiple determinants. Several ideas from other countries could be applied in South Africa. One recent innovation is "cash plus" programming, which combines cash transfers such as social grants with links to other services, such as behaviour change communication around good nutrition, feeding and hygiene practices. Also indicated are stronger investments in antenatal and post-natal health care, and in the nutrition of adolescent girls and pregnant and lactating women. Most important of all is to implement a holistic approach, by setting targets to reduce child malnutrition and adopting multisectoral coordination mechanisms to achieve the necessary improvements in incomes, diets, education, quality health care, clean water, sanitation and hygiene.

References

Agüero, J., Carter, M. and Woolard, I. (2007). 'The impact of unconditional cash transfers on nutrition: the South African Child Support Grant', *IPC Working Paper*, no. 39. Brasilia: International Poverty Centre.

Ahmed, A., Hoddinott, J., Roy, S., Sraboni, E., Quabili, W. and Margolies, A. (2016). *Which kinds of social safety net transfers work best for the ultra-poor in Bangladesh? Operation and impacts of the Transfer Modality Research Initiative*. Dhaka: IFPRI and World Food Programme.

Alderman, H., Hoogeveen, H. and Rossi, M. (2006). 'Reducing child malnutrition in Tanzania: Combined effects of income growth and program interventions', *Economics & Human Biology*, 4(1): 1–23.

Aliber, M. (2009). 'Exploring Statistics South Africa's national household surveys as sources of information about household-level food security', *Agrekon*, 48(4): 384–409.

Altman, M., Hart, T. and Jacobs, P. (2009). 'Household food security status in South Africa', *Agrekon*, 48(4): 345–361.

Aryastami, N. et al. (2017). 'Low birth weight was the most dominant predictor associated with stunting among children aged 12–23 months in Indonesia', *BMC Nutrition*, 3(16). doi: 10.1186/s40795-017-0130-x .

Banerjee, A., Duflo, E., Goldberg, N., Karlan, D., Osei, R., Parienté, W., Shapiro, J., Thuysbaert, B. and Udry, C. (2015). 'A multifaceted program causes lasting progress for the very poor: evidence from six countries', *Science*, 348(6236). doi: 10.1126/science.1260799.

Barrett, C. (2010). 'Measuring Food Insecurity', *Science*, 327: 825–828.

Barrios, P. and Hoffman, D. (2013). 'Relationship between household structure, maternal education and undernutrition in Brazilian children', (378.7). *FASEB Journal*, 28(1 Supplement): 378–7.

Black, R.E. et al. (2008). 'Maternal and child undernutrition: Global and regional exposures and health consequences'. *The Lancet*, 371(9608), 243–260.

Black, R.E. et al. (2013). 'Maternal and child undernutrition and overweight in low-income and middle-income countries', *The Lancet*, 382(9890): 427–451.

Branco da Fonseca, C.R. et al. (2014). 'Adequacy of antenatal care and its relationship with low birth weight in Botucatu, São Paulo, Brazil: A case-control study', *BMC Pregnancy and Childbirth*, 14(1): 255. doi: 10.1186/1471-2393-14-255.

Bwalya, B. et al. (2015). 'Factors associated with stunting among children aged 6–23 months in Zambia: Evidence from the 2007 Zambia Demographic and Health Survey', *International Journal of Advanced Nutritional and Health Science,* 3(1): 116–131.

Case, A. (2001). 'Does money protect health status? Evidence from South African pensions', *NBER Working Paper,* 8495: Cambridge, MA.: National Bureau of Economic Research.

Chambers, R. and von Medeazza, G. (2014). 'Reframing undernutrition: faecally-transmitted infections and the 5 As', *IDS Working Paper,* 450. Brighton: Institute of Development Studies.

Christiaensen, L. and Alderman, H. (2004). 'Child malnutrition in Ethiopia: Can maternal knowledge augment the role of income?' *Economic Development and Cultural Change,* 52(2), pp. 287–312.

Coetzee, M. (2013). 'Finding the benefits: Estimating the impact of the South African Child Support Grant', *South African Journal of Economics,* 81(3): 427–450.

Coetzee, M. (2014). 'Do poor children really benefit from the Child Support Grant?' Available at: www.econ3x3.org/sites/default/files/articles/Coetzee_2014_Child_grant_FINAL.pdf. Accessed: 27 January 2018.

Committee on World Food Security (CFS) (2012). *Coming to Terms with Terminology.* Rome: CFS.

Coutsoudis, A., Hussey, G., Ijsselmuiden, C., Labadarios, D., Harris, B., Robertson, H.L., van Middelkoop, A., deHoop, M., Kotze, J., Cameron, N. and Eggers, R.R. (1996). 'Anthropometric, vitamin A, iron and immunisation coverage status in children aged 6–71 months in South Africa, 1994.' *South African Medical Journal,* 86(4): 354–357.

de Montesquiou, A. and Sheldon, T. (2014). *From extreme poverty to sustainable livelihoods: A technical guide to the graduation approach.* Washington DC: CGAP and Ford Foundation.

Department of Health (DoH), Medical Research Council (MRC) and OrcMacro (2007). *South Africa Demographic and Health Survey 2003.* Pretoria: Department of Health.

Department of Social Development (DSD), South African Social Security Agency (SASSA) and UNICEF (2012). *The South African Child Support Grant Impact Assessment: Evidence from a survey of children, adolescents and their households.* Pretoria: UNICEF South Africa.

Devereux, S. and Waidler, J. (2017). 'Why does malnutrition persist in South Africa despite social grants?' *CoE–FS Working Paper,* #1. South Africa: DST–NRF Centre of Excellence in Food Security.

Duflo, E. (2003). 'Grandmothers and Granddaughters: Old-Age Pensions and Intrahousehold Allocation in South Africa', *The World Bank Economic Review,* 17(1): 1–25. doi: 10.1093/wber/lhg013.

FAO (2015). *Regional Overview of Food Insecurity: Africa.* Accra: Food and Agriculture Organisation of the United Nations.

FAO (2017). *Regional Overview of Food Security and Nutrition in Africa 2016: The challenges of building resilience to shocks and stresses.* Accra: Food and Agriculture Organisation of the United Nations.

FAO, IFAD & WFP (2015). *The State of Food Insecurity in the World 2015: Meeting the 2015 international hunger targets, taking stock of uneven progress.* Rome: Food and Agriculture Organization Publications.

Fernald, L.C., Gertler, P.J. and Neufeld, L.M. (2008). 'Role of cash in conditional cash transfer programmes for child health, growth, and development: an analysis of Mexico's *Oportunidades*', *The Lancet,* 371(9615): 828–837. doi: 10.1016/S0140-6736(08)60382-7.

Forero Ramirez, N. *et al.* (2014). 'Child malnutrition and prenatal care: Evidence from three Latin American countries', *Pan-American Journal of Public Health,* 35(3): 163–171.

Gillespie, S., Hodge, J., Yosef, S. and Pandya-Lorch, R., eds. (2016). *Nourishing Millions: Stories of Change in Nutrition.* Washington, DC: International Food Policy Research Institute.

Goga, A.E., Dinh, T.H. and Jackson, D.J. for the SAPMTCTE study group (2012). *Evaluation of the Effectiveness of the National Prevention of Mother-to-Child Transmission (PMTCT) Programme Measured at Six Weeks Postpartum in South Africa, 2010.* South African Medical Research Council, National Department of Health and PEPFAR/US Center for Disease Control and Prevention.

Hall, K., Meintjes, H., & Sambu, W. (2014). 'Demography of South Africa's children.' In Mathews, S., Jamieson, L., Lake, L. and Smith, C., eds., *South African Child Gauge 2014.* Cape Town: Children's Institute, University of Cape Town.

Hasan, M. T. *et al.* (2016). 'Long-term changes in childhood malnutrition are associated with long-term changes in maternal BMI: Evidence from Bangladesh, 1996–2011', *American Journal of Clinical Nutrition,* 104(4): 1121–1127. doi: 10.3945/ajcn.115.111773.

Hasan, M., Sores, T., Magalhaes, R., Williams, G. and Mamun, A. (2015). 'The role of maternal education in the 15-year trajectory of malnutrition in children under 5 years of age in Bangladesh', *Maternal and Child Nutrition.* Unicef, 2013: 1–11. doi: 10.1111/mcn.12178.

Headey, D., Hoddinott, J. and Park, S. (2016). 'Drivers of nutritional change in four South Asian countries: a dynamic observational analysis', *Maternal and Child Nutrition,* 12 (Supp. 1): 210–218.

Health Systems Trust (2013). 'District Health Barometer 2012/13', *DHB Supplement Series,* 2. Westville: Health Systems Trust. Available at: http://www.hst.org.za. Accessed: 28 January 2018.

Hendriks, S. (2014). 'Food security in South Africa: Status quo and policy imperatives,' *Agrekon,* 53(2): 1–24.

Hoddinott, J. and Yohannes, Y. (2002). 'Dietary diversity as a food security indicator', *FCND Discussion Paper,* 136. Washington, D.C.: International Food Policy Research Institute (IFPRI).

Ikeda, N., Irie, Y. and Shibuya, K. (2013). 'Determinants of reduced child stunting in Cambodia: analysis of pooled data from three Demographic and Health Surveys', *Bulletin of the World Health Organization*, 91(5): 341–349. doi: 10.2471/BLT.12.113381.

Jiang, Y. *et al.* (2015). 'Prevalence and risk factors for stunting and severe stunting among children under three years old in mid-western rural areas of China', *Child: Care, Health and Development*, 41(1): 45–51. doi: 10.1111/cch.12148.

Jonah, C. and May, J. (2017). *Associations between child stunting, maternal and household characteristics in children ten years and below: A four-wave analysis using South Africa's National Income Dynamics Survey (NIDS)*. Report prepared for the South African Poverty Assessment.

Labadarios D *et al.* (2005). 'The National Food Consumption Survey (NFCS): South Africa 1999', *Public Health Nutrition*, 8(5): 533–543. doi: 10.1079/PHN2005816.

Labadarios, D., Steyn, N. and Nel, J. (2011). 'How diverse is the diet of adult South Africans?', *Nutrition Journal*, 10(1): 33. doi: 10.1186/1475-2891-10-33.

Langendorf, C., Roederer, T., de Pee, S., Brown, D., Doyon, S., Mamaty, A-A., Toure, L.W., Manzo, M.L. and Grais, R.F. (2014). 'Preventing acute malnutrition among young children in crises: A prospective intervention study in Niger', *PloS Medicine*, 11(9): e1001714.

Li, N., Sando, M. M., Spiegelman, D., Hertzmark, E., Liu, E., Sando, D., ... and Fawzi, W. (2015). 'Antiretroviral therapy in relation to birth outcomes among HIV-infected women: A cohort study', *Journal of Infectious Diseases*, 213: 1057-1064.

Makoka, D. (2013). *The Impact of Maternal Education on Child Nutrition: Evidence from Malawi, Tanzania, and Zimbabwe*. Calverton, Maryland, USA: ICF International.

Makoka, D. and Masibo, P. K. (2015). 'Is there a threshold level of maternal education sufficient to reduce child undernutrition? Evidence from Malawi, Tanzania and Zimbabwe', *BMC Pediatrics*, 15(1). doi: 10.1186/s12887-015-0406-8.

May, J. and Jonah, C. (2017). *Non-income dimensions of poverty: The nexus between food security and nutrition, and income poverty in South Africa*. (Revised Draft 06/07/17.)

May, J. and Timæus, I. (2014). 'Inequities in under-five nutritional status in South Africa: What progress has been made?' *Development Southern Africa*, 31(6): 761–774.

Monteiro, C., *et al.* (2010). 'Narrowing socioeconomic inequality in child stunting: the Brazilian experience, 1974–2007', *Bulletin of the World Health Organisation*, 88: 305–311.

Nannan, N., Norman, R., Hendricks, M., Dhansay, M.A., Bradshaw, D. and South African Comparative Risk Assessment Collaborating Group (2007). 'Estimating the burden of disease attributable to childhood and maternal undernutrition in South Africa in 2000.' *South African Medical Journal*, 97: 733–739.

National Department of Health (NDoH), Statistics South Africa (Stats SA), South African Medical Research Council (SAMRC) and ICF (2017). *South Africa Demographic and Health Survey 2016: Key Indicator Report*. Pretoria: Statistics South Africa.

Nel, J. and Steyn, N. (2002). *Report on South African food consumption studies undertaken amongst different population groups (1983–2000): Average intakes of foods most commonly consumed.* Pretoria: Department of Health.

Ngure, F. M. *et al.* (2014). 'Water, sanitation, and hygiene (WASH), environmental enteropathy, nutrition, and early child development: Making the links', *Annals of the New York Academy of Sciences*, 1308(1): 118–128. doi: 10.1111/nyas.12330.

Oldewage-Theron, W. H., & Kruger, R. (2008). 'Food variety and dietary diversity as indicators of the dietary adequacy and health status of an elderly population in Sharpeville, South Africa.' *Journal of Nutrition for the Elderly*, 27(1–2):101–133.

Oxfam (2014). *Hidden hunger in South Africa.* Oxford: Oxfam International.

PACSA (2016). *PACSA Food Price Barometer Annual Report October 2016.* Accessed from www.pacsa.org.za/images/food_barometer/2016/2016_PACSA_Food_Price_Bar ometer_REDUCED.pdf, 06 June, 2018.

Qadir, M. and Bhutta, Z. (2008). 'Low Birth Weight in Developing Countries'. In Kiess, W., Chernausek, S. and Hokken-Koelega, A., eds., Small for Gestational Age: Causes and consequences. *Pediatr Adolesc Med.,*13: 148–162. doi: 10.1159/000165998.

Rahman, M. S. *et al.* (2016). 'Association of low-birth weight with malnutrition in children under five years in Bangladesh: Do mother's education, socio-economic status, and birth interval matter?', *PLoS ONE.* Public Library of Science, 11(6): e0157814. doi: 10.1371/journal.pone.0157814.

Roelen, K., Devereux, S., Abdulai, A., Martorano, B., Palermo, T. and Ragno, L. (2017). 'How to make "cash plus" work: Linking cash transfers to services and sectors', *Innocenti Working Paper,* 2017-10. Florence: UNICEF Office of Research.

Ruel, M. T. (2010). 'The Oriente Study: Program and Policy Impacts', *Journal of Nutrition.* 140(2): 415–418. doi: 10.3945/jn.109.114512.

Said-Mohamed, R., Micklesfield, L., Petifor, J. and Norris, S. (2015). 'Has the prevalence of stunting in South African children changed in forty years? A systematic review.' *BMC Public Health,* 15: 534.

Save the Children (2016). *Unequal Portions—Ending Malnutrition for Every Last Child.* London: Save the Children Fund.

Seidenfeld, D., Handa, S., Tembo, S., Michelo, S., Harland Scott, C. and Prencipe, L. (2014). 'The impact of an unconditional cash transfer on food security and nutrition: The Zambia Child Grant Programme'. Available at: https://opendocs.ids.ac.uk/o pendocs/handle/123456789/4385. Accessed: 28 June 2018.

Shisana, O. *et al.* (2013). *The South African National Health and Nutrition Examination Survey.* Cape Town: Human Sciences Research Council (HSRC) Press. Available at: http://www.hsrc.ac.za/en/research-outputs/view/6493.

Smith, L. and Haddad, L. (1999). 'Explaining child malnutrition in developing countries: a cross-country analysis', *FCND Discussion Paper,* No. 60. Washington DC: International Food Policy Research Institute.

Soares, F., Ribas, R. and Osório, R. (2010). 'Evaluating the impact of Brazil's Bolsa Familia: Cash transfer programs in comparative perspective', *Latin American Research Review,* 45(2): 173–190. doi: 10.1353/lar.2010.0017.

Stats SA (2016). *General Household Survey: 2015*. Pretoria: Statistics South Africa.

Stats SA (2017). *Poverty Trends in South Africa: An examination of absolute poverty between 2006 and 2015*. Pretoria: Statistics South Africa.

Sudfeld *et al.* (2015). 'Linear Growth and Child Development in Low- and Middle-Income Countries: A Meta-Analysis', *Pediatrics*, 135(5): e1266–e1275. doi: 10.15 42/peds.2014-3111.

Ulijaszek, S.J. and Kerr, D.A. (1999). 'Anthropometric measurement error and the assessment of nutritional status.' *British Journal of Nutrition*, 82(3): 165–177.

UNICEF (1990). *Strategy for Improved Nutrition of Children and Women in Developing Countries*. Policy Review Paper, E/ICEF/1990/1.6. New York: UNICEF.

Victora, C., Vaughan, J., Kirkwood, B., Martines, J. and Barcelos, L. (1986). 'Risk factors for malnutrition in Brazilian children: The role of social and environmental variables', *Bulletin of the World Health Organization*, 64(2): 299–309.

WHO (World Health Organisation) (2003). *Diet, Nutrition and the Prevention of Chronic Diseases*. Geneva: World Health Organisation.

WHO (World Health Organisation) (2006). *WHO Child Growth Standards: Length/height-for-age, Weight-for-age, Weight-for-length, Weight-for-height and Body Mass Index-for-age: Methods and Development*. Geneva: World Health Organisation.

Young, S. *et al.* (2012). 'Maternal nutritional status predicts adverse birth outcomes among HIV-infected rural Ugandan women receiving combination antiretroviral therapy', *PloS One*, 7(8): e41934. doi.org/10.1371/journal.pone.0041934.

Zere, E & McIntyre, D (2003). 'Inequities in under-five child malnutrition in South Africa.' *International Journal for Equity in Health* Vol.2: 7. www.equityhealthj.com /content/2/1/7. Accessed 6 July 2010.

CHAPTER 7
Tackling Undernutrition with a 'Cash Plus' Approach

Nicola Hypher, Luke Harman, Kerina Zvobgo and Oluwatosin Akomolafe

1. Introduction

The objective of this chapter is two-fold. Firstly, it aims to provide emerging evidence and learning on the impact of 'cash plus for nutrition' programmes on nutritional outcomes. This is based on wide recognition and coherent evidence that, although cash transfers have a range of outcomes beyond poverty reduction, including on food security and health, the impact on second-order outcomes of cash transfers alone, including on anthropometric outcomes, has been more limited. Secondly, drawing on evidence from recent 'cash plus for nutrition' programmes, the chapter provides some insights into the required design and implementation features of programmes in order to address the multiple drivers of undernutrition.

Globally, in 2011, acute malnutrition (wasting) affected an estimated 52 million children under five years old and contributed to around 800,000 child deaths, around 12 percent of all deaths of children under the age of five (UNICEF et al. 2017, The Lancet 2013). Chronic malnutrition (stunting) affected 155 million or 23 percent of children under five years old and contributed to between 1 to 1.17 million child deaths, around 15 to 17 percent of all child deaths (UNICEF et al. 2017, The Lancet 2013). Maternal undernutrition contributes to 800,000 neonatal deaths annually (Bhutta et al. 2013). Overall, undernutrition is the underlying cause around half of all child deaths, increasing the risk of death from infectious diseases, such as pneumonia, measles, malaria, as well as diarrhoea (Caulfield et al., 2004).

Acute malnutrition is characterised by low weight-for-height, or a mid-upper arm circumference (MUAC) of less than 12.5 cm, or the presence of oedema. It is a short-run indicator of undernutrition and is generally the result of recent rapid weight loss due to hunger and/or disease. Chronic malnutrition is defined in terms of having a low height-for-age and indicates inadequate nutrition over a long period of time and/or an indicator of frequent or repeated infection. Children who measure less than two standard deviations from the mean weight-for-height or height-for-age of a reference group of children experiencing normal growth are considered wasted or stunted respectively.

Evidence shows that good nutrition during the 1,000-days of pregnancy and the first two years of a child's life is essential for children to attain their development potential. Undernutrition during this period can lead to negative short and long-term physical, economic and social consequences that are difficult to reverse (Black et al. 2013, Dewey and Begum 2011). Children in humanitarian contexts are particularly vulnerable to undernutrition; humanitarian emergencies are often characterised by high and rising rates of acute malnutrition, as well as micronutrient deficiencies. In 2013, 65 percent of all children living in conflict zones were chronically undernourished and the prevalence of stunting and wasting is higher in fragile states (IFPRI 2015, IFPRI 2016).

Maternal undernutrition occurs when mothers have inadequate consumption or absorption of one or more nutrients, especially during pregnancy and lactation, which can lead to birth defects and permanent physical or mental delays (Black et al. 2013). Pregnant and lactating women are particularly vulnerable to micronutrient deficiencies, notably deficiencies in iron, Vitamin A and Zinc, mainly because they have a relatively greater need for vitamins and minerals and are more susceptible to the harmful consequences of deficiencies (WHO et al. 2006).

As outlined in Chapter 6 of this volume (by Devereux et al.), there are four underlying causes for child undernutrition: inadequate access to food; inadequate care for women and children; insufficient health services and unhealthy environment; and inadequate education. Income poverty is a major underlying driver of undernutrition in many contexts. Evidence from Asia shows that even in 'normal times' many poor households cannot afford a nutritious diet to prevent undernutrition in addition to essential non-food expenditure; on average, households would need to increase their annual income by almost 1.5 times to be able to afford a nutritious diet in addition to non-food expenditures (Self et al. 2017). Income poverty also undermines a household's potential to achieve a healthy environment and access health services due to costs related to water, sanitation, hygiene and health. Lastly, poverty affects time use and care, especially if pregnant and lactating women are required to work.

Despite the importance of income poverty, in most low-income contexts and many middle-income contexts, undernutrition is something that affects children across all wealth groups, due to the multiple drivers of undernutrition. For example, while the stunting rate among Zambia's least wealthy population quintile in 2013/14 was 47.3 percent, it was still 28.4 percent in the wealthiest quintile (Central Statistical Office, Zambia et al. 2014). A similar picture is found in Ghana and Bangladesh among others (Hong et al., 2006; Hong, 2007). This highlights the key role of non-financial determinants.

Estimates indicate global progress is off track to meet the Global Nutrition Targets 2025 (agreed at 2012 World Health Assembly) on stunting, and that urgent action is needed to scale-up approaches to meet the targets (World Bank et al. 2015). It is estimated that even if ten proven nutrition-specific interventions[1] were scaled up to cover 90 percent of children in countries with the highest burden of stunting, the prevalence of stunting globally would still only reduce by 20 percent and the total number of under-five child deaths by 15 percent (Bhutta et al. 2013, The Lancet 2013). To accelerate progress in reducing undernutrition, there is increasing recognition that nutrition-specific approaches must therefore be complemented with nutrition-sensitive approaches, such as social protection measures and cash transfer programming, which address the underlying drivers of undernutrition and incorporate specific nutrition actions and objectives (Ruel et al. 2013).

2. 'Cash plus for nutrition': An integrated approach to address the pathways of undernutrition

There is wide-ranging, robust evidence demonstrating that cash transfer programmes have positive impacts on poverty reduction and child development, including food security, dietary diversity, health and education (Roelen et al. 2017, Bastagli et al. 2016). In addition, in humanitarian emergencies, cash transfers are increasingly being used as alternatives to general food distribution and supplementary feeding programmes (Bailey and Hedlund 2012, REFANI 2015).

---

1   Nutrition-specific interventions include: folic acid supplementation; micronutrient supplementation in pregnancy and in children; promotion of breastfeeding; appropriate complementary feeding; as well as management of severe acute malnutrition and moderate acute malnutrition.

However, the impact on long-term, second-order outcomes, such as on anthropometric outcomes, has been more limited and has varied across different programmes (Bastagli et al. 2016, Manley, Gitter and Slavchevska 2013, Roelen et al. 2017). Of the 13 studies identified in a large-scale review of cash transfers that reported aggregate effects on stunting, just five found a statistically significant effect (all improvements) (Bastagli et al. 2016). In terms of wasting, just one of five studies reporting impacts in this area found a statistically significant improvement, while just one of eight studies found a statistically significant effect on children being classified as underweight (Bastagli et al. 2016). Although cash transfer design and implementation, including ensuring sufficient transfer values, timely transfers and access to health clinics, is critical, the evidence points to the conclusion of likely needing to complement cash transfers with other actions in order to see more consistently positive effects in improving anthropometric measures (Bastagli et al. 2016, Roelen et al. 2017).

'Cash plus' is a term that is gaining considerable traction and has been applied in programmes to improve a wide range of outcomes (Roelen et al. 2017). The theory of change behind 'cash plus' programming is that behavioural aspects may constrain impacts of cash transfers. Therefore, additional inputs or linkages to services may improve the effectiveness of the cash transfer programme in achieving second-order outcomes by inducing behavioural changes or addressing supply-side constraints (Roelen et al. 2017). Conditionalities are sometimes introduced to cash transfer programmes in the attempt to improve human development outcomes (Bastagli et al. 2016).

'Cash plus for nutrition' aims to reduce the prevalence of stunting and wasting by addressing the nutrition pathways, encompassing the financial and non-financial barriers to household food security, caring practices for women and children, as well as health environment and services. The non-financial barriers may be more related to behaviour and structural constraints. 'Cash plus for nutrition' programmes have two core components. Firstly, a nutrition-sensitive cash transfer, which is designed and implemented taking into account nutritional considerations. Secondly, nutrition-specific interventions and linkages to other sectoral services to improve Infant and Young Child Feeding (IYCF) practices in the first 1000 days, as well as health-seeking behaviour and hygiene and access to treatment of acute malnutrition. By integrating cash transfers with nutrition-specific interventions, 'cash plus for nutrition' interventions help to ensure that households have access to a minimum necessary income to support their purchase of a nutritious diet and other child-related expenditure, particularly related to child health. In addition, nutrition-specific interventions ensure that poor and vulnerable groups have access to nutrition services and interventions that promote behaviour change in support of health and nutrition outcomes. The nutrition-specific interventions may include behavioural change communication (BCC), referrals to health and nutrition services, food or micronutrient supplementation or improve health and nutrition services. Chapter 6 of this volume (Devereux et al. 2018) provides analysis on persistent undernutrition in South Africa, which is a reflection of widespread poverty and non-income drivers. One of the potential responses highlighted in the chapter is cash plus programming with behavioural change communication around good nutrition, feeding and hygiene practices.

There are two main types of 'cash plus for nutrition' programmes: (i) preventative ones that provide income support throughout the first 1,000 days, generally as part of social protection to prevent stunting and wasting; (ii) those that aim to prevent acute malnutrition; and (iii) those that are targeted specifically to children already affected by Moderate or Severe Acute Malnutrition (MAM or SAM) to improve recovery and reduce relapse (Langendorf et al., 2014, Grellety et al., 2017).

3.   Evidence from 'cash plus for nutrition' programmes

This section presents evidence from several programmes that have sought to improve child nutrition outcomes to complement other emerging evidence that cash transfers are more effective on specific child outcomes, and specifically on nutritional outcomes, when complemented with nutrition-specific interventions (Bailey and Hedlund 2012, Ruel et al. 2013, Holmes and Bhuvanendrah 2013). The evidence provided in this chapter demonstrates the impacts on nutritional outcomes from taking a 'cash plus for nutrition' approach, in some cases providing a comparison with cash only. This evidence supports the contention that, if designed and implemented appropriately, cash transfers with an appropriate mix of nutrition-specific interventions can have powerful effects in reducing the incidence of stunting and wasting relative to cash or nutrition-specific interventions alone. The examples of 'cash plus' programmes below were selected from a review carried out by the authors, which identified a total of 26 'cash plus for nutrition' programmes.

The programmes included below were selected based on the following criteria: (1) programme incorporating a cash transfer and nutrition-specific interventions with clear linkages (sometimes as a conditionality) between the two interventions; (2) impact evidence available through rigorous evaluation design, and (3) a predominant focus on Africa given the theme of this edited volume. Table 1 provides a summary of the core features of the programmes. Although all of the programmes aimed to broadly address child undernutrition, they are characterised by different objectives and intervention designs. For example, whereas the primary outcomes of interest in the short-term interventions related to tackling wasting in contexts of crisis, the longer-term programmes are more focused on addressing chronic malnutrition (i.e. stunting). Table 2 provides a summary of the main impact findings from the longer-term programmes.

Table 1.   Summary of programmes included in the review

Programme and country	Evaluation method & study duration	Location and Reach	Cash Transfer element	Nutrition-specific element
Child Development Grant Programme (CDGP) (Nigeria)	Cluster-RCT [Midline evaluation: 2 yrs]	Zamfara and Jigawa states in Northern Nigeria; 70,000 beneficiaries	Unconditional cash transfer of NGN 4,000 provided to pregnant women until their children reach the age of 2	Social and behavioural change communication through food demonstrations, nutrition messaging (via posters, text messages and radio) and health talks. Nutrition support groups and 1:1 counselling also provided in some communities.
Niger Safety Net Project (*Projet Filets Sociaux*)	Cluster-RCT [Endline evaluation: 3 yrs]	Impact evaluation focused on Dosso and Maradi region; 10,000 households.	Unconditional US$20 a month for 24 months. Delivered with various accompanying measures, including activities that encourage households to save & develop income-generating activities	Behavioural change communication to increase community knowledge of children's nutrition and development issues, and to encourage positive parenting practices. Topics based on UNICEF's "Essential Family Practices" modules. Promoted: exclusive breastfeeding for the first six months, adding nutritious foods to a child's diet, and sleeping under insecticide-treated mosquito nets.
Filets Sociaux Jigisémèjiri programme (Mali)	Cluster-RCT [Midline evaluation: 2 yrs]	Six regions (Sikasso, Segou, Mopti, Koulikoro, Kayes, Gao), plus the district of Bamako; 62,000 households	Unconditional transfers of 30,000 FCFA every quarter over a 3-year period (USD 50)	'Accompanying Measures' of two training sessions per month provided by NGOs, covering topics including: use of cash transfers, exclusive breastfeeding, health, complementary feeding, child rights, nutrition practices, WASH.
Transfer Modality Research Initiative (TMRI) (Bangladesh)	Cluster-RCT [Endline evaluation: 2 years]	Selected *upazilas* (sub-units in districts) in North-West and South of Bangladesh; 4,000 ultra-poor women	Conditional cash transfers BGT 1,500 or equivalent food transfers to women with at least one child under the age of 24 months.	Behavioural change communication through group trainings (to participants, household members and communities) and household follow-up visits.

Learning, Evidence Generation & Advocacy for Catalysing Policy (LEGACY) (Myanmar)	Cluster-RCT (Midline evaluation: 1 yr)	Rural villages in three townships (Pakkoku, Yesagyo and Mahlaing) in central dryzone to around 7,000 women	Unconditional cash transfers of 10,000 MYK (increased to 15,000 MYK) to pregnant women until their children reach the age of 2.	Social and behavioural change communication on nutrition and health-seeking topics through mother-to-mother support groups and community nutrition sessions.
Short-term interventions				
Prospective Intervention Study, (Niger)	Quasi-random prospective study (Final evaluation: 5 months)	48 rural villages located within 15 km of a health centre supported by *Forum Santé Niger*, *Medecins Sans Frontieres* in Madaorunfa health district (Maradi region). 5,395 children	Among the seven treatment arms four groups received cash: (1) Cash only group received J43/month ($59); (2) J38/month ($52) with supplementary foods.	Six treatment groups each received different supplementary foods (plus one receiving cash only).
Cluster-randomised trial, (Democratic Republic of the Congo)	Cluster-RCT (Final evaluation: 6 months)	Commune of Bipemba in the city of Mbuji-Mayi, Kasaï-Oriental province. 1481 children formed part of the study.	Unconditional cash transfer of US$40 each month during treatment and follow-up for a total of 6 months. Amount calculated to provide 70 percent of monthly household income for a household of seven people in a 'very poor' household.	Children received treatment according to the national protocols. Included: weekly take-home ration of Ready to Use Therapeutic Foods and routine medicines; measles vaccination and anti-malarial treatment where necessary; weekly follow-up at the health centres; counselling on Infant and Young Child Feeding in the household during a home visit; cooking sessions during the first 3 months.

Sources: e-Pact (2017); World Bank (2016); Hidrobo et al. (2018); Akhter et al. (2016); IPA (2017); Langendorf et al. (2014); Grellety et al. (2017). Chapter 6 of this volume written by Devereux et al

Sources: e-Pact (2017); World Bank (2016); Premand et al. (2016); Hidrobo et al. (2018); Akhter et al. (2016); IPA (2017); Langendorf et al. (2014); Grellety et al. (2017). **Note:** any impacts reported are statistically significant

Table 2.   Impacts: Longer-term programmes

Programme	Health-seeking and antenatal care (ANC)	Knowledge on care and feeding practices	IYCF practices	Child growth outcomes
CDGP, Nigeria	Increase in use of antenatal care (36 per cent in CDGP compared to 20 per cent in non-CDGP)	Positive impacts across a wide range of indicators e.g. increase in knowledge about early initiation; 69 per cent of women and 44 per cent of men in CDGP (compared to 42 per cent for women and 32 per cent for men in non-CDGP)	Increase in exclusive breastfeeding; 70 per cent in CDGP compared to 28 per cent in non-CDGP. Minimum dietary diversity (6-23 months) increase; (52 per cent in CDGP vs. 40 per cent in non-CDGP)	Stunting—decrease in percentage of children born after CDGP classed as stunted (65 per cent in CDGP vs. 71 per cent in non-CDGP)
Safety Net Project, *Projet Filets Sociaux*, Niger	Health—5 percentage points decrease in child illness; 6 percentage points increase in health centre use if sick	Not mentioned in evaluation.	Exclusive breastfeeding—22 percentage point increase; (40 per cent for cash only compared to 62 per cent for cash plus)	No impact
Filets Sociaux Jigisémèjiri, Mali	Health—caregivers 10 percentage point more likely to seek treatment for range of symptoms in their 6–23-month-old child.	Maternal knowledge score (health & nutrition)—No impact	Breastfeeding—2.5 percentage point reduction in proportion of children ever breastfed. Exclusive breastfeeding could not be measured. Timely introduction of (semi-) solid and soft foods—11 percentage point increase. Minimally acceptable diet- 3.6 percentage point increase children 6–23 months. Child dietary diversity score—No impact.	No impact

TMRI, Bangladesh	At least 4 visits to skilled health professional—7 percentage points difference between treatment and control	Maternal knowledge of correct breastfeeding practices (six of more questions answered correctly)—increase by around 30 percentage points compared to baseline for the modalities with BCC. No impact for cash or food only.	Early introduction of water—decrease by around 30 percentage points compared to baseline for modalities with BCC. Likelihood of pre-school children consuming fresh foods and eggs—increase by 22 percentage points and 36 percentage points respectively for 'cash plus' BCC. Diet quality[2]—increase 24 percentage points for 'cash plus' BCC (compared to 7–9 percentage points for other modalities)	Modalities with BCC components led to a significant reduction in stunting (reduced by 7.3 percentage points)
LEGACY, Myanmar		Knowledge across range of indicators—10 percentage points increase—impacts greater for 'cash plus' BCC compared to cash only	Significant positive impact in early initiation of breastfeeding (among others)	Not measured at midline (though preliminary endline results indicate improved anthropometrics)

Sources: e-Pact (2017); World Bank (2016); Premand et al. (2016); Hidrobo et al. (2018); Akhter et al. (2016); IPA (2017); Langendorf et al. (2014); Grellety et al. (2017). **Note:** any impacts reported are statistically significant

1   Consuming 4 food groups and recommended number of meals for a specific child age
2   Measured by the World Food Program's (WFP's) Food Consumption Score

3.1 Impacts on access to and uptake of healthcare and child health outcomes

Two studies reported impacts on use of ANC, with both finding significant improvements in use of ANC. The Child Development Grant Programme (CDGP in Nigeria led to a dramatic increase in the use of ANC by women who were pregnant at the time of the midline survey of 80 percent (16 percentage points, significant at 1 percent level) compared to the control group (36 percent for CDGP compared to 20 percent) (e-Pact 2017). In LEGACY in Myanmar, the 'cash plus' group were 7 percentage points more likely to attend at least four ANC visits. This was despite a short time frame at midline of around 5 months of pregnancy. There was an increase in newborn care, with an increase in the proportion of mothers attending at least one visit to a skilled health professional among those receiving 'cash plus' BCC (IPA 2017).

There were also positive impacts on child health from the programmes. In the Safety Net Project in Niger, illness decreased by 5 percentage points for children whose families received the behavioural change component and they were more likely to visit a health centre when they were sick, an increase by 6 percentage points (World Bank 2017). CDGP in Nigeria was associated with an 8 percentage point decrease in children who had any illness or injury in the previous 30 days. Caregivers that participated in Jigisémèjiri in Mali were 10 percentage points more likely to seek treatment for their child (e-Pact 2017, Hidrobo et al. 2017). In CDGP, there were significant increases in vaccinations, in particular 45 percent of CDGP children had a measles vaccination, compared to 31 percent for non-CDGP (e-Pact 2017). LEGACY had few significant impacts on childhood illness and health-seeking behaviour, which is likely to be due to short timeframe at midline. The programme was associated with a significant decrease in the proportion of mothers that who borrowed money to pay for healthcare (IPA 2017).

3.2. Impacts on knowledge on infant and young child feeding (IYCF)

Of the four programmes that reported on this area, three found significant improvements across a range of indicators. Participation and exposure to BCC interventions appears to be critical to these improvements, which is explored in more detail in the next section. CDGP had large positive impacts on women's and men's knowledge about health and nutrition. For example, 69 percent of women recalled messaging on early initiation of breastfeeding (compared to 42 percent in non-CDGP communities)[1] and there was an 11-percentage point increase in the proportion of men that said that the best place to give birth is at a health facility (41 percent for CDGP communities compared to 29 percent for non-CDGP) (e-Pact 2017).

In the case of LEGACY, there were also substantial impacts on knowledge of IYCF, which were stronger for participants that received 'cash plus' BCC. There was an increase in knowledge on optimal length of breastfeeding of 12 percentage points for both treatment groups, with a slightly larger increase for those that received 'cash plus' BCC (14 percentage points compared to 11 percentage points for cash only). For knowledge on timing for introducing complementary feeding the impacts were only found for mothers that received 'cash plus' BCC (IPA 2017).

For TMRI in Bangladesh, the modalities that were accompanied with BCC saw large and significant impacts on maternal knowledge on nutrition and care related practices, of around 30 percentage points, with no impacts for cash or food only, indicating that the nutrition BCC components increased maternal knowledge, selected hygiene and nutrition (Akhter 2016). Jigisémèjiri' in Mali had no observable impact on knowledge relating to health and nutrition. The authors of the evaluation note that this is very likely due to the fact that there was a limited exposure of mothers to the 'accompanying measures' that would have improved knowledge (Hidrobo et al. 2018).

3.3. Impacts on IYCF practices and dietary diversity

All five programmes report on indicators in this area, with strong positive improvements, albeit with more limited improvements in the case of Jigisémèjiri'. In Jigisémèjiri', an 11-percentage point increase is found in timely introduction of complementary feeding, though the authors believe that this change is due more to increased resources as opposed to increased knowledge as more than half of mothers did not demonstrate accurate knowledge in this area. Although there was a small improvement (3.6 percentage points) in children aged 6–23 months consuming a minimum acceptable diet, there was no significant impact on the child dietary diversity score. The authors highlighted that the targeting of the

---

1   It was found that spillover effects between communities did occur, meaning that impact estimates likely underestimate the true effect of the programme.

cash transfer and accompanying measures to household heads and minimal exposure to accompanying measures in general likely played a role in this (Hidrobo et al. 2018).

All other programmes reported a range of very encouraging improvements in IYCF and dietary diversity. CDGP, for example, found as much as 70 percent of women in intervention areas engaging in exclusive breastfeeding for the first 6 months, which is an improvement of over 200 percent compared to control areas. The programme was also associated with a 31 percent improvement relative to the control group in the proportion of children aged 6 to 23 months receiving the recommended number of food groups (e-Pact 2017). The Niger Safety Net Project recorded exclusive breastfeeding of 62 percent compared to 40 percent in cash only households, an increase of 55 percent, as well as significant increases in introduction of complementary foods for children aged 6 to 9 months old. There was an 11 percent increase in child diet diversity relative to the cash only group for children aged 12 to 23 months (World Bank 2017).

LEGACY led to significant improvements in children receiving a minimum acceptable diet, minimum meal frequency and early initiation of breastfeeding. The impacts were greater for 'cash plus' BCC compared to cash only, suggesting a greater influence of BCC. For example, the proportion of all children meeting a minimum acceptable diet increased from 10 percent to 42 percent (increase of 32 percentage points) for 'cash plus' BCC and to 24 percent for cash only (IPA 2017). In TMRI, mothers participating in the BCC component were significantly less likely to report introducing foods and liquids early, mothers were 29 percent less likely to report early introduction of water in the BCC study arms in the North. TMRI saw increases in child consumption of fresh foods (22 percentage points) and eggs (36 percentage points) and household Food Consumption Score increasing by 24 percentage points relative increases of 7–9 percentage points for the non-cash plus groups (Akhter et al. 2016).

3.4. Impacts on child growth outcomes

When it comes to the main outcomes of interest—improvements in child anthropometric measures—of the four studies that measures indicators in this area, two find very promising significant impacts. CDGP reported a reduction in stunting of 6 percentage points after just two years, and TMRI found a reduction in stunting of 7.3 percentage points after the same period (e-Pact 2017 and Akhter et al. 2016).[2] To give a sense of the magnitude of this impact, the reduction in TMRI represents a reduction of almost three times the national average decline over the same period. In Nigeria, stunting has in fact been increasing in recent years, making the reductions even more remarkable. Interestingly, in the case of CDGP, a small decrease in weight-for-height was observed among beneficiary households (e-Pact 2017). Current thinking is that this may be related to the improvements in stunting, with children being taller for their age, but then relatively thinner for their (increased) height. No impacts were found in TMRI on weight-for-height scores.

While both the Niger Safety Net Project and Jigisémèjiri found no impact on child growth outcomes, both evaluations are instructive in terms of what may be behind this. As highlighted above in the case of Jigisémèjiri, the weak behaviour change communication component appears to have undermined improvements in knowledge and practices relating to child feeding and health, and so it is not surprising that there was no meaningful impact on child nutrition status (Hidrobo et al. 2018). As for the Niger Safety Net Project, the authors point to major weaknesses in the provision of health and social services and a severe lack of adequate water and sanitation.

---

2   At the time of writing, preliminary results of the endline of LEGACY also indicate statistically significant reductions in malnutrition.

Table 3.   Short-term interventions addressing wasting

Programme	Impacts			
	Food security	Incidence of MAM or SAM	Recovery & relapse	Mortality
Cluster-randomised trial, (Democratic Republic of the Congo)	**Food Consumption Score:** 20 (treatment) vs. 6 (control) **% households with 'Acceptable' Food Consumption Score** 93% (intervention) vs. 66% (control)	Not reported.	**Full recovery:** Higher in cash group (hazard ratio for full recovery from SAM 35 percent higher in cash group). **Relapse:** Lower in cash group (adjusted hazard ratios in cash group for relapse to MAM and SAM were 0.21 and 0.30 respectively)	No difference (data insufficient to show any statistical difference)
Prospective Intervention Study, (Niger)	Not reported.	Lowest incidence of MAM and SAM observed in groups receiving cash with their food supplements. MAM twice as low for groups receiving cash with supplements compared to cash only strategy or supplementary food only. SAM three times lower in the group with cash plus supplementary foods, compared with supplementary food only group.	Not reported.	Mortality in three of the groups receiving supplements plus cash significantly reduced compared to the cash-only strategy.

Sources: Langendorf et al. (2014); Grellety et al. (2017). **Note:** any impacts reported are statistically significant.

3.5. Summary of impacts from the short-term interventions

Table 3 summarises impacts of the two short-term interventions. The study in the Democratic Republic of Congo (DRC) found that combining regular treatment with a monthly cash transfer improved household food consumption (to an 'Acceptable' Food Consumption score) for 93 percent of households receiving the cash. This is a significant difference when compared to the just 66 percent of households in the non-cash group who had an 'Acceptable' Food Consumption score (Grellety et al. 2017). The prospective study in Niger found that incidence of MAM and SAM were significantly lower in groups that received cash along with a food supplement compared to cash only or supplement only groups. For example, SAM was as much as three times lower in the group receiving supplementary foods with cash, compared to supplementary foods only (Langendorf et al. 2014). In the DRC programme, children in households receiving cash transfers alongside regular treatment were significantly more likely to experience full recovery from SAM and less likely to relapse back to MAM and SAM (Grellety et al. 2017). Only the study in Niger was able to measure impacts on mortality and found that mortality was significantly reduced among groups that received cash in addition to the nutritional supplements (compared to cash alone) (Langendorf et al. 2014).

4.   Learning on design and implementation of 'cash plus for nutrition'

The programmes included in this review demonstrate that 'cash plus for nutrition' programmes can have large, positive improvements across a wide range of nutrition indicators, relating to improved IYCF knowledge and practices as well as improvements in anthropometric measures such as stunting. The evidence also shows that it is possible to reduce the incidence of moderate and severe acute malnutrition far more effectively by combining either treatment or food supplements with cash transfers. Related to this, although the evidence base is limited, it appears that 'cash plus' approach can also save lives, with the prospective study in Niger finding it led to reduced mortality compared to cash alone (Langendorf et al., 2014). However, given that targeting of the latter type of 'curative' programme is based on acute malnutrition status, it would be beneficial for future research to look at the possibility of any potential adverse incentives arising.

The evidence indicates that design and implementation of programmes, in terms of key aspects of the cash transfer as well as the BCC activities, is critical for ensuring this impact (REFANI 2015). Design of 'cash plus for nutrition' programmes should aim to address the multiple drivers of undernutrition, across the nutrition pathways, in that context and should be based on a causal analysis.

The environment in which the 'cash plus' programme is implemented and continued existence of other drivers of undernutrition are likely to have implications on the design of the intervention and the potential impact. For example, in Niger Safety Net Project, although there were improvements in behaviours, the limited impact on child growth may well be due to the inability of the 'cash plus' positive parenting training to overcome the other drivers of malnutrition, particularly where access to clean water and health services were limited (World Bank 2017). Similarly, in LEGACY, there was no evidence of change in WASH practices or childhood illness related health seeking behaviour, leading the authors to recommend that more focus should be placed on sanitation/hygiene practices and treatment of childhood illness (IPA 2017). The following section provides some insights and lessons on design and implementation of 'cash plus for nutrition' programmes, based on a review of the literature, as well as programme experiences and impacts from the programmes included in this review.

4.1. Targeting of interventions

As demonstrated in the studies included in this review, 'cash plus for nutrition' programmes that aim to reduce prevalence of stunting should target the first 1000 days. All the long-term programmes included in the study reached children under the age of two, and both LEGACY and CDGP also reached women during pregnancy. In the case of CDGP, the evaluation only found an impact on stunting for those children born after the household started to receive the programme interventions, which may provide further evidence of the critical importance of the first 1000 days, including reaching women during pregnancy. By reaching women during pregnancy, the pregnant women will be better able to access a nutritious diet in pregnancy, will receive early messaging on nutrition and health as well as in receiving antenatal care, especially if the health centre is involved in targeting of the programme. CDGP and LEGACY are implemented in areas with high levels of stunting and therefore, opted for a universal approach of mothers in those areas. This was based on evidence from these areas that large proportions of the population experience affordability gaps in meeting the cost of a nutritious diet and high stunting levels across wealth groups (Save the Children 2016, Save the Children 2017). This is supported by other evidence on some of the challenges of narrower poverty-based targeting (Kidd 2013).

Two different approaches were followed in the short-term programmes. The Prospective Intervention study in Niger aimed to prevent non-malnourished children from becoming MAM as well as to prevent children that are already classified as MAM from becoming worse or transitioning to SAM and therefore targeted children age 6 to 24 months, with length taken as a proxy of age (Langendorf et al. 2014). The programme in DRC aimed to improve recovery from SAM and therefore, was targeted to children with uncomplicated SAM (Grellety et al. 2017). Both interventions were based around the catchment areas of health centres (Langendorf et al. 2014; Grellety et al. 2017).

Evidence indicates that the programme beneficiary within the household may influence the impact on nutrition, particularly through potential impacts on household care and investment in children. Many cash transfer programmes transfer resources to the primary caregiver, predominantly mothers, to increase the use of the cash transfer on food and care for the pregnant woman or child in the first 1000 days (Pellerano and Barca 2014, Bastagli et al. 2016). The evidence is mixed on the potential impact on nutrition, including on the potential for perpetuating intra-household tensions or negative impact on child care (Hagen-Zanker et al. 2016). In the majority of programmes considered in this review the mother was the primary beneficiary. In the case of CDGP, the evaluation found that women generally retained control over the transfer with over 90 percent of mothers being part of decisions on how to spend the transfer, and around 70 percent being the predominant decision-maker (e-Pact 2017). Similarly, in LEGACY, women reported exercising control of how the transfers were used. Although in CDGP the primary beneficiary was the mother, a proxy was identified who would be able to collect the transfer on behalf of the main recipient, especially for late in pregnancy.

In Jigisémèjiri, the household head was the primary person engaging with the programme and deciding how to use the cash transfer (Hirobo et al. 2018). In all five long-term programmes, the BCC components were targeted to the main recipient of the programme. However, the majority of programmes also aimed to reach other household members and community members more broadly.

4.2. Cash transfers

The design and implementation of cash transfers shapes the potential impact on nutrition, by improving the positive impacts and mitigating negative impacts on household investment in children and childcare practices. These considerations include the choice of modality, amount, frequency and duration of transfers. The TMRI study included a comparison of food and cash transfers. While both modalities combined with BCC had large and significant impacts on knowledge and practices related to nutrition, cash was used more readily to diversify diets (Akhter et al. 2016).

For nutritional impact, cash transfers are distributed regularly, typically monthly, in order to smooth consumption and allow for year-round consumption of nutritious foods and health coverage (Bastagli et al. 2016). The programmes included in this review, such as CDGP, LEGACY, TMRI and Jigisémèjiri, were characterised with regular cash transfers as intended, typically monthly except for Jigisémèjiri, which provided transfers quarterly. Beneficiaries tended to receive the correct transfer amounts (e-Pact 2017, Hirobo 2018, Akhter et al. 2018, IPA 2017).

Evidence shows that the transfer size and duration are critical for determining impacts on nutrition in the first 1000 days (Bastagli et al. 2016). In CDGP and LEGACY, the cash transfer amount was informed by analysis to determine the cost of a nutritious diet (Save the Children 2016, 2017). For CDGP and LEGACY, cost of diet analysis found that the transfer made a significant impact in the affordability of a nutritious diet for the household and particularly for the mothers and children's diets from six months (Save the Children 2016, 2017). However, the values did not fully close the affordability gap and in both cases the transfer values have increased since the evaluation and there is some potential to further improve affordability (Save the Children 2016, 2017). The cash transfer amounts tended to be higher in the short-term interventions that aimed to prevent or address acute malnutrition during a crisis.

The payment mechanism, either physical distribution of cash or electronic payment mechanisms, may affect impact on nutrition. Electronic payment mechanisms may reduce the direct and indirect costs of accessing the cash transfer, with impacts on nutrition, due to changes in childcare and feeding practices (Bastagli et al. 2016). Several of the programmes included in this study used mobile money or banking-based payment mechanisms, including MCCT, TMRI, CDGP and Jigisémèjiri. This demonstrates that although electronic payment mechanisms pose challenges in terms of network coverage and illiteracy, they can be used in challenging environments that are characterised in these programmes. In CDGP, voice and text messaging were also used as a channel for nutrition messaging and around 40 percent of beneficiaries reported receiving messaging from this channel (e-Pact 2017).

4.3. Nutrition-specific activities

Similarly, it is important to combine the cash transfer with well-designed and implemented nutrition activities. These activities play a key role in improving health and nutrition knowledge and practices as well as in promoting access to health and nutrition services. In order to promote nutritional outcomes, programmes can use a combination of supplementary feeding, BCC and explicit referrals to health and nutrition services (Roelen et al. 2017).

BCC activities are based on a recognition that lack of knowledge may undermine programme impacts, and that the outcomes may be strengthened by awareness raising around the use of the transfer to purchase nutritious foods as well as on a range of nutrition and health related behaviours and practices (Roelen et al. 2017). The design of BCC will need to be informed by analysis into knowledge, attitudes and practices as well as an understanding of the main barriers in a specific context.

The programmes included in this review demonstrate the importance of high levels of participation in BCC despite transfers not being conditional on participation (except in TMRI). This supports the assertion that combining cash transfers with other interventions may be sufficient to ensure beneficiaries participate in BCC (Pellerano and Barca

2014, Bastagli et al. 2016). In most cases, BCC is targeted to beneficiaries, particularly women; influential household members, such as husbands and to the wider community. In Jigisémèjiri the BCC, known as 'accompanying measures' were not targeted and were available to any household. This section summarises the strategies undertaken by the programmes included in this review and draws some lessons from the implementation and impact of the BCC components.

In CDGP, community volunteers delivered BCC to mothers, husbands and community members in the form of food demonstrations, messaging via text, calls or posters, health talks as well as for a subset of beneficiaries more intensive BCC through support groups and one-to-one counselling. LEGACY provided messaging on nutrition and health-seeking through mother-to-mother support groups and community nutrition sessions. In TMRI, there were participant group trainings, trainings for family members and communities and follow-up household visits on nutrition and WASH delivered by community nutrition workers. The Niger Safety Net project provided meetings and home visits by community educators, following training and supported by refresher courses and NGO coaching (World Bank 2017). Jigisémèjiri conducted two training sessions a month in each village that were organised in groups of themes, with the full curriculum taking six months. This information is also presented at cash transfer distributions.

The BCC components demonstrate some successes and challenges, from which useful lessons can be learned. In the Niger Safety Net Project, participation was very high, with 92 percent of cash transfer beneficiaries taking part regularly and many who did not receive the cash transfers also participated in community meetings (World Bank 2017). In TMRI, participants on average attended 48 sessions per year (Akhter et al. 2016). In CDGP 90 percent of women and 83 percent of men recalled being exposed to at least one BCC channel. The multiple channels within CDGP was critical as men and women accessed BCC channels differently. Women mainly accessed messaging from posters and food demonstrations, both with around 70 percent of women exposed to the channels; whereas men were far less likely to attend health talks or food demonstrations and mainly accessed messaging from radio, followed by posters (e-Pact 2017). For TMRI, the evaluation stated that delivery of the BCC was initially weak but improved over time and the programme was characterised with a well-developed curriculum. Participation in BCC sessions was 89 percent in the implementation areas in the north and 70 percent in the south of the country, with the latter reportedly affected by illness. In the north, 92 percent of respondents reported that a community nutrition worker visited them at home if they missed a session, as stipulated in the guidelines. In Jigisémèjiri, about 60 percent of beneficiary households reported attending at least one accompanying measure session but the number they reported attending on average was low (for example, in Sikasso, beneficiaries on average attended 6 sessions compared to 30 sessions that were scheduled).

Several challenges with delivery of BCC were identified. Firstly, in some cases it took time to develop and implement an effective BCC component. This was the case in TMRI and CDGP and includes challenges around recruitment and training of the community volunteers and nutrition workers that play a critical role in implementing the programme (Akhter 2017; Save the Children 2015). Similarly, in Niger's Safety Net Project, 25 percent of community educators didn't have the required knowledge to effectively conduct activities, in part due to widespread illiteracy, and some home visits were shorter and less interactive than planned (World Bank 2017). There are critical trade-offs between the scale and intensity of BCC. The findings of Niger's Safety Net Project highlight that the delivery model was designed to allow implementation at scale in low income settings. In CDGP, although two intensities of BCC were implemented, the evaluation found minimal differences in terms of participation and impact across the two approaches.

Referrals and linkages provide automatic access or facilitate access to services that are critical to improved impacts on nutrition, for example through improved case management, such as through a functioning Management Information System (MIS) (Roelen et al. 2017). This may include antenatal and postnatal care, treatment of wasting through Community Management of Acute Malnutrition (CMAM), child health services as well as sanitation and hygiene supplies and products. Evidence from the cash transfer programme in DRC demonstrated the impact of strengthening the linkages between a cash transfer and CMAM, in terms of improved recovery and reduced relapse (Grellety et al. 2017). Nutritious supplementary food has also been shown to improve impact on nutrition. There is positive evidence of providing nutritional supplements with a cash transfer in Niger; relative to cash alone, the impact was a halving of moderate acute malnutrition (Langendorf et al. 2014).

5. Conclusion

Drawing on recent evidence from 'cash plus for nutrition' programmes, this chapter demonstrates multiple impacts of such programmes on nutrition practices and outcomes. There appears to be consistent impacts on IYCF knowledge and practices and some evidence of impacts on anthropometric measures, such as stunting. Notable positive impacts were found on use of antenatal care (ANC), children's health, as well as in breastfeeding practices and dietary diversity for children aged between 6 and 24 months. Where the evaluations provided a comparison with cash only, 'cash plus for nutrition' programmes demonstrated greater impacts or enabled an impact where there wasn't otherwise an impact. For the two programmes that reported impacts on stunting, there were significant positive impacts of around 6 percentage points for 'cash plus' BCC interventions. For short-term programmes aiming to prevent, or to improve treatment of, wasting, there was reduced incidence of wasting.

The chapter also provided insights into the key aspects of effective design and implementation to improve impact of nutrition by drawing on the design of these programmes and learning from the evaluations. 'cash plus for nutrition' programmes comprise of a cash transfer that is designed and implemented, taking into account nutrition considerations as well as nutrition-specific interventions that promote improved nutrition practices and access to services. 'Cash plus for nutrition' programmes work by addressing the nutrition pathways and, therefore, should be based on contextual causal analysis.

'Cash plus for nutrition' programmes aim to reach mothers and infants during the critical window of the first 1000 days. It may be particularly critical to reach mothers during pregnancy in ensuring impact on stunting, due to improvements in pregnant women's diets and improvements in use of ANC. Although there is mixed evidence on the impact of targeting programmes to mothers as the primary caregiver, for the programmes included in this review, it was found that women did retain control of the cash transfer and were able to decide how to use the transfer.

The programmes in this review were implemented in challenging and remote contexts. Despite this, the programmes provided regular transfers of the intended transfer amount. In addition, several of interventions used electronic payment mechanisms, such as bank or mobile phones, which improved convenience for the recipients, potentially limiting the possible negative impact on childcare and, in some cases, provided an additional channel for distributing nutrition messaging.

It is important that the behavioural change component (BCC) is well-designed and implemented. Behavioural change communication activities should be designed to ensure high levels of participation among primary caregivers, with activities that also reach other family and community members. Multiple channels may be useful in ensuring maximum update across a broad range of participants and effective communications requires well-trained nutrition workers or volunteers. Lastly, the environment in which the 'cash plus' programme is implemented and continued existence of other drivers of undernutrition, particularly with respect to health and WASH, is likely to have implications on the design and potential impact of the intervention.

References

Ahmed, Akhter; Hoddinott, John; Roy, Shalini; Sraboni, Esha; Quabili, Wahidur; Margolies, Amy (2016). "Which Kinds of Social Safety Net Transfer Work Best for the Ultra Poor in Bangladesh?" Operation and Impacts of the Transfer Modality Research Initiative. International Food Policy Research Institute (IFPRI) and World Food Programme (WFP).

Bailey S, Hedlund K (2012). *The impact of cash transfers on nutrition in emergency and transitional contexts: A review of the evidence.* London: Overseas Development Institute.

Bastagli, F.; Hagen-Zanker, J.; Harman, L.; Sturge, G.; Barca, V.; Schmidt, T.; Pellerano L.; (2016). *Cash transfers: What does the evidence say? A rigorous review of impacts and the role of design and implementation features.* Research report. London: Overseas Development Institute (https://www.odi.org/sites/odi.org.uk/files/resource-documents/11316.pdf).

Benhassine et al. (2013). *Turning a shove into a nudge? A 'labeled cash transfer' for education.* Working Paper 19227. Cambridge, MA: National Bureau of Economic Research.

Bhutta ZA, Das JK, Rizvi A, Gaffey MF, Walker N, et.al. (2013). "Evidence-based interventions for improvement of maternal and child nutrition: what can be done and at what cost." *The Lancet* Vol.382, no 9890. 452–477.

Black, R.E., et al. (2013). "Maternal and Child Undernutrition and Overweight in Low-income and Middle-income Countries." *The Lancet*. Vol. 382, no. 9890: 427–451.

Caulfield, L.; de Onis, M.; Blössner, M.; and Black, R. (2004). "Undernutrition as an underlying cause of child deaths associated with diarrhea, pneumonia, malaria, and measles." *American Journal of Clinical Nutrition* 2004; 80:193–8.

Central Statistical Office (CSO) [Zambia], Ministry of Health (MOH) [Zambia], and ICF International (2014). *Zambia Demographic and Health Survey 2013–14*. Rockville, Maryland, USA: Central Statistical Office, Ministry of Health, and ICF International.

Dewey, K. G. and Begum, K. (2011). "Long-term consequences of stunting in early life." *Maternal & Child Nutrition*, 7: 5–18. doi:10.1111/j.1740-8709.2011.00349.

e-Pact Consortium (2016). Child Development Grant Programme Evaluation: Qualitative Midline Report. Oxford Policy Management, ITAD and Institute of Fiscal Studies. Oxford. https://www.opml.co.uk/files/Publications/8214-evaluati on-child-development-grant-programme/cdgp-qualitative-midline-report.pdf?no redirect=1.

ePact (2017). Child Development Grant Programme Evaluation: Quantitative Midline Report.Oxford Policy Management, ITAD and Institute of Fiscal Studies. Oxford. https://www.opml.co.uk/files/Publications/8214-evaluation-child-development-grant-programme/cdgp-quantitative-midline-report-volume-i.pdf?noredirect=1.

Grellety, E., Babakazo P., Bangana A., Mwamba G., Lezama I., Zagre N. and Ategbo E. (2017). "Effects of unconditional cash transfers on the outcome of treatment for severe acute malnutrition (SAM): A cluster-randomised trial in the Democratic Republic of the Congo." *BMC Medicine*. 15:87.

Hagen-Zanker, J., Bastagli, F., Harman, L., Barca, V., Sturge, G., Schmidt, T. (2016). *Understanding the impact of cash transfers: the evidence*. ODI Briefing. London: Overseas Development Institute.

Hidrobo, M., Roy, S., Huybregts, L., Njee-Bugha, L., Sessou, E., Kameli, Y. (2018). *Filets Sociaux (Jigisémèjiri) Program Midline Report*. Jigisémèjiri. International Food Policy Research Institute (IFPRI), Institut de Recherche pour le Développement (IRD).

Hoddinott, John (2016). *The economics of reducing malnutrition in Sub-Saharan Africa*. Global Panel on Agriculture and Food Systems for Nutrition Working Paper.

Holmes, R. & Bhuvanendrah, D. (2013). *Social protection and resilient food systems: The role of cash transfers*. London: Overseas Development Institute.

Hong, R. (2007). "Effect of economic inequality on chronic childhood undernutrition in Ghana." *Public Health and Nutrition*. 10(4): 371–378.

Hong, R., Banta, J., and Betancourt, J.; (2006). "Relationship between household wealth inequality and chronic childhood undernutrition in Bangladesh." *International Journal of Equity in Health*. Dec 5: 5–15.

Innovations for Poverty Action (IPA) (2017). *LEGACY Project—Randomised Controlled Trial—Midline report*. IPA and Save the Children.

International Food Policy Research Institute (IFPRI) (2015). *2014–2015 Global Food Policy Report*. Washington DC. IFPRI.

International Food Policy Research Institute (IRPRI) 2016. *Global Nutrition Report 2016: From Promise to Impact, Ending Malnutrition by 2030*. Washington, D.C. http://dx.doi.org/10.2499/9780896295841.

Kidd, Stephen (2013). "Rethinking 'Targeting' in International Development." *Pathway's Perspectives on Social Policy in International Development*. Issue No. 11. Oxford: Development Pathways.

Langendorf C, Roederer T, de Pee S, Brown D, Doyon S, et al. (2014). "Preventing Acute Malnutrition among Young Children in Crises: A Prospective Intervention Study in Niger." *PLOS Medicine* 11(9): e1001714. https://doi.org/10.1371/journal.pm ed.1001714.

Manley, J., Gitter, S., and Slavchevska, V. (2013). "How effective are cash transfers at improving nutritional status?" *World Development*, Vol. 48: 133–155.

Pellerano L and Barca V. (2014). *Does one size fit all? The conditions for conditionality in cash transfers*. OPM Working Paper 2014-1. Oxford: Oxford Policy Management.

Premand, P., Barry, O., Smitz, M. (2016) Transferts monétaires, valeur ajoutée de mesures d'accompagnement comportemental, et développement de la petite enfance au Niger: Rapport de l'évaluation d'impact à court terme du Projet Filets Sociaux. Washington, D.C. World Bank Group. http://documents.worldbank.org /curated/en/122221467609922455/Transferts-monétaires-valeur-ajoutée-de-mesures-daccompagnement-comportemental-et-développement-de-la-petite-e nfance-au-Niger-Rapport-de-lévaluation-dimpact-à-court-terme-du-Projet-Filets.

REFANI Consortium (2015) *Literature review: Research on Food Assistance for Nutritional Impact*. Action Against Hunger (ACF), Concern Worldwide, Emergency Nutrition Network, University College London (UCL).

Roelen, K, Devereux S, Abdulai A, Martorano B, Palermo T and Ragno L (2017). "How to Make 'Cash Plus' Work: Linking Cash Transfers to Services and Sectors." *Innocenti Working Paper 2017-10*. Florence: UNICEF Office of Research.

Ruel, Marie T et al. (2013). "Nutrition-sensitive interventions and programmes: How can they help to accelerate progress in improving maternal and child nutrition?" *The Lancet*, Vol. 382 (9891): 536–551.

Save the Children (2012) *State of the World Mothers*. Westport and London. Save the Children.

Save the Children (2015a). *Malnutrition in Bangladesh: Harnessing Social Protection for the most vulnerable*. London. Save the Children.

Save the Children (2015b). *Child Development Grant Programme. Implementation Manual and Programme documents*. Abuja, Nigeria.

Save the Children (2016). Rapid Market Analysis to update the CDGP Cost of Diet Report 2015. Abuja. Nigeria.

Save the Children (2017). *A Cost of the Diet analysis in the Dry Zone, Myanmar: Pakokku, Mahlaing & Yesagyo townships*. Yangon, Myanmar.

Self, V., Childs, R. and Swift, L. (2017). *How families Cope with Poverty in Asia.* London. Save the Children.

Smith, L., and Haddad, L., (2014). "Reducing Child Undernutrition: Past Drivers and Priorities for the Post-MDG Era." IDS Working Paper 2014 No 44. Brighton: Institute of Development Studies.

The Lancet (2013). Executive Summary of The Lancet Maternal and Child Nutrition Series. *The Lancet* Vol.382, no 9890. 452–477.

UNICEF (2017). "UNICEF Data on Malnutrition" https://data.unicef.org/topic/nutrition/malnutrition/. Accessed 28th December 2017.

UNICEF, WHO and World Bank Group (2017). *Joint Child Malnutrition Estimates; Key findings of the 2017 Edition.* https://www.who.int/nutgrowthdb/estimates2016/en/. Accessed 17th February 2019.

WHO, WFP and UNICEF (2006) *Preventing and controlling micronutrient deficiencies in populations affected by an emergency.* Joint statement by the World Health Organization, the World Food Programme and the United Nations Children's Fund Geneva. 2006.

World Bank (2017) NIGER: Can cash and behavioral change programs improve child development? For Evidence to Policy. Washington D.C. World Bank.

World Bank, Results for Development, 1000 days, The Children's Investment Fund Foundation (CIFF) and The Bill and Melinda Gates Foundation (2015). *Reaching the Global Target to Reduce Stunting: How Much Will it Cost and How Can We Pay for It?* Policy Brief (accessed 17 February 2019) http://thousanddays.org/tdays-content/uploads/Stunting-Costing-and-Financing-Overview-Brief.pdf.

CHAPTER 8
Unconditional Cash Transfers and Business Grants: Do Transfer Amounts and Labels Make a Difference for Children?[1]

Billow Hassan, Stephen Mutiso and Munshi Sulaiman

1. Introduction

Poverty is strongly negatively associated with many child wellbeing indicators such as education, health and protection. Households with higher incomes tend to have children who eat better, are healthier and are more likely to go to schools than households with lower income. Therefore, it is often assumed that interventions that are successful in increasing household income will also benefit children. Cash transfers are also often used as an instrument for supporting poor households to increase their income through self-employment. However, the extent to which cash transfers or increased income through economic strengthening stand to benefit children directly is debatable (Roelen, 2015; see also Chapter 6 in this volume).

In the protracted humanitarian context of Somalia, evaluations of cash transfers are usually limited to comparing changes in household food security before and after transfers. There has hardly been any effort towards measuring the impacts of the transfers (such as nutritional and learning outcomes), let alone systematic comparison of effectiveness of possible variations in cash size, frequency or transfer modality. While there are several studies that assess the impacts of lump-sum cash transfers on stimulating micro-entrepreneurship, increasing income of poor households and on reducing poverty (Sulaiman, 2018)[2], the downstream effects of these intervention on children's wellbeing is particularly under-studied. This study compares the extent to which the

1   We are grateful to active support from the teams of Save the Children in Mogadishu and Hiran under BRCiS consortium. Special thanks to Abdullahi Arays, Abdulahi Alasow Hilowle and Abdulkadir Abdi for their active roles in implementation of the research. The study involved projects supported by UKAID, DEVCO and German Federal Foreign Office. All errors are ours.
2   Sulaiman (2018) includes a meta-analysis of 11 studies on cash transfers to compare against other anti-poverty interventions.

provision of different amounts of cash transfers lead to short-term impacts on household investment in businesses, income, and food security as well as on children's education, health, and nutritional status.

Small businesses are everywhere in developing countries, with hundreds of millions of people engaged in some form of self-employed, micro-entrepreneurial activity (Kushnir et al., 2010). These micro-entrepreneurs face complex financial decisions each day—how much to invest, what to invest in, and where and how to find work on a daily basis. There are many challenges in running a business, such as limited access to credit, stagnant growth, and low business survival (Bruhn et al., 2010; McKenzie and Woodruff, 2016). At the same time, studies find that businesses have opportunities of making profitable investments, ranging from 5–20 percent per month (De Mel et al., 2008; Udry and Anagol, 2006; McKenzie and Woodruff, 2008; Banerjee and Duflo, 2014; Fafchamps et al., 2014). More recently, a number of studies look at cases when cash is provided with "no strings attached," and find that unconditional cash transfers can significantly increase business investment and sales (De Mel et al., 2008; Udry and Anagol, 2006; McKenzie and Woodruff, 2008; Fafchamps et al., 2014). GiveDirectly, an NGO set up for cash transfer with very low operational costs, have conducted randomized experiments in Kenya on giving out cash to poor households—an unconditional cash transfer—and these were found to lead to large investments into the home, business, and health of the family (Haushofer and Shapiro, 2016).

Unconditional cash transfers (UCT) have become a common feature in social protection and humanitarian programming. However, there is a key distinction between transfers being made in small instalments over a longer period, compared to lump sum business grants being provided with the objective to start or expand micro-enterprise. The GiveDirectly study find that lump sum transfers are more likely to be spent on household durables and building assets compared to monthly transfers (Haushofer and Shapiro, 2016). A more recent study by Bastian et al. (2017) in northern Nigeria compares the provision of transfers of the same amount with varying frequencies of payment, namely monthly versus quarterly disbursements. This study finds similar effects across food security and assets outcomes and conclude in favour of lumping transfers to improve cost-effectiveness.

Most of these studies on business grant and unconditional cash transfers are focused on understanding the constraints that poor households face in sustainable increases of their income. However, very few studies look at the "downstream" effects of their interventions on children, which this study aims to do. It also considers the additional effect of labelling.

This study was conducted in Somalia to test the marginal effects of additional capital transferred to micro-entrepreneurs. The cash size was randomly varied at individual level whereby beneficiaries received a "small" ($100–250), "medium" ($500) or "large" ($1,000) size of cash grant.[3] The group receiving small transfers was divided into a group whose grants were labelled as unconditional cash transfers, and another group receiving it as income generating activity (IGA) or business grants. Medium and large transfers were labelled as business grants.

We find that the small transfers labelled as business grants had positive impacts on business income, food security and savings, compared to small transfers that were labelled as unconditional transfers. A quarter of the capital transferred through medium and larger business grants is found to have been invested in business, and has resulted in higher income from business. However, the larger transfers have not yielded substantial effects on children, at least not within the short period of this evaluation. We do not find any impact on child nutrition or health. The only significant effect is a six percentage point increase in school enrolment for primary school-aged children for the households having received the large cash transfer.

With this introduction, Section 2 explains the study design, data collection and analysis methods. Section 3 discusses household level findings—economic activities, assets, consumption and food security. Section 4 focuses on measuring child level outcomes to show whether these household level impacts commensurate with the effects on children. Section 5 discusses robustness of the results and some limitations. Section 6 concludes the chapter.

---

3   Cash transfers were done in USD, which is a common practice in Somalia. We use $ sign to refer to USD.

2.   Evaluation design

This study was conducted by leveraging two projects implemented by Save the Children in Somalia. Both projects, "Humanitarian Support and Re-Integration of IDP and Returnees in Mogadishu," supported by German Federal Foreign Office (FFO) and "Building Resilience in Hiran," supported by International Cooperation and Development (DEVCO) of European Commission, included support for micro-business establishment or expansion. Despite the humanitarian and development orientation of the two projects, the support for micro-business development was identical. This study randomly varied the size of cash grants received by the selected beneficiaries to measure the marginal effects of larger transfers.

2.1 Context and participants' profile

With decades of conflict and severe drought at regular intervals, Somalia has been in chronic humanitarian crisis. The country is consistently ranked among the lowest in most social indicators where data is available, e.g. life expectancy, maternal and infant mortality (UNDP, 2018). Basic social services such as education, health and nutrition are still predominantly reliant on humanitarian agencies. The economy is heavily dependent on livestock rearing and remittances. Agriculture is limited to small parts of the country, and highly dependent on rainfall. Consequently, humanitarian support, in the form of UCT or food vouchers, are common phenomena for the country. In recent years, there has been increased focus on resilience building among the agencies working in the country.[4] Creating economic opportunities through small businesses is one of the tools for such initiatives. Given that a large portion of the population lives at various internally displaced person (IDP) camps for years on end, humanitarian support often focuses work in these areas. Another contextual factor to consider is the severe drought that affected the whole country during the study period.

The study was conducted at fourteen IDP camps in Mogadishu and in five urban communities in Hiran region. Baseline data shows low levels of economic opportunities for the population. Only approximately one-

---

4   Although there is no universally accepted definition of resilience, the general idea of this approach is to build ability for the households to better cope with shocks and recover faster from any shock that they experience.

third of all households had any form of wage income, predominantly casual labour, in the month preceding the survey. Only 20 percent of households had any income from micro-businesses, and over 40 percent of the households did not have any cash earning in the previous month. With average household size of 6.4 members and 0.7 earners per household, these households live in extreme poverty. However, beneficiaries selected from the urban communities in Hiran did have better economic status than their counterparts did from the IDP camps of Mogadishu.

Given the low income and lack of public social services, children from these households suffer from various deprivations. School enrolment rates of the primary school aged children (6–13 years) were only 16 percent in Mogadishu and 55 percent in Hiran. Girls in both sites were found to be less likely in school than the boys (12 percent vs. 20 percent in Mogadishu, and 53 percent vs. 57 percent in Hiran). Because of poor nutritional status, children frequently suffer from various illnesses. At baseline, 8 percent of the children (aged less than 18 years) were reported to have suffered any illness in last two weeks. More importantly, over 40 percent of these children did not seek any healthcare for their illnesses. Using mid-upper arm circumference (MUAC) as a proxy, we found extremely high level of malnutrition in these households with 26 percent of the 6–59 months-old children being malnourished at baseline. Only 22 percent of the 12–59 months-old children received full immunization.

2.2. Treatment groups

This study used randomization approach to measure the marginal effects of "lumpy" and larger cash grants compared to a "typical UCT". Because of ethical as well as feasibility concerns in not providing any support to a portion of study participants, we did not include a pure control group. Field officers of the two projects identified eligible beneficiaries following standard selection process.[5] The community was informed that the

---

5   Beneficiary selection is done by forming a village relief committee in each community consisting of clan leaders and people respected in the communities. This committee organizes open meetings attended by Save the Children field officers. They collectively identify the characteristics of vulnerable households and determine the eligible beneficiaries. Verification of the eligible beneficiaries is done by the project team based on project specific criteria.

transfer amounts received by the households are to be determined at a later stage, but that all the selected households will receive grants. The cash was transferred through mobile money, which is very common in Somalia as most humanitarian agencies use this for delivery of UCT. After the selection process was completed, the allocation of transfer types was determined through a public lottery that was attended by the beneficiaries. There were four types of transfers included in the lottery.

As Figure 1 shows, the size of transfers for households in Groups 1 and 2 varied between the two sites. This was due to budget constraints of the two projects and the programmatic necessity of disbursing the amounts within the project timeframe. In Mogadishu, the small transfer was $250 whereas in Hiran it was $100. However, in both cases, the same approach was adopted to make the transfer in two monthly instalments (Group 1) and one instalment (Group 2). Transfer sizes for Groups 3 and 4 were $500 and $1,000 respectively. The transfer took place in January and February of 2017 after the baseline survey.

Figure 1.   Randomized treatment groups by site

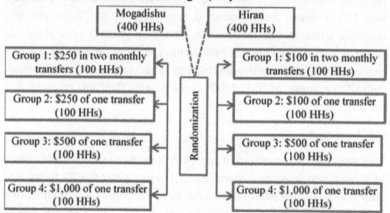

In addition to the variation in transfer sizes, there is another important difference for Groups 2, 3 and 4 compared to Group 1. For Group 1, the transfer was framed as an unconditional cash transfer, whereas the other three groups were told about the transfers as business grants. Beneficiaries of these three business grant groups also participated in week-long business training conducted by a consultant for 1–2 hours per day. The training covered generic modules on planning, accounting, costing and marketing. This training took place after the business grants were disbursed, and there was no conditionality attached for the use of cash.[6] The participants were aware that they could spend the cash for any purpose although they were encouraged to use this for investment.

2.3. Data and impact measurements

Baseline data was collected between December 2016 and January 2017 after the beneficiary selection was done. Out of the 800 selected households, 795 households could be interviewed at baseline. The public lottery took place after the baseline survey was conducted. The cash transfers were done in late January and February 2017, and the business training was rolled out in February and March. We conducted a follow-up survey in May–June 2017. Therefore, the study measures short-term effects of the cash transfers.

Table 1.   Attrition rate between baseline and follow-up

	Baseline Sample	Attrition rate (%)		
		Mogadishu	Hiran	Total
Group 1 (UCT)	200	7.0	2.0	4.5
Group 2 (low cash)	200	5.1	1.0	3.0
Group 3 ($500)	200	4.2	18.0	11.2
Group 4 ($1,000)	200	6.0	0.0	3.0
Total	800	5.6	5.3	5.4

In the follow-up survey, we managed to interview 752 of the baseline households with a 5 percent attrition rate (i.e. households who could not be interviewed at the follow-up survey). Given the limited focus on collecting panel data in most evaluations in Somalia, this can be considered as a good attrition rate. As mentioned earlier, this has been a period of severe drought for the whole country, which caused many households to migrate to different locations. The attrition rates are similar between the two sites (5.6 percent in Mogadishu and 5.3 percent in Hiran). However, there is significant difference in attrition rate between the treatment arms (Table 1). The medium sized business grant recipients of Hiran (Group 2) had an attrition rate of 18 percent, which is remarkably

---

6   The study also embedded a "cross-cutting" randomization in baseline survey whereby half of the participants answered five additional questions related to use of cash and business income in order to better the lives of their children. This was done as an exploratory work and further details of the results are available on request. Overall, this "nudge experiment" did not produce major positive effects.

higher than the rest of the groups. We could not find any valid explanation for this differentially high attrition rate for this particular group.

We used randomization to identify the impacts attributable to the different cash sizes. In addition, we included baseline values of respective outcome indicators and site dummy as control variable in the following regression.

$$y_{iF} = \alpha + \beta_1 SBG_i + \beta_2 MBG_i + \beta_3 SBG_i + \delta_1 y_{iB} + \delta_2 S_i + \varepsilon_i$$

Where y_{iF} are the outcome indicators for household i at follow-up period, and y_{iB} are the corresponding values at baseline, δ_2 is the fixed effects for Hiran. In this specification, β_1 measures the marginal effect of receiving the small cash transfers in one instalment and the business training. β_2 and β_3 measures the *marginal effects* of receiving the additional cash and the business training. Given the differential attrition, we used inverse probability weight factors in all regressions following Wooldrige (2002). This method gives more weight to the types of households who were likely to have been lost in the follow-up. However, given the very small rate of attrition, the choice of using weights does not have qualitative implications with respect to the results. To address the effects of possible outliers, for all monetary outcomes, we winsorized the top 5 percent values.[7] This is done by applying the income (or expenditure) value of the 95th percentile to the top 5 percent of the observations.

There is an important point to note in interpreting the results from this analysis. We are able to measure additional effects of lumping two instalments into one (Group 2 vs. Group 1), and the effects of the additional grants made to Group 3 and 4. Since we use the two instalments of small cash transfers (which is equivalent to typical UCT in the county) as our control group, we are not able to measure the effect of that transfer. Our assessment is focused on whether the three treatments have any effect on household and their children "over and above" the impact of UCT.

---

7   Winsorizing is the transformation of statistics by limiting extreme values in the statistical data to reduce the effect of possibly spurious outliers.

3.   Impacts at household level

Since the interventions are intended as business grants to support micro-enterprise growth, we present the impacts on labour supply and income followed by the effects on assets, savings and food security. The impacts on several child level outcomes are presented in a separate section.

3.1.   Labour supply, micro-business management and income

Table 2 shows the impact findings on labour supply. As discussed in measurement methods, the coefficients for Groups 2, 3 and 4 shows the average differences for the three groups from Group 1 (i.e. unconditional transfer). As we can see, there is no significant impact on the number of individuals from the households who are involved in earning activities or the amount of work. In other words, at household level, the additional transfer or lump sum amount do not increase labour supply. It is important to note that the total labour supply by the households is extremely low, which is determined by limited work opportunities.

However, we find significant increase in the likelihood of households earning income from non-farm businesses because of larger size of IGA grants as well as lump sum transfer. Getting the same amount as the UCT (Group 1) as one-off grant (instead of two transfers) and the IGA training increased the likelihood of the households earning profit from non-farm businesses by 11 percentage points. This suggests possibilities of leveraging cash transfers to build resilience. When comparing the effect size among the IGA grant recipients, additional capital also increased the likelihood of generating income from non-farm businesses. The effect sizes are 18 and 20 percentage points for $500 and $1,000 grant recipients respectively. While the effect size for the large cash transfer (Group 4) is also statistically significantly different from the 11 percentage point effects on Group 2, the difference in effect sizes between Group 3 and Group 2 is not.[8] Considering the fact that 45 percent of the households had little business income at baseline, the effects are remarkable. It is also noteworthy that around 35 percent of the medium and large cash recipients did not have any income from non-farm business at the follow-up survey.

---

8   P-value of the differences in coefficients are 0.08 for Group 2 vs. Group 4, and 0.20 for Group 2 vs. Group 3.

Table 2.   Impact on labour supply and income sources

	Number of HH members worked	# of days worked by all HH members	# of hours worked by all HH members	Earned from non-farm business	Earned from wage work
	(1)	(2)	(3)	(4)	(5)
Group 2 (One-off low cash)	−0.005	−0.054	6.438	0.109**	−0.068*
	(0.061)	(1.588)	(15.651)	(0.051)	(0.040)
Group 3 (Medium cash)	0.037	1.202	17.731	0.176***	−0.024
	(0.060)	(1.551)	(16.032)	(0.052)	(0.043)
Group 4 (High cash)	0.084	1.752	14.620	0.196***	−0.043
	(0.058)	(1.507)	(14.861)	(0.050)	(0.041)
Group 1 (mean)	0.66	14.20	128.66	0.45	0.22
Observation	752	752	752	752	752
R-square	0.091	0.083	0.056	0.019	0.075

Note: *, ** and *** denote significance from the control group at 10 percent, 5 percent and 1 percent respectively. Average value for Group 1 is taken from the follow-up survey for assessing the magnitude of impacts. Total number of days and hours are calculated for the last month preceding the survey date.

Equally importantly, we do not observe any significant reduction in the likelihood of medium and large transfer groups' earning wage income, compared to UCT groups. In other words, the medium and large IGA grants groups have been able to increase their involvement in non-farm activities, but are still reliant on wage work. Estimated impact on total number of days worked by all household members is small (less than two days in last month) and statistically not significant. This shows that business grants resulted in some shift in their type of work, but not necessarily increasing total employment. In terms of other economic activities, there is very limited scale of livestock rearing by the study population (only 4 percent and 3 percent at baseline and follow-up survey respectively), and agriculture or fishing are even lower.

In Table 3, we look at the impact on non-farm business management to assess the contribution of business training in this study. The IGA training emphasizes on keeping written business records, and we find significant positive effects on this indicator. The effect size is between 11 and 16 percentage points compared to the average of 24 percent for the households in Group 1, and there is no significant difference among the three groups (who received the training). This indicates the observed effects are driven by the training rather than the size of business capital. The businesses are almost exclusively petty trading of different sorts (e.g. groceries, vegetable, charcoals, tea stalls etc.), which are managed by household members. During key informant interviews of the project staffs, it was reported that some of the IGA grants recipients are creating employment opportunities for others by hiring people. However, we do not find any significant effects of the additional grants on hiring (Column 2 in Table 3). In fact, about 90 percent of the businesses do not hire anyone for operating their businesses.

Table 3.   Impact on business management practices

	Keep written records of business	Hired anyone for the business	Sought loan for business	Did any credit purchase for business	Value of businesses (USD)
	(1)	(2)	(3)	(4)	(5)
Group 2 (One-off low cash)	0.122***	0.001	–0.007	–0.041	36.854
	(0.047)	(0.027)	(0.036)	(0.040)	(24.607)
Group 3 (Medium cash)	0.110**	–0.006	–0.049	0.006	83.988***
	(0.048)	(0.028)	(0.035)	(0.041)	(26.799)
Group 4 (High cash)	0.157***	–0.004	–0.085**	–0.021	217.654***
	(0.048)	(0.028)	(0.034)	(0.040)	(30.971)
Group 1 (mean)	0.24	0.09	0.19	0.25	167.19
Observation	752	752	752	748	752
R-square	0.016	0.060	0.159	0.182	0.154

Note: *, ** and *** denote significance from the control group at 10 percent, 5 percent and 1 percent respectively. Average value for Group 1 is taken from the follow-up survey for assessing the magnitude of impacts. The business practices questions were added at follow-up survey, and hence the regression does not control for baseline value.

Column 3 and 4 present the effects of the transfer on taking cash loan for business (expansion or as working capital), or buying and credit from wholesalers. On the one hand, additional capital can relax their credit constraint and thereby reduce the extent of borrowing. Conversely, having larger amount of working capital in their businesses through the IGA grants can increase their creditworthiness to lenders or wholesalers. The impact estimates show the net results of these two possible effects. The impact evidence suggests that credit constraints are a relatively stronger force; the recipients of large cash transfers (Group 4) are significantly less likely to seek cash loans (less by 9 percentage points when compared to the small transfer UCT beneficiaries).

Column 5 shows the estimated impacts on the total value of their businesses. To measure business values, the respondents were asked to consider all capital items (furniture, shops etc.) and stocks for their businesses. The estimates can be used to interpret how much of the additional IGA grants are invested. The effect is the largest for Group 4 at $218, with significantly larger effect than on Group 3 ($84) and Group 2 ($37). This shows that the additional $500 (after the first $500) results in an impact of $134 dollars, which is about a quarter of the additional $500 grant. This rate of investment is similar when we compare Group 1 vs. Group 3, which is about 26 percent for the additional 350 dollars.[9] This propensity to investment accounting suggests a linear pattern. Although not significant at conventional levels, the effect of $37 for Group 2 is interesting as this suggests potential value of combining multiple UCT into lump-sum with IGA training, which is aligned with impacts on profit from businesses.

To measure impacts on income, we collected information on their income from various sources in the last 30 days as well as total profit from businesses in the last six months. Estimated impact on income (Table 4) correspond to the effects observed on their labour supply and business management. The four cash transfer groups do not have any significant difference in their last months' wage income. Compared to the UCT beneficiaries (Group 1), last month income from non-farm businesses are significantly higher for all the other three groups. The impact estimates are $5, $10 and $16 for Groups 2, 3 and 4 respectively. Similar trends are observed when we look at the impacts on their total last month's income (Column 3). There is a significant difference (by $24) between Groups 1 and 2 in business income in the last six months reinforces the earlier conclusion of improving grant effectiveness by combing transfers for supporting IGAs (Column 4). Using the impact estimates of the additional capital, we find that the $500 grant recipients (Group 3) need to maintain the additional $10 income from business for 2.7 years to equalize the additional $325 transfer whereas the $1,000 grant recipients need to

---

9   The accounting is "84/(500-175)" done by taking average of 250 and 100 dollars transferred to UCT group.

maintain their extra income for 4 years. The corresponding figures are 3.6 and 4.2 years if we use the impact estimates for last six months' income. From this short-term impact, $500 of IGA grant appears more cost-effective than $1,000 grant.

Table 4.   Impact on household income

	Last month income from wage work	Last month profit from micro-business	Total income in last month	Profit from micro-business in last 6 months
	(1)	(2)	(3)	(4)
Group 2	−2.373	5.428*	3.115	23.942*
(One-off low				
cash)	(2.807)	(2.900)	(4.474)	(13.943)
Group 3	1.887	10.329***	12.774***	44.864***
(Medium cash)	(3.071)	(3.102)	(4.786)	(14.694)
Group 4	−0.370	16.727***	19.828***	97.448***
(High cash)	(2.871)	(3.262)	(4.939)	(16.711)
Group 1 (mean)	11.97	18.09	32.74	83.69
Observation	752	752	752	752
R-square	0.018	0.090	0.060	0.127

Note: *, ** and *** denote significance from the control group at 10 percent, 5 percent and 1 percent respectively. Average value for Group 1 is taken from the follow-up survey for assessing the magnitude of impacts.

3.2. Assets

We look at the impacts on household physical and financial assets. As noted earlier, very few of the households in this study own livestock, and there is no significant difference for the three treatment groups compared to Group 1 (Table 5). For household assets, we counted number of asset items owned out of 13 items.[10] We find significant positive effects on asset ownership for Group 4.

---

10   The assets counted are mobile phone, radio, television, watch, charcoal stove/jiko, wheelbarrow, vacuum flask, kerosene lamp, mat, bed, Somali stool and sitting cushion/pillow.

Table 5.   Impact on assets and savings

	Whether own any livestock	Number HH assets owned	Have any outstanding loan	Amount of outstanding loans (USD)	Have any savings	Amount of savings (USD)
	(1)	(2)	(3)	(4)	(5)	(6)
Group 2 (One-off low cash)	−0.005	0.185	0.019	2.942	0.083**	7.707**
	(0.017)	(0.163)	(0.034)	(8.510)	(0.040)	(3.607)
Group 3 (Medium cash)	0.003	0.100	−0.008	−1.722	0.093**	10.552***
	(0.018)	(0.168)	(0.033)	(8.642)	(0.041)	(4.027)
Group 4 (High cash)	0.009	0.314*	−0.015	−5.094	0.170***	17.693***
	(0.019)	(0.162)	(0.033)	(8.501)	(0.043)	(4.317)
Group 1 (mean)	0.03	5.40	0.14	30.35	0.15	9.84
Observation	752	752	752	752	752	752
R-square	0.015	0.316	0.131	0.212	0.032	0.030

Note: *, ** and *** denote significance from the control group at 10 percent, 5 percent and 1 percent respectively. Average value for Group 1 is taken from the follow-up survey for assessing the magnitude of impacts.

There is no significant effect on outstanding loans, either at the extensive margin (likelihood of having outstanding loan in Column 3) or at the intensive margin (amount of outstanding loan, Column 4). However, we find significant differences for all three IGA grant recipients compared to UCT groups at both margins. While 15 percent of the UCT group reported having any cash savings, the effects of IGA grants are 8, 9 and 17 percentage points for Groups 2, 3 and 4 respectively. Impact on amount of cash savings is between $8 and $18, corresponding to the likelihood of having savings. This impact on savings, especially for Group 2, reinforces the potential benefit of IGA grant over UCT. The primary goal behind UCT is to enable households to maintain a minimum level of consumption, and there is ample evidence on the critical role of savings in consumption smoothing. With the same amount of cash transfers, an IGA grant is able to better influence savings, when compared to UCT. Although the $8 difference seems small in absolute value, this is substantial compared to the average $10 savings for the UCT group. Larger IGA grants (Groups 3 and 4) yielding higher impact on cash savings is expected, but the magnitude of the effects ($11 and $18 for Groups 3 and 4 respectively) are not substantially large to influence cost-effectiveness comparisons.

3.3. Food security and wellbeing

While income and assets are the immediate outcomes of IGA grants, it is important to look into the impacts on food security and household wellbeing for proper comparison with UCT. In Table 6, we present the impacts of IGA grants on household expenditure. We categorized the household expenditures into three groups—food expenditure (in the last one month), recurrent non-food expenses (such as fuel, transport, children's education in the last one month) and lumpy expenses that are incurred occasionally (such as clothes, utensils, ceremonial expenses in the last 6 months). We do not find any impact on any of the three indicators (Columns 1–3) for Group 2. However, both medium and high IGA grants recipients have spent larger amounts for all three types of consumption. The large IGA grant recipients (Group 4) made additional purchases on $30 lumpy expenses, when compared to UCT. Using per capita expenditure as a household wellbeing indicator, we find that both Groups 3 and 4 are better-off than the UCT group (Column 4 and 5).

Table 6.   Impact on consumption expenditure

	Last month food expenditure	Monthly non-food recurrent expenses	Last 6 months' lumpy expenses	Per capita monthly food expenditure	Per capita monthly total exp.
	(1)	(2)	(3)	(4)	(5)
Group 2 (One-off low cash)	0.423	2.511	8.395	0.187	−0.008
	(2.761)	(6.386)	(8.492)	(0.574)	(1.486)
Group 3 (Medium cash)	11.065***	17.022**	13.233	2.431***	3.051**
	(3.083)	(6.829)	(9.154)	(0.627)	(1.506)
Group 4 (High cash)	5.258*	15.966**	30.024***	1.173*	3.641**
	(2.862)	(6.719)	(9.688)	(0.600)	(1.529)
Group 1 (mean)	58.53	108.48	55.99	10.79	22.19
Observation	752	752	752	750	750
R-square	0.042	0.161	0.164	0.238	0.121

Note: *, ** and *** denote significance from the control group at 10 percent, 5 percent and 1 percent respectively. Average value for Group 1 is taken from the follow-up survey for assessing the magnitude of impacts.

Table 7 shows impacts of IGA grants on household food security. We use dietary diversity as indicator of food security, which were measured separately for the households and children (aged 2–17 years). There is no significant difference across the treatment arms in either of the indicators. The difference in food expenditure and lack of difference in dietary diversity indicates that there is high level of food insecurity in general, and additional income is used for increasing the amount of food consumption rather than improving the diet. To assess the adequacy of food consumed, we asked the household if every member of their household had enough food to eat in the last one week. We find significant effects of IGA grants on this indicator. Compared to UCT beneficiaries, the IGA grant recipients are 11–15 percentage points more likely to have reported eating enough last week.

Table 7.   Impact on food security

	HH dietary diversity score	Dietary diversity score for children	Had enough food last week	Have at least 1 week's food stock	Coping strategy index
	(1)	(2)	(3)	(4)	(5)
Group 2 (One-off low cash)	0.186	0.022	0.106**	0.008	−0.792*
	(0.264)	(0.288)	(0.046)	(0.038)	(0.407)
Group 3 (Medium cash)	−0.133	−0.263	0.143***	0.034	−1.397***
	(0.249)	(0.276)	(0.045)	(0.039)	(0.380)
Group 4 (High cash)	0.215	−0.061	0.151***	0.067*	−1.204***
	(0.255)	(0.284)	(0.044)	(0.040)	(0.406)
Group 1 (mean)	5.65	5.50	0.66	0.23	2.66
Observation	752	697	752	752	752
R-square	0.086	0.104	0.043	0.242	0.057

Note: *, ** and *** denote significance from the control group at 10 percent 5 percent and 1 percent respectively. Average value for Group 1 is taken from the follow-up survey for assessing the magnitude of impacts.

In the high food insecurity context of the country, the amount of food stock available at the house is an important indicator (Column 4 in Table 7). We find significant effects only for the large IGA grants on the likelihood of households having food that can last for at least a week. While 23 percent of the UCT recipients reported having one week's of food stock, the rate is 7 percentage points higher for Group 4. Coping strategy index (CSI) is another commonly used indicator in order to assess the food security situation in Somalia. Higher value in CSI indicates lower ability of the households to meet their food needs since they rely on more undesirable options for securing food such as borrowing or eating less preferred food items. All three groups of IGA grant recipients demonstrate better coping ability compared to small transfer UCT recipients. Although each indicator of food security has its limitations, a general conclusion that can be drawn is that larger transfers increase the amount of food but that they have no measurable effect on diversity of diet. This partly contravenes findings for South Africa in Chapters 3 (Sambu and Hall) and 6 (Devereux et al.), which indicate that larger cash transfers may improve dietary diversity.

4.   Impact on children

Although household poverty is strongly associated with child specific outcomes, various evaluations of anti-poverty interventions have shown that the positive impacts on household income or expenditure do not necessarily translate into better wellbeing for children (see also Hypher et al., Chapter 7 in this volume). As we have already seen in household food security, positive impacts on business ownership and income from larger sized grants did not translate into greater dietary diversity. In this section, we look at various other child specific outcomes and indicators reflective of child wellbeing.

In Table 8, we see that children in households of IGA grant groups do not have a greater number of meals than the children in the UCT group. There is also no effect on household expenditures on children's education, although we find a small positive effect on enrolment rates (Table 9). We find positive impacts on household expenditures for children's healthcare for the medium and large IGA grants (Groups 3 and 4), albeit small in magnitude. Access to sanitary latrines and safe drinking water are household level outcomes, but can have direct implications for children. We do not find any effect of additional grants on either of these two indicators.

Table 8.   Impact on investment in children

	Number of meals taken yesterday by children (6–17 years)	Expenses for children's education last month	Expenses for children's healthcare last month	Whether use sanitary toilet/latrine	Whether treat water before drinking
	(1)	(2)	(3)	(4)	(5)
Group 2 (One-off low cash)	0.098	–1.111	–0.402	0.037	–0.045
	(0.063)	(1.624)	(0.832)	(0.041)	(0.051)
Group 3 (Medium cash)	0.096	–1.497	2.162**	0.024	–0.048
	(0.070)	(1.631)	(0.973)	(0.042)	(0.052)
Group 4 (High cash)	0.067	1.923	2.061**	–0.009	–0.018
	(0.061)	(1.690)	(0.905)	(0.043)	(0.050)
Group 1 (mean)	2.16	13.02	6.83	0.79	0.61
Observation	617	752	752	752	752
R-square	0.076	0.307	0.255	0.010	0.007

Note: *, ** and *** denote significance from the control group at 10 percent, 5 percent and 1 percent respectively. Average value for Group 1 is taken from the follow-up survey for assessing the magnitude of impacts.

Acquiring human capital through more education is one of the important pathways out of intergenerational poverty. While an increase in income can give households greater ability to send their children to schools, IGA grants may lead to unintended consequences such as increasing child labour (either for business or at home) that can indirectly influence school enrolment.

Table 9.   Impact on children's schooling and labour

	Children of school going age (6-13)			Household have any child labour
	Enrolled (All)	Enrolled (Boys)	Enrolled (Girls)	
	(1)	(2)	(3)	(4)
Group 2 (One-off low cash)	−0.040 (0.032)	−0.024 (0.046)	−0.059 (0.045)	0.001 (0.011)
Group 3 (Medium cash)	−0.037 (0.034)	−0.060 (0.047)	−0.012 (0.048)	0.001 (0.011)
Group 4 (High cash)	0.063* (0.034)	0.070 (0.049)	0.059 (0.046)	−0.010 (0.007)
Group 1 (mean)	0.32	0.32	0.32	0.01
Observation	1,483	755	728	752
R-square	0.064	0.050	0.089	0.016

Note: *, ** and *** denote significance from the control group at 10 percent, 5 percent and 1 percent respectively. Average value for Group 1 is taken from the follow-up survey for assessing the magnitude of impacts. Child labour is measured by whether any household member who is less than 18 years old worked outside home for cash or payment in the month preceding the survey.

Nevertheless, we find a positive effect of the large IGA grant (Group 4) on school enrolment of children in primary school age. Overall, the enrolment rate for children is very low at 32 percent, and the estimated effect size for Group 4 is 6 percentage points. When we look at the effects on male and female separately, the point estimates are similar (7 and 6 percentage points for male and female, respectively). Although this is not statistically significant, this may be influenced by the smaller sample size when disaggregated by sex. There is no significant difference in child labour among the treatment groups. Overall, only 1 percent of the households reported to have any child involved in earning activities. This is contrary to a general narrative of widespread child labour at IDP camps and urban areas in the country. However, given the very limited economic opportunities in these sites, it is not surprising to find low levels of child labour.

Table 10.   Impact on children's health and nutrition

	Children (2–17 years)			Children (6–59 months)	
	Whether suffered from illness	Sought healthcare (male)	Sought healthcare (female)	Weight-for-height z-score	Weight-for-age z-score
	(1)	(2)	(3)	(4)	(5)
Group 2 (One-off low cash)	0.008	−0.172	−0.159	−0.044	−0.134
	(0.019)	(0.207)	(0.129)	(0.141)	(0.161)
Group 3 (Medium cash)	−0.001	−0.228	0.125	−0.060	0.128
	(0.018)	(0.201)	(0.123)	(0.145)	(0.172)
Group 4 (High cash)	0.015	0.173	0.218**	−0.085	−0.121
	(0.019)	(0.154)	(0.103)	(0.142)	(0.160)
Group 1 (mean)	0.084	0.72	0.76	−0.416	−0.663
Observation	1,819	72	91	894	910
R-square	0.003	0.139	0.132	0.011	0.006

Note: *, ** and *** denote significance from the control group at 10 percent, 5 percent and 1 percent respectively. Average value for Group 1 is taken from the follow-up survey for assessing the magnitude of impacts. WHZ and WAZ data were collected only at endline.

In terms of impact on child health, we do not find any effects on morbidity. Eight percent of the children in UCT group reported suffering from any illnesses in the last two weeks, and the rates are same among all the treatment groups. However, we find significant effect of large IGA grant (Group 4) on health seeking of female children. Although we find that girls were 22 percentage points more likely to have received any treatment in the large transfer group, our sample size of children that suffered from illness is too small to draw strong conclusions.

For measuring impacts on child nutrition, anthropometric data was collected at follow-up survey. We do not find any significant effect on weight-for-height or weight-for-age z-scores for children aged 6–59 months. Since the grants do not have any major effect on dietary diversity, the lack of impact on nutrition is not surprising. With a few exceptions (e.g. IFPRI, 2016), there is a major gap in assessing the impact of anti-poverty programmes on child nutrition. A review of the evidence on comparative cost-effectiveness analysis by Gentilini (2016) concludes that the overall evidence base of impacts of cash transfers on child malnutrition is still limited. Among the few studies that assessed nutritional impacts in Sub-Saharan Africa, Langendorf et al. (2014) find that cash transfers alone are not as effective as combining cash with supplementary food. Similarly, small or no significant effects of cash transfers on child nutrition are observed by Berhane et al. (2016) in Ethiopia, Evans et al. (2014) in Tanzania and OPM (2016) in Kenya. Several other systematic reviews do not find robust evidence of impact of cash transfer on child nutrition (e.g. Manley et al., 2012; de Groot et al., 2017). Chapters 6 (by Devereux et al.), and 7 (by Hypher et al.) in this volume explore options for making anti-poverty programmes more effective in tackling undernutrition.

5.   Robustness and limitations of the study

There are several concerns that could influence the interpretation of these results or generalisation of findings. In this section, we discuss implications of various concerns. Firstly, resource sharing by the households with their neighbours can have significant influence on the results. For example, if the recipients of larger business grants share cash with others who were less lucky in the lottery, the results could be downward biased. Similarly, informal resource sharing with non-beneficiaries can also influence the differences observed in relation to assets. However, in our analysis of information resource sharing, we find that only 11 percent of the households gave out money (as gifts or credit) to other households. More importantly, there are no significant differences between the four treatment groups in their likelihood of resource sharing or in patterns of informal sharing (either cash or in-kind).

A second concern in interpreting differences as causal influence following differences in grant sizes is the possibility that the grant sizes influence the receipt of other types of support. It is plausible that the recipients of large grants (Groups 3 and 4) are supported in fewer other programmes in the locality compared to small grant recipients (Groups 1 and 2). In the follow-up survey, we asked the households to report all types of support that they had received from formal or informal sources. We find that the cash grants received from the Save the Children projects constituted a major component of any support that they received, and that there is no significant difference in support received from other sources.

In the study design, the amounts of cash transferred to the small grants groups in Mogadishu and Hiran varied (see Figure 1). It is not possible to distinguish the differences due to the variation in cash size within the small grants groups from the site level differences. Although we control for site fixed effects in the analysis, it is of interest to explore whether the effects varied between the sites. With the concern of smaller sample size for site level disaggregated results, we find that the directions of the main results (i.e. positive effects on business ownership, business income, assets, savings and consumption, but limited impact on children) to be qualitatively similar. The magnitude of effects on business income is larger in Mogadishu compared to Hiran, although the differences between UCT and other treatment groups in Mogadishu were lower than those in Hiran. This could possibly be influenced by higher level of economic opportunities in Mogadishu.

In randomized experiments that involve public lottery, there are often concerns about "discouragement effects" on the beneficiaries who receive smaller supports. Although our discussion with field officers did not reveal such concerns, it is not possible to rule out the possibility of such effects. Finally, the results observed in this study may not be generalizable for substantial scale of the same business grant supports.

This study measures short-term effects of business grants comparing to UCT. It can be argued that changes in the indicators for child wellbeing will require longer time to take place. While we cannot rule out that possibility, the results show that additional business income does not have many short-term benefits for children.

6. Conclusion

Cash transfers are a major component of most social protection programmes, and have become more common in both development and humanitarian programming in recent years. Unconditional cash transfers (UCT) made in monthly instalments is expected to support households with consumption smoothing, and various studies confirm its effectiveness in improving food security. However, such transfers do not necessarily have much impact on household asset building. Business grants, on the other hand, are found to be effective in assisting households to build their asset base and foster income growth, which are key elements for household resilience building. However, the effects of most of these programmes (either UCT or business grants) on children are usually limited and are generally not significant, with the major exceptions for conditional cash transfers.

In this study, we compare the livelihood and children level outcomes of four types of transfers to measure the marginal effects of business grants compared to UCT about five months after the transfers completed. We find that small business grants have positive effects on business ownership, business income, savings and food security compared to monthly UCT. Therefore, lumping monthly UCTs into "chunky" transfers can be considered as an option to improve cost effectiveness of such transfers. Larger grants have positive returns in term of business income and household assets. Based on the effects on income, we find that a grant of $500 is more effective than a large grant of $1,000, in terms of maximising the social return, and considering the impacts on income and food security.

In terms of effects on children, we find a positive effect on school enrolment for the large business grants group and some increase in money spent for children's healthcare. We do not find any significant effect on dietary diversity or nutrition status of children despite significant increases in household income. This finding corroborates with many other empirical studies that show weak impacts of "cash transfer only" approach on children.

References

Banerjee, A. V. and Duflo, E. (2014). "Do firms want to borrow more? Testing credit constraints using a directed lending program", *The Review of Economic Studies*, vol. 81(2): 572–607.

Barhane, G., Devereux, S., Hoddinott, J., Hoel, J., Roelen, K., Abay, K., Kimmel, M., Ledlie, N. and Woldu, T. (2016). "Evaluation of social cash transfer pilot programme, Tigray region, Ethiopia: Endline report", Unicef Ethiopia.

Bastian, G., Goldstein, M. and Papineni, S. (2017). "Are cash transfers better chunky or smooth? Evidence from an impact evaluation of cash transfer program in Northern Nigeria", Policy Brief 21, Gender Innovation Lab, World Bank, Washington D.C.

Bruhn, M., Karlan, D., and Schoar, A. (2010). "What capital is missing in developing countries?" *The American Economic Review*, vol. 100(2): 629–633.

De Groot, R., Palermo, T., Handa, S., Ragno, L. P. and Peterman, A. (2017). "Cash transfers and child nutrition: Pathways and impacts", *Development Policy Review*, vol. 35: 621–643.

De Mel, S., McKenzie, D., and Woodruff, C. (2008). "Returns to capital in microenterprises: Evidence from a field experiment", *The Quarterly Journal of Economics*, vol. 123(4): 1329–1372.

Duflo, E., Kremer, M., and Robinson, J. (2011). "Nudging farmers to use fertilizer: Theory and experimental evidence from Kenya", *The American Economic Review*, 101(6): 2350–2390.

Evans, D. K., Hausladen, S., Kosec, K., and Reese, N. (2014). "Community-based conditional cash transfers in Tanzania: Results from a randomized trial", World Bank, Washington D.C.

Fafchamps, M., McKenzie, D., Quinn, S., and Woodruff, C. (2014). "Microenterprise growth and the flypaper effect: Evidence from a randomized experiment in Ghana", *Journal of Development Economics*, vol. 106: 211–226.

Gentilini, U. (2016). "The Other Side of the Coin: The Comparative Evidence of Cash and in-kind transfers in Humanitarian Situations", World Bank, Washington D.C.

Haushofer, J. and Shapiro, J. (2016). "The short-term impact of unconditional cash transfers to the poor: Experimental evidence from Kenya", the *Quarterly Journal of Economics*, vol. 131(4): 1973–2042.

IFPRI (2016), "Channelling Social Protection Programs for Improved Nutrition in Bangladesh: Outcomes of the Transfer Modality Research Initiative", International Food Policy Research Institute (IFPRI), Washington D.C.

Kremer, M., Lee, J., Robinson, J., and Rostapshova, O. (2015). "Rates of return, optimization failures, and behavioral biases: Evidence from Kenyan retail shops", downloaded from https://economics.stanford.edu/sites/default/files/shops_draft_8apr16.pdf on Aug 20, 2017.

Kushnir, K., Mirmulstein, M. L. and Ramalho, R. (2010.) "Micro, small, and medium enterprises around the world: How many are there, and what affects the count?" World Bank/IFC.

Langendorf, C., Roederer, T., de Pee, S., Brown, D., Doyon, S. and Mamaty, A. (2014). "Preventing Acute Malnutrition among Young Children in Crises: A Prospective Intervention Study in Niger", *PLOS Medicine*, vol. 11(9): 2–15.

Manley, J., Gitter, S., & Slavchevska, V. (2012). *How effective are cash transfer programmes at improving nutritional status? A rapid evidence assessment of programmes' effects on anthropometric outcomes.* London: Institute of Education, University of London.

McKenzie, D. and Woodruff, C. (2008). "Experimental evidence on returns to capital and access to finance in Mexico", *The World Bank Economic Review*, vol. 22(3): 457–482.

McKenzie, D. and Woodruff, C. (2014). "What are we learning from business training and entrepreneurship evaluations around the developing world?" *The World Bank Research Observer*, vol. 29: 48–82.

McKenzie, D. and Woodruff, C. (2016). "Business practices in small firms in developing countries", Working paper no. 265, The University of Warwick.

OPM (2016). *Evaluation of the Uganda Social Assistance Grants for Empowerment (SAGE) Programme: Impact after one year of programme operations 2012–2013.* Oxford: Oxford Policy Management.

Roelen, K. (2015). "The two-fold investment trap: children and their role in sustainable graduation", *IDS Bulletin* 46(2): 25–34.

Sulaiman, M. (2018). "Livelihood, cash transfer and graduation approaches: How do they compare in terms of cost, impact and targeting?", Background Paper, Annual Trends and Outlook Report 2018, International Food Policy Research Institute (IFPRI), Washington D.C.

Udry, C. R. and Anagol, S. (2006). *The Return to Capital in Ghana.* Yale University Economic Growth Center Discussion Paper No. 932.

UNDP (2018). *Human Development Indices and Indicators: 2018 Statistical Update.* United Nations Development Programme (UND), New York: United Nations.

Wooldrige, J. M. (2002). "Inverse probability weighted M-estimation for sample selection, attrition and stratification", *Portuguese Economic Journal*, vol. 1(2): 117–139.

PART THREE
Transitions from Childhood into Adulthood

CHAPTER 9
Gaining Ground with Gatekeepers: Leveraging the Proximal Enabling Environment to Support Youth Livelihood Development

Nikhit D'Sa, Sarah Press, Anna Du Vent, Ahmed Farahat and Sita Conklin

1. Introduction

Of the 1.8 billion young people aged 10–24, 90 percent live in low- and middle-income countries (LMICs) (Gupta et al. 2014). They make up one-fourth of the working-age population and nearly half of the unemployed (ILO 2012, 2016). Although youth in LMICs are staying in school longer, and more are entering higher education (ILO 2015), they often enter the formal labour market underprepared (International Youth Foundation 2014; Palmer 2007). In response, over the last two decades, governments and non-government organizations have increased labour supply-side and demand-side livelihood interventions to promote youth entry into decent work: "productive work in which rights are protected, which generates an adequate income, with adequate social protection" (ILO, 2015: 61). However, the success of these interventions has been mixed. There is limited evidence on the efficacy of labour supply-side interventions and the mechanisms that are most effective.

In this chapter we argue that in order to strengthen the impact of labour supply-side interventions, practitioners must focus on the proximal enabling environment: the family and community that immediately surround youth and support them to maximize their assets, agency, access to services, and opportunities, as well as their ability to avoid risks and be protected (USAID 2017). We focus on evidence about the importance and influence of the proximal enabling environment on youth livelihood development, evidence generated over six years of implementing a youth livelihood development programme in Burkina Faso, Egypt, Ethiopia, Malawi, and Uganda. We use this evidence to build a case for the importance of having strategic and explicit intervention components that focus on the proximal enabling environment.

2.   Evidence on labour supply-side and demand-side interventions

Broadly speaking, livelihood development programmes for youth in LMICs have focused on two areas of intervention: (i) labour supply, and/or (ii) demand-side programing (James-Wilson 2008; Olenik et al. 2013; Butler, Taggart, and Chervin 2012). In Table 1 we present a brief overview of the main types of labour supply-side and demand-side interventions that have been used in LMICs (Flynn et al. 2017; Kluve et al. 2016; Lippman et al. 2015; Lopez et al. 2015; United Nations 2007; Olenik et al. 2013).

Table 1.   Overview of common types of labour supply-side and demand-side interventions

Intervention focus	Intervention type	Description	Socio-ecological Focus
Labour supply-side interventions	Education	Generally catering to out-of-school youth, interventions focused on raising the academic (literacy and numeracy) knowledge of youth through in-school or accelerated learning activities	Individual
	Training	Interventions focused on building key technical and non-technical skills in youth to prepare them for specific labour market opportunities	Individual
	Entrepreneur-ship promotion	Interventions specifically focused on training youth to research, resource, develop, run, and grow their own business venture	Individual
	Micro-insurance and microcredit schemes	Provision of small loans to individuals in low-resource, low-income communities to use as start-up capital for a small business	Individual Community
Labour demand-side interventions	Wage/ employment subsidies	Employers are offered financial incentives or support for creating more jobs or hiring specifically trained youth	Labour market
	Social funds	Developed by the World Bank in the late 1980s, focused on low-income communities selecting from competing public works contracts that create employment opportunities	Community Labour market

Cash-for-work schemes	Response to early food-for-work schemes, these interventions are a conditional cash transfer; individuals in low-resource communities given cash for taking up specific community public works or rehabilitation projects.	Individual Labour market
Public works	Primarily used in situations of high or chronic under-employment or un-employment, these schemes create public work opportunities for individuals in primarily rural low-resource contexts. National governments generally run these.	Individual Labour market

Labour supply-side interventions largely focus on building employment and livelihood skills in individual youth. The aim is to ensure that youth in low-resource contexts in LMICs have the requisite knowledge and training to find decent work. Labour demand-side interventions "are broad-based, micro- and macro-economic growth programmes including national youth employment policies, value chain development, public works programmes, wage subsidies, minimum wage, and tax breaks for employers" (Olenik et al., 2013: 5). They target the policies and norms in the larger labour market that define the social and economic factors that affect youth livelihood development (Butler, Taggart, and Chervin, 2012). While there are multiple policy documents that highlight the importance of the balance between labour supply-side and demand-side interventions (AfDB et al. 2012; UNDP 2014), most interventions over the last two decades have focused on the former (Olenik et al. 2013). In a systematic review of interventions of youth livelihood programmes, Kluve and colleagues (2016) found that half of the 107 studies they looked at were focused on education and skill building in youth, with an additional 14 percent focused on entrepreneurship promotion.

Overall, the evidence on the success of youth livelihood interventions, both supply-side and demand-side interventions, is mixed. A recent USAID review (2013) demonstrated that livelihood development programmes can increase employment opportunities for youth as well as boost short-term earnings, especially in LMICs. However, the review conducted by Kluve and colleagues (2016) found that only 30 percent of the reviewed programmes demonstrated success in labour market outcomes. This finding suggests a need to reconsider programmatic approaches for youth livelihood development.

3.   Focusing on the proximal enabling environment

One explanation for the limited success of youth livelihood programmes is the bias toward labour supply-side interventions, which are the focus of the majority of studies and policies on youth livelihood development (Flynn et al. 2017; Kluve et al. 2016). While these labour supply-side interventions aim to—and often do—increase youth knowledge and skills (Olenik et al. 2013), they do not always result in youth participation in decent work. The most successful programmes have targeted specific youth, or groups of youth, and have ensured there are sufficient support systems in place to guide youth from training into jobs (Kluve et al., 2016). In other words, labour supply-side interventions need to focus more strategically on youths' immediate, proximal environment (Clemensson and Christensen 2010; Youth Policy Labs 2015).

The response has been to blend supply-side and demand-side programming through "bridging strategies" (Butler, Taggart, and Chervin 2012), strategies that link trained youth to the labour market through mentorship, career counselling, access to financial services, or similar employment services. Nine percent of the studies that Kluve and colleagues (2016) reviewed focused on some component of employment services that bridged the supply and demand side of the youth labour market. But the focus on bridging strategies in the proximal enabling environment are still focused primarily on youth and their interactions with stakeholders in their immediate environment, rather than a defined intervention on the proximal enabling environment itself. It is much less common for labour supply-side interventions to explicitly and strategically intervene with peer groups, families, and communities (France et al. 2016).

There is a broader discourse in youth livelihood programming that views youth as primarily individualistic agents (Dejaeghere and Baxter 2014; Flynn et al. 2017). While this discourse fits well with the skill-building focus of labour supply-side interventions it does not sufficiently recognize, or programme for, the ways in which peer groups, families, and immediate communities act upon youth agency (Flynn et al. 2017; Youth Business International 2016). In order to strengthen the impact of labour supply-side interventions and more fully capitalize on bridging strategies between supply-side and demand-side interventions, we need to focus on how the proximal enabling environment impacts youth livelihood development (Youth Business International 2016). Indeed, other contributions in this volume, notably Chapters 10 (by Porter et al) and 12 (by Ogawa et al), also reflect on the importance of contextual and social factors for shaping employment and livelihood opportunities of young people.

Focusing strategically on peer groups, families, and communities has a theoretical and substantive foundation. From a theoretical perspective, a focus on the proximal enabling environment draws on ecological systems theory (Bronfenbrenner 1977; Bronfenbrenner and Morris 1988). Youth are nested within inter-related settings that affect how youth develop. Research has highlighted how a focus on the relationships that youth have in the settings around them can be beneficial for their development (Lerner et al. 2005; Scales, Roehlkepartain, and Shramko 2016; Benson et al. 2012). From this developmental perspective, workforce readiness is not simply a matter of preparing the individual with skills, but in also shaping environments to promote broad wellbeing that supports the acquisition and/or development of particular skills relevant for work success. Additionally, a growing body of research has highlighted how intervening directly with peers, families, and communities can have a positive impact on livelihood outcomes for youth, especially in rural communities in LMICs (France et al. 2016; Youth Business International 2016; Dejaeghere and Baxter 2014; Youth Policy Labs 2015). From a substantive perspective, several policy documents also point out the importance of targeting the social embeddedness of youth in livelihood development programming (Olenik et al. 2013; ILO 2015; UNDP 2014). But programmes have yet to catch up (Youth Policy Labs 2015). We need to go "beyond looking at how social relationships have instrumental value. It must include a focus on young people's social position, both within the family and in society at large" (Flynn et al., 2017: 39).

4.   Study design

4.1. Context

The data for this chapter was collected in the context of a youth education and livelihood development programme: Youth in Action (YiA). Started in 2012, YiA is a six-year programme implemented by Save the Children in partnership with the Mastercard Foundation. YiA supports out-of-school youth (12–18 years old) in rural Burkina Faso, Egypt, Ethiopia, Malawi, and Uganda, helping to enhance their existing capacity and build new knowledge and skills. For the first four months youth are arranged into groups of mixed literacy levels to work on literacy, numeracy, financial literacy, work readiness skills, business planning, and social assets. The curriculum is designed to help young people increase these skills quickly and develop transferable skills that will enable them to take advantage of and/or create livelihoods opportunities. Once they complete the learning cycle, youth enter the action phase. During this phase youth build on their existing livelihood skills; youth receive a small cash transfer and work on starting a business, taking up an apprenticeship, or attending a technical training programme. Younger youth may also choose to return to school.

There are a few important points to consider before we delve into the findings. First, YiA was not initially designed as a programme that explicitly focused on the proximal enabling environment. Like the programmes we critique in this chapter, YiA was designed as a labour supply-side intervention that had a few bridging strategies that connected youth to the labour market. However, over the course of implementation, and through the analysis of qualitative and quantitative research, we began to understand the deep influence of the proximal enabling environment and modified the programme to reflect this. Second, YiA focused on out-of-school youth; all project youth had been out of school for at least five months. This meant that we needed to incorporate significant foundational skill building (like literacy and numeracy). Third, YiA communities in the five countries were rural, between a one to four hour commute from the nearest urban hub. Unsurprisingly, in many of the communities there were few, if any, formal labour opportunities. After in-depth market assessments and a few months of trial-and-error, we decided that a large demand-side intervention was beyond the scope of the project and so we focused more fully on the proximal enabling environment and youth self-employment opportunities.

4.2. YiA and the proximal enabling environment

YiA encouraged positive shifts in the proximal enabling environment through engagement, demonstrative, and reflective strategies. This three-pronged approach was designed to simultaneously improve youths' perceptions of their environments, improve adults' perceptions of youth, and strengthen relationships and networks that would allow youth to enter and thrive in the labour market.

Engagement strategies encouraged active participation of family and community members in programming. Advisory panels of community business leaders and parents provided regular input on programming and labour market integration. Additionally, local entrepreneurs participated as mentors and trainers of apprentices during the action phase. The programme also engaged local service providers (example: microcredit establishments) to support youth financial inclusion. In cases where youth were not able to receive direct cash transfers due to legal restrictions, parents were asked to be co-recipients. Family and community members also participated directly in YiA programming both within sessions (example: assisting with youth-led market assessments) and through home-based and community-based activities (example: providing childcare for youth who were parents).

Demonstrative strategies provided youth with opportunities to display their engagement with families and communities as well as their appreciation for their support. Youth prepared presentations on their families and communities that they shared on Family and Community Celebration days. Through these presentations, youth highlighted what they learned through interviews and other investigative activities, and celebrated community achievements. Youth also planned and implemented community improvement projects that served both to increase their own engagement with community affairs and to demonstrate their competence and responsibility to their communities. Finally, upon completion of their plans for the future, youth presented their business plans to the advisory panels and family members for their approval and support. The principal purpose of the demonstration strategies was to improve community perceptions of youth, in order to increase the likelihood of support for youth as they transitioned out of YiA programming and into livelihoods or further training opportunities.

Reflective strategies provided different YiA stakeholders an opportunity to reflect on how youth were maturing and how they themselves could best support youth livelihood development. Youth were provided with opportunities to reflect on how they presented themselves and were perceived in their community, on their roles within their family and communities, on the strengths and resources around them, and in turn what strengths youth offered their communities. Reflective strategies among parents and communities included the opportunity to reflect on how to support youth during Family and Community Celebration days, following business plan presentations, and in regular consultations with the advisory panel.

4.3. Research questions

The data in this study was not initially collected to explicitly understand the influence of the proximal enabling environment on youth livelihood development. However, for this chapter we conducted a secondary analysis of the data to answer the following research questions:

- What was the status of family and community support for youth livelihood development in the YiA communities during the early stages of programme implementation?
- How did family and community support for youth livelihood development change over the period of YiA implementation?
- How was the change in family and community support related to improvements in skill building for youth?

4.4. Study design

The evidence that we draw on for this chapter come from multiple sources, from multiple countries, over five years. However, we offer a brief overview of the scope and depth of the research that we use for the secondary analysis in this chapter in Table 2.

Table 2.   Overview of data sources

Name of study		Description	Method	Country	Sample	Date	Citation
ENT	Enterprise Development Study	Operations research to understand how youth used the cash transfer to develop a business and what support youth received from family and community members.	Youth surveys as well as interviews and focus groups with YiA youth, non-YiA youth, parents, community leaders, and programme facilitators. Purposive sampling to maximize variation across enterprise types.	EG	316	Aug-17	(Gebrehiwot 2017; Farahat 2018)
				ET	203	Jul-17	
				MA	238	Jul-17	
				UG	273	Jan-17	
GEN	Rapid Gender Study	Operations research to identify the specific gender barriers to participation of male and female youth in YiA and explore how YiA has or could remove these barriers.	Interviews and focus groups with YiA youth, parents, and community leaders. Mixed sampling strategy with some convenience sampling.	BF	71	Nov-16	(Maina and Asencios 2017)
				EG	144	Jul-16	
				MA	78	May-16	
				UG	48	Nov-16	
POS	Programme Outcomes Study	Summative research to understand how work readiness skills—financial literacy, academic skills, transferable life skills, and self-employment skills—change for a sample of youth over the 8–10 month programme period, and the relationship of these changes to socioeconomic outcomes.	Pre-test and post-test survey data collected from 1-2 cohorts in each country once the programme was running as implementers intended. No control or comparison group.	BF	804	Feb-18	(D'Sa et al. 2018a)
				EG	798	Nov-17	(D'Sa et al. 2017a)
				ET	634	Nov-17	(D'Sa et al. 2017b)
				MA	579	Jan-18	(D'Sa et al. 2018b)
				UG	688	Aug-17	(D'Sa et al. 2017c)

SKL	Transferable Skills Study	Operations research to understand which transferable life skills youth used in their work and how family and community influenced the use of these skills.	Interviews and focus groups with YiA youth, non-YiA youth, parents, community leaders, and programme facilitators. Used purposive sampling to maximize the variation in participant characteristics in the sample.	MA	148	Dec-15	(D'Sa, Agaba, and Mchenga 2017)
				UG	115	Dec-15	
TRC	Tracer Study	Summative research to understand the socioeconomic outcomes—work status, income, savings, entrepreneurship capabilities, mentor support, and family support—for a sample of youth who graduated from the programme a minimum of nine months previously.	Retrospective survey data from a representative sample of YiA youth from all cohorts who completed the full programme cycle at least nine months prior to data collection	BF	204	Dec-17	(Leer and D'Sa 2017a)
				EG	487	Nov-17	(Leer and D'Sa 2017b)
				ET	382	Nov-17	(Leer and D'Sa 2017c)
				UG	494	Nov-17	(Leer and D'Sa 2017d)

Note: BF: Burkina Faso, EG: Egypt, ET: Ethiopia, MA: Malawi, UG: Uganda

5.   Findings

5.1. Limited family and community support for livelihood development

One of the primary findings from our data review was that prior to program implementation families and communities struggled to provide youth with substantial financial, material, and/or emotional support for livelihood development. As a baseline in the Programme Outcomes Study (POS; see Table 2), we asked youth about whether they felt that their family and community helped them learn the skills they could use in decent work, supported their ideas on how to earn money, or helped them plan for decent work that could help in the future. YiA youth in all five countries reported low levels of support or help from their family and community; this ranged from 43 percent of the youth in Egypt to 19 percent in Ethiopia. Additionally, survey data from the Tracer study (TRC; see Table 2) demonstrated that, prior to YiA, less than a third of youth received monetary, material, or emotional support from their families. This was especially concerning since nearly 95 percent of the youth in all five POS country samples also reported that they did not have sufficient access to material assets, credits, or savings to develop a decent business.

5.2. Family and community members are gatekeepers

In trying to understand the reasons for this low level of family and community support for work, we drew on two different types of evidence. First, we drew on the Transferable Skills Study (SKL) conducted in Malawi and Uganda early in the programme to understand how youth developed decent work and business opportunities. Second, we looked back on the Rapid Gender Assessments (GEN) conducted in four YiA countries to understand if the mechanisms affecting family and community support for youth livelihood development differed for male and female youth.

The sample of youth, family members, and community members in the SKL and GEN studies highlighted the fact that family and community members are the gatekeepers for youth building work readiness skills, starting/developing a business, or finding decent work in their community. Families are the first and most important gatekeepers to youth participation in both training programmes and in the market. In analysing the data from the GEN studies, we found that youth participation in a training programme like YiA was dependent on parental approval and that parents tend to be far more reticent in providing approval for their daughters than for their sons. This is due to multiple factors, including gender expectations—boys were expected to earn wages, whereas girls were expected to perform household duties—and concerns for the safety of adolescent girls. For example, in the GEN studies in Burkina Faso and Egypt, parents cited religious reasons for restricting their daughters' participation in skill-building programmes like YiA, as well as persistent beliefs that male youth had a greater capacity to make decisions, and that female youth needed protection and were safer at home. These perceptions about safety and restricted mobility have been validated by other recent research (Pereznieto et al. 2018).

In addition to serving as gatekeepers for skill-building opportunities, family and community members were the potential employers that youth contacted when they needed a job, and were the supports that youth drew on when starting a business. For example, participants in the SKL study described how community members sometimes helped youth build market-relevant skills. One community member from Malawi noted that "when time and space permits, we invite the youth and teach them skills such as making bricks as well as how to behave in the community." Youth could then turn these skills into an actual business. But the employment opportunities and help that community members provided were different for male and female youth. SKL study interviews with employers revealed a preference for hiring boys for physical labour, which was the most prevalent type of labour. The types of labour identified as "female" were typically unpaid, such as childcare or household duties, further restricting girls' access to wages. However, there were also examples in which female youth received specific support and job opportunities in their communities, such as cases in which female Malawian youth were hired by local restaurants to prepare food.

5.3. Negotiated reputation is important in youth livelihood development

The family and community support for skill development and employment opportunities was founded on a complex relationship between youth and community members. The discourse among community members from the SKL and GEN studies indicated that both male and female youth were perceived as lazy and not dependable. In the SKL study in Uganda, older community members commented that the current generation of youth were largely entitled, disrespectful, and did not heed the advice of elders: "Young people today lack determination; they take things for granted. Whenever they get money they think of spending it... and when you try to direct them, they do not understand. It is a generation that is wasted." This perception had a direct effect on whether community members helped youth gain market-relevant skills, meet self-employment goals, or find work. During the SKL study an employer from Malawi noted, "How can you employ someone who is known for being weak and not determined? To get employed, you need to show the employer that you can do [the work]" and "lazy youth are not good employees."

Youth attempted to counter this perspective by building a reputation for themselves in their community as hard-working and responsible individuals. The SKL data from Malawi and Uganda revealed that youth tried to build this reputation for themselves in three ways: using work and free time appropriately, getting additional training, and demonstrating independence. These strategies were signals to community members that a youth would make a good employee or that support for a youth-run business would pay off.

Although some parents were reticent to send their youth, especially their daughters, to training programmes like YiA, these training programmes served an integral role in building youths' negotiated reputations in their communities. Participation in YiA or similar trainings were viewed by community members as a signal that youth were serious about livelihood development, and youth themselves viewed these programmes as a good investment in their future. Data from the SKL studies in Malawi and Uganda highlighted the fact that youth believed that attending YiA reassigned value to them; because they had left school, they believed that adults viewed them as "troublemakers" or "slackers." Attending YiA allowed them to renegotiate this reputation. One young male YiA attendee in Uganda explained: "Because of [YiA], I have an opportunity to continue with school. I really wanted to stay in school, but we did not have money anymore. When you enter [YiA] you count yourself lucky, you know at least you are learning something to make yourself better." Additionally, data from SKL and GEN highlighted that many female youth who were not in school were confined to participation in household and religious activities, and were viewed negatively by the community if they engaged in other social or community activities. Participating in YiA provided some female youth an essential opportunity to engage in socially accepted behaviours. One parent from Uganda (SKL) provided the following explanation: "...my neighbour's daughter, she messed around with some [motorcycle taxi] man and she got pregnant... At least now when you see her going to [YiA] you know that maybe she can do something for her family."

5.4. Evidence of increased support through participation in YiA

Quantitative data from the TRC allowed us to identify notable changes in family and community support for youth after their participation in YiA[1], which we found especially pertinent given the low levels of family and community support reported at baseline (see evidence from POS above).

In terms of monetary support, in Egypt and Ethiopia one in four youth reported receiving money from their family before YiA to start or grow a business. Several months after graduating from YiA more than half the youth reported receiving some kind of monetary support from their families. In Burkina Faso and Uganda, however, the percent of youth who reported receiving money from their family to support their work remained unchanged. While the improvements in monetary support were mixed across the four TRC countries, we found marked improvements in three other types of support: material and emotional support from family, and work support from a community mentor. We illustrate these findings in effect size units in Figure 1.

---

1   We controlled for the differential effect of age, gender, household wealth, years of education, and YiA pathway in all our fitted regression models. Table of fitted models available upon request.

Figure 1.   Effect sizes for gains in family material and emotional support, and mentor work support

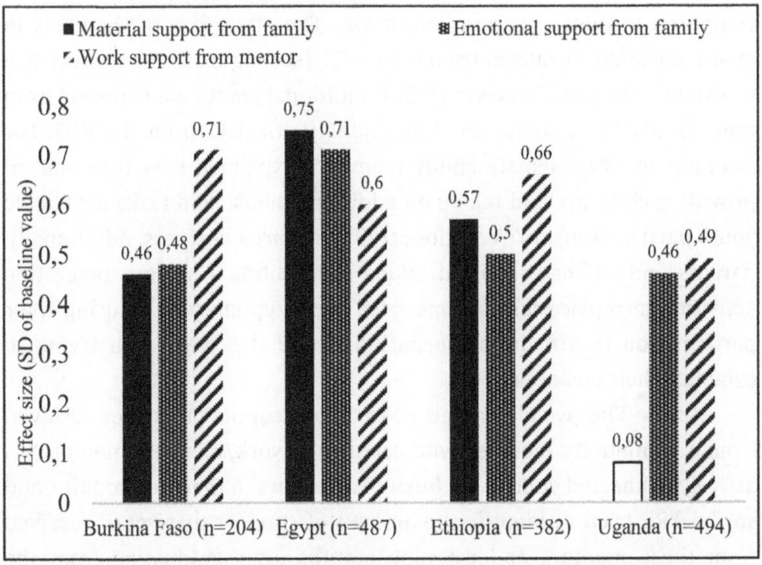

Note: Unshaded white bar represents gains that were statistically but not practically meaningful.

In terms of material support, in the TRC, we asked youth if their family gave them access to land, space in the home, tools/raw materials (e.g. grain for animal fattening), or animals. We created an index of the number of types of material support youth reported receiving. Youth in Burkina Faso, Egypt, and Ethiopia reported marked increases in their families' contribution of material support. The effect size of the gains was between 0.46–0.75 (see Figure 1). This effect size translates into youth receiving 0.5–1 additional material supports from their family several months after having graduated from the programme. We triangulated this finding with data from the Enterprise Development Study (ENT). For example, in Burkina Faso, 77 percent of youth in the ENT study (38 percent female), reported that their family provided them with land—between ¼ hectare and ½ hectare—to start an agricultural business after their participation in YiA.

The same was true for emotional support. In the TRC, we asked youth if their family helped them learn new skills, supported their work ideas, gave them sufficient time to finish their work, and helped them manage their business. We created an index of the number of types of emotional support youth reported receiving. Youth reported substantive improvements several months after graduating from the programme, as compared to their situation before YiA. The effect size of the gains in emotional support ranged from 0.46–0.71 (see Figure 1). This effect size translates into youth receiving 0.5–1 additional emotional supports from their family. We triangulated this finding with data from the ENT. For example, in Egypt female family members explained how they started providing childcare and taking on additional household tasks for female youth participating in YiA or those trying to start a business. Additionally, parents and siblings reported taking on additional income generating activities to replace lost income from the Egyptian youth during their participation in YiA or in the period where they were still trying to establish their business.

In the TRC, we also asked youth about support that they received from a community member who acted as a work/business mentor. YiA actively connected youth with business mentors in their community, and so the TRC tried to identify the amount of support that youth received from these mentors at least nine months after graduating from the programme. We defined support as receiving information about market resources, emotional support through work challenges, help in building work confidence, instruction on new skills, and advice about work issues. We created an index of the number of types of support youth reported receiving from their mentor. Forty-two percent of youth reported having a mentor before starting YiA. Several months after graduating from the programme, almost 80 percent of youth still had a business mentor. Additionally, in Burkina Faso, Egypt, Ethiopia, and Uganda youth reported an increase of 1–1.5 support behaviours from their mentor, an effect size of 0.49–0.71 (see Figure 1).

5.5. Family and community support predicts skill building

Lastly, we wanted to understand if the improvements in family and community support were associated with improvements in the skills youth built during YiA. In the POS, we created a measure of family and community support from items focused on youth perceptions of family and community support, safety, and trust. In all the YiA countries we found that for youth who reported high levels of this family and community support before the programme, they also reported higher levels of financial literacy, internal assets (e.g. social competencies, positive values, and positive identity), communication skills, and self-employment capabilities (e.g. business planning)[2]. We did not find this relationship when it came to pre-YiA levels of literacy and numeracy.

However, pre-test levels of family and community support were negatively associated with gains in financial literacy, internal assets, communication skills, and self-employment capabilities. This means that youth who had lower levels of family and community support prior to YiA were actually able to gain more in terms of foundational skills through the programme. If we view the levels of family and community support as an equity factor, this finding highlights the fact that the skill building in YiA worked best for the youth who needed it the most, the youth with the lowest levels of family and community support.

Lastly, gains in family and community support over the programme period were positively associated with gains in financial literacy, internal assets, communication skills, and self-employment capabilities. This could be a reflection of the "signalling effect" of participating in livelihood programmes like YiA. Youth who participated in YiA sent a signal to their family and community that they were responsible and dedicated; this could have resulted in additional support for skill building during the programme from family and community members.

6. Discussion and implications

In the rural contexts where YiA was implemented in Burkina Faso, Egypt, Ethiopia, Malawi, and Uganda, parents and community members are the gatekeepers for youth building labour market skills, finding decent work, or starting a business. Youth are often negotiating their reputation in their community for being hard working and responsible, a reputation that is linked to family and community members supporting youth livelihood development. One way in which youth can build this reputation is by participating in programmes like YiA. Indeed, in all the YiA countries youth who participated in YiA reported increased support from their family for livelihood development in the form of space for a business, land,

---

2   We controlled for the differential effect of age, gender, household wealth, and work status prior to YiA in all our fitted regression models. Table of fitted models available upon request.

tools, and/or emotional support. Additionally, family and community support were associated with the skills youth gained through the programme. High levels of family and community support prior to the programme were associated with higher levels of work readiness skills. However, YiA helped level the playing field: youth who had lower levels of family and community support prior to YiA were actually able to gain more in terms of foundational skills through the programme and gains in support over the programme period were positively associated with gains in work readiness skills.

As we demonstrated through our secondary analysis, the relationships in the proximal enabling environment—especially the family and immediate community—are essential to ensuring youth access to training or other educational activities and later success in income-generating activities. Supply-side interventions need to focus more explicitly on the proximal enabling environment, especially when it comes to working with youth in rural communities in the five countries where YiA is implemented. We provide more information on some of these strategies below.

- Improve family and community perceptions of youth

Our analysis highlighted the importance of positive perceptions of youth: when young people are viewed as responsible and hard-working, adults in the community are willing to provide financial, emotional, and additional supports to their entry into the labour market. Providing opportunities for youth to demonstrate their learning is a key strategy for promoting improvements in adult perceptions of youth. More importantly, engaging family and community members as active participants of programme activities and attempting to change normative perceptions through targeted social behaviour change communication can help communities perceive youth as responsible, hard-working agents of change in their community.

- Increase parental and community-wide engagement

Effective skill-building programmes recognize that the skills learned in one context, such as youth learning sessions, are acquired more efficiently and effectively when they are practiced in other contexts (Pellegrino and Hilton 2012; Brown et al. 2015). When families and communities are involved in programmatic skill building, they are able to provide opportunities for youth to practice those skills outside of sessions. Additionally, strong, supportive relationships increase the likelihood that mentorships and apprenticeships will result in the desired outcomes. Regular engagement with parents and other community members in programme activities as sources of information, teachers of skills and competencies, role models, and generally valued and respected programme stakeholders could result in increased support for youth skill building and income-generation. This is a fundamental strategy for ensuring that youth have continued, sustainable opportunities for growth beyond the lifespan of a particular intervention.

- Promote recognition of the proximal environment

In YiA we found that there is a tendency among youth and families from rural areas to underestimate the significance of the tangible and intangible supports available in their communities. Youth and their families may believe they have no access to credit because there are no local formal financial institutions, or that non-monetary resources are inconsequential. However, these inputs can be extremely pertinent in determining youth livelihoods outcomes, and are often more readily available than formal services. Youth livelihood programming should include activities that allow families, communities, and youth themselves, to identify locally available resources, and encourage adults to make those resources available to youth. For example, the creation of informal savings networks can substitute formal lending institutions, and even minimal parental financial contributions can have significant impact on youth start-up activities.

7. Conclusion

Programming that addresses youth livelihoods in LMICs must recognize the importance of families and immediate communities to youth participation and success in skill-building and market-based activities. Linking youth to the market through "bridging strategies" is a step in that direction, but true engagement with parents and communities requires strategic interventions that target them specifically. Interventions that aim to improve family and community perceptions of youth, increase parental and community engagement in skill-building and market-based activities, and engage families and communities as stand-ins where institutions and policy implementation is largely absent, can be successful in fostering an enabling proximal environment. Further research is needed to determine whether these findings hold true in other contexts, however existing extant literature suggests the importance of the proximal environment to youth livelihood success in different LMIC contexts (Youth Business International, 2016; Youth Policy Labs, 2015). We encourage programme developers to integrate a strategic and explicit focus on the proximal enabling environment in their work with youth livelihoods, in order to increase their likelihood of attaining positive outcomes for youth.

References

AfDB, OECD, UNDP, and UNECA. 2012. *African Economic Outlook 2012. Special Theme: Promoting Youth Employment.* Paris, France.

Benson, Peter L., Nancy Leffert, Peter C. Scales, and Dale A. Blyth. 2012. "Beyond the 'village' Rhetoric: Creating Healthy Communities for Children and Adolescents." *Applied Developmental Science* 16 (1): 3–23. https://doi.org/10.1080/1088 8691.2012.642771.

Bronfenbrenner, Urie. 1977. "Toward an Experimental Ecology of Human Development." *American Psychologist*, 32 (7): 513–31.

Bronfenbrenner, Urie, and Pamela A Morris. 1988. "The Ecology of Human Developmental Processes." In *Handbook of Child Psychology: Volume 1: Theoretical Models of Human Development*, 5th ed.: 993–1028. Hoboken, New Jersey: John Wiley & Sons Inc.

Brown, AN, K Rankin, M Picon, and DB Cameron. 2015. *The State of Evidence on the Impact of Transferable Skills Programming on Youth in Low- and Middle-Income Countries.* New Delhi, India: International Initiative for Impact Evaluation.

Butler, Erik Payne, Nancy Taggart, and Nancy Chervin. 2012. "Education, Earning, and Engagement for out-of-School Youth in 26 Developing Countries: What Has Been Learned from Nine Years of EQUIP3?" *Journal of International Cooperation in Education* 15 (2): 129–58.

Clemensson, Martin, and Jens Dyring Christensen. 2010. *How to Build an Enabling Environment for Youth Entrepreneurship and Sustainable Enterprises.* Geneva, Switzerland: International Labor Organization. http://ilo.ch/public/english/re gion/eurpro/moscow/info/publ/employment/build_enabling_environment_ye se.pdf.

D'Sa, Nikhit, Selah Agaba, and Promise Mchenga. 2017. "Influence of Community on Youth Transferable Skills in Livelihood Development: A Case Study from Rural Malawi and Uganda." In *Adolescent Psychology in Today's World: Global Perspectives on Risk, Relationships, and Development*, edited by M. Nakkula and A. Schneider-Muñoz. Santa Barbara, CA: Praeger.

D'Sa, Nikhit, Eliel Gebru, Peter C. Scales, and Chen-Yu Wu. 2017a. *Effect of Youth in Action on Work Readiness and Socioeconomic Outcomes: Findings from Egypt.* Washington, DC: Save the Children.

———. 2017b. *Effect of Youth in Action on Work Readiness and Socioeconomic Outcomes: Findings from Ethiopia.* Washington, DC: Save the Children.

———. 2017c. *Effect of Youth in Action on Work Readiness and Socioeconomic Outcomes: Findings from Uganda.* Washington, DC: Save the Children.

———. 2018a. *Effect of Youth in Action on Work Readiness and Socioeconomic Outcomes: Findings from Burkina Faso.* Washington, DC: Save the Children.

———. 2018b. *Effect of Youth in Action on Work Readiness and Socioeconomic Outcomes: Findings from Malawi.* Washington, DC: Save the Children.

Dejaeghere, Joan, and Aryn Baxter. 2014. "Entrepreneurship Education for Youth in Sub-Saharan Africa: A Capabilities Approach as an Alternative Framework to Neoliberalism's Individualizing Risks." *Progress in Development Studies* 14 (1): 61–76. https://doi.org/10.1177/1464993413504353.

Farahat, Ahmed. 2018. *Learning Narrative: Family Support and Youth Livlihood Development.* Toronto, Canada: Save the Children.

Flynn, Justin, Philip Mader, Marjoke Oosterom, and Santiago Ripoll. 2017. *Failing Young People? Addressing the Supply-Side Bias and Individualisation in Youth Employment Programming.* London, UK.

France, Jonathan, Vistoria Pelka, and Laura Kirchner. 2016. *Youth Entrepreneurship in Rural and Remote Areas : A Study of the Challenges and Possible Solutions.* London, UK: Youth Business International & BG Group.

Gebrehiwot, Yosef. 2017. *Learning Narrative: Youth-Led Enterprise Development.* Toronto, Canada: Save the Children.

Gupta, Monica Das, Robert Engelman, Jessica Levy, Gretchen Luchsinger, Tom Merrick, and James E. Rosen. 2014. *The Power of 1.8 Billion Adolescent, Youth and the Transformation of the Future.* Washington D.C: UNFPA.

ILO. 2012. *Global Employment Trends for Youth 2012.* Geneva, Switzerland: International Labour Organization. http://www.ilo.org/wcmsp5/groups/public/---dgreports /---dcomm/---publ/documents/publication/wcms_412015.pdf.

———. 2015. *Global Employment Trends for Youth 2015: Scaling up Investments in Decent Jobs for Youth.* Geneva, Switzerland: International Labour Organization. https://doi.org/92-2-113360-5.

———. 2016. *World Employment Social Outlook: Trends for Youth.* Geneva, Switzerland: International Labour Organization.

International Youth Foundation. 2014. *Strengthening Life Skills for Youth: A Practical Guide to Quality Programming*. Baltimore, MD: International Youth Foundation.

James-Wilson, David. 2008. *Youth Livelihoods Development Programme Guide*. Washington D.C: USAID.

Kluve, Jochen, Susana Puerto, David Robalino, Jose Manuel Romero, Friederike Rother, Jonathan Stöterau, Felix Weidenkaff, and Marc Witte. 2016. "Do Youth Employment Programs Improve Labor Market Outcomes? A Systematic Review." *IZA Discussion Paper Series*, no. 10263.

Leer, Jane, and Nikhit D'Sa. 2017a. *Youth in Action: Burkina Faso Tracer Study*. Washington, DC: Save the Children.

———. 2017b. *Youth in Action: Egypt Tracer Study*. Washington, DC: Save the Children.

———. 2017c. *Youth in Action: Ethiopia Tracer Study*. Washington, DC: Save the Children.

———. 2017d. *Youth in Action: Uganda Tracer Study*. Washington, DC: Save the Children.

Lerner, Richard M., Jason B. Almerigi, Christina Theokas, and Jacqueline V. Lerner. 2005. "Positive Youth Development A View of the Issues." *The Journal of Early Adolescence* 25 (1): 10–16. https://doi.org/10.1177/0272431604273211.

Lippman, Laura H., Renee Ryberg, Rachel Carney, and Kristin A. Moore. 2015. *Key 'soft Skills' that Foster Youth Workforce Success: Toward a Consensus across Fields*. Washington D.C: USAID.

Lopez, Veronica, Susana Puerto Gonzalez, Peter Glick, Nelly Mejia, Francisco Perez-Arce, and Mattias Lundberg. 2015. *Toward Solutions for Youth Employment: A 2015 Baseline Report*. Washington DC: S4YE Coalition.

Maina, Nelly, and Raquel Asencios. 2017. *Learning Narrative: Gender Mainstreaming in Youth Livlihood Programs*. Toronto, Canada: Save the Children.

Olenik, Christina, Caroline Fawcett, Jack Boyson, and USAID. 2013. *State of the Field Report: Examining the Evidence in Youth Workforce Development*. Washington D.C.: USAID.

Palmer, Robert. 2007. "Skills for Work?: From Skills Development to Decent Livelihoods in Ghana's Rural Informal Economy." *International Journal of Educational Development* 27 (4): 397–420. https://doi.org/10.1016/j.ijedudev.2006.10.003.

Pellegrino, James W, and Margaret L Hilton. 2012. *Education for Life and Work: Developing Transferable Knowledge and Skills in the 21st Century*. National Academies Press. https://doi.org/0-309-25649-6.

Pereznieto, Paola, Rachel Marcus, Matthew Maclure, Nandini Archer, and Anna Mdee. 2018. *Gender and youth livelihoods programming in Africa*. Toronto, Canada: Mastercard Foundation.

Scales, Peter C., Eugene C. Roehlkepartain, and Maura Shramko. 2016. "Aligning Youth Development Theory, Measurement, and Practice across Cultures and Contexts: Lessons from Use of the Developmental Assets Profile." *Child Indicators Research* 10 (4): 1145–78. https://doi.org/10.1007/s12187-016-9395-x.

UNDP. 2014. *Empowered Youth, Sustainable Future: UNDP Youth Strategy 2014–2017*. New York: United Nations.

United Nations. 2007. *The Employment Imperative: Report on the World Social Situation 2007*. New York: United Nations.

USAID. 2017. *A Systematic Review of Positive Youth Development Programs in Low- and Middle-Income Countries, Vol. 1*. Washington D.C: USAID.

Youth Business International. 2016. *Supporting Young Entrepreneurs: What Works? An Evidence and Learning Review from the YBI Network*. London, UK: Youth Business International.

Youth Policy Labs. 2015. *From Rhetoric to Action: Towards an Enabling Environment for Child and Youth Development in the Sustainable Development Goals*. Highlights from the Report Commissioned by the Case for Space Initiative. Berlin, Germany. https://doi.org/10.1017/CBO9780511996405.

CHAPTER 10
Physical and Virtual Mobility for Youth Employment in Malawi: Reflections on Findings from Two Research Projects

Gina Porter, Kate Hampshire, Alister Munthali and Elsbeth Robson

1. Introduction

Young people's access to livelihoods in sub-Saharan Africa is of vital importance to the next development decade: jobs and opportunity for young people are consistently at the top of the development agenda in virtually every African country (World Bank 2014; UK Department for International Development 2017). With half of sub-Saharan populations under 25 years of age, a projected half a million more reaching the age of 15 each year in the years between 2015 and 2035, and concerns about youth's potential role in social unrest (especially given the Arab Spring experiences), this is hardly surprising (World Bank 2014). A growing proportion of young people have higher expectations than their parents for employment and are prepared to move across and beyond the continent as they search for meaningful work. In this context, understanding the role of mobility in shaping opportunities and frustrations is likely to be critical, as efforts are made by governments and international donors to devise policies that can improve young lives and livelihood trajectories within Africa.

This chapter explores the roles played by both physical and virtual mobility in young people's endeavours to access income-earning opportunities and make a better life. It draws on findings from two interdisciplinary, mixed-methods research studies with young people in sub-Saharan Africa, in which young people themselves played a key role as peer investigators. The first project (www.dur.ac.uk/child.mobility/), conducted between 2006 and 2010, focused principally on the daily physical mobility patterns of children aged 9–18 years; the second (www.dur.ac.uk/child.phones/), conducted between 2012 and 2015, worked with an extended age cohort (9–25 years) and examined the impact of the virtual mobility facilitated by mobile phones. Although both studies were conducted in three countries (Ghana, Malawi, South Africa), space limitations dictate that the main focus in this chapter is the poorest country of the three, Malawi.

Our work in eight different research sites across Malawi provides clear examples of how physical and virtual mobilities (and intersections between them) have been playing out on the ground over the last decade in diverse contexts, urban and rural; this has significant implications for young people's livelihood experiences and trajectories.

The first study on daily physical mobilities demonstrates how physical mobility and (poor) access to transport helps not only to define or limit the locations available for work but also the labour tasks assigned to young people in Malawi. Many work activities in Malawi are generated as a result of transport failures: the need to carry water in the absence of water pipes; fuel in the absence of electricity; other goods such as maize or fertilizer when motorised transport is too costly or unavailable. Often such tasks are unpaid, sometimes physically harmful, and may well reduce access to formal schooling. However—as we will demonstrate—they also contribute to building a repertoire of knowledge and skills and valuable social networks that may be utilised subsequently to obtain informal sector paid employment.

The second study shows how young people in our Malawi study sites are benefitting from the potential new flexibilities between physical and virtual mobilities afforded by mobile phones. The significance of mobile phones in an employment context lies in their potential to leapfrog physical distance (across neighbourhoods, regionally across the country, or even internationally). Mobile phones can help connect those looking for work with information about work, with potential employers and, if they set up an independent micro-enterprise, with customers. Phones may thus reduce expensive and potentially hazardous journeys undertaken when searching for or undertaking work. They are also used to connect with transport providers when transport is required in the course of such endeavours.

Issues associated with the roles of location and gender in the search for work and the nature of available work interlace both mobility stories. Our investigations of physical mobility in diverse sites, ranging from remote rural to high density urban places, highlight the particular difficulties that young people face in more remote locations as they try to access education that will improve their future job prospects, and later as they look to enter the full-time labour market; the hurdles that girls must overcome are particularly great. The second study shows that, while some young people can enhance connections across their networks through the opportunities that mobile phone usage offers for leapfrogging locational constraints, thus allowing them to modestly progress their working lives, gender continues to play a significant role in the shaping of the employment opportunities available.

We start this chapter with a short review of the context of youth employment and post-schooling transitions in sub-Saharan Africa and Malawi. A brief description of the research sites and the innovative methodology employed in the two studies follows. Findings are then presented firstly regarding opportunities for, and constraints on, daily physical mobility that affect access to work and, secondly, our more recent work on the impact of mobile phones as a potential game-changer for youth as they pursue work opportunities.

2. Youth employment and post-schooling transitions in sub-Saharan Africa and Malawi: some contextual information

One of Africa's most pressing problems is young people's poor employment prospects, as is also highlighted in Chapters 9 (D'Sa et al.) and 12 (Ogawa et al) in this volume. In most sub-Saharan countries, open unemployment is relatively low, especially in rural locations, but there is much "working poverty" (Filmer et al. 2014). This is certainly the case in Malawi: in a survey of 3,000 children aged 9 to 18 years we conducted across 24 sites in Ghana, Malawi and South Africa in 2013/14 (in connection with our child mobility research described further below), 91 percent of those young people in Malawi aged 9–25 not enrolled in education had undertaken some livelihood activity in the 12 months prior to the survey. This figure was considerably higher than that for our other study countries (with Ghana at 77 percent and South Africa at 52 percent; see Porter et al. 2018). In Malawi's rural areas the figure was even higher at 95 percent. Work in both rural and urban areas here, as in most African countries, is typically in the informal sector—temporary, low-paid and with poor working conditions (World Bank 2012: 206; World Bank 2014).

Even while still in school, many young people across sub-Saharan Africa start to build experience in the informal sector, working in family enterprises (often unpaid) or elsewhere, before and after school and at weekends or during school holidays (Andvig 2001; Spittler and Bourdillon 2012). While such work tends to be low-skilled, it may still offer training, experience and entry into networks that can shape future work opportunities (Porter et al. 2018). Boys, for instance, may learn construction skills, while girls help family members trading in local markets, or perhaps sell snacks in the school playground during break times. For most girls across the continent, however, work opportunities tend to be more limited than for boys, and as the following discussion demonstrates in Malawian contexts, much of their work comprises unpaid domestic labour. In many cultural contexts across Africa it is girls, alongside women, who bear primary responsibility for carrying domestic water and firewood, in the absence of alternative low-cost modes of transport (Porter 2011; Porter et al. 2012a).

In Africa's rural areas, life on family farm holdings is clearly very hard (see Morrow et al. 2014: 142–8 for rural Ethiopia). Urban areas are often seen as the key to a better life, not least through improved educational and job opportunities; such perceptions prevail not only among young people themselves, but among their elders. This amounts to what Quayson in a Ghanaian context, has described as "enchantment" (2015: 151): the self-making and prosperity potential of the city. Unsurprisingly, then, many rural youth and their elders see migration to the city as a logical move. It will potentially bring not only money but also knowledge and status (Hashim and Thorsen 2011: 48). The comment that, "there is nothing good that can be an advantage to my children here … I hope they finish school and get jobs and live a good life in town," which came from a mother of two boys in remote rural Malawi, expresses a sentiment that resonates among rural people in many locations across the continent.

For some young rural Africans, the first taste of urban life comes when they move to access educational opportunities, especially the secondary education which is perceived as so key to formal sector jobs (Hashim and Thorsen 2011: 49–53). Staying with family members can be helpful in negotiating this first taste of the city—renting a room independently and without recourse to family support in the vicinity tends to be more challenging, financially and socially. Subsequently, as their search for full-time employment intensifies, many more rural youth migrate city-ward with the hope of finding more secure and better paid work and greater opportunity for advancement. In the case of Malawi this may be to locations within the country itself (often the main commercial city Blantyre, or the capital city Lilongwe), or beyond, with South Africa a common destination. Here, their employment hopes and frustrations mirror those of many other young people recorded across the continent (Hansen 2005; Chant and Jones 2005; Langevang and Gough 2009; Mains 2007; Weiss 2005; Archambault 2012).

A national dialogue on the future of work in Malawi, opened by the government last year, observed the depth of the crisis for young people: as the official opening the dialogue observed:

> Youth unemployment is at 23 percent ... A deeper analysis will reveal that most of the employment and work is in the informal sector which faces serious work deficits. The youth find themselves in this sector because they have no alternative means of livelihood ... they are in this sector not by choice but rather for survival. (Malawi Nyasa Times, July 17th 2017)

While there are various programmes in place to try to improve the situation—including a new government programme to set up community colleges in all districts, aimed at providing youth with technical skills— there is unlikely to be a dramatic change in conditions so long as the national jobs market remains stagnant. It is important to bear this broader employment context in mind as we consider the place of physical and virtual mobility in shaping young people's access to employment in Malawi.

3.   A review of research sites and methodology

3.1 The research sites

Our comparative research on young people's mobility in 24 sites across Malawi, Ghana and South Africa commenced in 2006 with a study of the physical mobility of children aged 9–18 years. In Malawi (as in the other two study countries) we worked in eight sites spread across two agro-ecological zones: four in the very densely populated Shire Highlands region in and around the city of Blantyre in southern Malawi; and four in the (slightly less) densely populated plains region in and around the country's capital, Lilongwe, in central Malawi. In each of these regions we worked in one remote rural settlement with no services (not even a primary school), one rural settlement with services (minimum of a primary school and/or health centre), one peri-urban settlement located on an all-weather road, and one high density poor urban neighbourhood.

In the two remote rural sites the nearest primary school is 3–5 km away. In the case of the Blantyre remote rural site, the nearest secondary school is over 5 km away and in the case of the Lilongwe zone site it is 10 km away. There is no public transport serving these areas and few private vehicles reach either settlement. Villagers grow maize, vegetables and some keep some small livestock or cattle on their highly dispersed smallholdings, with assistance from their children. Some are also involved in the production of charcoal which will subsequently be sold in district trading centres or directly to city-based dealers. Educational and work opportunities in such remote sites are minimal.

The remote rural settlements are each linked by poor laterite track to a village with services, 3–5 km away, which we also studied. Dirt roads then link onward to our peri-urban study sites which are (seasonally) accessible by motor transport from these villages. However, most people must walk or cycle to reach the main tarmac road 5–9 km away, in the absence of regular public transport services. In the villages with services there are at least primary schools and basic clinics or regular visits by mobile health workers. Opportunities to pursue secondary education and develop income-earning opportunities are also a little more favourable than in remote rural locations, given closer access to roads where transport is likely to be at least occasionally available. This slightly improves young people's potential to reach secondary schools and the trading centres where there is more likelihood of finding regular paid work.

In the peri-urban research sites educational and work opportunities are substantially stronger. There are government primary and community day secondary schools, private schools, health centre, post office, some electricity, some boreholes and public transport links to the city by paved road. Trading centres in these locations provide opportunities to sell goods to residents, incoming city dealers and road travellers passing through. There is also work to be had at local bars and hotels, in construction work, in sex work, or as porters, bicycle transporters and suchlike.

The two urban research sites are located respectively in Blantyre, Malawi's commercial centre and Lilongwe, Malawi's administrative capital. Both research sites are poor, high density neighbourhoods with local primary and secondary schools (including some private schools) and various other facilities, including regular but relatively expensive public transport within a radius of 3 km. Both urban study sites have experienced substantial in-migration because the potential for educational and work opportunities is seen to be so much greater here than elsewhere in the country. Unsurprisingly, they are also more ethnically mixed than other sites.

During our initial physical mobility research (completed in 2010), new and potential complexities arising through young people's access to mobile phone were beginning to emerge (Porter et al. 2012) and led to our second study focused on young people's virtual mobility via mobile phones which commenced in 2012. We continued to work in the same research locations, but this time with an extended age-range of 9–25 years, thus enabling us to follow our initial cohort six years on. This also allowed us to engage with many more young people who had left school and were now working or at least attempting to find work.

3.2 Methodology

We maintained the same mixed-methods approach in both studies (and across all 24 sites in the wider research project): a two-strand approach, in which a more conventional adult academic research study (with qualitative and quantitative components) was complemented by an innovative "young researcher" strand. We commenced both studies with the "young researcher" strand, as this helped us select key issues for further investigation in the subsequent "academic-led" strand. Thus, in Malawi in 2006, 24 young researchers (secondary school pupils aged between 14 and 22 years) from six locations were recruited through their schools (with parental, school and child/young person's consent) and given a basic training in research methods, for our "young researcher" strand. They selected the research tools they were comfortable with and conducted their studies among peers in places convenient to them (Robson et al., 2009). Their findings were gathered through informal interviews, group discussions, diaries, photographic journals of children's travel to school and at work using disposable cameras, and accompanied walks. These findings fed into and complemented the adult academic researcher strand, which explored the questions the young researchers raised, together with wider issues suggested by the literature and our previous work with young researchers on this theme (Porter and Abane 2008). The academic research team followed on with in-depth interviews, focus group discussions, ethnographic diaries and accompanied walks with young people, and with in-depth interviews, life histories and focus group discussions with their parents and other key informants. There also was a quantitative survey of just over 1000 child respondents aged approximately 9–18 years (c. 125 per site).

When we commenced the new virtual mobility (phones) research study in 2012, we were able to contact most of the 24 young researchers we had trained in 2006; many had continued to keep in touch over the intervening period. Those who were in a position to do so participated from time to time in the new study, according to their availability (Porter 2016). This time, some of the young researchers played an even larger part in the research, with contributions extending from pilot work in the peer research phase (where key questions for the academic strand were identified, as in the child mobility study), to direct engagement in the main phase of work, both through in-depth interviewing and through administering survey questionnaires. By this time, as university graduates and/or workers for non-governmental organisations (NGOs), with research experience from the previous phase, they felt confident to do this work and produced excellent results.

In the main "academic-led" component of the phones study, in-depth interviews were conducted firstly using a story-based approach, covering education, livelihoods and a wide range of other issues, followed by "call register interviews" focused on young people's contact lists and recent phone-based interactions (including calls, texts, use of social network sites). Other qualitative research included: focus groups (some with older people 40 years old and older); key informant interviews with settlement leaders and others; life histories with a small number of people in their late 20s–30s; and essays written by school children. Approximately 60 to 100 qualitative interviews were completed in each of the Malawi sites, totalling in all just under 700 interviews, while the questionnaire survey covered 1,000 9–18 year-olds, as in the earlier child mobility study, plus an additional 500 young people aged 19–25 years, split as evenly as possible across sites. Survey respondents (as in the earlier physical mobility study) were selected by enumerators working along transects across each settlement (i.e. working first in one direction, then crossing the settlement again in another direction, in order to pick up any significant differences associated with location within the settlement, such as concentrations of particular ethnic groups).

4. Daily physical mobility and access to work

Individual experiences of employment and post-schooling transition among young people in Malawi are shaped by many factors, but our data suggest that location and gender commonly play particularly significant roles in influencing the potential for physical access to remunerative work. So far as location is concerned, young people living in remoter rural areas are particularly disadvantaged. As noted earlier, transport services in our remote rural sites are extremely poor, irregular and unreliable; much travel must be entirely on foot. Consequently, education for most rural children is limited to primary level (and in the remote rural study sites even primary schools require a long trek to the nearest village with services). This is because secondary schools tend to be located at a distance, in peri-urban and urban centres. Such limited exposure to formal education limits subsequent work opportunities for most young people.

Once young people leave school, poor access to transport has further impact, reducing the locations available for work to the local environs—in remoter rural areas this essentially means agricultural labour, petty trade and/or charcoal production. The combination of poor access to transport and jobs encourages city-ward migration (especially among young men); even so, once ensconced in a poor urban neighbourhood, young people's physical mobility as they search for or engage in employment is often constrained by the relatively high cost of public transport.

Female gender brings further constraints on a young person's mobility for education and meaningful work. Parental and family concerns about girls' vulnerability to the hazards of independent travel are often mixed with other concerns regarding their potential for sexual activity (Porter 2011). Such attitudes are widespread and particularly potent when combined with family demands for unpaid domestic labour. They lead to greater surveillance and less mobility for girls compared with boys.

Local transport failures bring particular burdens to young girls from an early age. They are generally expected to carry water, maize and firewood for domestic use on a regular basis, in addition to the other domestic tasks commonly assigned to females (cooking, cleaning, help with child care etc.). Boys, by contrast, are usually entirely exempt from domestic load-carrying once they reach their mid-teens. As one father in a remote rural site observed, as he reflected on the differing mobility characteristics of his four daughters and two sons:

> Boys have more freedom than girls ... girls work hard more than boys, hence boys have more time to move around ... girls ought to stay home and look after the house and cook.

Among 16–18-year-olds in the Malawi survey, 84 percent of girls reported carrying water daily, compared to just 34 percent of boys. Among 7–11-year-olds, the gender differences were less pronounced (59 percent of girls and 27 percent of boys carried water daily) but still considerable. As fathers in one peri-urban focus group observed, "we send girls of good age [to collect water], as boys in most cases refuse." Older boys are often embarrassed to be seen collecting and carrying water. In the peri-urban sites, where most households still have no access to piped water, three-quarters of girls surveyed carried water every day, compared to just one-third of boys (Porter et al. 2012, 2017; Robson et al. 2013). Such water carrying is one of those domestic tasks that regularly delays girls' travel to school, resulting in punishments for late arrival, poor performance associated with reduced lesson time in school, and the consequent likelihood of early drop-out. Without a satisfactory school leaving examination certificate, the likelihood of obtaining even a low-paid job is small.

Fuelwood collection represents another burden which falls more heavily on girls: overall, 41 percent of Malawian girls in the survey reported having carried fuelwood at least once in the preceding week, compared with 16 percent of boys. In the 16–18 year age group this burden on girls was even more pronounced with comparative figures of 51 percent for girls, yet just 16 percent among boys. Although firewood does not usually have to be collected every day, loads can be substantially heavier than for water, and firewood collection may require excursions to remote, isolated areas with difficult terrain such that many girls reported fears for their safety.

Carrying heavy loads of maize to the grinding mills and returning with a headload of flour is another job predominantly allocated to girls. As with water carrying, maize porterage and firewood collection reduce the time that girls have available for school, with similar consequences to those noted in the water context. However, effective learning in class is likely to be even further reduced when girls have been carrying very heavy loads. They often arrive at school not merely late but exhausted (Porter et al. 2012). Over 30 percent of boys and nearly 40 percent of girls surveyed reported pains incurred from load-carrying, with the highest proportions in rural areas. The extent to which such experiences damage children's health outcomes and associated capacity to engage in employment in the longer-term are unknown (Porter et al. 2013). Even so, in rural Malawi, some parents suggested that carrying domestic loads benefited their children. One mother observed: "They get knowledge about how to work [and] ... it makes them strong."

For many girls, especially those living in remoter areas of Malawi, domestic chores—not least those associated with the transport gap—are so substantial that schooling is limited to a few years at the closest local primary establishment. Moreover, those who manage to pass the examination to proceed to secondary education are often denied that opportunity. In addition to the costs entailed, and a tendency to prioritise boys' education over girls', attending secondary school would require lengthy and potentially hazardous pedestrian travel to a distant (often urban) school or "home-boarding" (independent renting of accommodation). The latter strategy is said to result, too often, in lone girls being targeted by older men and returning home pregnant. Back in the village, with a child to care for, there is little potential for such girls to access the kinds of employment they have often dreamed of when they left the village for secondary school.

In view of the constraints observed above that limit girls' formal and informal education severely, most are only qualified to enter the very lowest level of paid employment once they leave school, wherever they find work: cleaning, porterage, petty trade and other casual day labour (*ganyu*) are the most common options available. Thus, even when girls in such circumstances go to find work in the city, their options will still be very limited, as eighteen-year-old Elizabeth, interviewed in rural Blantyre, described. Some years prior to our meeting, the hunger at home had become such that Elizabeth could no longer concentrate at school—this had driven her to leave home for a low-paid house-girl's job in Blantyre city, washing, cleaning and looking after children. The returns were so low, however, that eventually she decided to return home to her ageing parents in the village. Meanwhile, city parents still worry about their young daughters' vulnerability to harassment, attack and sexual assault; boys are considered more able to take care of themselves. One urban-based father of ten children observed that, "to raise a girl child properly, you need to have a keen eye on her always;" while an 18-year-old school girl in this urban neighbourhood was aware that her "movements are strictly monitored at home." Such parental concerns inevitably impact on young women's mobilities, whether they are resident in urban or rural areas, with significant potential impact on their search for, and uptake of, better employment opportunities.

5.   Mobile phones as a potential game-changer for youth employment

In sub-Saharan Africa, where landlines had mostly been the preserve of the elite, mobile phones have dramatically changed the opportunities for connectivity over the last decade. Their arrival has generated considerable optimism regarding their potential as a game-changer, not only for youth employment in general, but for women and girls' empowerment and access to jobs in particular (Porter et al. 2018).[1] Phones present an accessible and affordable tool for leapfrogging distance, and one which has been re-envisioned to suit African contexts through adapted low cost modes of usage: SMS, "buzzing" and, more recently, social media and money transfers. Young people have been at the forefront of this adoption, as they are keen embracers of the new technology. Even in 2006, it was evident that phones were starting to change the mobility context in our study countries, albeit with less impact at that time in Malawi than either Ghana or South Africa. When we conducted our 2007/8 (child mobility project) survey, only 9.3 percent of the 9–18 year-old respondents in our Malawi research sites had used a

---

1   See also http://www.huffingtonpost.co.uk/kathy-calvin/more-than-a-phone-mob
ile-empowering-women_b_4849761.html. 26/04/2014.

phone in the week prior to survey (varying from 0.4 percent in the remote rural sites to 21.6 percent in the urban sites)[2].

Since that first survey, usage in Malawi has expanded considerably, though ownership and usage is still lower than our other study countries, an unsurprising fact given Malawi's especially low status in wealth rankings (184th out of 189 countries in the world).[3] In the early days, many handsets had arrived in Malawi as gifts from family members working in South Africa; these were mostly basic phones, though by 2013/14 a few urban youth had their own internet-enabled phones (and 5 percent of those surveyed across Malawi had used an internet-enabled phone in the previous month). When we conducted the 2013/14 survey, overall phone use in the week prior to survey among the 9–18 year cohort had risen to 34.7 percent, varying from 13.8 percent in remote rural sites to 58.6 percent in urban sites. The extent to which phone usage has been able to facilitate youth access to work inevitably also varies, not just with reference to location but also with gender.

Location still plays a factor in accessing employment opportunities since phone networks remain so much poorer in the more remote rural areas than elsewhere: the coverage exclusion that Buys et al. (2009) observed "for low density rural populations that are off-road and uphill" has reduced but still pertains to some degree. Similarly, gender continues to play a role in shaping the potential that young people have to access or pursue employment via the phone, since females of all ages typically have fewer resources to buy a handset, or even to pay for airtime if they can manage to borrow a phone. In 2013/14, 10 percent of boys but only 6 percent of girls aged 9–18-years-old owned a phone, while 48 percent of men but only 31 percent of women aged 19–25 owned one. In rural areas (where only around 1–2 percent of girls under 19 years-old owned phones in 2014), girls told us that if they owned a phone they might be labelled a prostitute. In urban areas, meanwhile, many girls' mothers said they were reluctant to let their daughters own phones, as they linked phone ownership with teen pregnancy. So far as usage in the week prior

---

2   Usage was (and is) a better indicator of phone impact than ownership since so many people here, as elsewhere, share phones (Porter et al. 2012, 2015).

3   Projected GDP per capita, October 2016, from International Monetary Fund World Economic Outlook (October-2016) http://statisticstimes.com/economy/count ries-by-projected-gdp-capita.php.

to survey was concerned, there was a relatively small gap between boys and girls aged 9–18 in 2013/14 (36 percent as opposed as to 33 percent), but among those 19–25 a larger disparity was evident (62 percent of men as opposed to 49 percent of women), which probably relates to women's lower access to handsets and resources to purchase airtime. Unsurprisingly, there is some knock-on impact with reference to job search and livelihoods as we describe below.

Our phones research project explored young people's phone usage in diverse aspects of livelihood construction: in the conduct of job searches; phone-related work as a direct income source such as airtime sales, etc.; the use of phones to start or build micro-enterprise; and the way they may be used even among those without work for building a safety net—garnering resources through the pursuit of network capital. In 2013/14 in Malawi, among 9–25 year-olds not enrolled in school, 19 percent in Malawi (compared to 24 percent in Ghana and 46 percent in South Africa) had used a phone to try to find work over the past year. However, girls and young women were less likely than boys and young men to have done so (i.e. only 14 percent of females compared to 24 percent of males in Malawi). As might be expected, given the dominant role of the informal sector (and absence of internet connectivity for the vast majority), this was done almost entirely through calls to personal contacts (92 percent in the case of males, 100 percent in the case of females). One young woman now living in the city recalled how, when she was still staying at home in the village, one day an uncle living nearby had received a call from her elder sister in the city, to advise that a housemaid's post was available. Her uncle immediately rushed to inform her, and she quickly went to look for transport to take her to town that same morning. On arrival at the city outskirts she went to a telephone bureau to call her sister, who came to meet her at the bus depot and took her immediately to the employer's house. Having access to a phone in such circumstances was clearly key to the successful employment of the young woman concerned, but we only rarely met such stories.

Mobile phones are often identified as a business opportunity in themselves, but gender still shapes the potential opportunities available within this sector. We found that phone-related businesses in urban areas were reported as most successful where they involved phone repair and phone-charging—both seemingly exclusively male businesses. Poor quality handsets made in China regularly fall into disrepair, as one 20 year-old recounted, thus providing a lucrative income for those with repair skills. Charging phone batteries meanwhile, is a popular service in areas without mains electricity and is often combined with barbering. Hawking airtime is another common phone-related business, and one that requires little entry capital, but profits are much lower and thus, unsurprisingly, this work is often in the hands of women in urban areas. In rural areas, however, even much of this business is in male hands: men often run small grocery stalls where airtime is also sold; this is frequently in conjunction with phone-charging using small solar panels, a growing phenomenon.

Mobile phones are also now beginning to play a role in setting up and running some non-phone-related small businesses. Of those young people who had managed to set up their own business or were self-employed, in Malawi just 8 percent of women, but 29 percent of men, said that the phone had played a role in this process. In micro-enterprises the phone is used for diverse purposes: for building relations with customers/suppliers; for placing/receiving orders (especially in rural contexts); for booking transport (personal or freight); sometimes to obtain bank notification of payments; and for chasing debts. The advantages in trading contexts, where reductions in travel can improve profits substantially, were regularly observed in both urban and rural locations:

> Before I started using the phone in my business, sometimes I used to travel [to town] only to come back without anything because ... people have not started selling their produce or the prices are too high. (Woman, 22 years old, farmer/groundnut dealer, remote rural Lilongwe)

> Instead of me travelling [to town] without any knowledge of the thing's availability, I call them first. (Man, 22 years old, grocer, peri-urban Lilongwe)

> I used to sell [cloth] wrappers to my customers on credit. I was supposed to collect the money in instalments every month end. But I used to spend the money travelling to collect the debts ... When I got my phone, I got phone numbers of my customers [and could check that they were ready to pay before he went to collect the money]. In that way I minimised on transport expenses. (Man, 21 years old, hawker, peri-urban Lilongwe)

However, many such businesses are so precarious that they regularly fail, and many young people—male and female—related how they had to sell their phone to buy essentials such as food or, in rural areas, fertilizer and seed at the start of the planting season. But for those living a precarious existence it is important to retain access to a phone (and preferably a personal sim card too), even if one no longer has ownership. Phones can help significantly in the provision of a safety net, since distress calls may bring resources, monetary or material, that enable the recipient to "get by." In Malawi, nearly half (45 percent) of the young people aged 9–25 years old who we surveyed had contacted someone by phone to request money as a gift or loan for their personal use in the 12 months prior to the 2013/14 survey; 39 percent had requested material goods (shoes, clothes, books, food etc.), with little variation by gender. The level of requests for money (almost entirely made to relatives) was particularly high in the peri-urban and urban sites (52 percent and 55 percent respectively, compared to 29 percent in remote rural and 33 percent in rural with service sites). This probably reflects the high cost of living in those locations, especially for those without secure paid work.

There is thus only very limited evidence to date in Malawi that mobile phones are proving the game-change that has been hoped for across Africa. Certainly, they aid communication in rural as well as urban areas, and in better-networked rural areas they allow small businesses in hitherto unconnected service centres to improve their access to supplies when these are required, reducing time and travel costs. This benefits young men in particular, since they are more likely to have the resources and a modicum of education to establish these small enterprises in the first place. Mobile phones also enable many young people who have no paid work—men and women—to obtain help from their social networks at times when they are in desperate need of assistance. The potential of phone ownership or phone access to generate major improvements in livelihoods, however, is still significantly constrained by wider economic precariousness across the country as a whole.

6. Conclusion

Our two studies explored the potential for mobility—physical and virtual—to shape youth employment opportunities. Our data for Malawi show that across urban and rural areas there is an extensive informal sector where young people find occupation of a sort. From the age of around eight years old, work commonly takes place alongside formal education and, while this often entails unpaid assistance to family members, it may offer some training and experience which can be beneficial when school days are left behind and paid work sought. Most will then have to depend entirely on the informal sector for employment, albeit much of the work on offer is low paid and temporary. Physical mobility to access school and paid work is particularly difficult in rural areas, because motorised transport services are typically sparse, costly, irregular and unreliable. This restricts most young people in rural areas to those places and opportunities accessible on foot from their place of residence, unless they decide to migrate to the city. However, even in the poor city neighbourhoods where they are likely to reside, transport is costly. Girls and young women experience further mobility constraints in both urban and rural areas, associated with societal perceptions not only of their vulnerability to attack, but also their supposed potential for promiscuous behaviour (Porter et al. 2011).

In these conditions, the arrival of mobile phone technology and its potential to leapfrog distance, overcoming physical mobility constraints, has been widely viewed as a potential game-changer. Certainly, it is helping many young people in Malawi "get by" through the possibility it presents for accessing family resources in times of hardship. It has also helped some entrepreneurial young people—particularly young men—to build a better livelihood, whether through direct work in the mobile phone sector, or through the way phones can facilitate improved distance management and reduced costs, especially among those working in the trading sector. However, rural location, female gender and the overlying cap which constrained national economic conditions and a demographic youth bulge impose on the employment sector, all currently continue to limit the potential for significant improvement in the livelihoods and life chances of Malawian youth.

These experiences from Malawi are replicated across much of sub-Saharan Africa. Given the size of the youth bulge, current economic structures and ongoing sparsity of good-quality education, it seems likely that the majority of this generation's workers across the continent will remain in the informal sector throughout their working lives (World Bank 2014: 5). Indeed, this and the widespread evidence of already excessive pressures on service provision in most major urban centres, leads the World Bank (ibid) to suggest that African governments will have to refocus their attention once more on the rural sector and agriculture if they are to absorb the large numbers of new job seekers coming into the market. However, the rural-urban flow of youth will be difficult to stem, unless agricultural and associated rural informal sector employment can be repackaged as dynamic and relatively high-status. Higher quality rural education and training must be in place to support this, and feelings of rural isolation need to be reduced (including through more low-cost, regular, reliable and safe rural transport services). In this latter respect, as our Malawi example has shown, mobile phones can play a significant complementary role in rural areas. As phone networks continue to expand, if mobile phones can be better harnessed to support improved rural service provision, including not only transport services organisation but also rural education, skills training and health services, their potential could be considerable. For those many rural young women who face substantial constraints on their physical and virtual mobility, however, accessing meaningful employment arguably requires a whole host of confidence-building skills to enable them to challenge the social norms that currently limit their mobility and employment potential. In the short-term we can look to small improvements, such as the spread of solar power, community-based child care centres and more fuel efficient stoves, which may bring some beneficial reduction of domestic labour demands and associated time expenditure. If such time savings can be used to access skills training specifically geared to girls' needs, using mobile phones, hopefully incremental benefits will emerge over time.

References

Andvig, J.C. (2001). *Family controlled child labour in sub-Saharan Africa: A survey of research.* Washington: World Bank, Social Protection Unit.

Archambault, J. (2012). 'Travelling while sitting down': mobile phones, mobility and the communication landscape in Inhambane, Mozambique. *Africa* 82,3: 393–412.

Buys, P., Dasgupta, S., Thomas, T. S., Wheeler, D. (2009). Determinants of a digital divide in sub-Saharan Africa: a spatial econometric analysis of cell phone coverage. *World Development* 37: 1494–1505.

Chant, S., Jones, G.A. (2005). Youth, Gender and Livelihoods in West Africa: Perspectives from Ghana and The Gambia. *Children's Geographies* 3, 2: 185–199.

Hansen, K. T. (2005). Getting stuck in the compound: Some odds against social adulthood in Lusaka, Zambia. *Africa Today* 51,4: 3–16.

Hashim, I. and Thorsen, D. (2011). *Child Migration in Africa.* London: Zed Books.

Langevang, T. and Gough, K.V. (2009). Surviving through movement: The mobility of urban youth in Ghana. *Social and Cultural Geography* 10, 7: 741–56.

Mains, D. (2007). Neoliberal times: Progress, boredom, and shame among young men in urban Ethiopia. *American Ethnologist* 34, 4: 659–73.

Morrow, V., Tafere, Y., Vennam, U. (2014). Changes in rural children's use of time: evidence from Ethiopia and Andhra Pradesh. In Bourdillon, M. and Boyden, J. (eds), *Growing Up in Poverty: Findings from Young Lives*. London: Palgrave Macmillan.

Porter, G. and Abane, A. (2008). Increasing children's participation in transport planning: reflections on methodology in a child-centred research project. *Children's Geographies* 6, 2: 151–167.

Porter, G. (2011). 'I think a woman who travels a lot is befriending other men and that's why she travels': Mobility constraints and their implications for rural women and girl children in sub-Saharan Africa. *Gender, Place and Culture* 18, 1: 65–81.

Porter, G. (2016). Reflections on co-investigation through peer research with young people and older people in sub-Saharan Africa. *Qualitative Research* 16, 3: 293–304.

Porter, G., Hampshire, K. Munthali, A. and Robson, E. (2011). Mobility, surveillance and control of children in the everyday: Perspectives from sub-Saharan Africa. *Surveillance and Society* 9 (1/2), 114–131.

Porter, G., Hampshire, K., Abane, A., Munthali, A., Robson, E., Mashiri, M., Tanle, A. (2012). Youth, mobility and mobile phones in Africa: Findings from a three-country study. *Journal of Information Technology for Development* 18, 2: 145–162.

Porter, G. Hampshire, K., Abane, A., Munthali, A., Robson, E., Mashiri, M., Tanle, A., Maponya G., Dube, S. (2012). Child porterage and Africa's transport gap: Evidence from Ghana, Malawi and South Africa. *World Development* 40, 10: 2136–2154.

Porter, G., Hampshire, K., Dunn, C., Hall, R., Levesley, M., Burton, K., Robson, S., Abane, A., Blell, M., Panther, J. (2013). Health impacts of pedestrian head-loading: A review of the evidence with particular reference to women and children in sub-Saharan Africa. *Social Science and Medicine* 88: 90–97.

Porter, G. with Hampshire, K., Abane, A., Munthali, A., Robson, E., Mashiri, M. (2017). *Young People's Daily Mobilities in Sub-Saharan Africa: Moving Young Lives*. London: Palgrave Macmillan.

Porter, G., Hampshire, K., De Lannoy, A., Bango, A., Munthali, A., Robson, E., Tanle, A., Abane, A., Owusu, S. (2018). Youth livelihoods in the cell phone era: Perspectives from urban Africa. *Journal of International Development* 30, 4: 539–558.

Quayson, A. (2015). *Oxford Street, Accra: City Life and the Itineraries of Transnationalism*. Durham: Duke University Press.

Robson, E., Porter, G., Hampshire, K., Bourdillon, M. (2009). 'Doing it right?': Working with young researchers in Malawi to investigate children, transport and mobility. *Children's Geographies* 7,4: 467–480.

Robson, E., Porter, G., Hampshire, K., Munthali, A. (2013). Heavy loads: Children's burdens of water carrying in Malawi. *Waterlines* 32, 1: 23–35.

Spittler, G., Bourdillon, M. (eds) (2012). *African Children at Work*. Berlin: IAS.

UK Department for International Development (2017). *Economic Development Strategy: Prosperity, Poverty and Meeting Global Challenges*, January 2017.

Weiss, B. (2005). The barber in pain: Consciousness, affliction and alterity in East Africa. In F. De Boeck and A. Honwana (eds), *Makers and Breakers: Children and Youth in Postcolonial Africa*. Oxford: James Currey.

World Bank (2012). *World Development Report 2013: Jobs*. Washington DC: World Bank.

World Bank (2014). *Youth Employment in Sub-Saharan Africa*. Washington DC: World Bank.

CHAPTER 11
Disentangling Urban Adolescents' Vulnerability to Age- and Gender-Based Violence through a Capability Lens in Ethiopia and Rwanda

Nicola Jones, Umutoni Marie Francoise, Bekele Tefera, Ernestina Coast, Workneh Yadete, Roberte Isimbi, Guday Emirie and Kassahun Tilahun

1. Introduction

Despite considerable progress over the past two decades in advancing the visibility of the rights of children and adolescents to bodily integrity and a life free from violence, the transition from childhood to adulthood remains fraught for girls and boys in low- and middle-income countries (LMICs) (Patton et al., 2016). Emerging evidence suggests that adolescents often experience a range of discriminatory gendered and age-related social norms and practices, which may negatively affect their wellbeing and longer-term development trajectories (International Center for Research on Women (ICRW), 2016; Fulu et al., 2017; Harper et al., 2017). The evidence base on adolescent experiences and perceptions of violence is thin and fragmented, and research on the age-based and gender-specific patterning of violence in different settings (household, school, community)—as well as the availability and appropriateness of formal and informal channels of response and redress—is limited in many contexts (UNICEF, 2014a; Fulu and Kerr-Wilson, 2015; Pankhurst et al., 2016a; Chant et al., 2017; Yount et al., 2017).

This chapter contributes to efforts to fill this evidence lacuna by exploring how adolescent girls and boys experience age-based and gender-based violence in two East African low-income countries: Ethiopia and Rwanda. It draws on qualitative research conducted in 2016 in two marginalised urban geographies, in Ethiopia (West Hararghe zone) and Rwanda (Musanze district), with approximately 200 adolescent girls and boys—covering those in early adolescence (10–12 years old), mid adolescence (13–15 years old) and older adolescence (16–19 years old)—as well as their peers and caregivers. The data is part of the multi-country Gender and Adolescence: Global Evidence (GAGE) longitudinal policy research programme (2015–2024) funded by the UK Department for International Development (DFID).

2. Conceptualising violence against children

The World Health Organization (WHO)'s 2006 World Report on Violence Against Children represented the first systematic attempt to bring violence against children into public view. WHO (2006) defines violence against children as:

> ... all forms of physical and/or emotional ill-treatment, sexual abuse, neglect, or negligent treatment or commercial or other exploitation, resulting in actual or potential harm to the child's health, survival, development or dignity in the context of a relationship of responsibility, trust or power.

The WHO framework identified four types of child maltreatment (physical abuse, sexual abuse, emotional and psychological abuse, and neglect) and five settings in which violence against children occurs (home and family, schools and educational settings, care and justice systems, work settings, and in the community) (Pinheiro, 2006: 9), and highlighted a lack of evidence to drive policy.

Over the past decade, the scope and magnitude of violence against children has come become clearer, as researchers have set about generating the evidence needed to drive policy (UNICEF, 2014b; WHO, 2016, 2017; Hillis et al., 2016, 2018; Butchart et al., 2018; Pais, 2018). Links have been identified between child maltreatment and a range of negative child and adult outcomes—including not only injury, but also illness, school dropout, adolescent pregnancy, substance use, mental illness, unemployment, intergenerational violence, and suicide (UNICEF, 2014b; Hillis et al., 2016, 2018; WHO, 2016; Pais, 2018). Attention is also being paid to developing frameworks that link socio-ecological risk factors for violence with institutional and structural drivers of violence (Maternowska et al., 2016), and interrogating the boundary between rights-based approaches and cultural differences (Chandran et al., 2011; Laird, 2016; Devries et al., 2017). Although data availability is still limited, there is also growing attention to exploring the ways in which violence against children is gendered and varies by children's developmental stage (UNICEF, 2014b; Maternowska et al., 2016; Hillis et al., 2016, 2018; WHO, 2016; Devries et al., 2017). WHO (2016), for example, has reworked its typology of violence against children; it now includes intimate partner violence (most common for adolescent girls) and delineates between bullying and peer violence (most common for adolescent boys).

Despite progress, however, conceptualisations of violence against children remain fractured. While policy makers and researchers regularly note that intimate partner violence "commonly occurs against girls within child and early/forced marriages," and observe that some cultures engage in harmful traditional practices (HTPs), there have been few attempts to call out child marriage and HTPs as forms of violence against children in and of themselves (WHO, 2016: 14)[1]. Indeed, UNICEF's statistical compilation (2014b: 7) notes that the "report does not cover certain forms of violence that take place within the context of shared community, cultural or social norms and values." In addition, while Hillis et al. (2016) observe that violence against children is the focus of two Sustainable Development Goal (SDG) targets that call for total elimination (e.g. Goal 16.2: "end abuse, exploitation, trafficking, and all forms of violence against children," and Goal 5.2: "eliminate all forms of violence against women and girls"), Hillis et al. fail to include two other targets that address violence against children (e.g. Goal 5.3: "eliminate all harmful practices, such as child, early and forced marriage and female genital mutilation," and Goal 4.a: "provide safe, nonviolent, inclusive and effective learning environments for all.")

3. Adolescent capabilities and the factors that shape them

Reflecting the importance of a life-course and socio-ecological approach, GAGE's conceptual framework pays careful attention to the interconnectedness of what we call the "3Cs": capabilities, change strategies, and contexts. It focuses on the ways in which adolescents evolve over the second decade of life and how their individual development trajectories are shaped by family, peer, community, national and global-level factors (Figure 1).

GAGE's focus on capabilities emphasises investments in the person as a whole, and has evolved as a broad normative framework exploring the kinds of assets (economic, human, political, emotional and social) that expand the capacity of individuals to achieve valued ways of "doing and being" (Sen, 1984; Kabeer, 2003; Sen, 2004; Nussbaum, 2011). Importantly, the approach encompasses the ways in which the acquisition of key capabilities during adolescence is a deeply gendered process; it is

---

1   For an important exception, see Vohito (2018)

the time when gendered norms become increasingly enforced and personally salient, as girls (and, in different ways, boys) reach puberty. And indeed, for the purposes of this chapter, with its focus on the capability domain of bodily integrity, our aim is to explore how adolescents' experiences of age-based and gender-based violence evolve and why.

Our definition of age-based and gender-based violence incorporates diverse forms of violence experienced within the home, perpetrated by parents, siblings or (in the case of married adolescents) spouses and in-laws, as well as violence experienced en route to or within schools by strangers, peers or teachers, and violence from within the community perpetrated by strangers or acquaintances. It also includes early, forced and child marriage as well as HTPs (e.g. female genital mutilation and cutting (FGM/C) and labia elongation).

GAGE's approach further emphasises that in order to nurture transformative change in adolescents' capabilities and broader wellbeing, potential change strategies must simultaneously intervene at different levels, weaving together interventions that support adolescents, their families and their communities while also working to effect service delivery and system-level changes. For the capability domain of bodily integrity, we focus on exploring the extent to which programme interventions help adolescents to access the knowledge, skills, resources and support they need to avoid violence and to seek appropriate redress should they be subjected to violence. GAGE's approach also includes attention to the ways in which interventions can create a more enabling environment, from the micro through to the meso and macro levels, and to support adolescents to reach their full capabilities and potential.

The third component of the GAGE conceptual framework relates to contexts. This article focuses on two countries that have relatively supportive policy and legislative environments, but where efforts are chronically under-resourced in terms of implementation capacities. We also explore the particular vulnerabilities facing adolescents in urban contexts, recognising that there is a dearth of evidence on adolescent experiences of age-based and gender-based violence in urban contexts in the global South (see also McIlwaine, 2013: 69).

Figure 1: GAGE "3Cs" conceptual framework

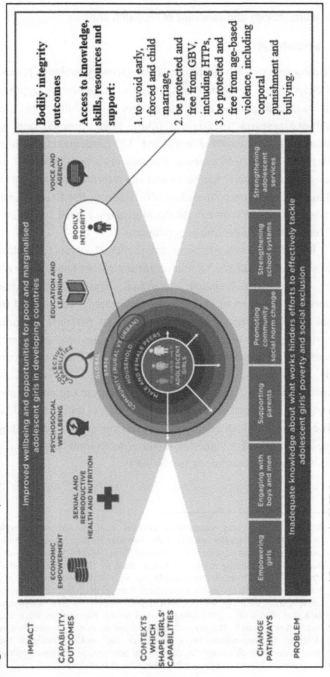

Source: Conceptual Framework, GAGE Consortium, 2017

4.   Methodology and overview of research sites

4.1. Methodology

Following research ethics approvals,[1] the primary evidence presented in this chapter was generated using a range of qualitative approaches—individual and group—with adolescents and adults. The formative qualitative research in Ethiopia (Chiro town, Oromia) and Rwanda (Musanze district) involved more than 360 participants, including 240 adolescents aged 10–15 years. It also involved a sample of their parents, other adult community members and key informants at the community and sub-national levels, including officials from the Health, Education, Justice and Gender/Women's Affairs Ministries, as well as implementers and recipients of adolescent programming.

Researchers used interactive and participatory tools to explore, with adolescents and adults, what adolescent transitions look like for girls and boys. These tools included: individual decision-making charts to understand the types of decisions that adolescents are allowed to make about their own lives, from relationships to personal aspirations; a "worries" exercise to explore the sorts of things that adolescents are concerned about and how they access support to mitigate those concerns; body mapping, to understand how adolescents feel about puberty transitions and the risks they face as they grow up; community mapping, to understand the spaces in which adolescents feel safe and unsafe, as well as the extent to which adolescents access services and how they view these services; and a vignettes exercise, to explore how social norms impact adolescent transitions (see Table 1).

---

1   Ethical clearance was sought and received from the Overseas Development Institute (ODI) Ethics Review Board, the Rwandan National Ethics Committee and the Ethiopian Addis Continental Institute of Public Health (an Institutional Review Board (IRB) certifying body that is approved by the Government of Ethiopia Ministry of Science and Technology). In line with ethical principles of carrying out research with children, assent was secured from adolescents (as legal minors) and consent from their parents or guardians. All transcripts were anonymised, and data was stored on a password-protected server. Researchers were trained on conducting research ethically with children and on how to handle disclosures of violence. All respondents were also given the contact details of the GAGE programme in each country in case of any concerns or questions following the interview, and these mobile numbers were monitored daily.

Table 1.   Number of respondents per method

Method	Type	Respondents in Chiro Town, Ethiopia	Respondents in Musanze District, Rwanda
Individual interviews	Younger girls, 10-12 years	9	8
	Younger boys,10-12 years	3	3
	Mid-teen girls,14-15 years	6	4
	Mid-teen boys,14-15 years	3	3
Community mappings (groups of 8)	Younger girls,10-12 years	1	1
	Younger boys,10-12 years	1	1
	Mid-teen girls, 14-15 years	1	1
	Mid-teen boys,14-15 years	1	1
Body mapping (groups of 8)	Younger boys,10-12 years	8	8
	Mid-teen girls, 14-15 years	8	8
	Mid-teen boys,14-15 years	8	8
	Younger girls,10-12 years	8	8
Focus group discussions (groups of 8, unless specified)	Younger girls, 10-12 years	8	6 (1 group of 6)
	Younger boys, 10-12 years	8	8
	Mid-teen girls, 14-15 years	8	8
	Mid-teen boys 14-15 years	8	8
	Mothers of 10-12 years adolescents	8	8
	Fathers of 10-12 years adolescents	8	8
Individual interviews	Mothers of 10-12 years old girls	7	8
Community mapping (groups of 8)	Women aged >35 years	8	8
	Men aged> 35	8	NA
Community timeline (groups of 8, unless specified)	Civil society	NA	6 (1 group of 6)
	Women aged > 35 years	8	8
	Men aged > 35 years	8	8
Key Informants interviews	Key informants	14	14
Total		**186 individuals**	**181 individuals**

4.2. Research site overview

Table 2 provides a snapshot of the key characteristics of the two urban research sites. There is one critical difference between them: West Hararghe (Ethiopia)—the zone in which Chiro is located—is a child marriage hotspot (Jones et al., 2016), whereas in Musanze (Rwanda), there is (officially at least) no child marriage. (Marriage is considered illegal in Rwanda below 21 years of age, and there are no recorded cases of child marriage—although there are adolescent pregnancies and informal unions.) In terms of adolescent programming in the two sites, the programmes referred to are those that respondents were either aware of or were participating in. In Chiro, there were no active programmes targeting adolescents at the time of data collection, while in Musanze, there were several initiatives but at limited scale.

Table 2.   Overview of research sites and key characteristics

	Chiro town, Oromia, Ethiopia	Musanze district, Rwanda
Population	67,000	368,267
Livelihoods	Chat cash crop[2]	Cash farming (potatoes and sorghum) and tourism
Food security	Drought-affected	Productive land
Migration	In-migration for domestic work, petty trade, chat economy; out-migration to Middle East	Limited migration
Religion	Muslim, Orthodox Christian, Catholic, Protestant	Majority Christians (Catholics, Protestants) and Muslim
Child marriage	32.3% of girls under 18 are married[3]	No national data available on child marriage rates; marriage under age 21 is illegal and thus there are no available data. There are adolescents living in marriage-like partnerships – but no data on this.
Adolescent programming	No current programming	DFID-funded 12+ programme for adolescent girls, Compassion International and Red Cross working with adolescent girls and boys

To contextualise our research findings, it is also critical to understand the broader national policy environment that shapes adolescent experiences of violence and bodily integrity risks. Table 3 outlines the policy context of age-based and gender-based violence in Ethiopia and Rwanda, focusing on adolescents. It is important to note that neither country has a specific government adolescent policy (covering young people aged 10–19 years of age) so we have pieced together relevant information from child- and youth-related policies. Ethiopia arguably has a broader set of provisions to address the multiplicity of forms of violence and threats to bodily integrity that adolescents face (including, in particular, recognition of school violence and HTPs). However, as we discuss in the next section, the resourcing in place in both countries to ensure that these policy provisions are translated into action and justice for adolescents in impoverished urban settings is highly inadequate.

Table 3.   National policy environment

	Ethiopia	Rwanda
Child and youth strategy/policy	The National Child Policy approved in 2017 covers a diverse range of issues relating to young people but is generally not adolescent-specific. It discusses the importance of technical and vocational training (TVET) for adolescents.	The 2013–2018 Youth Sector Strategic Plan has limited discussion of violence. The policy mainly focuses of empowerment of youth in the education and employment sector.
Gender-based violence strategy /policies/laws	In 2010, the Strategic Plan for an Integrated and Multi-Sectoral Response to VAWC (Violence Against Women and Children) and Child Justice in Ethiopia and the Operational Plan for an Integrated and Multi-Sectoral Response to Violence against Women and Children and Child Justice in Ethiopia were issued. Both emphasise the importance of cooperation between the justice, health, education and social welfare sectors. UNICEF is working with the government of Ethiopia to develop and scale up a VAWC system, including coordination mechanisms, referral pathways and one-stop centres.	The National Policy against Gender-Based Violence, adopted in 2011, lays out services for survivors, punishment for perpetrators, recognises the centrality of gender norms and calls for community sensitisation. Law No. 59/2008, on the Prevention and Punishment of Gender-Based Violence (GBV), is aimed at prevention and treatment.

Child marriage/harmful traditional practices (HTPs) and adolescent sexual and reproductive health (SRH) strategies/policies/laws	The 2000 Revised Family Code established 18 as the legal minimum age of marriage for boys and girls, and the Criminal Code stipulates punishment and prison terms for perpetrators. The 2005 Code also deals with a ranges of HTPs, including FGM/C. The government launched the National Alliance to End Child Marriage and the National Strategy and Action Plan on Harmful Traditional Practices.	The Adolescent Sexual Reproductive Health and Rights Policy, adopted in 2012, aims to ensure that teens have age-appropriate access to gender-sensitive SRH services.
School violence strategies/policies	There is a Gender Strategy for the Education and Training Sector and UNICEF is working with the Ministry of Education to mitigate GBV in schools through this strategy.	No strategy or policy addressing school violence.
Child justice/child protection policies.	The 2017 National Child Policy discusses the need to support children living in difficult circumstances (including those subject to sexual violence).	The National Integrated Child Rights Policy, adopted in 2011, recognises a plethora of children's rights and the government's responsibility to fulfil them (including children who are abused, working, on the street, etc.)

5.   Findings on adolescents' risks and experiences regarding bodily integrity and freedom from violence

We now discuss our findings, framing our analysis according to the "3Cs" conceptual framework introduced earlier. Regarding the first "C"—capabilities—we explore adolescent girls' and boys' experiences regarding bodily integrity and freedom from violence, discussing four sub-components of this capability domain: (1) age-based violence; (2) sexual and gender-based violence (SGBV); (3) harmful traditional practices (HTPs); and (4) child, early and forced marriage. In this discussion, we weave in the second "C"—contextual factors—by highlighting the particular threats to adolescents' bodily integrity from within their families, schools and communities. We discuss the third "C"— change strategies—by looking at the extent to which services and programmes in these urban settings mediate adolescents' experiences of bodily integrity, identifying gaps in prevention and redress services.

5.1. Adolescent capabilities: bodily integrity and freedom from violence

5.1.1. Age-based violence

Age-based violence is widespread. Hillis et al. (2016) estimate that in Africa, 50 percent of children aged 2–14 have experienced physical violence. The same rate applies for adolescents aged 15–17, but as older children tend to experience different forms of discipline, rates of violence do not rise when the forms of violence change.

Our research found that age-based violence was a widespread concern among adolescent boys and girls in both research sites— perpetrated within families, schools and the wider community. Beginning with family settings, many adolescent respondents—especially those from very poor families—highlighted that physical violence was a common form of discipline, meted out by parents as well as older (especially male) siblings. In Chiro town (Ethiopia), beatings by parents were commonplace and often severe:

> My mother is easily angry with me. The neighbour tries to help me when she beats me. I cry when she beats me and the neighbours come and protect me from her. (In-depth interview (IDI), 11 year-old girl)

> Here there are parents who tie the hands of their children together and bitterly punish them. Some parents punish their children of our age. Some of them even burn their body with a burning knife or spoon. (Body mapping, 14–15-year-old boys)

> I have been bitterly punished. When I quarrel with other children, my father punishes me with a stick. He stops punishing me after he becomes tired of hitting me. He stops to punish me only when he thinks that he is satisfied with his action. (Boy, 14 years).

Interviews with adolescents (especially young adolescents) as well as with key informants highlighted that this type of violence is generally normalised. This cycle of violence within families is perpetuated by parental stress, economic poverty, limited coping strategies for anger management, and social norms that permit and perpetuate the use of violence by parents as well as older siblings (especially brothers) to discipline children.

In school settings, violence typically takes two forms: peer-to-peer and teacher-to-child. Teacher-to-child violence is mainly in the form of corporal punishment—typically beatings or extended periods of kneeling or other painful and humiliating forms of punishment. While corporal punishment is officially illegal in Ethiopia (according to the Constitution, the 2004 Criminal Code, and reiterated in Ministry of Education guidelines and the 2017 National Child Policy), adolescent respondents emphasised that teachers routinely use physical violence, as well as severe beatings (sometimes with sticks or electric wires) and physical punishments to discipline children:

> The teachers [...] punish students with sticks and plastic pipes. They beat students when students become late and talk in the class. They beat on the inside of the hand. (12 year-old girl, Chiro)

> Once, one teacher (I was in grade 3) bitterly beat me and my hand became swollen. He beat me with a stick. My mother became upset. She brought me to school and she entered into an argument with the teacher. The principal told the teacher that he made a mistake for bitterly beating me. Still, students are beaten with pipes and sticks in school. It has not stopped. (15 year-old girl, Chiro)

> Teachers punish students when they are absent from school without permission. They also punish disruptive students and when we are late. (14 year-old boy, Chiro).

Contributing factors to teacher violence include overcrowded classrooms and lack of training in non-violent positive discipline approaches.

School-based violence also emerged as a key concern among adolescents in Musanze (Rwanda). Corporal punishment of children is not explicitly prohibited in Rwanda; however, children are legally protected from "severe" and "excessive" corporal punishment by the Penal Code 2012 and Law No. 54 Relating to the Rights and Protection of the Child 2011. Presidential Order No. 48/01 of 10/3/2009 states that punishment should be commensurate with the age of the child and the severity of the misconduct, and should be aimed at educating the student. A conference organised by UNICEF and supported by the Rwandan government, Stop Violence Against Children, held in Rwanda in 2011, recommended that corporal punishment should be prohibited in all settings, including homes and schools (Ministry of Gender and Family Promotion, Republic of Rwanda, 2011).

Adolescents (of all ages) interviewed in Musanze reported being beaten at school, for reasons that included: arriving late; delay in paying school fees and/or other school charges; misbehaving at school (e.g. shouting in class, fighting with other children); not answering correctly in class; not having a haircut in line with school policy; and not having the necessary school materials (pens, books, etc.).

Young adolescent girls (aged 10–12 years) mentioned that they were more likely to be beaten by teachers for making noise in class and poor performance in course work. However, some mentioned receiving painful and severe punishment for the same reason, such as being beaten on the head with a sugar cane. Mentors for the 12+ Adolescent Girls Empowerment Programme in Rwanda (funded by DFID) were reported as beating girls who were beneficiaries if they made noise during the sessions.

When recalling important events that had happened in their lives, adolescent boys tended to recount more positive events related to school and education, while positive experiences for girls tended to be related to their families. Young adolescent girls were more likely than boys to report negative events related to school—for example, beatings and bullying.

Beating by teachers per se was not considered problematic, either by older adolescents or parents; indeed, parents and children alike felt that it was appropriate for teachers to beat students under certain circumstances, including if they were late for school. However they did not see it as appropriate in other instances, such as when they did not have books or other equipment, as parents felt this was their responsibility and not the child's.

The routine beating of children by teachers appears to be partly related to gendered divisions of household labour. Girls reported being beaten after arriving late at school because of having to do household chores before they left home.

Beatings were also reported to be one of the reasons why girls drop out of school:

> This [having dropped out of school] makes me sad. Also my other elder sister was beaten when she was at school and this made her drop out of school as well. It makes me feel bad to know that I was forced to quit school for the same reason. (14 year-old girl, Musanze)

Beyond the school environment, age-based violence within the community emerged as an important theme that affected many adolescents in Ethiopia but not in Rwanda. In Chiro, adolescent boys often mentioned the risk of violence and a sense of insecurity:

> If a boy goes to the forest alone, he might get robbed. After robbing, the gangsters even can kill the boy as they might be afraid of the fact that the boy might report the case to police. (Body mapping, 14–15-year-old boys, Chiro)

> Children from other villages come and beat us. Recently, the children from other places stopped coming to this place because we brought bigger boys there after they beat us a few months ago. We took the big boys in order to beat these children. Thus, we play freely because the bigger children from other places were stopped. (14 year-old boy, Chiro)

Some adolescent boys also expressed fears about ongoing political uprisings and police action against young people:

> Sometimes, there have been uprisings in our country. Young people engage in uprisings. I strongly fear when there is disorder in the area. Once there was an uprising in the city and I became so frightened. I fear that the police officers will beat me with their strong stick. (12 year-old boy, Chiro)

> Last summer there was an uprising in this community. The federal police came and took measures on young people involved in the uprising. (10 year-old boy, Chiro)

5.1.2. Sexual and gender-based violence (SGBV)

Evidence on the incidence of SGBV largely comes from national Demographic and Health Survey (DHS) data and is thus limited to adolescents over the age of 15. Devries et al. (2017) note that for girls, intimate partners are the third most common perpetrators of violence (after household members and other children) and that across countries, approximately 7 percent of 15 year-old girls and 13 percent of 19 year-old girls have experienced physical or emotional violence at the hands of a partner in the past year. In Ethiopia, of girls aged 15–19, 3.5 percent reported ever having experienced sexual violence (CSA and ICF, 2017); in Rwanda, that figure is 2.8 percent (National Institute of Statistics of Rwanda (NISR) et al., 2016). Hillis et al. (2016) report that Violence Against Children surveys in Africa found much higher rates of sexual violence than those reported by national DHS data, at 27–38 percent (girls) and 9–18 percent (boys).

Our research found that overall, the risk of SGBV perpetrated against adolescents in the community and while travelling to school or to access other services emerged as a widespread concern among adults and adolescents alike, and especially among older adolescents. Girls (particularly those in the mid- and older adolescent age groups) risked experiencing rape and sexual violence while travelling to and from school—and, in some cases, within school—or while engaged in petty trading and service industry jobs in towns. More generally, a number of key informants commented that, given the rise of a new culture of sexuality and the erosion of traditional customs around female sexual purity before marriage, levels of SGBV are increasing as a reaction to these changes.

In school settings, the risk of gender-based violence perpetrated by peers or teachers was a frequent theme among adolescents and their parents. Girls complained frequently about violence by male peers:

> I developed a negative attitude towards boys starting from my childhood. When I was a child, I saw one boy beat many girls, and I was beaten by him and other boys when I was in grade 3 and 4. (10 year-old girl, Chiro)

> Boys prevent girls from using the water at school. They push us when we want to drink water. Thus, most of the time, we bring water from home using the plastic containers. Smaller children in particular could not get access to water so that they are forced to bring water from home. (12 year-old girl, Chiro)

In focus group discussions, adolescents spoke of sexual violence perpetrated by older pupils in school grounds, noting that rather than being supported to report the case officially, the survivors had been silenced by the school authorities. In one case, a 12 year-old girl had been sexually assaulted by an older male student, but when she reported it, the school principal allegedly sought to cover up the incident rather than prosecute the perpetrator, fearing that the school's reputation would be tarnished as a result.

Adolescent girls of all ages reported being bullied by male students at school. They reported being beaten by boys, often for no apparent reason. Other bullying behaviours by classmates included stealing school materials such as pens and notebooks—particularly problematic if this is the cause of being sent home, as this also often led to being beaten by their parents.

Girls also reported being mocked if their family circumstances were somewhat atypical. Some examples of different circumstances included:

being raised by a grandmother when the mother was working as a domestic worker outside the community; growing up without a known father when born to a young mother; or having a father in prison.

SGBV also emerged as a key concern for girls outside of school, in the wider community. In Chiro, adolescent girls highlighted the risks of being outside in the evenings in the town or other urban areas, or away from adult supervision near the river—a preferred recreational spot for young people locally:

> Girls may face different things during the evening. One of these is rape. We fear that our female children will face rape during the evening. We do not send female children outside the home during the evening. Sometimes, they rape girls in groups. Only girls working in hotels and bars can stay outside the home during the night. (Mother of adolescent girl, Chiro)

> The neighbours raped her. The girl did not report the case to her mother but the mother asked her daughter after seeing the changes in her behaviour [...] Now boys lobby girls, buying them biscuits and money. Most of the time, children in urban areas do not accept the advice of their parents. (Mother of adolescent girl, Chiro)

Some interviewees also linked the rising problem of sexual assault to substance abuse, especially given that West Hararghe, where Chiro is situated, is a major *khat*-producing area:

> Many of the young boys chew khat, which encourages them to rape girls. (Mother of adolescent girl, Chiro)

Moreover, when asked to identify unsafe spaces for girls, the *khat* and *areke* (local alcohol) houses were cited as among the riskiest places. This was especially the case for migrant girls who lack supportive social networks and safe income-generating options.

Concerns about sexual violence were not limited to girls; adults and adolescents alike commented that boys are also at risk of sexual assault:

> It is a major problem. I saw that a girl of 12 years old was raped; her father raped a 13-year-old girl [...] There are young boys which take girls to the river and rape them. Men also rape boys. One of my neighbour's boys was raped and the perpetrator is not in prison. I am very careful with my children. The child is about 14 years old. (Mother of adolescent, Chiro)

In Musanze, adolescents reported experiencing violence within the community, perpetrated by neighbours and others. This happened in various public spaces, including on the way to and from school. Two specific forms of community-based violence reported by respondents were rape and poisoning. More broadly, adolescents and adults alike identified some of the vulnerabilities associated with paid employment as a source of potential violence.

Most of the adolescents who participated in our study aged 10–15 years, female and male, were engaged in some form of activities that generated money. Adolescent girls were very concerned that some of the income-generating activities they did—such as collecting stones from the river for construction and selling fruit and vegetables—put them at greater risk of sexual violence, mainly because they had to travel through unsafe places such as forests and urban centres, which posed the risk of meeting "bad people" on the way. Some girls had heard of one girl having been raped while she had gone to collect stones.

Finally, the "sugar daddy" phenomenon (older men having sexual relationships with adolescent girls in return for money or gifts) was another key concern that emerged in discussions on community violence, particularly among adolescents and adults in Rwanda (who also mentioned "sugar mummies", although to a much lesser extent).

> We have called them sugar daddies and sugar mummies. They played a big role in destroying our youth. The challenge we have is that these sugar daddies tempt the girls who are at the same age with their daughters. Although the government is fighting against this, these sugar daddies and sugar mummies persist. (Religious leader, Musanze).

Sexual relationships between older men (sugar daddies) and adolescent girls were reported in Musanze. However, the type of relationships described by adolescent girls included those with much older and richer men, and with less well-off men (bus conductors, construction workers, aid workers, small kiosk owners) who groomed girls into sexual relationships by giving them gifts.

Some community members used the sugar daddy phenomenon as an excuse to victimise young girls who fell pregnant, with a frequent narrative that the girl just wanted more things than her family could afford, and so had sex for money or other items. In such cases, the pregnancy was perceived to be a punishment for the girl, reducing her likelihood of receiving any psychosocial support.

Adolescent girls also reported being aware of sugar daddies, and attributed them to older men being in a position to provide girls with material things that they or their families could not afford:

> When you are lacking something and you don't have money and you find that there is a sugar daddy who can give it to you, you accept it, but at the end it may result into getting HIV/AIDS. (Body mapping, 14–15-year-old girls, Musanze)

In Musanze, sugar daddies were also seen by adolescent girls as a type of sexual harassment, especially if the man concerned was a teacher, because there were significant consequences for girls who refused their advances:

> There are some teachers who are sugar daddies and who want to date you [...] When he asks you to have sex and then you refuse, it can be a source of conflict. He can send you back home to bring your parents or even beat you. (14-year-old girl)

Adults in the community were concerned that sugar daddies could tempt younger adolescent girls to become sexually active in return for gifts, including mobile phones and other popular items.

5.1.3. Harmful traditional practices (HTPs)

As noted above, HTPs have generally not been defined as a form of violence against children. Indeed, until quite recently, such practices have been largely taboo and have attracted little research. For example, questions about prevalence and types of FGM/C were not added to the Ethiopian DHS until 2016, while the number of published studies on labia elongation in Rwanda (which is classified by the WHO as a form of FGM) appears to be less than a dozen (Koster and Price, 2008; Perez et al., 2016).

In Ethiopia, FGM/C takes different forms (from symbolic nicking to total infibulation), is carried out on girls of different ages (from infancy through to adolescence), and incidence varies considerably by geographical region—ranging from 24 percent (Tigray) to 99 percent (Somali). On a national level, FGM/C is declining: 47 percent of girls aged 15–19 have been cut, compared with 75 percent of women aged 35–49. The incidence of labia elongation in Rwanda is unknown.

Respondents in our research in both Ethiopia and Rwanda revealed that HTPs present considerable risks to adolescents' bodily integrity. In Chiro (Ethiopia), the key risks identified were human trafficking and FGM/C, while in Musanze (Rwanda), labia elongation was the most common HTP risk reported.

FGM/C emerged as a significant concern for adolescents in Chiro, where the practice is typically undertaken when girls are between 7 and

10 years old.[2] It may involve a two-stage process beginning with a mild cut, but then a more invasive procedure during which girls are forcefully tied down and at risk of severe bleeding (according to a key informant at the district Women's Bureau). Despite growing awareness that FGM/C is officially banned, it continues and has largely been driven underground, as the head of the *woreda* (district) health office explained:

> The main problem here in our *woreda* is circumcision. Mothers have 1:5 organisations [government-organised groups at village or neighbourhood level to share information and mobilise community action] so we talk about the problem. Mothers agree not to carry on the practice but they allow their daughter to undergo circumcision all the same [...] In one neighbourhood recently there were two cases. Girls were circumcised three times. One of the girls was circumcised once and her friend was in the second stage. They later got sick because of the circumcision and came to the hospital. She was told not to report her situation as her mother had forced her to get circumcised. The girl could not recover completely. She was bleeding badly [...] People say that they are no longer circumcising their daughters but there are still cases and they go to other areas for it. People say that an uncircumcised girl means she may bring bad luck and break things—they believe that uncircumcised girls refuse orders and create problems at home. The girls themselves are convinced to hide the situation from us, so it creates a problem for us to control it. (*Woreda* health office head, male).

Officials are uncertain about how widespread the practice is as there are no accurate data available because families are increasingly keeping all arrangements secret or hidden; officials and service providers only tend to learn about it when girls experience health complications such as fistula or severe bleeding.

Evidence from our study in Rwanda revealed a range of practices, knowledge and beliefs relating to labia elongation. Traditionally, older females are responsible for teaching young girls, starting around the age of 9 years, how to stretch their labia minora using herbal medicines. There are strong socio-cultural norms that prevent mothers from discussing labia elongation with their daughters; one mother reported asking an older friend of her daughter to tell the girl about labia elongation.

The practice of labia elongation highlighted some important dissonances in reported attitudes and behaviours. In community discussions, at first, people would frequently deny that any such practice

---

2   The age at which circumcision takes place varies widely in Ethiopia, from early infancy through to mid-adolescence (see Stavropoulou and Gupta-Archer, 2017).

306   Jones et al.

existed; but subsequent discussions would reveal support for it, as undergoing the practice was considered to make a woman more sexually attractive. Pressured by the husband, the wife will reach out to an aunt or friend to have the conversation with her daughter. Government officials, too, are aware of the practice, describing it as "not healthy" for adolescents because of assumptions of the spread of infection due to a lack of hygiene.

Some adolescent girls reported knowing about labia elongation, and some reported having done it. Some girls reported having been told by their peers that labia elongation would help them deliver babies with less pain. Others reported being told that it would make them more adult and more able to make their (future) husband happy.

Within schools, there were conflicting feelings about the practice. While teachers were not supposed to discuss or promote labia elongation with students, some felt that girls should know about it, while others had to deal with questions from students:

> I used to encourage the labia elongation practice in my discussions with primary 6 female students, as the teacher in charge of female students. I considered it as an important culture. However, after I attended a workshop by Care International, we were told how dangerous the practice was, in terms of HIV transmission risks; I stopped telling the girls to do labia elongation. (Female teacher, Musanze)

For those adolescents who either knew about or had done labia elongation, their main sources of information were other female relatives and their peers.

5.1.4. Child marriage

As already stated, conceptualisations of violence against children have typically noted that marriage increases girls' risk of violence—especially sexual violence—but have failed to consider child marriage to be a form of violence in and of itself, even as policy attention to the topic has grown exponentially. That said, vulnerability to child marriage is one area where our two case study countries vary markedly. Rwanda is one of the few countries in the region that has very low child marriage rates (the most recent DHS found rates so low that they cannot be calculated for girls aged 15–19), while in Ethiopia, 40 percent of young women aged 20–24 were married before the age of 18 (CSA and ICF, 2017). Moreover, Chiro is situated in West Hararghe, a zone that has been identified as a hotspot in terms of very high child marriage rates (Jones et al., 2016).

Echoing findings from other recent studies on Ethiopia, our research found considerable changes in terms of child marriage practices in Chiro (ibid.; Pankhurst et al., 2016b). Community key informants highlighted that although awareness of the Family Code (which criminalises child marriage) is very low, awareness of the risks of child marriage had increased and arranged marriages in Chiro are declining. However, a number of focus group discussants noted that this change was not necessarily a wholesale departure from the past—in part, because practices have become more covert.

> Early marriage is common among the Christians and the Muslims. Wedding ceremonies have been declined because young people engage and marry without preparing wedding ceremonies. (Mother of adolescent, Chiro)

A common complaint by parents was that young people were increasingly entering into relationships voluntarily rather than through arranged marriages, but at the cost of their future development trajectories—as this reflection from a participant in a mothers' focus group discussion highlights:

> They start to marry at 16 or 17. During our time, early marriage was there but they married without having started sexual relationships. Now there is no need to abduct the girls because the girls are voluntarily having relationships with the boy. Now the legal age for marriage is 18 years old, the law also encourages girls to marry voluntarily. The main challenge is that young people marry without having any job and economic resources to lead an independent household. When they start to live together without having a job, they marry, drop out from school and they may be divorced. (Mother of adolescent, focus group discussion)

Other focus group discussants highlighted the growing phenomenon of marriage brokers, who are paid to match-make either by prospective grooms or by a girl's family.

> There are brokers who lobby girls to accept a marriage proposal. They urge girls to marry, saying that instead of becoming a domestic servant for their parents, they should marry and lead an independent household [...] Overburdened girls are the most exposed to early marriage and marriage through lobbying. (Key informant interview with *woreda* Women and Children's Officer)

However, the risks for girls who enter into relationships in this way may be very high. In practice, brokered relationships may be for sexual relations rather than for marriage, and if a relationship does not end in marriage, the adolescent girl risks being disowned by her family. This risk was, according to key informants, particularly the case with well-off men who may engage brokers to, in effect, deceive adolescent girls. Such relationships are also resulting in increased sexual and reproductive health problems, including higher rates of HIV, unwanted pregnancies and obstetric fistula.

> Brokers are involved in lobbying the girls to accept the marriage request of the husband. He receives money for playing the role in convincing the girl to accept the marriage request. The broker may get the girl around school or somewhere outside her home. Parents do not know such hidden moves of the brokers, which play key roles in convincing the girl to marry. Marriage conducted in this manner can last for a long time but it also may end up with divorce because the man may not have the resources to lead a family life. Sometimes, the man may be an adult person, and the women may become exposed to health problems such as fistula and complicated problems during child delivery. (Key informant interview, *woreda* health office)

So, while the form of adolescent marriage may be evolving, deeply ingrained gendered social norms mean that adolescent girls perceive they have limited alternative adult trajectories outside of marriage, thereby curtailing the realisation of their full potential—educational and economic.

5.2. Change strategies to tackle risks to adolescents' bodily integrity

While gender-based and age-based violence and HTPs are a key concern of adolescent girls in particular and also of boys, effective responsive services and justice mechanisms were perceived to be limited, in both Ethiopia and Rwanda.

In Ethiopia, adolescents, parents and key informants all highlighted deficits in awareness about legal rights and services, while key informants also underscored a major disconnect between ambitious policy and programmatic commitments and highly limited resourcing on the ground. Adolescent respondents lamented that there were no empowerment programmes available to them either within or outside of school, and that even school-based girls' clubs were often inactive.

In Chiro, opportunities to access formal justice were also very limited. In the case of child marriage, part of the challenge is that marriages are increasingly happening voluntarily between adolescent males and females of similar ages:

> Most of the time, marriage is arranged traditionally so that only a few people take it to the court for approval. Even at the court, the main issue is whether the two are volunteering to marry or not. The issue of age is not the main concern in the area. If the boy and the girl agree to marry, the law does not create a problem for them. (Key informant interview, female health extension worker)

Generally, adolescents and adults reported that there is almost no culture of reporting child marriage or HTPs, and that in urban areas, people still prefer to deal with injustices through informal, traditional mechanisms. As one mother in Chiro town noted: "There is no police but we have our own way of dealing with problems in the *kebele* [neighbourhood]." Some focus group discussants also noted that *kebele* committee members could be bribed to keep knowledge of an impending marriage quiet.

In both countries, justice for rape survivors was also highlighted as being very limited. In Ethiopia, a key concern related to the shortcomings in the law whereby prosecutors have to bring evidence beyond a reasonable doubt, which necessitates three witnesses. One boys' focus group discussion cited the example of a 12 year-old girl who witnesses had seen crying and bloodied following a rape. Even when she was taken to the police station afterwards with shreds of the assailant's shirt to report the case, without three witnesses willing to testify, the case could not be taken to court. The same boys' focus group discussion further complained that the local police and courts are corrupt and may release perpetrators after a week or so in exchange for a monetary bribe. In other cases, sentences are reportedly very low—with respondents citing examples of a 500 birr (17.6 USD) fine only or a 3-month sentence. A health extension worker similarly recounted that services are seeing a number of HIV-positive cases among young adolescents resulting from rape attacks, but in the absence of reliable witnesses, access to justice remains impossible. The Women and Children's Affairs Bureau noted that budgeting to investigate and follow up cases (including transportation to undertake follow-up interviews) is negligible.

In Rwanda, despite laws punishing rape, sexual violence, gender-based violence and sexual harassment, reporting of such offences is limited. Settling matters through informal channels was again reported as the preferred option for victims' families and perpetrators, in order to reduce future conflicts and threats that might arise for retaliation. Limited reporting was attributed to victim-blaming, especially for rape, because a girl would be blamed for provoking the attack. When respondents discussed cases of rape, issues relating to the disclosure and reporting of cases—including delays—were common:

> In a community, it [rape] can happen, but we have a problem with virginity tests because girls say that they have been raped after many days and the proof can't be found, and the person who was accused directly becomes innocent. (Female teacher)

Limited capability and resources to provide proof of rape is also a hindrance to proper punishment of perpetrators:

> Yes, there was a headmaster who raped his student and they put him in Ruhengeri prison but after days they freed him because the doctor said there was no proof. So we think the problem is with the capacity of doctors in finding proof, but the police do their work very well. (Key informant, community leader)

Young and older adolescent girls in our study reported knowing where to go in case of rape, such as going to the police or the Isange One Stop Centre. This Centre is an initiative to help survivors of rape and sexual assault, which has been implemented at district and national levels by the Ministry of Gender and Family Promotion in collaboration with the Ministry of Health and the Rwanda National Police.

6.   Conclusions and implications for policy, programming and future evidence generation

Overall, our study contributes to a still fledgling but expanding body of literature on the multi-dimensionality of adolescents' experiences of violence. The observation that no other chapters in this volume discuss issues of violence highlight the need for such a contribution. Our findings highlight a number of issues in both countries, well as country-specific risk factors to urban adolescents' rights to bodily integrity and freedom from age-based and gender-based violence; these risk factors in turn jeopardise adolescents' ability to realise their full capabilities and development trajectories.

These factors operate at the micro, meso and macro levels. Within the family, key risk factors for age-based violence include parental stress, poverty, limited coping strategies for anger management, and social norms that permit and perpetuate use of violence by parents (as well as older siblings, especially brothers) to discipline their children. At the school level, key risks include a lack of awareness among teachers of alternative, non-violent forms of discipline, as well as a lack of effective reporting channels and impunity for peer bullying and violence, whether perpetrated by older students against younger students, or by male students against female students.

SGBV risks include: a dearth of safe spaces for adolescents, especially for adolescent girls and migrants who lack supportive social networks; very limited safe income-generating options; and commonplace consumption of *khat* or alcohol. In terms of HTPs and child marriage, risks include: deeply ingrained (albeit evolving) gendered social norms whereby adolescent girls perceive they have limited alternative adult trajectories outside of marriage. Another gendered social norm is that girls must comply with practices to alter their bodies so that they conform to culturally acceptable standards and related behaviours (FGM/C in Ethiopia and labia elongation in Rwanda). There is also a dearth of effective reporting and response mechanisms and impunity for perpetrators of sexual violence. Income generating options can be exploitative, and there are many social practices through which adults seek to benefit economically or sexually from adolescents' vulnerability (the "sugar daddy" phenomenon in Rwanda, marriage brokers and human trafficking rings in Ethiopia). All of these community-level risks of age-based and gender-based violence limit the agency of adolescents (particularly adolescent girls) within the urban environment.

As noted by WHO (2016), which lays out seven strategies for ending violence against children, and Chandran et al. (2011), who offer a prevention framework more tailored to LMICs, future progress in tackling violence depends on evidence about what works and for whom. To that end, our research explored with both adults and adolescents what change strategies are available to them—and how they perceive those strategies to be working for different groups of adolescents and different forms of violence. Our findings underscore the need for multi-sectoral stakeholders to promote a deeper understanding of adolescents' complex vulnerabilities and to work harder to provide the support adolescents need to make healthy and successful transitions into adulthood.

The multi-layered risk factors at family, school and community levels that have been highlighted by our qualitative research provide important contextual evidence for programming, as well as for the refinement and revision of existing policies. Currently, in Ethiopia and Rwanda, there is limited policy attention to adolescence as a critical stage of the life course, and especially the specific challenges that urban adolescents face. However, given demographic realities—rapid urbanisation and an unprecedented "youth bulge" in both countries— there is an urgent need to strengthen evidence-informed policy and programming to tackle age-based and gender-based violence and their broader effects on adolescent wellbeing and development.

While there is growing awareness on the policy stage of the need to tackle age-based and gender-based violence (including child marriage), the multiplicity and often overlapping nature of the forms of such violence requires urgent attention. School violence remains an area where policy guidance and related programming is particularly limited: in Rwanda, specific policies are absent; while in Ethiopia, awareness among teachers, parents and students about the policies and strategies designed to combat school-based violence is very low. This suggests a pressing need to simultaneously: (1) harness research evidence on adolescent experiences of violence to inform specific policy guidance and related resourcing for implementation; and (2) invest in sensitisation and behavioural change activities among all community members to promote children's right to a life free from violence. These steps will likely make some progress in addressing the context-specific ways in which those rights are currently being violated, and will strengthen mechanisms for prevention, reporting and redress.

References

Butchart, Alexander, Hillis, Susan, and Burrows, Stephanie 2018. "INSPIRE: Using the Best Evidence to Prevent Violence Against Children." In Lenzer, Gertrud (ed.) *Violence Against Children: Making Human Rights Real*. New York and Oxon: Routledge.

Chandran, A. Jaya, Puvanachandra, Prasanthi, and Hyder, Adnan A. 2011. "Prevention of Violence Against Children: A Framework for Progress in Low- and Middle-income Countries." *Journal of Public Health Policy*. Vol. 32, No. 1: 121–134.

Chant, Sylvia, Klett-Davies, Martina, and Ramalho, Jordana 2017. *Challenges and Potential Solutions for Adolescent Girls in Urban Settings: A Rapid Evidence Review*. London: GAGE.

Central Statistical Agency (CSA) [Ethiopia] and ICF 2016. *Ethiopia Demographic and Health Survey 2016*. Addis Ababa, Ethiopia, and Rockville, Maryland, USA: CSA and ICF. https://dhsprogram.com/pubs/pdf/FR328/FR328.pdf accessed 29 October 2018.

Devries, Karen, Knight, Louise, and Petzold, Max, et al. 2017. "Who Perpetrates Violence Against Children? A Systematic Analysis of Age-specific and Sex-specific Data." *BMJ Paediatrics Open* 2: e000180.

Fulu, Emma, and Kerr-Wilson, Alice 2015 *What Works to Prevent Violence against Women and Girls Evidence Reviews. Paper 2: Interventions to Prevent Violence against Women and Girls*. London: What Works to Prevent Violence against Women and Girls, UK Department for International Development. https://www.whatworks.co.za/documents/publications/35-global-evidence-reviews-paper-2-interventions-to-prevent-violence-against-women-and-girls-sep-2015/file accessed 29 October 2018.

Fulu, Emma, Miedema, Stephanie, Roselli, Tim, McCook, Sarah, Chan, Ko Ling, Haardörfer, Regine and Jewkes, Rachel 2017. "Pathways between Childhood Trauma, Intimate Partner Violence, and Harsh Parenting: Findings from the UN Multi-country Study on Men and Violence in Asia and the Pacific." *The Lancet Global Health* Vol. 5, No 5: e512–e522.

GAGE Consortium 2017. *Gender and Adolescence: Why Understanding Adolescent Capabilities, Change Strategies and Contexts Matters*. London: GAGE Consortium.

Harper, Caroline, Jones, Nicola, Marcus, Rachel, Ghimire, Anita and Kyomuhendo Bantebya, Grace (eds.)2017. *Empowering Adolescent Girls in Developing Countries: Gender Justice and Norm Change*. London: Routledge.

Hillis, Susan, Mercy, James, Amobi, Adaugo, and Kress, Howard 2016. "Global Prevalence of Past-year Violence Against Children: A Systematic Review and Minimum Estimates." *Pediatrics*. Vol. 137, No. 3: e20154079.

Hillis, Susan, Mercy, James, Kress, Howard. and Butchart, Alexander 2018. "Violence against Children: Endemic, Detrimental, Preventable." In Lenzer, Gertrud (ed.) *Violence Against Children: Making Human Rights Real*. New York and Oxon: Routledge.

International Center for Research on Women (ICRW) 2016. "Child Marriage Facts and Figures". www.icrw.org/child-marriage-facts-and-figures accessed 29 October 2018.

Jones, Nicola, Tefera, Bekele, Emirie, Guday, Gebre, Bethelihem, Berhanu, Kiros, Presler-Marshall, Elizabeth, Walker, David, Gupta, Taveeshi, and Plank, Georgia 2016. *One Size Does Not Fit All: The Patterning and Drivers of Child Marriage in Ethiopia's Hotspot Districts.* London: UNICEF and ODI.

Kabeer, Naila 2003. *Making Rights Work for the Poor: Nijera Kori and the Construction of 'Collective Capabilities' in Rural Bangladesh.* IDS Working Paper 200. Brighton: Institute of Development Studies.

Koster, Marian, and Price, Lisa Leimar 2008. "Rwandan Female Genital Modification: Elongation of the Labia Minora and the Use of Local Botanical Species." *Culture, Health & Sexuality* Vol. 10, No. 2: 191–204.

Laird, Siobhan 2016. "Protecting Children from Nutritional and Medical Neglect in Sub-Saharan Africa: A Five-country Study." *International Journal of Social Welfare* Vol. 25, No. 1: 47–57.

Maternowska, Mary Catherine, Potts, Alina, and Fry, Deborah 2016. *The Multi-Country Study on the Drivers of Violence Affecting Children: A Cross-Country Snapshot of Findings.* Florence, Italy: UNICEF Office of Research.

McIlwaine, Cathy 2013. "Urbanization and Gender-based Violence: Exploring the Paradoxes in the Global South." *Environment and Urbanization,* Vol. 25, No. 1: 65–79.

Ministry of Gender and Family Promotion, Republic of Rwanda 2011. *Stop Violence Against Children Conference.* Background paper. Ministry of Gender and Family Planning, Republic of Rwanda.

National Institute of Statistics of Rwanda (NISR), Ministry of Finance and Economic Planning, Ministry of Health, and ICF International 2016. *Rwanda: Demographic and Health Survey 2014–2015.* Rockville, Maryland, USA: NISR, MoH and ICF International. https://dhsprogram.com/pubs/pdf/FR316/FR316.pdf accessed 29 October 2018.

Nussbaum, Martha 2011. *Creating Capabilities: The Human Development Approach* Massachusetts: Harvard University Press.

Pais, Marta Santos 2018. "Violence Against Children: From a Hidden Phenomenon to a Global Concern." In Lenzer, Gertrud (ed.) *Violence Against Children: Making Human Rights Real.* New York and Oxon: Routledge.

Pankhurst, Alula, Negussie, Nathan, and Mulugeta, Emebet 2016a. *Understanding Children's Experiences of Violence in Ethiopia: Evidence from Young Lives.* Florence, Italy: UNICEF Office of Research.

Pankhurst, Alula, Tiumelissan, Agazi, and Chuta, Nardos 2016b. *The Interplay between Community, Household and Child Level Influences on Trajectories to Early Marriage in Ethiopia: Evidence from Young Lives.* Oxford: Young Lives.

Patton, George, Sawyer, Susan, Santelli, John, Ross, David, Afifi, Rima, Allen, Nicholas, Arora, Monika, Azzopardi, Peter, Baldwin, Wendy et al. 2016. "Our Future: a Lancet Commission on Adolescent Health and Wellbeing." *The Lancet* Vol. 387, No 10036: 2423–2478.

Perez, Guillermo Martinez, Bagnol, Brigitte, Chersich, Matthew, Mariano, Esperanza, Mbofana, Francisco, Hull, Terence, and Hilber, Adriane Martin 2016. "Determinants of Elongation of the Labia Minora in Tete Province, Central Mozambique: Findings of a Household Survey." *African Journal of Reproductive Health*, Vol. 20, No. 2: 111–121.

Pinheiro, Paulo Sérgio 2006. *World Report on Violence Against Children: United Nations Secretary-General's Study on Violence against Children*. Geneva: United Nations.

Sen, Amartya Kumar 1984. *Commodities and Capabilities*. Oxford: Oxford University Press.

Sen, Amartya Kumar 2004. "Capabilities, Lists, and Public Reason: Continuing the Conversation." *Feminist Economics* Vol. 10, No. 3: 77–80.

Stavropoulou, Maria, and Gupta-Archer, Nandini 2017. *Adolescent Girls' Capabilities in Ethiopia: The State of the Evidence*. London: GAGE/ODI.

UNICEF 2014a. *A Statistical Snapshot of Violence against Adolescent Girls*. New York: UNICEF.

UNICEF 2014b. *Hidden in Plain Sight: A Statistical Analysis of Violence against Children*. New York: UNICEF.

Vohito, Sonia 2018. "Violence against Children in Africa." In Lenzer, Gertrud (ed.) *Violence Against Children: Making Human Rights Real*. New York and Oxon: Routledge.

World Health Organization (WHO) 2016. *INSPIRE: Seven Strategies for Ending Violence against Children*. Geneva: World Health Organization.

Yount, Kathryn, Krause, Kathleen, and Midemna, Stephanie 2017. "Preventing Gender-based Violence Victimization in Adolescent Girls in Lower-income Countries: Systematic Review of Reviews." *Social Science & Medicine*, Vol. 192: 1–13.

CHAPTER 12
Social Connectedness and Youth Transitions: Reflections on a South African Programme[1]

Marlene Ogawa, Shirley Pendlebury and Carmel Marock

1. Introduction

The population comprising youth in South Africa is fractured by profound inequalities along the lines of race, class, gender and geographical location. Almost half of South Africa's population is under the age of 25; just over 20 percent are between 15 and 24 years old. More than half of all young people live in income poverty, experience high levels of unemployment, low levels of education and restricted access to social security (Hall and Sambu, 2016; Marock and Harrison, 2018). Failure to reduce high levels of youth unemployment and to provide young people with broader opportunities not only threaten South Africa's democratic gains (National Planning Commission, 2012) but "feed the intergenerational cycle of exclusion and poverty" (De Lannoy et al., 2015: 22). Much as interrupting the transmission of poverty depends on structural interventions, it also depends on young people's agency and capacity to frame their own lives. For this reason, De Lannoy et al. argue, programmes aimed at breaking the intergenerational cycle of poverty must "help young people access a range of different kinds of capital" (ibid.: 26), including social capital, to support their transitions to adulthood.

In this chapter we examine the relationship between social connectedness, social capital and resilience in opening transitional pathways for youth. Much of the exploration is conceptual, with an evaluative case to consider how, if at all, the intentional strengthening of

1   This work is made possible thanks to funding from the Samuel Family Foundation. The Social Connectedness Programme emerged from thinking advanced by Kim Samuel in her collaboration with the Oxford Poverty and Human Development Initiative and through her visionary leadership as President of the Samuel Family Foundation. The authors thank: City Year South Africa (CYSoA), the staff and service leaders who participated in the evaluation; and Jacqui Bagwiza Uwizeyimana who assisted with the 2016 interviews and survey. Thanks are also due to the editors and anonymous reviewers for helpful comments on earlier versions of the chapter.

young people's social connectedness may help them to access a range of "capitals" to realise their aspirations. The case is drawn from a youth development initiative in Johannesburg and represents a small slice of a much larger Social Connectedness Programme in southern Africa.

The Social Connectedness Programme grew from a collaboration between Synergos[2] South Africa, Kim Samuel, the Samuel Family Foundation, Canada and researchers from the Missing Dimensions of Poverty Data research at the Oxford Poverty and Human Development Initiative (OPHI). The Missing Dimensions of Poverty work at OPHI aims to give an account of human flourishing that is grounded in poor people's experiences of poverty. People living in poverty talk about isolation and associated shame and humiliation as important aspects of their lived experiences (Narayan et al., 2000; Bantebya et al., this volume), yet until recently there have been scant data on these aspects. In this sense, social connectedness has been a "missing dimension" within poverty analysis (Mills, Zavaleta and Samuel, 2014; Samuel, Alkire, Hammock, Mills, and Zavaleta, 2014).

OPHI's research on social connectedness provided the impetus and main conceptual grounding for the Social Connectedness Programme. The programme aims to promote awareness of the importance of social connectedness for wellbeing; to understand and reduce chronic relational deprivation as a dimension of poverty; and to deepen the social connectedness of children, youth and their caregivers. It pursues these aims through partnerships with selected organisations to embed social connectedness within their practices and activities. The case presented in this chapter focuses on the role of social connectedness in youth development in one partner organisation, City Year South Africa (CYSoA).

We begin with an account of key concepts, followed by a review of some widely-held but contested notions concerning youth. We then give a brief overview of the Social Connectedness Programme in practice before presenting the case in detail. A discussion of the case considers linkages between social connectedness, social capital and resilience in young people's transitions, with particular attention to their employability, employment and assets for critical life transitions.

---

2   Synergos Institute, a global non-profit organization, brings people together to solve complex problems of poverty through systemic change. In southern Africa, the Social Connectedness Programme is central to this endeavour.

2. Social connectedness, social capital and resilience

While OPHI's work on social connectedness frames the Social Connectedness Programme, over time the concepts of social capital and resilience have also come to shape it. We consider each of these concepts in turn and, along the way, sketch some conceptual connections and tensions among them.

2.1. Social connectedness: countering shame, humiliation and isolation

The theme of social connectedness brings together three related strands of experience cited by people living in poverty—shame, humiliation and social isolation—which are only beginning to be recognised as measurable dimensions for poverty research and policy development (Samuel et al. 2018). Yet shame has a long history in debates about poverty (Roelen, 2017). An early OPHI working paper, alludes to this history in its title "The ability to go about without shame" (Zavaleta, 2007). Here, taking a cue from Adam Smith (1776) and from Sen's argument that the ability to go without shame is a key capability whose deprivation lies at the heart of absolute poverty (Sen, 2000), Zavaleta conceptualises and proposes internationally comparable indicators of shame and humiliation.

Shame and humiliation are distinct, although they may occur together. Shame involves a personal judgment of failure or inadequacy and the belief that one deserves the shame. Humiliation rests on a belief that one does not deserve to be treated in a particular way; it involves the perception of one's dignity being lessened, that one is being unjustly demeaned. Typically, while humiliation arouses hostility, shame prompts withdrawal. The reflex of shame "is to hide from the eyes of those who will see one's deficiency" (Nussbaum, 2001: 196). Where poverty-induced shame or humiliation result in withdrawal or hostility, this may cause or deepen a person's social isolation by hindering their participation in the practices that maintain social bonds (Narayan et al., 2000). Evidence from a large cross-country study implicates shame as a factor in increasing the persistence of poverty: respondents not only despised poverty but "frequently despised themselves for being poor" (Walker et al., 2013: 224). Humiliating treatment by others—in the family, community, school and officialdom—externally reinforced respondents' internalisation of shame. Such experiences also extend to children, as explored in Chapter 2 (Bantebya et al.) in this volume.

Coupled with social isolation and a sense of not belonging, shame impairs agency and wellbeing, and severs connections with systems of support. In this way, shame, humiliation, social isolation and poverty interact in a causal nexus of mutual reinforcement. Although experienced individually, shame and shame-induced isolation are structurally and systemically shaped and embedded (Roelen, 2017; Walker et al. 2013).

Rather than addressing shame and humiliation directly, the Social Connectedness Programme focuses on overcoming social isolation (or relational deprivation) and deepening social connectedness. Social isolation can be defined as "the inadequate quality and quantity of social relations with other people at the different levels where human interaction takes place (individual, group, community, and the larger social environment)" (Zavaleta, Samuel and Mills, 2014: 6). It has both internal and external aspects. External isolation refers to a paucity of relationships with other people; internal isolation refers to the distress resulting from a felt divergence between ideal and experienced social relationships. Internal isolation may be experienced as loneliness or a persistent sense of being unable to approach others to find comfort, seek advice or engage physically or emotionally (Samuel et al., 2018). For instance, the shame felt by poor children who are stigmatised as lazy, unclean or deviant can lead to self-chosen exclusion, isolation and loneliness (Schweiger and Graf, 2015). Their relational deprivation occurs in both its external and internal aspects.

Relational deprivation is intrinsic to capability poverty and also a cause of diverse capability failure (Sen, 1999; 2000). It is intrinsic to capability poverty because people have good reasons to value connectedness with others (Sen, 2000) and because affiliation between people is a social basis for respect and non-humiliation (Nussbaum, 2000). Relational deprivation can result in other deprivations and can compromise people's capabilities. For children and youth, relational deprivation, especially when it is associated with other deprivations of multidimensional poverty, is a grave impairment to human development and well-being. Overcoming social isolation, and associated shame and humiliation among children and youth in poor or vulnerable communities, is a vital endeavour.

The concept of social connectedness seeks to address a richly layered and nuanced set of circumstances. Social connection operates at multiple levels and refers to the meaningful relationships individuals have with others and the community, as well as with state authorities, civil society groupings, employers so on. A person may be excluded from the economic system and yet continue to experience strong social connections. It is also the case that those with low levels of social connectedness who are also poor tend to suffer the effects of poverty most, and become vulnerable to more complex forms of marginalisation, exclusion and disconnection.

The overlapping literature on social cohesion, social exclusion and social capital draw attention to the importance of social connectedness (Zavaleta, Samuel and Mills, 2014). This literature provides multifaceted evidence of the positive impact social connections can have on a person's life as health, education, job opportunities and access to resources (Berkman and Glass 2000; Coleman 1988; Grootaert 1998; Putman 2000; Woolcock 1998). However, research on social capital concentrates on the instrumentality of social connections and tends to overlook their intrinsic value. Dominant research strands on social capital also tend to disregard the "meaningful social relations within which 'social capital' subsists" (Du Toit, Skuse and Cousins, 2007: 524).

In short, the notion of social connectedness incorporates the intrinsic and instrumental value of meaningful social connections (Zavaleta et al. 2017). From a capabilities' perspective, it is central to people's effective opportunities to be and to do what they have reason to value, and is constitutive of human wellbeing (Samuel, 2016; Zavaleta, Samuel and Mills, 2016).

2.2. Social capital

For present purposes, social capital is a useful concept precisely because of its instrumentality. As an analytic lens, it illuminates how social connectedness may support young people to use social networks as a resource for access to and persistence in employment or further education.

Social capital refers to the significance that social connectivity has in enhancing a person's ability to gain access to power or resources and to collaborate towards common ends. Three categories of social capital may be distinguished: bonding, bridging, and linking capital (Bourdieu, 1986; Putnam, 2000; 2001; Woolcock, 2010; Yeboah, 2017). Bonding social capital occurs within groups. It nurtures and arises from ties between people of similar backgrounds or interests. Bridging capital occurs across socially heterogeneous groups, such as institutional and social networks, and produces a flow of resources for advancing aspirations (Yeboah, 2017). Linking capital is produced by vertical links to people in authority or in a position to provide access to political and other resources (Woolcock 2010).

Bonding social capital is central to southern African Indigenous Knowledge Systems (IKS) researched in the *Imbeleko* study (NMCF, 2014). Within a broadly shared communitarian worldview that values wholeness, harmony, spiritual wellbeing and interdependency, each IKS in the studied communities had customs for acquiring, processing and sharing different kinds of knowledge. People applied their collective skills, experiences and insights to maintain or improve their livelihoods, and used their collective social capital as a resource for survival and development. Indigenous practices expand the realm of relatedness beyond the domain of the living to include ancestral relationships. In such a continuity of connectedness, cultural and spiritual "capital" are as important as social capital. In the studied communities, individual economic well-being appeared to be less important to Indigenous notions of poverty than the number and quality of social connections (NMCF, 2014).

Bonding social capital is a primary means of identity formation in youth culture. Bonding networks support young people's resilience in the face of risk or persistent challenges to their wellbeing (Theron, 2012). However, bonding networks can also restrict opportunities. Within strongly bonded groups, the totality of resources possessed by members may constrain or enable the reciprocity exchanges of social capital (Yeboah, 2017). Strongly bonded networks may also deter the exercise of agency for positive ends. Within disadvantaged communities especially, the flow of information within bonding networks may support risky or criminal behaviour (Yeboah, 2017) which in turn fuels the moral panic that infuses popular conceptions of youth as a "ticking time-bomb."

Over time, young people may be able to diversify their networks to augment bonding capital with bridging networks that create the broader identities and reciprocity required to "get ahead" (Putnam, 2000) and access a wide range of informational resources relevant to job seeking or educational opportunities. Bridging networks also foster connections across social divisions and strengthen young people's collective ability to act in concert towards a common goal. Where bonding and bridging networks cannot offer young people all the support they need, linking networks play an important role in assisting them to navigate towards resources and opportunities for work and continuing education (Yeboah, 2017).

How far the Social Connectedness Programme has been able to promote all three kinds of social capital is a question we raise in the illustrative case. In posing the question, we are mindful that the social relations in which social capital inheres cannot be separately understood from the "meaning-giving practices" with which they are entwined and the micro- and macro-level processes that empower some and marginalise others (Du Toit, Skuse and Cousins, 2007). Understood thus, the notion of social capital invites critical attention to the structure and dynamics of these relationships, within the "shifting terrains of political economy" (Du Toit, Skuse and Cousins, 2007).

2.3. Resilience

The Social Connectedness Programme assumes that being socially connected enables children and young people to participate in activities that build resilience and give them a sense of belonging. In everyday terms, resilience is understood as "bouncing back" in the face of adversity; more formally, it is a process and an outcome characterised by positive adaptation or adjustment to significant adversity (Theron, 2012).

In South Africa, resilience research has been subject to critical scrutiny, on the grounds that interventions towards resilience prolong a status quo of adversity because, it is argued, as long as the youth are resilient, societies are not compelled towards transformation. Internationally, criticisms of resilience research are levelled at a conception of resilience as a personal attribute, which can result in blaming youth for not making positive adjustments to adverse circumstances. Both critical concerns are answered in an approach that conceptualises resilience as an "eco-systemic transactional process" rather than a personal attribute (Theron, 2012; Unger, 2011; 2013). On this conception, resilience involves two jointly necessary capacities: (i) the capacity of individuals in contexts of significant adversity "to navigate their way to the 'psychosocial, social, cultural, and physical resources that sustain their wellbeing'" and (ii) their individual and collective capacity "to negotiate for these resources to be provided and experienced in culturally meaningful ways" (Ungar 2008: 225). Here the discourse of resilience becomes one of process and resource provision: when navigation towards resources is thwarted, or when the resources provided lack meaning, "it is more likely that the environment will fail in its facilitative role" (Ungar, 2011: 11).

Even when young people have the personal resilience to persist in pursuing work opportunities without losing hope, their success requires an ecosystem that can provide the resources and environment to support them (Marock and Harrison-Train, 2018). Social capital networks are part of such a supportive ecosystem. Indeed, social capital can be regarded as a defining feature of community resilience, along with physical infrastructure and "culturally embedded patterns of interdependence" (Ungar, 2013).

In this section, we have sketched the concepts of social connectedness, social capital and resilience, and some linkages and overlaps among them. The next section critically considers three concepts that permeate much youth development work.

3.   Thinking about youth

In its report *Development and the Next Generation,* the World Bank (2006) identifies five critical life transitions for youth: continuing to learn, starting to work, developing a healthy lifestyle, starting a family, and exercising citizenship. Three notions from the report infuse a prevailing narrative that "justifies and orients policy around youth and employment": the youth bulge, youth as a demographic dividend, and youth transitions to adulthood (Ayele, Khan and Sumberg, 2017: 2). A youth bulge occurs when children and young adults comprise a large share of the population. In theory, where an economy can provide productive employment to young people, there is a potential demographic dividend in economic productivity. If an economy cannot provide productive employment, it foregoes any demographic dividend from the youth bulge. This narrative is evident in South Africa's *National Youth*

Policy which emphasises the potential economic benefits of youth for the country (RSA, 2015).

Where the potential demographic dividend of youth cannot be realised, the youth bulge may be seen as a threat to social stability, a "ticking time bomb." Characterising the youth bulge in terms of a binary opposition between ticking time bomb and demographic dividend has become something of a cliché in the mass media. Research and critical commentary present a more complex picture of youth, the youth bulge and conditions for a healthy transition to productive adulthood (Arnot & Swartz, 2012; De Lannoy, Leibbrandt & Frame, 2015; Lefko-Everett; 2012). The binary opposition ignores the fluid, lived realities of young people and their aspirations (see also Chapter 9 by D'Sa et al. and Chapter 10 by Porter et al. in this volume). It ignores, too, the extent to which young people have a sense of hope, even in the face of adversity, and are able to navigate the multiple disadvantages that limit their lives (Marock & Harrison-Train, 2018).

The notion of secure transitions to adulthood is problematic for at least two reasons. Firstly, it assumes that youth will achieve adulthood once and for all. Yet in situations of extensive social crisis, many young people may be unable to acquire the social status of adulthood. For some, youth is a "permanent condition" (Hansen, 2005). In terms of a transition to an orthodox form of adulthood, a large number of young people in South Africa have not completed this by their early 30s (Seekings, 2013). South African Youth Policy extends the category of youth to 35 years in recognition of the impediments to achieving adulthood. Yet the idea of an extended transition to full future adulthood may be misleading. Characteristics regarded as markers of youth in transition may instead characterise "a new form of adulthood" where most young people in their 20s "are already living the kind of life that they will probably lead for the rest of their lives" (Seekings, 2013: 19). Precarious, intermittent employment is a feature of such a life.

Secondly, "secure transitions to adulthood" implies a move from dependence to autonomous selfhood. Equating autonomy and adulthood as a universal sociological state ignores the understanding—in many societies—of adulthood in terms of interdependence, where "people are considered to become less rather than more independent as they mature"

(Jeffrey, 2010: 498). Interdependence is a central ethical tenet of IKS in sub-Saharan Africa and in the rural communities involved in the Social Connectedness Programme (NMCF, 2014).

Nonetheless, the notion of transitions remains helpful because common-sense perspectives and policy frameworks use transitions to structure young people's life trajectories. Transitions are a socially constructed "reality" that the young must manage. In any case, studies of transition need not be narrowly linear or severed from an integrated analysis of the role of relationships, cultural practices and the political-economy in shaping young people's life courses.

4.   The Social Connectedness Programme in practice

Across its reach in southern Africa, the Social Connectedness Programme has two main achievement criteria, outcomes and impact. Intended medium- to long-term outcomes are: (i) a cohort of practitioners across sectors has a deeper understanding and integrates social connectedness into practice; (ii) key institutions integrate knowledge of social connectedness, scale up and replicate best practice models of social connectedness through deep and broad engagement with programmes and practice; and (iii) a cadre of leaders from various sectors promote the work on social connectedness. The intended impact is that the resilience of children, youth and their caregivers is developed through social connectedness interventions, and this is given expression in their different life spaces, and in their ability to access resources, services, and opportunities.

Table 1.   Social Connectedness Programme practice partnerships

Organisation	Model	Scope
Othandweni	Pairing infants and toddlers in residential care with gogos[3]	One residential care centre in Soweto
City Year South Africa (CYSoA)	Structured volunteer programme for developing youth leadership through support for school children	9 primary schools in Gauteng province
NACOSA	Community dialogues for awareness, action and change	30 organisations across 6 provinces in South Africa
REPSSI[4]	Accredited qualifications for community development workers and teachers.	Across the SADC (Southern African Development Community) region

The programme pursues its aims in partnership with organisations that work with children and youth living in poverty. Implementation began with four partnerships, shown in Table 1 above. Youth have a central role in two of these partnerships: City Year South Africa (CYSoA) and NACOSA (Networking HIV/AIDS Community of South Africa). In both, youth provide care and support services to children—on a volunteer basis in an urban context in CYSoA, and in paid employment in a largely rural context in NACOSA.

An evaluation of the Social Connectedness Programme partnerships with CYSoA and NACOSA yielded data on whether and how participating youth benefitted from social connectedness training. From this data set, Samuel and Bagwiza Uwizeyimana (2017)[5] developed two cases that show how deepened social connectedness and an awareness of isolation and its relationship to poverty can enable positive identity formation and resourcefulness among young people. They found that an important outcome for young care workers in NACOSA was an increase in bridging social capital. Some of the care workers created peer support groups who helped them to connect with community leaders and local government officials. In turn, these connections, together with the care workers' resourceful exercise of their agency, enabled them to assist children and

---

3   Gogo means grandmother in isiZulu.
4   Regional Psychosocial Support Initiative.
5   An unpublished Synergos working draft by Marlene Ogawa, Shirley Pendlebury and Jacqui Bagwiza Uwizeyimana served as a basis for the paper by Samuel and Bagwiza Uwizeyimana (2017).

their caregivers to get the social support and primary health care. Although these services are theirs by constitutional right, they had been excluded from them through isolation, shame, stigma or lack of information.

This chapter uses data from the evaluation of the programme partnership with CYSoA to construct a case that explores linkages between social connectedness and youth transitions into adulthood. The presented case does not aim to cover all aspects of the CYSoA's sterling work in opening various pathways for participating youth. Rather it focuses on young people's employability, their access to employment, and their assets for critical life transitions. More broadly, the case relates to the impact criterion for the Social Connectedness Programme. Two co-authors of the chapter were involved in the evaluation. Carmel Marock led the external evaluation team, in consultation with Marlene Ogawa.

5.   Social connectedness and youth transitions: An illustrative case

City Year South Africa (CYSoA), a non-profit organisation with a "sister" body in the USA, is partly a response to South Africa's complex social history. Apartheid created structural inequalities in educational access, quality and outcomes. In the decades since the end of apartheid, the quality of education has not adequately addressed past imbalances. To address this educational legacy, CYSoA has developed a model of service in schools that seeks to improve the quality of education for primary school children and, simultaneously, to develop a cohort of young people as future leaders and active citizens.

At nine primary schools in disadvantaged communities in Gauteng province, youth volunteers (service leaders) run children's clubs, which provide an after-school programme on literacy, numeracy and life orientation, and offer homework support. During school hours, they also provide some individual support to children with learning difficulties. Each school has a site leader (a paid alumnus of CYSoA) who oversees the school activities and guides the service leaders. Service leaders come from lower income households with very limited access to employment opportunities and social mobility. Many of them join CYSoA to earn the small stipend and better themselves through leadership training. For a few, the stipend is the main income for their households.

Concurrently with their service in schools, the service leaders participate in a leadership development programme. Accredited courses and non-formal learning opportunities are designed to equip them with the tools to be active, responsible members of their community and country. Opportunities are designed to help participants to transition into salaried employment or further study on completing their year of voluntary service. Since 2014, social connectedness has been part of the core curriculum for leadership development. Service leaders receive a basic orientation on social isolation, social connectedness and poverty. In workshops, they reflect on case studies and their own levels of social connectedness, and engage with material on the linkages between poverty, social isolation and healthy child development. An important aim is to help them understand how children in low-income environments might be at risk of social isolation, and how social isolation affects children's development. A practical aim is to hone service leaders' capacities for supporting the children in the after-school clubs, and to provide guidelines for referring children in need of social services.

5.1. Data sources

This case study draws on data collected in the 2015 evaluation and on additional data collected in 2016. The 2015 evaluation aimed to review the CYSoA partnership against the impact and outcomes for the Social Connectedness Programme. Data were collected through: in-depth interviews with CYSoA senior staff and Board members; a focus group with the nine site leaders; and a survey of service leaders. The survey was designed to assess the extent to which training on social connectedness had impacted service leaders' personal lives and their volunteer work at CYSoA. A total of 70 service leaders completed the 2015 survey, which comprised mainly quantitative tick-box responses, with some qualitative questions to obtain more nuanced data on changes in attitude, practices and behaviour. The majority of respondents (94 percent) were African, the remaining 6 percent self-identified as coloured; 57 percent were female and 43 percent male. The youngest was 19 years old and the oldest 26 years old; the majority (85 percent) were aged between 20–24 years. This distribution reflects the demographics of CYSoA participants.

In 2016, a Synergos intern conducted a focus group with 12 alumni (both site and service leaders) and in-depth interviews with eight alumni to probe the impact of their social connectedness training on their access to opportunities for work or further education. A follow-up survey, with items prepared by the evaluation team, was sent to alumni from the 2014 and 2015 cohorts. There were 44 respondents (10 out of 24 participants from 2014; 34 out 100 participants from 2015); 64 percent of respondents were female and 36 percent were male. The 44 respondents represent a tiny proportion (2 percent) of alumni since the inception of the CYSoA programme in South Africa.

The 2016 focus group reflection suggested that social connectedness training may have enabled service leaders to develop social networks that opened pathways to employment. An analysis of the 2016 survey provides some corroboration for this but also raises important questions about the programme.

5.2. Findings

For the purposes of this chapter, the findings presented here focus on data pertaining to service leaders' employment, social capital, and accrual of assets for their transition to work or continuing education. The programme evaluation at CYSoA also gathered data on how the young service leaders had incorporated their training on social connectedness into their volunteer work with children at participating schools.

5.2.1. Employment and employability

For youth volunteers in CYSoA, their year of service is part of a transitional pathway. In addition to the small stipend it provides, it opens opportunities for experiential learning, further study and, in some cases, paid employment.

The 2016 survey found that 13 out of the 44 responding alumni (30 percent) were employed, 5 (12 percent) were interns, 9 (20 percent) were studying, and 17 (39 percent) were unemployed. Those who were neither employed nor studying at the time of the 2016 survey had been unemployed for an average of 11.5 months, ranging from one month to 24 months. These findings are consistent with national youth unemployment figures and with youth unemployment rates in Gauteng province, where CYSoA is located. According to Statistics South Africa (2015), national youth unemployment (ages 15–34) stood at 36.1 percent in 2014 and 36.9 percent in 2015. In Gauteng province, the youth unemployment rate was

36.4 percent in 2014, with an increase to 39.8 percent in the first quarter of 2015. Of the 10.2 million individuals aged between 15 to 24 years in South Africa, one-third are not in employment, education or training (NEET).

Considered in relation to national rates of youth unemployment and more strikingly to Gauteng provincial rates, findings from the 2016 survey could be interpreted as an indication that participation in CYSoA had no appreciable effect on young people's employment access. Weighing against this conclusion is the fact that for the 2014 cohort, the percentage unemployed is lower than for 2015. Taken together with other data from the survey and focus group, this suggests that CYSoA graduates continue with their learning (through further education or internships) and after that access employment. Comments from CYSoA's Executive Director support this more nuanced interpretation: "For most of our service leaders, studying is their first preference after the programme. They believe they are young and need further formal education in order to achieve their long-term career goals. We do not only measure ourselves as youth employment pathway." (Personal correspondence, November 2018).

Both the 2015 survey and the smaller 2016 survey showed that the knowledge, attitudes and behaviours of those polled were influenced by their exposure to ideas about social connectedness. A substantial proportion of respondents in employment stated that their CYSoA experience and leadership training had given them the confidence to apply and secure the job they were in. Several specifically mentioned social connectedness: "Understanding the importance of social connectedness assisted me to access the opportunity for a job;" "Gave me the contacts I never had to get the job I have;" "Learning about social connectedness and how to build my network has really made a big difference to my getting this job."

In response to a question about how their experience at CYSoA had prepared them for work, attributes gained with the highest ratings in the 2016 survey were: discipline, positive attitude, energy, respect towards supervisors, and ability to work in a team; followed by the ability to communicate, problem-solving, attendance, and curiosity. Together these and other acquired attitudes, behaviours and skills comprise an employability repertoire.

While further education may enhance young people's employability repertoires, for at least one CYSoA alumnus (let us call her Zodwa, for ease of reference in the later discussion), study was a period of unwelcome delay in the transition to much-needed paid employment. Among those who were not yet employed but were continuing with formal education, almost all were studying in areas of their choice and believed that CYSoA had prepared them well for this transition. When asked how the CYSoA experience had prepared them effectively for their studies, from a tick-box list, respondents gave excellent to very good ratings to the following: a positive attitude, ability to read and write, punctuality, discipline, energy and ability to plan.

For young people from income-poor households, finding a job is especially onerous. One former service leader (whom we will call Ntombi) said: "I don't have the money I need to apply for a job (e.g. internet, taxi fares, phone airtime)." With this one exception, all the young people surveyed demonstrated persistence in their job seeking and remained upbeat about their prospects. Two-thirds had applied for more than 10 jobs since completing the CYSoA programme. Most of remaining third had applied for more than one job. In the response to the question "What will you do if you can't find a job?" half of the respondents replied that they would study; most of the others responded that they would find jobs; a few said they would start their own businesses. Encouraging as such optimistic views may be, it would be a mistake to regard them, on their own, as a mark of resilience. To do so would be to assume an individualised conception of resilience as a positive personal attitude towards adversity.

5.2.2. Networks and social capital

Two years after finishing, almost all of those surveyed are still in touch with people they had met at CYSoA and thought that the relationships they had formed there had helped them to extend their meaningful network circles. On reflection, the focus group discussions demonstrated how the shared experience of social isolation had opened the way for mutually beneficial relationships. During an in-depth interview in 2016, a young woman commented: "I realized we have a lot in common, we need each other, to support each other so we can achieve a future we want."

The 2016 poll showed that in their work-seeking most respondents drew either on new or already established bonding networks: "my friends and people the same age as me" (by far the most frequent response); "my parents or older relatives"; "someone in my church". However, responses to open-ended questions suggest that participants had also started to build bridging networks. One commented, "I engage with people of different ages and background on regular basis, so the experience has furnished the skill to socially connect with others in a good way." A young woman reflected on how connections could contribute to her personal growth: "I have started and learned to approach people and create meaningful networks that I hope will help me grow myself. I have started to be an outgoing person, attending 'women seminars' and growth events." Another observed that before volunteering at CYSoA, she had not been able to connect with others outside her group, but afterwards was able to apply the things she had learnt within the organizations she was participating in. These statements and other evidence from interviews and focus group reflections indicate a move towards strengthened and more diversified networks—from bonding to bridging.

There was little evidence of linking *networks,* although it is clear that many of the service leaders want to move up to the next level of networking towards making bolder, more strategic approaches to people in positions of power and authority.

The story of Tumelo, a 2012 alumnus, is instructive even although his service pre-dates the introduction of social connectedness in the CYSoA programme.

Tumelo's CCI Internship Experience: City Year Boston and Beyond[6]

South African student Tumelo Mosweu went to Boston for his exchange year with CCI at Bunker Hill Community College. As soon as Tumelo learned that part of the Community College Initiative Program included participating in an internship, he started searching for companies to work with.

In fact, Tumelo's search began before he even set foot in the United States and he reflected on how his current connections might help him find an internship. He reached out to City Year South Africa, an organization he had volunteered with in 2012, and after explaining about his opportunity to study abroad, City Year South Africa wrote a letter of recommendation to help him get an internship with a City Year organization in the U.S. At the time, City Year Boston was not looking for an intern, but Tumelo knew he could be useful and reached

---

6   https://blogs.nvcc.edu/cci/2017/03/21/tumelos-cci-internship-experience-city-year-boston-and-beyond/

out anyway. After a couple of months volunteering with them, Tumelo secured an internship with City Year Boston in October 2016.

Tumelo observes that City Year Boston "represents a model of business that I want to run," and his passion for education, volunteering, and business fits perfectly with the City Year organizational model.

Since starting his internship, Tumelo has contributed over 90 hours of work as a Development Intern. His work responsibilities include donor database administration, research, and event planning assistance. "Practically, I am learning how to run and operate a business—what I study at college is what I get to do at the office."

Tumelo has succeeded in cultivating that all-important measure of potential success, social capital, by drawing on bridging and linking capital through leveraging his contact with CYSoA and converting it into an opportunity abroad. His story prompts the question of whether and how the CYSoA programme could be strengthened to enable each cohort of service leaders to accrue bridging and linking capital.

5.2.3. Accruing assets for critical life transitions

Increased confidence, greater interpersonal skills and a sense of self-efficacy are important outcomes for young people who volunteer at City Year. The leadership development curriculum contributes directly to these outcomes, which are reinforced in practice through the schools service programme and the after-school programme (called the City Year Children's Clubs). These outcomes constitute assets accrued towards the critical life transitions identified by the World Bank (2006). None are material assets, but rather a "bank" of knowledge, skills, attitudes and experiences that can be deployed at home in the family, to contribute to the local community, and to motivate these young people to participate actively as citizens.

In the 2015 survey, respondents were asked to describe the things that they had started doing differently since the social connectedness training at CYSoA. Threaded through their responses are such themes as respect, care, trust, participation and sharing, withholding judgement, reciprocity, coming to understand others. These themes are evident in the following examples of respondents' comments on how the experiences at CYSoA had changed them. Each is taken from a different respondent.[7] Theme-markers are italicised in these extracts:

---

7   Identifying details of respondents' age, gender and race were not captured in the survey analysis.

Being alone, at first I was that kind of a person who would prefer to be in his own corner and wait for someone to come to me but now I can't do that anymore, as I am the one who would sometimes go "out there." What led to that in the beginning was that I needed to *understand the people around me* first, through the learning of social connectedness it has somehow changed how I see things.

I created a friendly environment with my family, in which *we rely on each other's strengths, hold each other accountable...* I now know how to treat people the way they should be treated with *respect.*

I have started asking the people in the location about what is it that they understand about SASSA/grant. I *share* the information about the grant and all other training I have acquired.

I am now *no longer judging* a person without walking in his or her moccasins.

I started *engaging myself to community projects* that are happening, *joined* a sports club so I can *understand different people* that are staying in my community; their lifestyle, their background and their plans for the future.

Many positive outcomes relate to the Children's Clubs. In the 2015 survey, service leaders provided examples of how they had used their understanding of social connectedness to support children to learn. They spoke of employing strategies like teamwork and group work and buddy pairs. Some responses indicated attention to providing individual support that was sensitive to a particular child and context. Play and thoughtful listening were used to build trust and mutual respect. Cultivating mutual respect and trust, and opening safe spaces for children to talk and be heard, are crucial ways of safeguarding them from shame and humiliation. For service leaders who are interested in a teaching career, or early childhood development work, experience in running the Children's Clubs is a pathway in professional education and later employment.

5.4. Critical reflections on the case

Social connectedness serves as an important framing idea for young service leaders at CYSoA. Through their participation in the programme, participants became more aware of the roles they could play in creating connections which strengthen their relationships with each other and encourage a practice of reaching out to others to deepen their networks. Bridging and linking social capital remained largely out of reach for them, despite a growing recognition of their importance. Nonetheless, the case indicates that social connectedness training played a crucial part in nurturing their resilience and the positive exercise of their agency, in concert and individually. By contributing towards one of the necessary conditions for these young people to do and be what they have reason to value, the programme enables their capabilities. It does so in part by facilitating their accrual of employability assets and a repertoire of knowledge and skills towards critical life stage transitions.

By design, City Year provides an opportunity for school-based work experience to young volunteers from disadvantaged communities, and includes opportunities that support their transition into successful employment. Yet only a small proportion of those polled from the 2014 and 2015 cohorts had found employment at the time of the 2016 survey. This could be taken to imply that the City Year programme fares no better than the myriad of other programmes (large and small) intended to address youth unemployment. Such a conclusion would be wrong on two counts. First, while City Year aims to open pathways to employment for youth, this is not the sole or central aim of the programme. Second, such a conclusion ignores the socio-economic context of youth unemployment in South Africa. Considered contextually, there is a more nuanced way of interpreting and learning from this small illustrative case.

Youth unemployment is increasing nationally, despite extensive government investment in programmes to address the problem, (Marock and Harrison-Train, 2018). The country's low economic growth is an obvious and serious impediment. This aside, race, age and gender are— not surprisingly—primary determinants in whether young people access employment; followed by whether a young person is affiliated to an organisation or secures some form of workplace experience. In their national study, Marock and Harrison-Train (2018) found that respondents aged between 25 and 34 years old were more likely to be employed than those aged between 15 and 24 years old. Most CYSoA service leaders fall within the younger age group, even a year or two after completing their volunteer year. Almost all service leaders from the 2014 and 2015 cohorts who had not found job placements were either continuing to study or had been placed in internships. Findings from Marock and Harrison-Train's (2018) national study, suggest that this is likely to increase their chances of finding employment.

Even so, the question arises about whether simply learning about the concept of social connectedness is enough to bring about meaningful change. In the context of structural unemployment and persistent educational, social and economic inequality, CYSoA will need to assess whether it is approaching social connectedness with too light a touch.

Because CYSoA is committed to addressing the nexus of leadership, poverty, and education, there may be value in deploying the language of "social capital" as the sharp end in the continuum of social connectedness. Social capital seeks to deal with the structural challenges facing the young people who volunteer for CYSoA. The hurdles these young people have to jump, and the responses that the introduction of social connectedness has yielded thus far, suggest the potential value of embedding this understanding through introducing a number of mechanisms to extend the service leaders' connections. There may be a place for more intentional transfer of social capital to young service leaders. For example, this might involve: more extensive alumni services, including support with references and interview preparation; connecting alumni with mentors working in the fields in which service leaders wish to specialise; and linking the service leaders to institutions with whom they can continue to relate after their CYSoA placement is over. These approaches, several of which have already been implemented at CYSoA, all have the potential to play a strategic role in clearing a stronger pathways to employment.

If we take Tumelo as the ideal, there is an evident need for broader and deeper engagement in the design and implementation of the social connectedness component of the CYSoA programme. Tumelo's story exemplifies resilience. It illustrates how he was able to use his social capital to navigate towards resources and opportunities for furthering his career plans, and to negotiate for opportunities that were meaningful for him. While CYSoA played an important part in helping him to establish linking capital, we surmise that other factors in Tumelo's social ecology may also have played a facilitative role. At the opposite extreme from Tumelo is the young women we have called Ntombi. We don't know Ntombi's story. Her comment that she has no money to cover the costs of job-seeking suggests that her social ecology has failed in its potentially facilitative role. As Ungar (2011) reminds us, a young person's navigation towards resources is thwarted if necessary resources are unavailable or when the person has not been able to negotiate for resources that are meaningful for her (Ungar, 2011).

Ntombi's is not an isolated case. For many young South Africans, the persistence of apartheid spatial planning traps poor and unskilled people in areas far away from job opportunities. High transport costs are a key barrier to young people's access to the labour market, as are other costs associated with work-seeking (Graham and Mlatsheni, 2015). Even if Ntombi found a job placement, would she earn enough to cover transport to work and meet the needs of her household? Much as the notion of capabilities directs attention to the multiple constraints that limit human lives, income remains important, as shown in Ntombi's situation and in Zodwa's view of further education as a period of unwelcome delay in transitioning to much-needed paid employment.

An in-depth, qualitative assessment with individual case studies might allow Synergos and CYSoA to delve deeper into how social connectedness functions and better understand the social ecologies that enable "capabilities for resilience" (Wilson-Strydom, 2017). Life histories and longitudinal studies could provide insight into the influences of social connectedness in young service leaders' longer-term capacity to navigate towards, and negotiate for, the resources and opportunities to support their critical life-stage transitions.

6. Conclusion

In this chapter, we have examined the relationship between social connectedness, social capital and resilience in the context of poverty, with a focus on youth transitions. In so doing we have sought to accomplish several tasks. The CYSoA case illustrates the linkages sketched in the conceptual overview and shows that greater connectedness was beneficial for many of the young participants in the programme, and for some it presents a turning point for moving out of poverty. A crucial reflection on the case considered, in particular, whether and how a programme intended to deepen social connectedness might support young people to find work, and suggested how it could do this better.

The case considered only a small slice of the more extensive social connectedness programme. The programme as a whole is animated by an understanding that social connections are intrinsically and instrumentally valuable in human lives, and that poverty can be both a cause and a consequence of deprivations of social connectedness, with potentially dire effects on the development and wellbeing of children and young people. If so, then there is good reason to advocate for policy and practices that help to overcome social isolation and enable the social ecologies that facilitate resilience.

But is social connectedness a strong enough mechanism to bring about the changes needed to reduce poverty and curb its intergenerational transfer? Not on its own. Prevailing poverty dynamics, left unchecked, are likely to be passed on through the transference of different "capitals" (De Lannoy, Leibbrandt and Frame, 2015). Such transfer is a product of a complex set of factors, both within and outside an individual's household. While social connectedness plays a pivotal role within this complex, it does not on its own deal with the structural conditions of poverty. This is a political task. From a capabilities perspective, the political task is to provide "support for human flourishing," for what enables people "to live a life they value" (Samuel et al., 2018: 93). This requires policies that help to create "facilitating environments which recognise and support interdependence" (ibid.). It requires, too, policies and programmes that are sensitive to power dynamics and the social ecologies that enable or impede individual and community resilience, and that respect the dignity and concerns of those whom policies are intended to support.

References

Alkire, S. (2007). *The Missing Dimensions of Poverty Data: An Introduction.* OPHI Working Paper 00. Oxford: Oxford Poverty and Human Development Initiative.

Arnot, M. and Swartz, S. (2012). Youth citizenship and the politics of belonging: Introducing contexts, voices, imaginaries. *Comparative Education*, 48(1): 1–10.

Ayele, S., Khan, S. and Sumberg, I. (2017). Introduction: New Perspectives on Africa's Youth Employment Challenge. In: Ayele, S., Khan, S. and Sumberg, J. (eds.) *Africa's Youth Employment Challenge: New Perspectives. IDS Bulletin* 48(3): 1–12.

Bourdieu, P. (1986). The forms of capital. In Richardson, J (Ed.), *Handbook of Theory and Research for the Sociology of Education.* Westport, CT: Greenwood Press: 241–258.

De Lannoy, A., Swartz, S., Lake, L. and Smith, C (eds.) (2015). *South African Child Gauge 2015.* Cape Town: Children's Institute, University of Cape Town.

De Lannoy, A., Leibbrandt, M. and Frame, E. (2015). A focus on youth: An opportunity to disrupt the intergenerational transmission of poverty. In: De Lannoy A, Swartz S, Lake L and Smith C (eds.) (2015) *South African Child Gauge 2015.* Cape Town: Children's Institute, University of Cape Town: 22–33.

Du Toit, A., Skuse, A. and Cousins, T. (2007). The Political Economy of Social Capital: Chronic Poverty, Remoteness and Gender in the Rural Eastern Cape. *Social Identities*, 13(4): 521–540. DOI: 10.1080/13504630701459180.

Graham, L. and Mlatsheni, C. (2015). Youth unemployment in South Africa: Understanding the challenge and working on solutions. In: De Lannoy A, Swartz S, Lake L and Smith C (eds.) (2015). *South African Child Gauge 2015*. Cape Town: Children's Institute, University of Cape Town: 51–59.

Grootaert, C. (1998). *Social capital: the missing link?* Social Capital Initiative working paper series; no. 3. Washington, D.C.: The World Bank.

Hall, K. and Sambu, W. (2016). Demography of South Africa's children. In: Delany A., Jehoma, S. and Lake, L. (eds.) (2016) *South African Child Gauge 2016*. Cape Town: Children's Institute, University of Cape Town: 106–110.

Hansen, K. (2005). Getting stuck in the compound: Some odds against social adulthood in Lusaka, Zambia. *Africa Today* 51(4): 3–16.

Hick, R. and Burchardt, T. (2107). Capability Deprivation. In: *The Oxford Handbook of the Social Science of Poverty*. DOI: 10.1093/oxfordhb/9780199914050.013.5

Jeffrey, C. (2010). Geographies of children and youth I: Eroding maps of life. *Progress in Human Geography* 34(4): 496–505.

Lefko-Everett, K. (2012). Ticking Time Bomb or Demographic Dividend? Youth and Reconciliation in South Africa. *SA Reconciliation Barometer Survey: 2012 Report*. The Institute for Justice and Reconciliation.

Marock, C. and Harrison-Train, C. (2018). *Next Generation: Listening to the Voices of Young People*, British Council, South Africa.

Mills, C., Zavaleta, D. and Samuel, K. (2014). Shame, Humiliation and Social Isolation: Missing Dimensions of Poverty and Suffering Analysis. *OPHI Working Paper* 71. Oxford: University of Oxford.

Narayan, D., Chambers, R., Shah, M. K. and Petesch, P. (2000). *Voices of the Poor: Crying Out for Change*. New York: Oxford University Press for the World Bank.

National Planning Commission (2012). *National Development Plan 2030. Our Future— Make it work*. Pretoria: The Presidency.

National Youth Development Agency (2015). *National Youth Policy 2015–2020*. Pretoria: NYDA.

NMCF (2014). *Imbeleko and social connectedness: Cultivating resourcefulness not dependency*. Report prepared for the Nelson Mandela Children's Fund (NMCF) by the Unit for Education Research in AIDS, University of Pretoria.

Nussbaum, M. (2000). *Women and Human Development: The Capabilities Approach*. Cambridge: Cambridge University Press.

Nussbaum, M. (2001). *Upheavals of Thought: The Intelligence of Emotions*. Cambridge: Cambridge University Press.

Pendlebury, S., Ogawa, M. and Morris, R. (2015). *Measuring Social Connectedness as a Constitutive Feature of Children's Wellbeing: Prospects and Pitfalls*. Paper presented at 5th Conference of the International Society for Child Indicators, University of Cape Town, South Africa, 2–4 September 2015.

Putnam, R. (2000). *Bowling Alone: The Collapse and Revival of American Community*. New York: Simon & Schuster.

Putnam, R. (2001). Social capital: Measurement and consequences. *Isuma: Canadian Journal of Policy Research, 2:* 41–51.

Roelen, K. (2017). Shame, Poverty and Social Protection. *IDS Working Paper No. 489,* Institute for Development Studies.

Samuel, K. and Bagwiza Uwizeyimana, J. (2017). Social Connectedness and Poverty Eradication: A South African Perspective. *Global Challenges Working Paper Series* No. 2. CROP: University of Bergen.

Samuel, K., Alkire, S., Zavaleta, D., Mills, C. & Hammock, J. (2018). Social isolation and its relationship to multidimensional poverty. *Oxford Development Studies,* 46(1): 83–97, DOI: 10.1080/13600818.2017.1311852.

Schweiger, G. and Graf, G. (2015). *A Philosophical Examination of Social Justice and Child Poverty.* Basingstoke: Palgrave Macmillan.

Seekings, J. (2013). *The Social and Political Implications of Demographic Change in Post-Apartheid South Africa.* CSSR Working Paper No. 328. Centre for Social Science.

Sen, A. (1999). *Development as Freedom.* Oxford: Oxford University Press.

Sen, A. (2000). Social Exclusion: Concept, Application, and Scrutiny. *Social Development Papers.* Manila: Office of Environmental and Social Development, Asian Development Bank.

Sen, A. (2009). *The Idea of Justice.* London: Allen Lane.

Smith, A. (1776). *An Inquiry into the Nature and Causes of the Wealth of Nations.* Oxford: Clarendon.

Statistics South Africa (2015). *National and Provincial Labour Market: Youth, Q1:2008–Q1: 2015.* Statistical Release P0211.4.2.

Theron, L. (2012). Resilience Research with South African Youth: Caveats and ethical complexities. *South African Journal of Psychology,* 42(3): 333–345.

Ungar, M. (2013). Community Resilience for Youth and Families: Facilitative physical and social capital in contexts of adversity. *Children and Youth Services Review 33*: 1742–1748.

Ungar, M. (2011). The Social Ecology of Resilience: Addressing contextual and cultural ambiguity of a nascent construct. *American Journal of Orthopsychiatry* 81(1): 1–17.

Walker, R. et al. (2013). Poverty in Global Perspective: Is shame a common denominator? *Journal of Social Policy,* 42 (2): 215–233.

Wilson-Strydom, M. (2017). Disrupting Structural Inequalities of Higher Education Opportunity: 'Grit', resilience and capabilities at a South African university. *Journal of Human Development and Capabilities* 18(3): 384–398.

Woolcock, M. (1998). Social Capital and Economic Development: Toward a theoretical synthesis and policy framework. *Theory and Society* 27(2): 151–208.

Woolcock, M. (2010). The Rise and Routinization of Social Capital, 1988–2008. *Annual Review of Political Science* 13: 469–87.

World Bank. (2006). *World Development Report 2007: Development and the Next Generation.* Washington, D.C.: World Bank.

Yeboah, T. (2017). Navigating Precarious Employment: Social Networks among Migrant Youth in Ghana. In: Ayele, S., Khan, S. and Sumberg, J. (eds.) *Africa's Youth Employment Challenge: New Perspectives. IDS Bulletin* 48(3): 79–94.

Zavaleta, D., Samuel, K. and Mills, C. (2014). Social Isolation: A conceptual and measurement proposal. *OPHI Working Papers* 67.

Zavaleta, D., Samuel, K. and Mills, C. (2017). Measures of Social Isolation. *Social Indicators Research* 131(1): 367–391.

CONCLUSION

Keetie Roelen, Richard Morgan and Yisak Tafere

This edited volume has sought to bring together high-quality research from across the African continent in order to deepen understandings of child poverty and its manifestations, causes and potential solutions. By presenting a wide range of empirical research from across disciplinary and methodological perspectives, it has aimed to inspire practical action for effective change and ultimately to improve the lives of children across Africa.

1. Key themes

This volume was structured along three themes, namely: (i) manifestations of child poverty; (ii) child-sensitive social protection; and (iii) transitions from childhood into adulthood.

Contributions within the first theme of manifestations of child poverty have provided various key insights. Firstly, there is need for nuancing understandings of child poverty beyond quantitative measures and rigid categorisations, pointing to the importance of acknowledging complexity and taking children's lived experiences to heart in designing policy responses. Secondly, issues of shame and dignity need to receive greater attention as they lie at the core of the experience of poverty and are pervasive across all aspects of children's lives. Thirdly, the persistent problem of childhood malnutrition can only be solved by recognising its intricate linkages with poverty, and also by furthering work around measurement and data collection in order to inform responses. Finally, richer insights into the fluid nature of child poverty require dynamic and multi-method analysis.

With respect to the second theme of child-sensitive social protection, contributions have focused on the design and implementation of interventions and how these play out for children. Firstly, the strong but nonetheless partial link between poverty and malnutrition calls for policies that move beyond addressing a lack of income. Secondly, and relatedly, a "cash plus" approach can offer a powerful extension of existing and combination of complementary interventions in order to promote or reinforce positive effects for children, including with respect to nutrition. Finally, the size and frequency of cash transfers matter, with regular transfers appearing to have a greater impact on children's lives than large lump-sum investments.

Contributions in relation to the third theme considered various aspects of the transition from childhood to adulthood. Firstly of all, family and community relations prove vital in supporting young people's abilities to build skills and find jobs. Related to this, the use of mobile phones and access to transport are also crucial for young people in connecting with employment opportunities. Thirdly, policies that support young people in their transitions to adulthood need to be cognisant of the fact that violence is often pervasive in adolescents' lives, and particularly those of adolescent girls, and respond to the complex interactions between economic deprivations and social norms that feed into harmful practices and exposure to violence. Finally, harnessing social connectedness can be powerful in supporting young people's moves out of poverty, although doing so can only represent part of a comprehensive package of support.

2.   Cross-cutting themes

In bringing these various contributions together, four topics strongly cut across all three key themes and are highlighted in many contributions. These are: (i) the significance of relationships; (ii) the importance of places and spaces; (iii) the prominence of the psychosocial side of poverty; (iv) the urgency of tackling malnutrition; and (v) the role of gender.

Relationships lie at the core of children's wellbeing and the fulfilment of their rights. Qualitative and participatory studies are particularly well-equipped to bring this to the fore. Ngutuku's research in Kenya provides evidence for the highly relational nature of childhood experiences, with children being part of complex and intergenerational systems in which they have to negotiate the receipt of care (e.g. by extended family members) and the provision of care (e.g. to siblings or elderly family members). At the same time, the quantitative cross-country investigation of how malnutrition is linked to family structures and community factors by Oluwaseyi et al. offers novel insight into the importance of parental presence for preventing malnutrition across sub-

Saharan Africa. With respect to policy, D'Sa et al. highlight the need for interventions to take account of the importance of social support and enabling environments as provided by families and community members in developing skills and stimulating youth employment. Ogawa et al. equally highlight the centrality of social connectedness in supporting young people's transitions to adulthood. Finally, Devereux et al. emphasise the centrality of the mother-child dyad in overcoming child malnutrition.

In relation to places and spaces, a commonly considered spatial fault line in analysing and understanding (child) poverty is the urban-rural divide. Many contributions in this volume highlight the importance of this divide and discuss the disadvantages that are experienced by children living in rural areas. Sambu and Hall confirm that the majority of income-poor children in South Africa can be found in rural areas, and that they are also more likely to experience substandard housing, poor environmental conditions, hunger and undiversified diets. Oluwaseyi et al. find similar patterns across sub-Saharan Africa, as do Woldehanna and Tafere in relation to multiple overlapping deprivations in Ethiopia. In their discussion of physical and virtual mobility for young people in Malawi, Porter and al. find that the wider context of living in rural areas, including limited economic opportunities and poor access to transport, shapes whether young people are able to find work and also what types of work they have access to.

A more systematic approach to the notion of places and spaces, in line with Bronfenbrenner's ecological model for human development, suggests that opportunities and challenges present themselves wherever children find themselves. The contribution by Bantebya-Kyomuhendo, Chase and Muhanguzi provides a spatial analysis of the psychosocial side of poverty, indicating how children experience shame as a result of deprivation at home, at school and in the community. Jones et al. attribute similar importance to home, school and the community as the spaces within which different types of violence may manifest themselves. At the same time the research presented by Bantebya-Kyomuhendo et al. offers a profound reminder of some of the universal aspects of child poverty: poverty-induced shame was experienced by children in both Uganda and the United Kingdom. Similarly, while types of violence differ markedly between Ethiopia and Rwanda, Jones et al. highlight how the experience is ubiquitous and commonplace in the lives of adolescent boys and girls in both countries.

A related and recurrent theme in narratives of poverty for children and youth refers to the psychosocial nature of poverty, highlighting the need to look beyond the material or immediately observable outcomes. The contribution by Bantebya-Kyomuhendo et al. speaks to this issue most directly as it investigates children's experiences of poverty-induced shame in Uganda and the UK. They highlight the centrality of shame in children's lives, thereby indicating that the psychosocial aspects of poverty should certainly not be considered as secondary to concerns about material needs. In addition, the contributions by Woldehanna and Tafere and Ogawa et al. offer powerful reflections of the role of humiliation and feelings of shame in relation to child deprivations in Ethiopia and negotiating adolescence in South Africa.

Other contributions provide further evidence on the pervasiveness of psychosocial elements of poverty, including stigma and stereotyping, and how children and their families adopt strategies for countering these. For example, the contribution by D'Sa et al. regarding the enabling environment for young people in building skills and finding work, shows that they may face strongly negative reputations within their families and communities, which they must fight hard to overcome. Elderly members label youth as being lazy and unreliable, and feel disinclined to employ them. Young people aim to overcome negative perceptions by seeking training, showing willingness to work and learn, and demonstrating independence.

The many contributions in this volume that speak to the issue of malnutrition provide testimony to its great urgency within the overall fight against child poverty in Africa. Progress towards undernutrition is lagging behind, hampering physical and cognitive development for millions of children. As highlighted in the contribution by Sambu and Hall, income poverty plays into many causes of malnutrition, such as low dietary diversity and frequent experiences of hunger. At the same time, poverty is only part of the picture. Oluwaseyi et al. elaborate on the role of families and communities in mitigating the effects of poverty on malnutrition, suggesting the potential of stronger roles for fathers and greater focus on social capital. Devereux et al. provide a detailed analysis of the mismatch between falling income poverty rates but fairly stable levels of stunting in South Africa, pointing towards the need for social protection to complement cash transfers with behaviour change communication (BCC), to include pregnant women in current social protection schemes, and to support more holistic programming that addresses multiple drivers of malnutrition simultaneously. In their contribution, Hypher et al. explore the role of "cash plus" interventions, and their particular design and implementation features, for tackling undernutrition. The importance of doing so is exemplified by the evaluation of cash transfers in Somalia by Hassan et al., showing that larger transfers do not translate into more diverse diets for children and do not reduce malnutrition. In combination, these contributions exemplify the complex interaction of multiple drivers underpinning malnutrition, and that viable policy solutions require more innovative and especially integrated approaches.

Finally, a number of contributions speak to the gendered nature of poverty among children, including adolescents. Jones et al. provide powerful testimonies of the brunt borne by adolescent girls in relation to child marriage in Ethiopia and labia elongation in Rwanda. Porter et al. offer analysis of how gender constrains the mobility of and opportunities for girls and young women in relation to work in Malawi. A combination of concerns for safety, fears of promiscuity and expectations in relation to domestic unpaid work on behalf of family members means that gender is an important factor in obtaining employment for young people. The contribution by D'Sa et al. suggests that youth livelihood programming may have a role to play in addressing gender inequality; while they find that parents are sometimes reluctant to send their girls to training programmes, their findings also indicate that attitudes to girls' employment became more favourable following participation in the programmes. The contribution by Hypher et al. reflects on women as main recipients of cash transfers and how this may increase nutritional impacts for children and empower women at the same time. While recognising that there is mixed evidence on the effect of designating women as main recipients of the cash transfers, Hypher et al. indicate that the studies under review found that women are able to retain control of the cash and make decisions about its use. As this goes hand-in-hand with improved outcomes for children, this appears a win-win approach.

3. Missing elements

Despite aiming to be comprehensive, this volume inevitably has gaps. We flag some of—what we consider to be—the main gaps in evidence here, thereby highlighting the need for further consideration in terms of both research and policy.

Firstly, this volume fails to shed light on the situation and potential policy options for some of the most vulnerable children, including children with disabilities, children affected by conflict and children living without family care. This gap is in large part reflective of the overall lack of information and robust data about these groups. Sambu and Hall highlight this lack of data in discussing the shortcomings of their research. They indicate that despite using three different data sets for their analysis, children that live outside of "private households," such as children in care institutions, boarding schools or on the streets, are excluded. The contribution by Oluwaseyi et al. offers important insights into the role of family structure in children's nutrition but the fact that the analysis is based on household survey data also means that children living outside of family settings are missing from the picture. Highlighting the gaps and limitations of current research should serve as reminders that truly inclusive solutions to fighting child poverty must ensure that these children are not forgotten.

Secondly, this volume does not address issues related to children who are "on the move" or otherwise affected by migration, including for economic reasons or as a result of conflict. Sub-Saharan African countries consistently experience some of the highest rates of migration in the world (Akeju, 2013). Economic migration holds strong ramifications for children "left behind," and it is unclear to what extent the economic benefits of parents' migration may outweigh negative consequences of being left with reduced or no parental care (Awumbila et al. 2015). Equally, there is a need to better understand the motivations and aspirations that influence the decisions of children and young people who are themselves migrating. The effects of conflict for children are unequivocally disruptive, and are widespread. In 2016, an estimated 21 percent of children in Africa were living in conflict areas (Save the Children, 2018). It is clear that the eradication of child poverty across the continent cannot happen without immediate and sustained support for these children and the simultaneous resolution of the root causes that underlie these conflicts.

4.   Call for Action

Following a **Call for Action** from the international conference *Putting Children First: Identifying Solutions and Taking Action to Tackle Poverty and Inequality in Africa* that was held from 23–25 October 2017 in Addis Ababa, we *recommend* the following **six priority measures** to combat child poverty; and call upon African governments, with their national and international partners, to take urgent action to implement them and improve the lives of children languishing in poverty, in the light of the huge challenges and opportunities facing African children today and in the spirit of the 2030 Agenda for Sustainable Development of "leaving no one behind":

1. ***Recognize child poverty*** as an explicit priority area in national strategies, policies and programmes, and as a distinct component of the struggle, in Africa as elsewhere, to eliminate poverty in all its dimensions. This will provide a basis for prosperous, equitable societies and sustainable national development in future generations.

2. ***Develop programmes specifically targeted*** to address poverty and deprivations among girls and boys at all stages of childhood. Proven initiatives include: child-sensitive social protection that is universal and that effectively reaches the poorest children and families; the delivery of basic services, including for early childhood, health, nutrition and education, that ensure access for the most marginalised children and population groups; and programmes aimed at secure transitions of adolescents and young people to adulthood with regard to education, decent work, family life and managing their aspirations.

3. ***Measure child poverty in its various dimensions.*** Routine national and local assessment and reporting on child poverty, as part of overall SDG monitoring, will be central to supporting progress. The "invisible" impacts of poverty on girls and boys, such as shame and stigma, also need much greater research and understanding. In all these efforts, it is vital to seek and listen to the voices and views of children themselves, and their caregivers, and involve them as key stakeholders.

4. ***Strengthen existing national information systems*** to focus on and distinguish the situation of the poorest families and most deprived children. National statistical systems need to be invested in and supplemented by cost-effective, locally-led innovations that address pressing gaps in information and knowledge. In doing so, particular emphasis should be given to information about children with disabilities, the psychosocial impacts of poverty, children affected by conflict and instability, those living without family care, and other children who are "invisible and uncounted."

5. ***Strengthen research and analysis*** on the many dimensions and causes of child poverty, to inform and motivate policy action. Every opportunity should be taken to build networks of learning on the causes of poverty and inequality among Africa's children and young people, and how their rights can practically be realized.

6. ***Establish an African Child Poverty Centre*** in Africa led by African researchers and supported by other associated networks. Such a Centre could focus on: local, national and cross-sectoral solutions; boosting knowledge and monitoring of children in poverty; and strengthening the linkages of research and evidence to policy to mobilize decision-making and action for the rights of the poorest children.

References

Akeju, D.O. (2013). Africa, Internal Migration. In: Ness, I (ed). The Encyclopaedia of Global Human Migration. United Kingdom: Wiley-Blackwell.

Awumbila, M., et al. (2015). Are Migrants Households Better Off than Non-Migrant Households? Evidence from Ghana. Migrating Out of Poverty Working Paper 28. Brighton: University of Sussex.

AUTHOR BIOGRAPHIES

Joshua Odunayo Akinyemi is Postdoctoral Fellow at the University of Witwatersrand in South Africa and Senior Lecturer at the University of Ibadan in Nigeria.

Oluwatosin Akomolafe is Knowledge Management Advisor at Save the Children in Nigeria.

Mesele Araya is Assistant Professor of Economics at Addis Ababa University in Ethiopia.

Grace Bantebya-Kyomuhendo is Professor at the School of Women and Gender Studies at Makerere University in Uganda.

Elaine Chase is Associate Professor in Education, Health Promotion and International Development at University College London, Institute of Education in the UK.

Ernestina Coast is Professor of Health and International Development at the London School of Economics and Political Science in the UK.

Sita Conklin is Regional Program Director for Youth in Action at Save the Children in the US. She holds a B.A. in French/Area Studies from American University.

Stephen Devereux is a Co-Director, Centre for Social Protection, Institute of Development Studies, Brighton in the UK; and NRF-Newton Fund (SA-UK) Research Chair in Social Protection for Food Security, affiliated to the Centre of Excellence in Food Security, University of the Western Cape in South Africa. His research is supported by the National Research Foundation of South Africa (Grant Number: 98411), and the Newton Fund, administered by the British Council.

Nikhit D'Sa is the Advisor for Research and Learning at Save the Children in the US.

Anna Du Vent is Senior Specialist for Knowledge Management at Save the Children in Canada.

Guday Emirie is an Assistant Professor in Social Anthropology at Addis Ababa University in Ethiopia.

351

Ahmed Farahat is Regional Monitoring Evaluation Accountability and Learning Manager for Youth in Action at Save the Children.

Adiam Hagos is an independent researcher in Ethiopia.

Katherine Hall is a Senior Researcher at the Children's Institute at the University of Cape Town in South Africa.

Kate Hampshire is at the Department of Anthropology, Durham University in the UK.

Luke Harman is Senior Social Protection Advisor at Save the Children in the UK.

Billow Hassan works with Save the Children International.

Nicola Hypher is Head of Programme Services at Save the Children in the UK.

Roberte Isimbi is the Managing Director of FATE Consulting Ltd in Kigali in Rwanda and the GAGE Rwanda Research Uptake and Impact Coordinator.

Coretta Jonah is a Postdoctoral Fellow, Institute for Social Development, University of the Western Cape in South Africa. Her research is supported by a National Research Foundation Grant, UID91490.

Nicola Jones is a Principal Research Fellow at the Overseas Development Institute (ODI) in London in the UK and is Director of the DFID-funded longitudinal GAGE research programme.

Carmel Marock is Monitoring and Evaluation Specialist at Singizi Consulting Africa in South Africa. Carmel has supported the evaluation of the Social Connectedness Programme.

Julian May is the Director, DST-NRF Centre of Excellence in Food Security, University of the Western Cape in South Africa. His research is supported by a National Research Foundation Grant, UID91490.

Richard Morgan is International Advocacy Director at Plan International.

Florence Kyoheirwe Muhanguzi is Senior Lecturer at the School of Women and Gender Studies at Makerere University in Uganda.

Alister Munthali is at the Centre for Social Research, University of Malawi in Malawi.

Stephen Mutiso works with Save the Children UK as a regional food security and livelihoods advisor for East and Southern Africa.

Elizabeth Ngutuku is a PhD candidate at the International Institute of Social Studies, The Hague in the Netherlands.

Clifford Odimegwu is Professor at the University of Witwatersrand in South Africa.

Marlene Ogawa is Social Connectedness Programme Manager at Synergos Institute in South Africa.

Shirley Pendlebury is Emeritus Professor at the University of Cape Town in South Africa and thought partner to the Social Connectedness Programme.

Gina Porter is at the Department of Anthropology, Durham University in the UK.

Sarah Press is Advisor for Adolescent Education at Save the Children in the US. She holds an M.A. in International Education Development from Teachers College, Columbia University.

Elsbeth Robson is at the Department of Geography at Hull University.

Keetie Roelen is a Research Fellow and Co-Director of the Centre for Social Protection at the Institute of Development Studies (IDS) in the UK.

Winnie C. Sambu is a PhD student at the School of Economics at the University of Cape Town in South Africa. Her research is supported by a National Research Foundation Grant, UID91490. She also wishes to acknowledge the Children's Institute at the University of Cape Town (UCT), the UCT University Research Committee and CROP for support to making her contribution possible.

Oluwaseyi Dolapo Somefun is an expert in public health with a large focus on adolescent health, and is a PhD candidate in Demography and Population Studies at the University of Witwatersrand, Johannesburg, South Africa.

Munshi Sulaiman works with BRAC and Makerere University Business School.

Yisak Tafere is the Coordinator of the Ethiopian Center for Child Research (ECCR) at Policy Study Institute (PSI) in Ethiopia.

Bekele Tefera is the Director of BT Consult in Addis Ababa in Ethiopia.

Kassahun Tilahun is an Instructor in Psychology at Debre Berhan University in Ethiopia and is the GAGE Ethiopia Qualitative Data Manager.

Marie Francoise Umutoni is a Senior Researcher at FATE (From Access to Equality) Consulting Ltd in Kigali in Rwanda and is the lead researcher for GAGE Rwanda.

Tassew Woldehanna is Professor of Economics at Addis Ababa University in Ethiopia.

Workneh Yadete is the GAGE Ethiopia Research Uptake and Impact Coordinator in Ethiopia.

Kerina Zvobgo is Senior Social Protection Advisor at Save the Children in Nigeria.